D0076278

FRENCH POLITICS
1774–1789

French Politics
1774–1789

From the accession of Louis XVI to the fall of the Bastille

JOHN HARDMAN

944.035
H264

LONGMAN
London and New York

Alverno College
Library Media Center
Milwaukee, Wisconsin

Longman Group UK Limited
Longman House, Burnt Mill,
Harlow, Essex CM20 2JE, England
and Associated Companies throughout the world.

*Published in the United States of America
by Longman Publishing, New York*

© Longman Group Limited 1995

All rights reserved; no part of this publication may be
reproduced, stored in a retrieval system, or transmitted
in any form or by any means, electronic, mechanical,
photocopying, recording, or otherwise without either the
prior written permission of the Publishers or a licence
permitting restricted copying in the United Kingdom issued
by the Copyright Licensing Agency Ltd.,
90 Tottenham Court Road, London W1P 9HE.

First published 1995

ISBN 0 582 23650 9 CSD
ISBN 0 582 23649 5 PPR

British Library Cataloguing-in-Publication Data

A catalogue record for this book is
available from the British Library

Library of Congress Cataloging-in-Publication Data
Hardman, John.
French politics, 1774–1789 : from the accession of Louis XVI to
the fall of the Bastille / John Hardman.
p. cm.
Includes bibliographical references and index.
ISBN 0-582-23650-9. -- ISBN 0-582-23649-5 (pbk.)
1. France--Politics and government--1774–1793. 2. France-
History--Louis XVI, 1774–1793. 3. Cabinet officers--France-
History--18th century. 4. Marie Antoinette, Queen, consort of
Louis XVI, King of France, 1755–1793. I. Title.
DC136.5.H37 1995
944'. 035--dc20   94-2957
                                             CIP

Set by 7A in 11/12 pt Garamond
Produced by Longman Singapore Publishers (Pte) Ltd.
Printed in Singapore

To my godson Tom Dunn and his family:

Tony, Ann and James Dunn,

Susie, Andrew and Duncan Bonfield

Contents

PART TWO

Separate Councils

Acknowledgements

I should like to express my thanks to Peter Campbell, for his warm encouragement and helpful suggestions (to which Chapter 7 on finance ministers is due); to Munro Price, for communicating his work on Vergennes to me; to Tony Dunn, who removed many of the infelicities and obscurities from the text; to Janet Snelson, for expert advice on word-processing and for retrieving all-but-lost discs; and finally to Pierre and Jacquemine de Tugny Vergennes, for their generous hospitality and for allowing me to photocopy the letters of Louis XVI to Vergennes.

Readers should note that in the footnotes the places of publication are Paris (for French works) and London (for English works) unless otherwise stated.

Il faut être roi et même roi de talent et de caractère fort pour produire un changement subit. Nous autres, ministres, instables dans nos emplois, nous ne pouvons que préparer les variations ou commencer les désuétudes.

(Miromesnil on Turgot)

Chronological synopsis

1774

May: Death of Louis XV from smallpox; succession of his grandson Louis-Auguste with the style of Louis XVI. The new king retains his grandfather's departmental ministers headed by the triumvirate of Maupeou, Terray and d'Aiguillon but recalls the Comte de Maurepas from exile to be his special adviser, without a portfolio. Louis XVI leaves Versailles, not to return for six months.

June: Marie-Antoinette forces d'Aiguillon to resign; king chooses Vergennes to succeed him as foreign secretary.

July: Maurepas transfers decision-making from the council to ad-hoc *comités.*

August: Louis finally capitulates to pressure from Maurepas to dismiss Maupeou and Terray, replaced by Miromesnil and Turgot respectively.

September: Turgot reintroduces limited free trade in corn.

November: Louis returns to Versailles and restores the old *parlement.* Slight restrictions placed on that body, which it observes. Miromesnil and Maurepas plan to manage the parlement through a *parti ministériel.*

1775

First shots fired in the struggle between England and her American colonists. Vergennes sends secret observer to America. Maurepas's cousin Madame de Polignac becomes *confidante* of Marie-Antoinette but remains Maurepas's political ally.

April–May: Guerre des farines (Flour War), bloodily suppressed by Louis and Turgot. The ministry considers the riots to have been fomented by supporters of Louis XV's former minister, the Duc de

1

Choiseul, who are backed by Marie-Antoinette. Lenoir, the lieutenant-général de police, dismissed for opposition to Turgot's measures.

June: Malesherbes appointed minister for the *maison du roi* in preference to Marie-Antoinette's candidate.

1776

January: Guines, the French ambassador to England and the queen's protégé, dismissed for incompetence and pro-English stance; government decides to give Americans secret subsidies.

March: Turgot's Six Edicts commuting the *corvée*, abolishing craft guilds, etc., registered in the parlement by *lit de justice*. Underhand opposition to Turgot's measures from Miromesnil.

May: Dismissal of Turgot and resignation of Malesherbes. Maurepas appointed chef du conseil royal des finances.

October: Necker appointed directeur-général of royal treasury under a nominal contrôleur-général.

1777

June: Necker directeur-général des finances.

1778

France enters War of American Independence. Necker sets up a pilot provincial administration in Berry.

1779

Congress of Teschen: France mediates in Austro-Prussian dispute over Bavaria and avoids threat of war on two fronts. Necker sets up a second provincial administration at Montauban.

1780

February: Necker freezes amount raised by the *taille*: any increase to be registered in the parlement.

October: Necker forces dismissal of the minister for the marine, Sartine, for overspending, and has him replaced by Castries. Maurepas loses control over ministerial appointments.

1781

February: Publication of Necker's *Compte rendu* falsely suggesting that royal finances are in surplus.

May: Resignation of Necker when the king refuses him 'conditional marks of confidence'. He is replaced by Joly de Fleury. Government's internal inquiry into *Compte rendu.*

October: English army capitulates to Franco-American forces at Yorktown; birth of a dauphin assures the succession and enhances Marie-Antoinette's authority.

November: Death of Maurepas; king leaves office of chef du conseil vacant and begins his personal rule.

1782

April: French naval defeat at the Battle of the Saints; Joly de Fleury exploits the patriotic fervour to impose a third *vingtième* – the last new direct tax imposed by the *ancien régime.*

1783

January: Peace preliminaries signed with England; France makes modest gains which, however, meet her war aims. Vergennes rewarded with office of chef du conseil royal des finances; his period of predominance. Castries protests at peace terms and keeps navy on wartime footing.

February: Joly inaugurates the comité des finances to control departmental expenditure, especially naval.

March: Joly succeeded by d'Ormesson.

August: D'Ormesson's memorandum to the king on restructuring taxation in 1787.

September: Bankruptcy of the Prince de Rohan-Guéméné for 30 million livres; Madame de Polignac succeeds Princesse de Guéménée as gouvernante des enfants de France. Run on the Caisse d'escompte.

October: D'Ormesson's abortive attempt to rescind the lease of the general farm.

November: D'Ormesson replaced by Calonne; end of the comité des finances. Breteuil made minister for the maison du roi through Marie-Antoinette's influence.

1784

October: Breteuil purchases Saint-Cloud for the queen without consulting Calonne – origin of destabilizing dispute between Breteuil and Calonne.

1784/1785

Austro-Dutch dispute over free navigation of the Scheldt; successful French mediation and signature of the Treaty of Fontainebleau (November) between France and Holland: this alliance with England's traditional ally is the highpoint of Louis XVI's diplomacy.

1785

March: Queen gives birth to the Duc de Normandie.

August: Arrest of Cardinal de Rohan and start of Diamond Necklace Affair.

December: Parlement mauls Calonne's loan and criticizes his re-coinage; Louis castigates parlement and dismisses Lefevre d'Amécourt as his political agent (*rapporteur du roi*) in the parlement.

1786

May: Acquittal of Rohan by the parlement; he is released from the Bastille but exiled by the king to Chaise-Dieu.

August: Calonne's unsuccessful attempt to break d'Aligre, premier président of the parlement; collapse of parti ministériel. Having lost control of the parlement, Calonne considers in earnest an Assembly of Notables to implement the reform of direct and indirect taxation planned since 1783. A uniform land tax is to be levied on all regardless of social and provincial privileges and to be assessed by provincial assemblies whose membership is to be determined by landed wealth not social status.

September–December: Calonne's projects discussed by a comité of the king, Calonne, Vergennes and Miromesnil; the conservative Miromesnil is in a minority of one. The king rejects his plea that the other ministers be consulted.

29 December: King announces the convocation of the Assembly of Notables as a *fait accompli* to the council. Breteuil tries to topple Calonne by manoeuvres in the parlement.

1787

January: Death of Vergennes; king leaves his office of chef du conseil royal vacant.

22 February: Assembly of 144 Notables meets. Immediate resistance to Calonne's measures, encouraged by Miromesnil.

1 April: Louis attempts to win popular support for his reforms by having the *avertissement* read from the pulpits.

4

8 April: King dismisses Calonne to save his programme and replaces Miromesnil with Calonne's candidate, président de Lamoignon. King's morale shattered.

May: Loménie de Brienne appointed chef du conseil royal through Marie-Antoinette's influence. Beginning of her sustained involvement in politics; she starts attending ministerial comités and becomes dangerously unpopular. Brienne attempts to get the heart of Calonne's measures endorsed by the Notables. Failure of this attempt and dismissal of the Notables.

June–August: Vain attempt by Brienne to get the measures through the parlement.

August–September: Parlement exiled.

26 August: Brienne made ministre principal.

September. Anglo-Prussian forces invade Holland; Castries proposes resistance but Brienne declines because of the financial situation; collapse of Louis XVI's diplomacy causes a further deterioration of internal situation. Parlement returns; negotiations on the basis that the king will levy five annual loans of 100 million livres and will summon the Estates-General, which had not met since 1614, for 1792.

23 November: Bungled *séance royale* in the parlement: at the last moment the king refuses to allow a free vote on the above proposals. The king's cousin Orléans exiled for declaring this procedure 'illegal'.

1788

3 May: Parlement enunciates the Fundamental Laws of France.

8 May: Coup d'état against the parlement. Its geographical jurisdiction curtailed and responsibility for registering royal legislation given to a *cour plénière.*

May–August: Resistance to government's measures in towns where there is a parlement and throughout Dauphiné and Brittany.

July: Breteuil distances himself from government measures by resigning. Brienne and Lamoignon revert to Calonne's policy of playing the third estate off against the nobility and clergy.

August: Date for meeting of Estates-General advanced to 1789. Treasury crisis, suspension of payments. Dismissal of Brienne (25th); Marie-Antoinette brings Necker back to the ministry, writing 'my fate is to bring misfortune'. Fatalism in royal entourage. Revival of policy-making role of council.

September: Dismissal of Lamoignon (replaced by reactionary Barentin) and unconditional return of the parlement. Parlement declares that the forthcoming Estates-General must have the same format as in 1614, which is taken to mean that the third estate will have only one-third of the seats.

November: Necker reconvenes the Notables to advise on this issue. Six of the seven bureaux advise against increasing the representation of the third estate.

December: Nevertheless the *résultat du conseil* (27th) grants them double representation without, however, specifying whether voting will be by head or by order. If the latter were adopted, *doublement* would be of little practical value as the nobility and clergy would be able to exercise a veto and paralyse the Estates-General as in 1614.

1789

Elections to the Estates-General by universal manhood suffrage. No attempt whatsoever by government to influence their outcome or the drafting of the *cahiers des doléances*, which in previous meeting of the Estates had served as basis for legislation.

7 May: Opening of the Estates. Neither king nor Necker rules on voting procedures. Wrangling between the orders on this issue continues for six weeks.

3 June: Death of the dauphin.

14–21 June: King's withdrawal to Marly.

17 June: Third estate declares itself the National Assembly.

20 June: 'Tennis Court Oath' not to separate until the Assembly had given France a constitution.

23 June: King tries to regain control of the situation by enforcing a compromise, which is rejected by the third estate. King capitulates but simultaneously summons troops.

11 July: Necker sent into exile; return of Breteuil as chef du conseil royal des finances. Questioned by the assembly about the troop movements, king proposes that it be translated to Soissons; he would take up residence nearby at Compiègne. The orders given to the troops are purely defensive but the Parisians believe that the new government plans to subdue Paris and dissolve the Assembly.

13–14 July: Armed rising in Paris, culminating in the storming of the Bastille. Fall of Breteuil's ministry and return of Necker's.

Introduction

The study of eighteenth-century French political history has been neglected, even despised, for most of the twentieth century. At the end of the nineteenth century and the beginning of the twentieth, fine works of scholarship were written by Chérest, Flammermont, Arneth and Marion. Then the curtain fell; little was written for fifty years. Only the late Jean Egret kept interest alive with works on the parlement under Louis XV, Necker, and especially the pre-revolution.[1] The creation of the chair in the history of the French Revolution at the Sorbonne had coincided with a period when French historians' preoccupations were dominated by Marxist concerns, which dictated not only their methodology but also their subject matter. In the early 1970s I remember being scandalized by the interest generated by some book on madness in Upper Normandy in the year II, considering that at that time no scholarly biography of either Louis XV or Louis XVI had been written. Things were not much better abroad, though a beacon in the darkness was provided by Albert Goodwin's seminal article on the 1787 Assembly of Notables (published in 1946).[2] When I was working at Edinburgh University I remember relating to Professor Maurice Larkin a reflection that Professor Goodwin had offered me: 'Let's face it, Calonne was far more important than however many thousand peasants in the Languedoc!' Professor Larkin replied that 'the material condition of the masses was the only thing that mattered'. 'You mean the most important', I said too reasonably. 'No', he replied, 'the only thing'.

That was only in 1980, but already things were changing and this process can only be helped by events in the late 1980s and early 1990s in eastern Europe which have helped to discredit Marxism in practice

1 For example A. Chérest, *La Chute de l'ancien régime, 1787–9*, 1884–6, 3 vols; J. Flammermont, *Le Chancelier Maupeou et les parlements*, 1883; M. Marion, *Le Garde des sceaux Lamoignon*, 1905; J. Egret, *Louis XV et l'opposition parlementaire*, 1970, and *Necker*, 1975.
2 A. Goodwin, 'Calonne, the Assembly of French Notables of 1787 and the origins of the "Révolte Nobiliaire"', *English Historical Review*, 1946, LXI, 202–34, 329–77.

and in theory. Work has now begun on the three main constituents of the 'structure of politics' during the ancien régime: the king, the ministers and, especially, the parlement, which has received attention in the United States from Echeverria, Joynes, Bailey Stone and Van Kley and in Britain from Doyle and in at present unpublished theses by Mansergh, Rogister and Swann.[3] The role of the king has been studied in Antoine's biography of Louis XV and my own biography of Louis XVI.[4] Studies of individual ministers have concentrated heavily on Necker, who is the subject of two by R.D. Harris and one by Egret, while H. Grange has devoted a study to his political ideas. Vergennes has been the subject of a study by Labourdette.[5]

The bulk of these recent works is English and American. Do they have anything in common? Is it possible to delineate the features of an Anglo-American school? Clearly the focus of attention is the parlement, rather than the government, and the reign of Louis XV rather than that of his grandson. The tone is less polemical than the earlier French treatment of the parlement, such detachment being perhaps easier for a foreigner to achieve. None of these studies treats the parlement either as selfishly defending its own vested interests under the guise of protecting the people (essentially the view of Antoine no less than of Marion before him) or as all that stood between France and enslavement to an encroaching bureaucratic despotism (the view of Flammermont), though the studies of Doyle and Rogister with more sophistication share something of this view. There has been interest and success in demonstrating precisely how a dynamic ideology of resistance was developed by Jansenist sympathizers out of old materials.[6]

There is general interest in the Maupeou coup d'état of 1771. This is neither new nor strange, considering its obvious importance, but whereas previous historians considered it merely as an event whose consequences for better or for worse ended with the restoration of 1774, these Anglo-Saxon historians signal a decisive change in the way people regarded the constitution of France. Echeverria signals the destruction of a consensus in favour of what one might call 'mixed absolutism', while Doyle argues that the parlement was permanently

3 D. Echeverria, *The Maupeou Revolution*, Baton Rouge, La., 1985; D.C. Joynes, 'Jansenists and ideologues: opposition theory in the Parlement of Paris, 1750–75', PhD thesis, Chicago University, 1981; B. Stone, *The Parlement of Paris, 1774–80*, North Carolina, 1981; D.K. Van Kley, *The Jansenists and the Expulsion of the Jesuits from France, 1757–65*, New Haven, Conn., 1975; M. Mansergh, 'The revolution of 1771', DPhil thesis, Oxford University, 1974; J.M.J. Rogister, 'Conflict and harmony in eighteenth-century France: a reappraisal of the pattern of relations between Crown and Parlements under Louis XV', DPhil thesis, Oxford University, 1972; J. Swann, 'Politics and the Parlement of Paris, 1754–71', PhD thesis, Cambridge University, 1988; W. Doyle, *The Parlement of Bordeaux and the End of the Old Regime, 1771–1790*, 1974.
4 M. Antoine, *Louis XV*, 1989; J. Hardman, *Louis XVI*, New Haven, Conn., 1993.
5 R.D. Harris, *Necker: Reform Statesman of the Ancien Régime*, Berkeley , Calif., 1979; R.D. Harris, *Necker in the Revolution of 1789*, 1986; H. Grange, *Les Idées de Necker etc*, Paris, 1974; J.F. Labourdette, *Vergennes*, 1990.
6 Van Kley, *The Jansenists*; Joynes, 'Jansenists and ideologues'.

weakened by what had happened and what might happen again but concludes also that this awareness made it seriously consider more durable buttresses against despotism, notably the Estates-General. Echeverria has justly observed that as a result of the coup, all sides, royalists, 'patriots', that is supporters of the parlement and what he terms 'independents', realized that the existing political arrangements were unsatisfactory.[7] Some advocated the resurrection of the old Estates; others, like Malesherbes, a more modern National Assembly; even the king experimented with new or revived forms – the provincial assemblies and ultimately the Assembly of Notables.

The parlement was the most characteristic feature of the ancien régime, the only central institution that did not survive it in any shape or form. Hence one can understand its fascination for historians. My own interest, however, lies rather with the ministers of the crown. The crown and the parlement together constituted the polity of the ancien régime under which France was governed without central representative institutions, without the Estates-General. This situation, which obtained between 1614 and 1789, gave rise to a series of characteristic problems which were solved when the Estates met in 1789, only to be succeeded by others of a different kind. Work on the ministers has been confined to three unpublished theses: P.R. Campbell's work on politics under Cardinal Fleury, Munro Price's on 'Politics and Reform' under Louis XVI and my own study of 'ministerial politics' in the years before the Assembly of Notables.[8] The present book seeks to explore the triangular relationship between the king, the ministers and the parlement in the fifteen years between the accession of Louis XVI and the fall of the Bastille. It is not an institutional history such as Michel Antoine's magisterial *Le Conseil du Roi sous le règne de Louis XV*, but a political history.[9] Institutional history is primarily concerned with describing the operation of the well-oiled machine which ran more smoothly under Louis XV than under his grandson, politics with the stops and starts, the appointment and dismissal of ministers rather than their achievements. By politics I mean not politics in the Platonic sense of 'the art of government' but what is sometimes called 'pure' politics, a contest to acquire and exercise power.

There was ample scope for politics under Louis XVI because jurisdictions were ill defined and overlapped, whether, say, one is talking about the competence of the grand conseil and that of the parlement, or that of the contrôleur-général des finances and the

7 Echeverria, *The Maupeou Revolution*, esp. 301–4.
8 P.R. Campbell, 'The conduct of politics in France in the time of the Cardinal de Fleury, 1727–43', PhD thesis, London University, 1985; M. Price, 'The Comte de Vergennes and the Baron de Breteuil: French politics and reform in the reign of Louis XVI', PhD thesis, Cambridge University, 1988; J.D. Hardman, 'Ministerial politics from the accession of Louis XVI to the Assembly of Notables, 1774–87', DPhil thesis, Oxford University, 1972.
9 M. Antoine, *Le Conseil du Roi sous le règne de Louis XV*, 1970.

minister for the maison du roi; also because major issues of public policy had not been settled, such as whether the crown had the right to tax the nobility in peacetime; finally because of the independence of many of the players: the judges of the parlement (even, according to Miromesnil, the premier président) could not be dismissed without violence or trial; each ministre-ordonnateur was financially independent and free of the discipline of a budget, the king working alone with each minister in the weekly *travail* constituting an autonomous unit. At the same time *parlementaires* lived in constant dread of another Maupeou coup (one was attempted in 1788), while ministers were, as Miromesnil put it, 'instables dans leurs emplois', so that the fight to maintain office was often as fierce as that to acquire it. In 1783, the Austrian ambassador, Mercy-Argenteau, said that for Vergennes this fight 'preoccupied him to the exclusion of everything else'. Vergennes admitted to the king that it was preventing him from concentrating on his work.[10]

In highlighting the play of 'pure' politics, I am not seeking to minimize the importance of policy-making: under Louis XVI, men of dedication and intelligence sought to implement far-reaching measures. Nor were they without altruism. Turgot and Malesherbes come to mind; but Calonne (even Calonne) told the king with apparent sincerity that 'he would not mind if he himself fell victim to the enterprise' he was proposing, provided the reforms themselves were implemented. Nevertheless, the more wide-reaching a measure was, the more controversial and there was never a question – is there ever? – of the king sitting down in his council secure in the knowledge that provided they could work out the wisest and most just course of action there would be no impediments. There was a politics of reform: the recall of the parlement in 1774, Calonne's programme and the organization of the Estates-General, all were acutely political decisions which will be discussed in Chapter 8 on decision-making.

One of the difficulties encountered in writing about politics at the end of the ancien régime is the lack of a familiar conceptual framework. This is an inevitable consequence of the neglect not only of political history but also of the contemporary belief that in a theoretically absolute monarchy there was no place for politics: *la politique* is generally translated as 'foreign policy', the politics of the powers. Of course by 1774 politics existed (just as did the influence of public opinion which K.M. Baker argues should also not have existed) and probably always had.[11] Nevertheless, ministers talked about what we would call political conventions in an embarrassed and

10 A. d'Arneth and J. Flammermont (eds) *Correspondance secrète du Compte de Mercy-Argenteau avec l'Empereur Joseph II et le Prince de Kaunitz*, 1891, 2 vols, I, 227; A.N. K164 no. 3, 1785 no. 5, 6 February.
11 K.M. Baker, 'Politics and public opinion', in K.M. Baker (ed). *The Political Culture of the Ancien Régime*, Chicago, 1987, 204.

euphemistic way: whether it was wrong, for instance, for ministers to present the king with a united front, what degree of pressure it was proper to put on him in the matter of ministerial appointments, and so on. The difficulty of getting measures through the parlement was treated as a fact of life, however: 'the great thing', Miromesnil (like an English political agent) told the king, 'is that your business gets through, and Your Majesty will judge everyone by his conduct'.[12] There was no pretence in the internal debates between ministers and the king that registration of royal legislation was merely the formal promulgation which the theory of absolutism proclaimed. In 1784, for instance, Miromesnil told the king that they should not anger senior parlementaires by encouraging Lamoignon's project for judicial reform because they were about to consider 'important legislation' from the king.[13]

In reconstructing the framework of political conventions, initial assistance has been sought from the contemporary English model. France and England were direct competitors and in many ways their political systems seemed to be converging until 1788 or 1789. Conventions have to reflect realities if they are to have any force and in many ways the reality of the situation of both countries – such as servicing the debt and financing the wars – was similar. Without wanting to overstate this similarity it was sufficient to suggest a way of looking at the still unfamiliar French political system, though the conclusions would obviously have then to be refined. Thus the rise under Louis XVI of the chef du conseil royal des finances has been compared with that of the English first lord of the treasury: both were largely ceremonial posts but both related to finance, which was at the heart of government. France had an older tradition of a formal prime minister but it did not accord with the fiction that Louis XVI maintained until 1787 that he was his own prime minister, whereas the chef du conseil could be so adapted. Other concepts familiar in the English context have been utilized, such as that of ministerial unity, while the English use of the inner cabinet invites comparisons with the comité system instituted by Maurepas in 1774.

This book is divided into two parts: Part One seeks to give the reason for the appointment and dismissal of every departmental minister in the period 1774–89; and gives genealogical and biographical details of each minister. Since his appointment and his dismissal (Louis XVI frowned on resignations) are the landmarks in a politician's life, these events make up a political narrative. The biographical and genealogical information serves to introduce the characters and can also be used to chart the changing social composition of the ministry; it may prompt reflections on the political

---

12 A.N. K164 no. 8. 4, letter of 11 December 1785.
13 A.N. K695 29 and 30, cited in Stone, *Parlement of Paris*, 52 n. 72.

consequences of such changes. Such an approach would have presented less interest during the reign of Louis XIV and most of that of Louis XV: ministers had generally passed up through the royal administration typically as maîtres des requêtes and intendants, had a common tradition of royal service and could be labelled with Ardaschef's useful phrase 'noblesse d'état'.[14] Under Louis XVI their backgrounds were more varied: there were ex-generals, ex-ambassadors, ex-parlementaires as well as ex-intendants and the question arises whether it is possible to talk of a ministerial corps with a set of values and assumptions.

Part Two, entitled Separate Councils, views these and other features in the political landscape from different perspectives, from the prime minister's, the finance minister's and the council's, from the king's and the queen's; then it looks out to the outside world, to the parlement and beyond to public opinion.

To examine how ministers achieved power and how they lost it without looking at what they did with it, except in so far as this determined their fall, may seem perverse but is not inappropriate in a study of politics rather than of administration. Viewing politics as a series of isolated entries and exits also underlines the artificiality of talking about the government or the ministry, although contemporaries did. Even with a change of reign and a major shift in policy, it took over a year for Louis XV's last ministry to be completely replaced, and all its members, with the exception of Maupeou and Terray – themselves rivals – fell separately. Ministerial unity – or rather the recognition of the need for it – came with the assemblies from 1787 onwards and the need to get business through them; hitherto it had existed, and then imperfectly, only during the heyday of Maurepas's political system, from 1776 to 1780.

Such an approach also serves to dispel one of the most common misunderstandings about government under the ancien régime, namely that the contrôleur-général was the most important minister. Most individual studies of ministers have been of contrôleurs-généraux, the main exceptions being Labourdette's study of Vergennes and Rampelberg's institutional study of the ministry of the maison du roi under Breteuil.[15] Yet the contrôleur's post was the most junior in status and the most insecure in tenure: the keeper of the seals, the minister for the maison and the foreign secretary deserve an equal consideration, while Castries as minister for the marine often played a decisive role.

The title of Part One, Le chagrin de l'exil, is taken from Marmontel's explanation of the suicide in 1789 of Lamoignon, the keeper of the seals. When a minister fell from office, whether because he had lost

14 P.M. Ardaschef, *Les Intendants de province sous Louis XVI*, 1909.
15 R.M. Rampelberg, *Le Ministre de la maison du roi 1783–1788: Baron de Breteuil*, 1975.

royal favour or, after 1787, because the king was forced to dismiss him, he often had to suffer the additional punishment of internal exile. This was often subject to elaborate conditions imposed by a *lettre de cachet* or by a simple *lettre ordre* from the king. Violence had not been employed since the 1720s, when Louis XV's governor, the Duc de Villeroy, had been conveyed into exile by twenty musketeers, and the prime minister, the Duc de Bourbon, had been escorted by one bodyguard. Conditions of exile varied enormously: generally the deeper the disgrace the further would be the *lieu d'exil* from Paris and the narrower the circle of friends who would be allowed to visit the exile. Thus in 1758 Louis XV allowed Cardinal de Bernis to retire to 'une de vos abbayes à votre choix', in 1787 the keeper of the seals, Miromesnil, sought Louis XVI's approval for his own choice of exile, whereas Calonne was sent to the confines of the kingdom and every visitor needed the king's express permission to go there: this exile required several clarifying letters and can be regarded as the perfection of the art. There were other variants; thus in 1771 the princes of the blood who had protested at the suppression of the parlement were simply forbidden the court, as was d'Aiguillon when his exile was mitigated in 1775. When the object of the king's wrath, say a refractory parlement, happened to live in the provinces different arrangements obtained. The parlement could be 'transferred' en bloc to another town or scattered in exile. Often, though, the practice was to summon the miscreant by a *veniat* to be 'à la suite du roi et de son conseil', which often entailed kicking his heels in a neighbouring village waiting to receive the royal rebuke.

At the start of the new reign Maurepas (a prominent victim of the system under Louis XV) and Miromesnil tried to persuade Louis XVI to end this barbarous practice, but Louis was reluctant to surrender a valuable weapon, though he did not bring to its exercise the black humour of his grandfather, whose relations with a minister were often at their most aimiable in the hours preceding his disgrace. In his *Réflexions sur mes entretiens avec M. la Duc de La Vauguyon*, written when he was dauphin, Louis gives an antiquated and formal rationale for the practice of exile, which he treats as the most natural thing in the world. He concedes that external exile is unjust (he would be driven to that too) but adds:

The sovereign can summon to his court those whom he judges to possess the talents necessary to perform the duties of the most important offices there and send away those whom he believes to be unworthy of his confidence on grounds of ingratitude or to merit his contempt for their vices. . . . a 'grand' dishonours himself in the capital, the king orders him to withdraw to his estates.[16]

---

16 *Oeuvres de Louis XVI*, ed. Sansovic de Jonc, 1865, 2 vols, I, 239.

In fact the real reason for the exile of ex-ministers stemmed partly from the ex-minister's possession of state secrets (he was in any case expected and sometimes explicitly enjoined to return all the king's letters under seal) and partly from the desire to prevent him from maintaining a faction and intriguing to return to office. Thus, Choiseul having been exiled to his estates at Chanteloup in 1770, the Duc de Croÿ could write: 'Since the Duc de Choiseul's party is being sustained by his friends, he is running a great risk of being sent further into exile'. The survival of internal exile meant that the ministers were as subject to the residual arbitrariness of the regime as anyone else

Part Two develops some of the themes thrown up in the first. There was a triangular relationship between the king, the queen, and the prime minister, each of whom is the subject of a chapter (Chapters 9, 10 and 6), in the sense that if Louis XVI had ruled in the way envisaged by Louis XIV there would have been no need for a prime minister and the queen would not have had any political influence. Maurepas told Louis XVI during his first audience that if he did not intend to be his own prime minister 'he must necessarily choose one'. The fact that Louis did not take this advice conditioned the whole political system of his reign: Maurepas had to devise an elaborate system which managed the king's susceptibilities and yet enabled himself to act as at least an 'ombre de point de réunion'. No one knew whether Maurepas was a prime minister or not. In this uncertainty his post of chef du conseil acquired a new significance.

The kind of premiership developed by Maurepas, one based on familiar access to the king, affected the relationship of the queen and the ministers to the king: essentially he acted as a screen between the king and anyone who wanted to discuss politics with him. In the case of the ministers this was effected formally by their conducting their weekly travail with the king only in Maurepas's presence. Maurepas could hardly insist on this in the case of the queen, but Mercy-Argenteau was still able to claim that 'the métier of a prime minister in France has always been to intercept and destroy the credit of the queens'.[17] 'Intercept' is the key word here; Maurepas had to make sure that Louis turned a deaf ear to Marie-Antoinette, potentially his chief rival in proffering the king general extra-departmental advice. Friction with Marie-Antoinette continued under Maurepas's ultimate successor as chef du conseil, Vergennes, and the problem was solved only when her nominee, Loménie de Brienne, became first chef du conseil and finally ministre principal. The rise in the queen's political influence (which Louis at first resisted) is charted principally in terms of her influence in the appointment of ministers who, in the words of

17 Letter to Maria-Theresa, 17 May 1774, in A. d'Arneth and M.A. Geffroy (eds) *Marie-Antoinette: Correspondance secrète entre Marie-Thérèse et le Comte de Mercy-Argenteau*, 2nd. edn, 1875, 3 vols, II, 147.

one of them, Breteuil, considered that their role was 'faire régner la reine'.[18]

The queen was also at the point of intersection between politics and the court. The mass of courtiers did not translate access to the king and queen into political influence because, as in the last reign, they exercised self-restraint in raising political questions with the sovereigns and if they forgot themselves they were reminded by Louis XVI's reprimand of silence. However, both Louis and Marie-Antoinette sought the relaxation of a normal life with a small group generally known as the queen's *société intime*, grouped round her favourite, Madame de Polignac, and this group did have an important, if greatly misunderstood, influence on politics. In addition, through her patronage of the remnants of the *parti Choiseul*, the queen was responsible for bringing courtiers into the ministry itself, over the dying body of Maurepas.

The title of Chapter 9 on the king, 'Louis XVI and the politicians', implies an antithesis; I suggest that there was no longer the identity of outlook between the king and his ministers that one imagines had existed in the formative period of the absolute monarchy. Ministers such as Castries distinguished between their duty to the king and their duty to the country. Miromesnil warned Louis in 1787 that he was pursuing divisive policies. Sartine considered that the ministerial corps did not have the king's backing. They in turn tried to make him take direct responsibility for unpopular or risky measures, while Louis, considering with some justification that many of his ministers did not share his conception of the absolute monarchy, treated them with suspicion and little affection.

Chapter 7 on the finance ministers underlines the paradoxes of their position. Generally considered to have been supreme, in fact they could not impose a budget on their colleagues and their administrative role was constantly threatened by that of the minister for the maison du roi, who was the true minister of the interior. Their very title was in a constant state of flux. Turgot was the last of the classical contrôleurs-généraux; the rise of Necker ushered in a period of experimentation, with changes in title, style and intent. Chapter 7 is concerned with the transformations that Necker made in the role of the finance minister and the painful adjustments made by his successors to them.

The decision-making process is considered in Chapter 8 on the council. This process was transformed by a politically inspired institutional change at the start of the reign: the transference of decision-making from the conseil d'état to ad-hoc ministerial committees which were called comités when presided over by the king and *conférences* in his absence. Antoine considered that the use

18 ibid., III, 36.

of comités to take decisions (rather than just prepare the work of the councils as under Louis XV) marked a stage in the degeneration of the regime.[19] Certainly some bad decisions were taken and we consider whether a deficient observance of the forms was the cause of this. The narrow basis of decision-making, particularly during the period of Louis's personal rule (1781–7), is underlined.

Chapter 11 on the crown and the parlement considers the relationship primarily from the point of view of the government. In particular it addresses Miromesnil's contention that the quarrels between crown and parlement merely reflect divisions within the ministry, rival ministers maintaining rival factions in the parlement rather than there being just one parti ministériel. Miromesnil's contention is examined against the background of the breakdown of relations between crown and parlement of 1785–6 which led to the convocation of the Assembly of Notables. We conclude that the destructive rivalry between Calonne and Breteuil that fuelled this crisis was a matter of pure politics and personality but that even without this a conflict over reform – particularly the imposition of equality in taxation – would inevitably have broken out both between Calonne and Miromesnil and between Calonne and the parlement.

Finally, there is a short chapter on the outside world as viewed by those in the ministerial milieu: their confused picture of public opinion; its influence on them and their attempts to influence it.

---

19 M. Antoine, 'Les Comités des ministres sous Louis XV', *Revue Historique de Droit français et étranger*, 1951: 193–230.

Le chagrin de l'exil or the appointment and dismissal of ministers

L'estime, et, en secret, la confiance du roi l'avoient suivi dans sa retraite de Bâville. Mais ou le chagrin de l'exil ou quelque peine domestique lui fit abandonner la vie (le 18 Mai 1789) et lui epargna des spectacles dont il seroit mort de douleur.

(Marmontel [III, 154] on the death of the garde des sceaux Lamoignon, found dead in the grounds of his château, a rifle by his side)

CHAPTER ONE

The six ministries: an overview

In the words of the Abbé de Véri, confidant of Louis XVI's chief minister, Maurepas:

The title of 'ministre' in the strict sense of the word is given only to those with the entrée to the conseil d'état where the king deals with foreign affairs. The contrôleur-général and the secretaries of state (with the exception of the one for foreign affairs) do not have this entrée ex-officio. In the ordinary language of the public 'ministre' means all those who have important departments.[1]

The appointments with which we shall be concerned were of ministers 'in the ordinary language of the public' to the 'important departments'. For in the reign of Louis XVI decisions tended to be taken in ad-hoc comités of departmental ministers rather than in the conseil d'état so that the importance of a ministre 'in the strict sense' was diminished to the point where membership of that body became little more than a *nullité honorable*.[2] In any case, ministres were not appointed: the king merely invited them to take a seat in the conseil rather than remain standing. (Before 1661 they had been appointed by *lettres patentes*.) Nor were they dismissed, possessing what the diplomat Bombelles called 'an indelible quality': the king ceased to summon them to the conseil but they remained ministres for life and continued to draw a modest *traitement* of 6,000 *livres* a year. The principal departmental ministers were the chancellor/keeper of the seals, the four secretaries of state (for the maison du roi, foreign affairs, war, and the marine) and finally the contrôleur-général des finances. They will be considered from the point of view not only of function but also of power, tenure and rank.

The chancellor's was the plum job for those ministers, still a majority in 1774, who had had a legal training. He was the king's alter ego

1 Abbé de Véri , *Journal, 1774–80*, ed. J. de Witte, 1928–30, 2 vols, I, 111.
2 A. d'Arneth and J. Flammermont (eds) *Correspondance secrète du Comte de Mercy-Argenteau avec l'Empereur Joseph II et le Prince de Kaunitz*, 1891, 2 vols, I, 201.

who, to emphasize the continuity of monarchy, alone did not attend the king's funeral or go into mourning; he occupied the king's *fauteuil* at meetings of the *conseil privé*. The chancellor was the voice of the king. In the Estates-General or Assemblies of Notables he spoke immediately after the king to develop his thoughts more fully. The flatness of Miromesnil's speech at the opening of the 1787 Assembly of Notables, which he did not bother to publish, and of Barentin's at the Estates-General in 1789 was significant.[3] He possessed one of the *grandes charges*; the others had either been abolished, for example the connétable in 1627 and the surintendant des finances in 1661, or lost their political importance. It was characteristic of such officers that they could not be dismissed; as Mercy-Argenteau put it:

The chancellor of France can only be removed with his consent as he cannot be dismissed without putting him on trial.[4]

The last chancellor to be so tried and stripped of office had been Poyet in 1545.

Such *inamovibilité* would have been more tolerable if the chancellor's functions had been confined to the honorific. However, his supreme responsibility for the administration of justice and the preparation of legislation made of him the main channel of communications between the king and the parlement. His was a highly political appointment over which the king needed unfettered control. Colbert had seen the abolition of an immovable office-holder of such eminence as a natural step in the development of royal authority; on 1 February 1672 Louis XIV announced his intention of dispensing with a chancellor and holding the seals himself, just as he was his own surintendant des finances. This experiment lasted for two years and was revived again under Louis XV from 1757 to 1761 and again in 1762. Louis XV found it soothing, pressing the seals into the hot yellow or black wax, and performed the act in public, presenting 'without cerebral fatigue, the noble and ostentatious appearance of a laborious prince'.[5] This kind of work satisfied him: though he was intelligent and spent longer hours at the desk than in the saddle or in the boudoir, he was intellectually lazy and spent a lot of time docketing and classifying his papers.

However, holding the seals himself was not a permanent solution and Louis XV also addressed the problem directly by attempting to make the office of chancellor *amovible*. As a first step, when Chancellor Lamoignon refused to resign he appointed Maupeou père vice-chancellor in 1763. The parlement refused to register the lettres

3 Abbé de Véri, MSS *Journal,* Archives départementales de la Drôme, Valence, unclassified, cahier 147.
4 A. d'Arneth and M.A. Geffroy (eds) *Mari-Antoinette: Correspondance secrète entre Marie-Thérèse et le Comte de Mercy-Argenteau,* 2nd. edn, 1875, 3 vols, III, 329.
5 P. Viollet, *Le Roi et ses ministres pendant les trois dernières siècles de la monarchie,* 1912, 185.

patentes and went through the show of sending commissioners to Lamoignon's *terre d'exil,* Malesherbes, to examine the sole question of whether he were physically fit enough to exercise his duties. They found him to be in rude health but it would have made little difference: Lamoignon did not in fact resign his office until after he had received the last rites of the church in September 1768. The status of the premier officier de la couronne symbolized the monarchy's inability to rid itself of the detritus of previous stages of its development.[6]

The unsatisfactory solution found by the regime to the problem of what to do with a chancellor disgraced but not dismissed was to exile him to his estates and assign his duties to a *garde des sceaux.* Exile was in any case the invariable lot of the disgraced minister. In 1782 Véri had a purely academic discussion with the garde des sceaux Miromesnil about what would happen if the disgraced and exiled chancellor Maupeou were to turn up in Paris:

'I [Véri] have always heard it said that if the chancellor were at Paris, he would automatically resume all his functions' – 'A false doctrine', he replied. 'Can any minister or leading official in France carry out the duties of his office when he does not have the ear of the king?' [7]

That may have been true but the encumbrance of a disgraced chancellor deprived the king of an important piece of patronage and diminished the prestige and authority of the acting head of the judiciary. For 'garde' in the phrase garde des sceaux connoted a temporary caretaker quality and, though Miromesnil was to be Louis XVI's longest-serving minister, he was much exercised by the instability of ministers and often thought he was about to be disgraced. When, for example, he was summoned to the king at the start of the Diamond Necklace Affair and was told by the valet de chambre that the minister for the maison had also been sent for, his first thought was 'le secrétaire d'état pour la maison du roi est l'agence ordinaire des disgrâces des ministres'. [8]

The minister for the maison du roi exercised this agency in virtue of his responsibility for issuing passports and lettres de cachet. Apart from his eponymous responsibility for the running of the court, the other functions of the minister for the maison du roi made him the nearest thing the ancien régime possessed to a minister for the interior – the title he was given when the ministry was reorganized during the Revolution. His duties included the general administration of the *pays d'états* and the affairs of Protestants. His control of passports and lettres de cachet stemmed from his responsibility for public order in

6 Comte de Luçay, *Les Secrétaires d'état en France depuis les origines jusqu'à 1774,* 1881, 65; Viollet, *Le Roi et ses ministres,* 184–5; J. Egret, *Louis XV et l'opposition parlementaire,* 1970, 136.
7 Véri, MSS *Journal,* cahier 109.
8 ibid., cahier 135; Castries, *Journal,* Archives de la Marine, MS 182/7964 1–2, I, fo. 297.

Paris, which he exercised with the help of his subordinate, the lieutenant-général de police, and which gave him his alternative title of minister for Paris. These functions gave the minister for the maison power without public exposure – 'il n'était pas jugé par l'opinion générale', wrote the lieutenant-général de police Lenoir.[9] No minister for the maison was simply dismissed in this period. Security of tenure was at a premium in an age of acute ministerial instability and this ministry was coveted by the 'noblesse de robe' (grand seigneurs did not possess the necessary administrative and legal expertise to run this department).

The remaining three secretaries of state, for foreign affairs, the marine, and for war, were peripheral to the making of general policy. The foreign secretary, however, had constant access to the king who regarded the conduct of diplomacy as his core function: the vast bulk of Louis XVI's surviving correspondence concerns this matter. This familiar access enabled Vergennes to gain the king's confidence and extend the field of his activities beyond his department. The foreign ministry and the two service ministries were of importance as the only ones that men from court families felt they could accept without *dérogeance* and this in itself increased their status. The service ministers were also considerable *ordonnateurs* (paymasters), second only to the contrôleur-général. Neither ministry was noted for its fixity of tenure. The war ministry changed hands several times during the baffling and demoralizing reorganization of the army which followed the defeats in the Seven Years War. Both ministries were judged by the public. In 1780 Véri notes, after a reverse in the American War:

The Parisian public blames this reverse on M. de Sartine [marine] . . . and speaks only of his dismissal from office. This will be the fate of every minister whose department is thrust into prominence without obtaining the success expected of it by the public.[10]

The secretaries of state were the descendants of the king's private secretaries, his amanuenses: 'of state' was added in the reign of Henri III. In our period they had long had secretaries of their own and the *premier commis* of a department was himself a high-ranking bureaucrat. The ministers' bureaux filled the first quadrangle of Versailles, the cour des ministres, and spilled over into Paris. The elevation of his secretaries, however, left the king bereft of secretarial assistance. Louis XV spent hours filing his documents. Louis XVI made his own copies of important letters, such as those from Charles III of Spain, and his almost daily correspondence with the foreign secretary, Vergennes, was written entirely in his own hand, whereas Vergennes usually employed secretaries. In 1785-7, the keeper of the seals, Miromesnil,

9 Lenoir Papers, Bibliothèque municipale d'Orléans, MSS 1421– 3, 1423, Résidus, 83.
10 Véri, *Journal*, II, 314.

wrote a number of letters to the king in his own hand, apologizing for his handwriting and excusing himself on the grounds that the letters were of such importance that he dare not trust a secretary. Perhaps Louis XVI regarded all his letters in that light. In order to cope with the burden, he employed great concision, which makes a refreshing contrast to the prolixity of Vergennes.

Simple histories of the reign often confine their attention to a list of the achievements and failures of the contrôleurs-généraux, yet his was the most junior of titles and the least stable of departments. His position was riddled with paradoxes: Véri could never make up his mind whether the contrôleur was merely a 'ramasseur d'argent' or the man without whose consent 'nul département ne peut aller'. The old surintendance des finances, which Louis XIV had suppressed together with its last incumbent, Foucquet, had had a seigneurial handle to it which had encouraged two ducs and four marshals of France to occupy it. However, the word *contrôleur* was associated with the menial task of auditing and connoted bourgeois attention to detail. There were also practical and legal differences between the surintendant and the contrôleur: the latter, unlike the surintendant and unlike the secretaries of state, could not 'signer en commandement', that is give executive authority to the king's wishes; unlike the surintendant again, he had to be sworn in before the chambre des comptes and thus be symbolically subject to that body. Finally, the signature of the surintendant had been both necessary and sufficient to authorize an order for payment by an ordonnateur: from 1661, the signature of the king was necessary and that of the contrôleur was not required: if the king did not coordinate expenditure, no one did. As a result of the changed status of the post, no grand seigneur ever became contrôleur-général and of the six ministries, the contrôle attracted men from the least prestigious families, measured by any yardstick, such as date of nobility, family alliances, posts held by recent ancestors.

Nor in point of function was the contrôleur necessarily the most powerful minister: we have seen that the real minister for the interior was the minister for the maison du roi, though his attributions overlapped with the contrôleur (to whom the intendants were primarily responsible) in a way that defies rational analysis. Even in purely financial matters, the contrôleur was hampered by the endemic deficit compounded by the king's inability to impose a budget on his colleagues. If Terray's budget for 1774 had been observed, there would have been a surplus of 5 million livres but all the ministers overshot. As Véri succinctly put it:

If the sovereign or his absolute minister does not forcibly reduce the ordonnateurs to expenditure which does not exceed revenue, the office of contrôleur-général is untenable in the long run.[11]

11 ibid., II, 383.

And so it was to prove: the average span of a contrôleur for the reign was fifteen months. The contrôleur was at the 'sharp end' of politics: because finance was the Achilles' heel of the ancien régime, political crises tended to be expressed in financial terms. This meant that most intelligent men did not want the job: only a fool or a knave would, as Maurepas was wont to say. It also meant, however, that when a contrôleur did acquire what was called *consistance*, as Calonne did, there was no stopping him within the ministry, ultimately no stopping him short of the forces of resistance to government itself. That consistance ultimately rested on the favour of the king based often on his recognition of an able contrôleur's indispensability in performing a thankless task.

Many in the governmental milieu thought that the contrôleur should be at once strengthened and restrained by the resurrection of the moribund conseil royal des finances. Maurepas, who gave the political system under Louis XVI many of its defining characteristics, gave the following assessment of how the contrôleur's fragile power without prestige ought to be exercised:

In time of peace, he believed that a contrôleur-général should have the main influence because the part [of the administration] he directed required it; the state had been badly governed when the contrôleurs had been too subjected or too opposed to other ministers.[12]

A time of war was not regarded as a calamity, except perhaps by the later Bourbons, but as something which succeeded a time of peace as naturally as night succeeded day. Like night, it was not a calamity but like night it required one to take the usual precautions and imposed a separate hierarchy of priorities. Véri elaborates on the position of the contrôleur in relation to the continuum of peace and war:

I am only speaking of the typical peacetime situation. If it were a question of ceding colonies, razing fortifications, cutting back on sappers or artillery, troops-of-the-line or the king's military household; châteaux or stables or stud or the grandes charges, then the choice of sacrifice must depend on the predilections and judgement of the master. That is something with which the finance ministry should not interfere.[13]

With the introduction of châteaux and grandes charges, Véri strays a little from his theme, or at least from purely military decisions. He would presumably have considered that the wholesale reform of the regime would also depend on the 'predilections and judgement' of the king.

12 ibid., I, 338.
13 ibid., II, 384.

CHAPTER TWO

The appointment and dismissal of ministers:
from the accession of Louis XVI to the death of Maurepas, 1774–81

MINISTERS LOUIS XVI INHERITED FROM LOUIS XV, MAY 1774

At his accession on 10 May 1774, Louis XVI decided to retain his grandfather's ministers. The departmental ministers were as follows.

Chancellor René Nicolas Charles Augustin de Maupeou (1714–92), Marquis de Morangles et Bully, Marquis de la Mothe (1767), Vicomte de Bruyères. Maupeou had spent his entire career in the parlement as conseiller (1733), président à mortier (1743) and premier président (1763) before succeeding his father as chancellor in 1768. For two years after his appointment as chancellor, Maupeou had continued the policy of entente between crown and parlement which he had observed as premier président. In 1771, however, he had expressed Louis XV's growing exasperation with the parlement by exiling it, restricting its jurisdiction by the creation of six conseils supérieurs, and replacing it with the grand conseil. Venality of office was abolished and three provincial parlements were suppressed.

Maupeou belonged to one of the leading families in the parlement. His ancestry and family alliances can most conveniently be given in the form of a genealogy:

I   Vincent Maupeou, notaire in the châtelet (1547).
*II   Pierre Maupeou, commissaire in the châtelet, auditeur in the chambre des comptes (1569). He was ennobled by lettres patentes in 1586.
III   René I de Maupeou (d. 1648), Seigneur de Bruyères, président in the chambre des comptes (1608).
IV   René II de Maupeou, Vicomte de Bruyères, président in the parlement.
V   René III de Maupeou (d. 1710), Vicomte de Bruyères, président in the parlement.

* In the following genealogies, with this representative, the family was ennobled.

VI   René Charles de Maupeou (1688–1775), Marquis de Morangles, premier président of the parlement (1743–57), garde des sceaux (1763–8), chancellor for a day in 1768. He married Anne Victoire de Lamoignon de Courson (from a branch of the great parlementaire family which served in the conseil d'état).

VII   René Charles Nicolas de Maupeou. In 1744 Maupeou married Anne de Roncherolles, only child and heiress of François, Marquis de Roncherolles, of a *chevaleresque* Norman family which enjoyed the honneurs de la cour. It was fairly common for a *robin* woman to marry into an ancient family but rare for the daughter of an old house to marry a robin.

VIII   René Ange Augustin de Maupeou became a président à mortier but then changed to a military career, becoming a maréchal de camp and a chevalier de Saint-Louis (1788). He married (1769) Anne Feydeau de Brou, sister of an intendant and scion of a famous family of royal administrators ennobled in 1608 by purchasing the office of secrétaire du roi.[1]

Contrôleur-général des finances Joseph Marie Terray (1715–78), a clerk in minor orders, Abbé de Saint-Martin de Troarn and of Notre-Dame de Molesnes. Terray had been a conseiller clerc in the first chambre des enquêtes of the parlement (1736) before being promoted to the grand' chambre (1754) and becoming rapporteur du roi, that is the king's political agent in the parlement, which provided invaluable experience for a career in government. In 1769 he became contrôleur-général des finances through the influence of Maupeou, though relations between the two men later cooled; further distinctions included ministre d'état (1770); secrétaire des ordres du roi (1770–4); directeur et ordonnateur des bâtiments du roi (1773–4).

Terray's ancestry is established from Barthélemy Tarray, a prosperous peasant from Boën in the Forez, who died *c.*1550. His son was an innkeeper and butcher and his grandson a merchant. The first member of the family to embark on a legal career was the minister's grandfather, Jean, who was appointed juge de la baronnie de Cousan in 1656. The family was ennobled with Terray's father, Antoine, who purchased the office of secrétaire du roi in 1720. Antoine was directeur des gabelles at Lyon in 1715 and from 1719 to 1720 was a farmer-general (a post which was less prestigious at this time than at the end of the century). The minister was the son of his father's second marriage (in 1705) to Marie Anne Dumas de Matel, the

---

1 F. Bluche, *L'Origine des magistrats du parlement de Paris au XVIIIe siècle*, 1956, 304–5; Jougla de Morénas, *Grand Armorial de France*, 1934–52, 7 vols, V, 20–1; Baron de Woëlmont de Brumagne, *Notices généalogiques*, 1923–8, 4 vols, IV, 517–30.

daughter of a Savoyard captain of light infantry. Terray's position as a *transfuge*, that is one who had moved from a career in a sovereign court to one in the conseil d'état, was confirmed by his brother's son (as a cleric Terray did not marry) who became a maître des requêtes and then an intendant des finances.[2]

Secretary of state for foreign affairs and war Emmanuel Armand de Vignerot du Plessis de Richelieu (1720–88), Comte, then Duc d'Agenois (1740), Duc d'Aiguillon (1750). D'Aiguillon had pursued a military career: colonel d'infanterie (1739); maréchal de camp (1748); lieutenant-général (1758). In 1753 he had been appointed commandant-en-chef in Brittany: his quarrels with the parlement of Rennes in this capacity were the immediate cause of Maupeou's coup d'état; n 1771 he had been appointed minister for foreign affairs and ministre d'état, largely through the influence of Madame du Barry; additionally he became minister for war in January 1774.

His family, the Vignerot, passed for one of noblesse d'extraction and though this was not conclusively proved, they enjoyed the honneurs de la cour before providing a minister (which automatically conferred this distinction). The rise to prominence of the family dated from the marriage of René de Vignerot, Seigneur de Pontcourlay, to the Cardinal de Richelieu's sister Françoise du Plessis. His grandson Jean Baptiste Amador, great-grandfather of our minister and a lieutenant-général in the army, assumed the surname du Plessis de Richelieu and was styled Marquis de Richelieu; his descendants regarded themselves as the custodians of the traditions of Cardinal Richelieu, especially in foreign policy, and as such opposed the 'diplomatic revolution' of 1756. Our minister's grandfather inherited the duchy of Aiguillon, but not the peerage. The *duché-pairie* of Aiguillon was revived by an *arrêt de conseil* of 1731 in favour of the minister's father, Armand Louis, who in 1718 had married Anne Charlotte de Crussol whose family were the 'premier pairs laïques de France'.

In 1740 the future minister married Louise Félicité de Bréhan de Plélo from a chevaleresque Breton family. Their only son Armand Désiré, famous for the part he played in the Night of 4 August 1789, married Jeanne Henriette de Navailles, heiress of the senior branch of a family which claimed descent from the premier barons de Béarn.[3]

Maupeou, Terray and d'Aiguillon are often referred to as the 'triumvirate', but a better analogy would be with a troika pulling in different directions and held together only by the restraining hand of Louis XV. Though their joint defection from Choiseul to Madame du

2 Bluche, *Origine*, 394–5; Jougla de Morénas *Grand Armorial*, VI, 279; Comte de Luçay, *Les Secrétaires d'état en France depuis les origines jusqu'à 1774*, 1881, 624–5.
3 F. Bluche, *Les Honneurs de la cour*, 1957; Jougla de Morénas, *Grand Armorial*, VI, 455 and 477; Luçay, *Secrétaires d'état*, 629.

Barry ushered in the last phase of Louis XV's reign, thereafter, Terray and d'Aiguillon tended to work against Maupeou and they were prepared for some sort of an accommodation with the exiled parlement. D'Aiguillon in particular felt hampered by the forfeiture of his peerage which the old parlement had declared against him when Louis XV had evoked his case to the council and seems to have felt that only the old parlement, or a section of it, could remove this stain. Louis XV had personally intervened to stop d'Aiguillon's manoeuvres.

Secretary of state for the marine Pierre Étienne Bourgeois de Boynes (1719–83), Seigneur de Boynes. Boynes had had a joint parlementaire and conciliar career: conseiller in the parlement (1739); maître des requêtes (1746); intendant of Besançon (1754–61) and conjointly premier président of the parlement of Besançon (1757–61): in his dual capacity Bourgeois asserted royal authority, retreating to the safety of being a conseiller d'état (1761) when Choiseul's rise put an end to forward policies against the parlements. His stance, however, had earmarked him for ministerial preferment on Choiseul's fall; he was appointed to the marine in 1771 and also made a conseiller d'honneur in the 'parlement Maupeou'. He was, in the words of Michel Antoine, a 'remarkable jurist',[4] but his lack of technical expertise led to blunders in running the marine, notably his attempt to give the navy an identical organization to that of the army. Nevertheless, in one of his last political acts, Louis XV had made him a ministre on 20 April 1774, possibly with the intention of counterbalancing d'Aiguillon's increased influence in the council and underlining his support for Maupeou's measures.

Boynes's nobility was of recent vintage as can be seen from the following genealogy:

I   Pierre Bourgeois (b. 1651), *avocat, juge* at Lyon.

*II   Étienne Bourgeois (1683–1754), *écuyer*, Seigneur de Boynes; treasurer of John Law's bank; with him the family became ennobled through the purchase of the office of secrétaire du roi. Pierre married (1718) Hélène de Francini, daughter of François, Seigneur de Grandmaison, grand prévôt de l'Île de France. The Francini family originated in Florence where they had belonged to the patriciate since 1318, becoming naturalized in France in 1600.

III   Pierre Étienne married (1749) Catherine Parat de Mongeron, daughter of Jérôme Louis Parat, Seigneur de Mongeron, receveur-général des finances for Lorraine. Her sister Françoise married the Baron de Breteuil (see p. 74), the future minister for the maison.

---

4 M. Antoine, *Louis XV*, 1989, 929.

IV   IV Armand Louis B. (1775–1853), Marquis de Boynes
            married (1806) Anne-Adèle, daughter of Jacques Balavoine
            de Chévigny de Vaux, from a family ennobled in 1755.[5]

Secretary of state for the maison du roi Louis Phélypeaux (1705–77),
Comte de Saint-Florentin, Marquis then hereditary Duc de la Vrillière
(by lettres patentes of 1771). La Vrillière, better known as the Comte
de Saint-Florentin, had been a minister from the age of 20: minister for
the maison du roi (1725); secrétaire (1736) then chancelier des ordres
du roi (1756); ministre d'état (1751).

His early advancement was due to his membership of a unique
ministerial dynasty, which had at least one member in the ministry
from 1610 until 1781. Chérin, the court genealogist, describes the status
of the family as follows:

La maison de Phélypeaux, illustre par les dignités de l'Église, par celle de
Chancelier de France, par onze secrétaires d'état et par des alliances avec les
1res. races du royaume.

La Vrillière's ancestry and alliances were as follows:

I   Louis I Phélypeaux, conseiller au présidial de Blois.
*II   Raymond P. (1560–1629), Seigneur de La Vrillière; secrétaire
            d'état (1621); ennobled by purchasing the office of
            secrétaire du roi. Founder of the La Vrillière branch of the
            family.
*II   Paul P. (1569–1621), Seigneur de Pontchartrain, secrétaire
(2nd son)   d'état (1610); he, like his brother, was ennobled by
            purchasing the office of secrétaire du roi; he founded the
            Pontchartrain-Maurepas branch of the family.
III   Louis II P., second son of Raymond, created Marquis de
            Tanlay by lettres patentes of 1671, conseiller d'état.
IV   Balthazar P. (d. 1700), secrétaire d'état.
V   Louis III P. (d. 1725), Marquis de la Vrillière, etc., secrétaire
            d'état. He married Françoise de Mailly, whose noble filiation
            was established from 1050; her son, our minister, quartered
            the arms of Mailly.
VI   Louis IV P., married Amelia Ernestine von Platen, natural
            daughter of George I of England. They had no children.[6]

La Vrillière was something of a Vicar of Bray; he would have had to
have been to have served for such an 'immense' period of time, as

5 Bluche, *Origine*, 102; Jougla de Morénas, *Grand Armorial*, I, 334, II, 227; Marquis de Granges
de Surgères, *Histoire nobiliaire, 2,500 actes de l'état civil et notarial concernant les familles de
l'ancienne France*, Nantes, 1895, 339 and 446; F.A. de La Chesnay des Bois, *Dictionnaire de la
noblesse*, 3rd edn, 1863–76, 19 vols, III, 828, and VIII, 60–1.
6 Bluche, *Origine*, 345–6; Jougla de Morénas, *Grand Armorial*, V, 271–2; Luçay, *Secrétaires
d'état*, 630.

Besenval put it, 'despite all that had been done to attack him and all that he had himself done to merit dismissal'.[7] Nevertheless, throughout all the struggles with the parlements, he was there discreetly on the side of royal authority. By making him a duc, as by making Boynes a ministre, Louis XV was laying down markers concerning his personal position. Furthermore the king was stressing the ennobling quality of service to the crown: if a duc could become a secretary of state, then a secretary of state could become a duc.

La Vrillière was the formative influence in the development of the department of the maison to the point where it was the recognizable antecedent of the ministry of the interior. Before his time, this ministry had been the most junior of the four secretaryships of state, symbolized by the fact that an incoming minister had to put up 400,000 livres whereas his colleagues put up 500,000. (Their salaries, however, were similar at about 200,000 livres a year.) La Vrillière was the first occupant of the maison to be made a ministre (in 1751). Crucially he was given responsibility for Paris in 1757: the lieutenant-général de police became his subordinate; the prévôt des marchands (mayor) was appointed by the king on his advice; his relations with the parlement were manifold, though not always manifest. Generally ministers for the maison spent Monday to Wednesday in Paris, which they administered from the Louvre. Thursday to Sunday (the most important working day) was spent at Versailles, for the weekly travail with the king, meetings of the conseil d'état and the conseil des dépêches, audiences and the public dinners that the ministers gave most days except during political crises.

During his fifty-year stint at the maison, La Vrillière became famous as the 'agence ordinaire de la disgrâce des ministres'. Croÿ reflects that 'it would be interesting to count the number of lettres de cachet and dismissals he has delivered or issued in his life' and he recounts the curious case of Choiseul-Praslin, who was dismissed from the war ministry in 1770:

The Duc de la Vrillière came to Paris to see the Duc de Praslin and give him his lettre de cachet, which was very frosty and exiled him to his estates. Praslin was ill, which was often the case, very fed up and saw no point in presenting a stiff upper lip. Instead he replied peevishly that he was ill and could not budge; that he could not imagine why he was being exiled since he had never interfered with anything; as for his job, he had been sick of that for a long time, but it was unfair to exile him. He was given until the end of the week, when he was obliged to depart, ill though he was and much as he detested both his wife and country life.[8]

Since the minister for the maison also administered the long oath to

7 Baron de Besenval, *Mémoires*, ed. Berville and Barrière 1821, 2 vols, I, 320–1.
8 Duc de Croÿ, *Journal 1718–84*, ed. Grouchy and Cottin, 1906–7, 4 vols, II, 457 and 461.

new ministers (which La Vrillière personally knew by heart) he was the midwife to the events of this chapter.

Fifth secretary of state (for agriculture, manufactures, etc.) Léonard Jean Baptiste de Bertin (1719–92), Comte de Bourdeilles. This ministry had been specially created for Bertin in 1763 after he had lost the contrôle-générale when the parlement had defeated his attempt to introduce a *cadastre* of landed wealth. Bertin, whose father had been ennobled by becoming a conseiller in the parlement of Bordeaux, had previously been a maître des requêtes (1745), intendant of Roussillon (1750–3) and of Lyon (1754–7). In 1757, under the protection of Madame de Pompadour, he became lieutenant-général de police with his own travail with the king. In 1759 at the king's insistence he became contrôleur-général on the understanding that he could resign at the conclusion of peace. In 1762 he was made a ministre d'état.[9]

1774: THE NEW APPOINTMENTS

The recall of the Comte de Maurepas

While retaining his grandfather's ministers, the 19-year-old king at the same time appointed a special adviser, La Vrillière's Phélypeaux cousin, Jean Frédéric, Comte de Maurepas and Pontchartrain (1701–81). Like his cousin, Maurepas's ministerial career had begun early: minister for the maison (1718) and for the marine (1723); secrétaire (1724) then grand trésorier des ordres du roi (1736); ministre d'état (1738). Maurepas was dismissed in 1749, allegedly for circulating some scurrilous verses about Madame de Pompadour, and exiled first to Bourges, where he stayed with his cousin, Cardinal de la Roche-foucauld, the archbishop. In 1752 he was allowed to move closer to Paris, to his estate of Pontchartrain, where he had remained ever since.

The ancestry and alliances of the Maurepas-Pontchartrain branch of the Phélypeaux can best be presented in the form of a genealogy:

I	Louis Phélypeaux, common ancestor of the La Vrillière and Pontchartrain branches.
*II	Paul P., Seigneur de Pontchartrain.
III	Louis P., Seigneur de Pontchartrain, président in the chambre des comptes (1650).
IV	Louis P. (1643–1727), Comte de Pontchartrain, secrétaire d'état, chancelier de France.
V	Jérôme P. (b. 1674), Comte de Pontchartrain, secrétaire d'état; married (1) in 1697 Christine de la Rochefoucauld de

9 M. Antoine, *Louis XV*, 1989, 792.

Roye, daughter of Frédéric Charles, lieutenant-général, who was made a peer of Ireland by James II in 1688; (2) Hélène Rosalie de l'Aubespine de Verderonne: their daughter Hélène married the Duc de Nivernais (see p. 34).

VI   Jean Frédéric P., married Marie-Jeanne de Phélypeaux de la Vrillière, sister of the future Duc de la Vrillière. There were no children, and no jobs for them if there had been.

Maurepas was the candidate of the *dévôt* faction at court: Louis XVI's father, the old dauphin, had headed this faction until his death in 1765 and his maiden aunts, Adélaïde and Victoire, Mesdames Tantes, who saw themselves as the custodians of their brother's policies, are generally considered to have been instrumental in the new king's choice of Maurepas in preference to the former contrôleur-général, Machault d'Arnouville, whom Louis XV had called 'l'homme selon mon coeur'. Louis XVI did not appoint Maurepas to anything: he merely removed the impediment of exile which had prevented him exercising his right as a ministre to sit on the conseil d'état. This placed Maurepas in an invidious situation *vis-à-vis* the departmental ministers. The Abbé de Véri, the companion of his exile and the chronicler of his second ministry, believed that he should leave the ministry 'unless he becomes its soul; having no department he would cut a ridiculous figure there'.[10] This meant that Maurepas, who (whatever his threats) had no intention of returning to Pontchartrain, had to replace the ministry and preferably with his own creatures. Maurepas's wife's cousin, d'Aiguillon, was the first to go but though this was referred to at the time as a *chasse cousin*, it was largely the work of the new queen, Marie-Antoinette.

The fall and replacement of d'Aiguillon

On 2 June 1774, d'Aiguillon resigned in anticipation of being dismissed from his two ministries of war and foreign affairs. Marie-Antoinette detested him for his open identification with Madame du Barry and for having supplanted Choiseul to whom she felt a chivalrous loyalty for having arranged her marriage to the king of France. For his part, Louis acknowledged to Maurepas that d'Aiguillon was a capable minister, 'but consider the door through which he entered [Madame du Barry] and the troubles which his spite has caused'.[11] Distancing himself, Maurepas replied: 'I will only act as his relation to the extent of obtaining from you some mitigation in his punishment'.[12] Maurepas asked the king to end the barbarous practice of exiling ex-ministers, of which he had himself been a prominent victim, and to make a start

10 Abbé de Véri, *Journal, 1774–80*, ed. J. de Witte, 1928–30, 2 vols, I, 111.
11 Lenoir Papers, Bibliothèque municipale d'Orléans, MS 1421–3, 1421, 11.
12 Véri, *Journal*, I, 99 and 101.

with d'Aiguillon. Louis agreed, though he had promised Marie-Antoinette that d'Aiguillon would be exiled.[13] Later, however, he changed his mind as a result of renewed pressure from Marie-Antoinette over d'Aiguillon's involvement in the Guines Affair (see pp. 205–6). However, at first d'Aiguillon had to go only to Veuvret, near Paris, and was spared the 'usual method of a lettre de cachet', being instead put on his honour to stay there.[14] The Baron de Besenval, who directed the queen's political excursions during the first eighteen months of the reign,[15] told her that the proximity of Veuvret

would leave [d'Aiguillon] with the facility of maintaining his faction, of directing his men, and of remaining as formidable as if he were in the centre of Paris; that it was necessary he went to Aiguillon [in Gascony] whose remoteness would make it impossible for him to continue his intrigues whose thread, once broken, could not easily be mended.[16]

Marie-Antoinette took Besenval's advice and was able to boast to a confidant:

This [d'Aiguillon's] departure is all my doing. The cup was overflowing; this evil man was conducting all sorts of espionage and spreading slander. He had tried to brave my wrath more than once during the affair of M. de Guines; as soon as judgement had been given in the case I asked the king to send him [d'Aiguillon] away. It is true that I did not want to employ a lettre de cachet but nothing has been lost since instead of remaining in the Tourraine, as he wanted, he has been requested to continue his journey as far as Aiguillon.[17]

For good measure, the king told La Vrillière, both as the minister for the maison and d'Aiguillon's uncle, how discontented he was with the disgraced minister. The way in which d'Aiguillon had been arbitrarily shunted about the country and the way in which the king's anger, naturally an immediate emotion, had been deferred, caused an outcry. Besenval notes that 'we heard nothing but the words *tyranny, hard justice, liberty of the citizen* and *legality*'. Later d'Aiguillon snubbed Marie-Antoinette by refusing the offer to return to Paris while he was forbidden Versailles.[18]

Having satisfied her vengeance, Marie-Antoinette took no interest in d'Aiguillon's replacements.

The only man considered for the war ministry was Louis-Félix de Félix (1711–75), Comte du Muy. Du Muy had an unusual career, beginning as a conseiller in the parlement of Aix before embarking on the profession of arms, becoming a lieutenant-général and

13 A. d'Arneth and M.A. Geffroy (eds) *Marie-Antoinette: Correspondance secrète entre Marie-Thérèse et le Comte de Mercy-Argenteau,* 2nd edn, 1875, 3 vols, II, 322.
14 Besenval, *Mémoires,* I, 314.
15 J. Arnaud-Bouteloup, *Le rôle politique de Marie-Antoinette,* 1924, 65; Véri, *Journal,* I, 337–9.
16 Besenval, *Mémoires,* I, 314.
17 Arneth and Geffroy, *Marie-Antoinette,* II, 362.
18 Besenval, *Mémoires,* I, 314–18.

commandant-en-chef of Flanders in 1762. His break had come when he was appointed a *menin* to Louis XVI's father, the old dauphin, to whom he was devoted.

The Félix family can be traced back to Claude Félix, a merchant at Avignon in 1493. They joined the nobility in the course of the following century but not by any of the regular methods of ennoblement (our minister's great-great-grandfather was contrôleur-général de la marine and his great-grandfather was premier consul of Marseille). Du Muy's father, Jean-Baptiste de Félix, was created Marquis du Muy by lettres patentes of 1697. He started his career, like his son, as a conseiller in the parlement of Aix, and like him became a soldier, ultimately becoming commandant-en-chef in Provence and a conseiller d'état d'épée. In 1735 he was nominated one of the two sous-gouverneurs of the dauphin; he married Marguerite, daughter of Charles d'Armand, Marquis de Mizon, whose nobility was chevaler-esque. Our minister did not marry but his brother, Joseph Gabriel, second Marquis du Muy and a lieutenant-général, married into the ancient Henin-Liétard family, which enjoyed the honneurs de la cour.[19]

After Choiseul-Praslin had been sent protesting into exile, du Muy had been offered the war ministry by Louis XV but had declined:

His principal motive [Croÿ informs us] was that having the ambition to be a Marshal of France and possessing only one remote estate, he feared to be exiled like the rest and to lose his baton for which he was in line through seniority. He had a discussion with the king on the subject during the course of which His Majesty promised not to hold it against him. [Du Muy, as a dévôt, did not want to have dealings with Madame du Barry, sentiments which La Vrillière] who had no desire to see him in office . . . delivered unvarnished to the king, who accordingly did not insist.[20]

In 1774, 'counting on the coming moral reformation',[21] he accepted office under the son of his revered friend.

The filling of the vacancy at foreign affairs was less straightforward. Public opinion seemed to designate Louis Mancini-Mazarini, the Duc de Nivernais and descendant of Cardinal Mazarin's heirs. He had married Maurepas's half-sister, and Maurepas, who was a dynast, would have liked his brother-in-law to have obtained the post. The king, however, failed to mention his name, probably because he had been one of the twelve peers who had signed the protest at the suppression of the old parlement.[22] When the post of grand aumonier

19 Bluche, *Honneurs de la cour*; Jougla de Morénas, *Grand Armorial*, III, 363–4, and I, 165; Marquis de Granges de Surgères, *Répertoire historique et biographique de la 'Gazette de France'*, 1902–6, 4 vols, II, 414–15; La Chesnay des Bois, *Dictionnaire*, I, 782–95, and VII, 898; M. Michaud, *Biographie universelle ancienne et moderne*, 1843–, 45 vols, XXIX, 662–3.
20 Croÿ, *Journal*, II, 459.
21 P. Burley, 'Louis XVI and a new monarchy', PhD thesis, London University, 1981, 442.
22 Véri, *Journal*, I, 10–6.

fell vacant in September, Maurepas said he would have 'la force d'exclure mais non d'inclure', that is a veto; in making ministerial appointments this relationship with the king was often reversed, the king applying an often silent veto.

The king's choice finally alighted on Charles Gravier (1717–87) Chevalier, then Comte de Vergennes (1765). Vergennes, who studied law, was destined for a legal career: years later Mercy-Argenteau was to say of him 'le barreau perce partout'. However, when his uncle, Théodore Chevignard de Chavigny, a diplomatic soldier of fortune, was appointed ambassador to Portugal, he took his young nephew with him as his conseiller d'ambassade. In 1755 Vergennes was appointed ambassador to Constantinople but in 1768 was recalled by Choiseul for contracting what a colleague was to call an 'indecent' marriage to a woman 'prise parmi le peuple'.[23] Vergennes sought the protection of Maupeou who probably secured him the prestigious Stockholm Embassy in 1771, after Choiseul's fall.

Vergennes was third-generation noble, the family having been ennobled by *charge de robe* in the chambre des comptes de Dijon, the process starting in 1681. His father was a conseiller in that body and Vergennes was his second son. Vergennes's mother was the daughter of a notaire from Beaune, Jean Chevignard, Seigneur de Charodon. Vergennes married Anna, daughter of Henri de Viviers, a Savoyard *hobereau*, and widow of a doctor called Testa. She was not presented at court until Vergennes was at the height of his power, in 1783. Their eldest son, Constantin, was a diplomat and married Louise de Lentilhac, daughter of Louis, Comte de Sédières, brigadier des armées, whose noble filiation was established from 1500. Their second son, Charles-Joseph, married a rich creole.[24]

The choice of Vergennes, as of du Muy and indeed of Maurepas himself, was probably made personally by the new king: all three had been on a list bequeathed to him by his father the dauphin. Mayer's *Vie (éloge) de Vergennes*, dedicated to the king in May 1789, stresses that both du Muy and Vergennes had been Louis's personal choice.[25] Vergennes was also in the rare position of being acceptable both to Maupeou, who was in a sense his patron and the ideas of whose coup he had 'exported' to Sweden in 1772, and to Maurepas. Véri at least records detailed discussions in which the choice had lain between Vergennes and the Baron de Breteuil, the ambassador to Naples, who had the queen's tepid endorsement. According to Véri, both Louis XVI and Maurepas were inclined towards Breteuil but Véri warned against

23 Castries, *Journal*, Archives de la Marine, MS 182/7964 1–2, I, fo. 218.
24 Louis XV, *Correspondance secrète inédite*, ed. M.E. Boutaric, 1866, 2 vols, II, 424; for Vergennes's ancestry and career see Bluche, *Honneurs de la cour*, Marquis de Chastellux, *Notes prises aux archives de l'état civil de Paris brûlées le 24 mai 1871*, 1875, 313; Granges, *Répertoire*, IV, 427–8.
25 De Mayer, *Vie (éloge) de Vergennes*, 1789, 90–1.

his ambitious and cantankerous character (qualities he was indeed to display when he finally did become a minister) and persuaded Maurepas to plump for Vergennes, since he wanted a 'ministère harmonieux'.

The likelihood, however, is that Maurepas was rationalizing a fait accompli. The composition of the ministry after d'Aiguillon had been replaced did not favour him and indeed enabled Croÿ to talk of 'le début où le Chancelier domina'.[26] The king, Maupeou, Vergennes and du Muy had a near identity of interests. All were deeply religious, though only du Muy had the ostentatious religiocity of the dévôt. All believed in the traditional absolute monarchy and believed it was under threat from the *philosophes*. Finally Vergennes and du Muy were allies both in supporting Maupeou and in defending the *secret du roi*, which had been Louis XV's attempt to continue traditional policies after the 'diplomatic revolution'.[27] Though Louis XVI was appalled at its bizarre mechanisms, its spirit was to inform his own foreign policy;[28] he was to find in Vergennes his ideal minister.

Louis XVI's letter appointing Vergennes is worth quoting as a rare survival of the genre:

La Muette, 5 June 1774
Monsieur, the Duc d'Aiguillon having given me his resignation from his offices, the good reports of you that I have heard from all sides and your diplomatic skills have prompted me to choose you to replace him in the department of foreign affairs. So, come as quickly as you can; in taking your leave of the King of Sweden, you will give him my compliments; I much look forward to seeing you.

It is instructive to compare this flat letter with the one Louis XIV sent Pomponne, also ambassador to Sweden, in identical circumstances a hundred years before:

On receiving this letter, you will experience a wide range of emotions. Surprise, joy and [financial] embarrassment will strike you all together, because you never expected that I would pluck you out of the frozen fastnesses of the North to make you a secretary of state. Such a great distinction and the choice made of you out of all France must touch a heart such as yours and the money which I am ordering you to put up may cause a moment of embarrassment to a man who has less riches than other qualities. So much by way of preamble.[29]

Comparing Louis XVI's bland letter with Louis XIV's lively one, hovering between self-importance and self-parody, self-absorbed and yet sensitive to feelings a king will never have to experience, one

26 Croÿ, *Journal*, III, 131.
27 A.N. K164 no. 3, Du Muy and Vergennes to the king, 3 February and 3 March 1775.
28 J. Hardman, *Louis XVI*, New Haven, Conn., 1993, 88–100.
29 Archives de Vergennes, *Lettres de Louis XVI*, Louis XIV to Pomponne, 16 September 1671, published by Luçay, *Secrétaires d'état*, 73 n. 1.

could be forgiven for feeling that an age of bronze had succeeded an age of gold.

The rise of Turgot

Whereas Louis XVI's first two departmental appointments had been of men who shared his political and religious beliefs, Maurepas, under the influence of Véri, wanted to introduce two men into the ministry, Turgot and Malesherbes, who were philosophes and who ultimately wanted a radical restructuring of the monarchy. Maurepas wanted Turgot as contrôleur-général but the king, who had a good head for figures, had too high an opinion of Terray's abilities for this to be accomplished immediately: as a preliminary, Bourgeois de Boynes was forced to yield the marine to Turgot in July.

Anne Robert Jacques Turgot (1727–81), Seigneur de Brucourt, Marquis de l'Aulne, had become a maître des requêtes in 1753 and since 1761 had been intendant of Limoges, a long spell in a low-ranking généralité, sparse in population and resources. Turgot represented the tenth generation of nobility in his family, his ancestor Jean Turgot, Seigneur des Tourailles, having been ennobled in 1472 in virtue of possessing a noble fief (agrégation par fiefs). Nevertheless, the family rose to prominence through robe offices and these at first were junior and local: the fourth of the line, Loÿs (d. 1588) was a conseiller au présidial de Caen; his son, Antoine, graduated to the parlement of Rouen, but as a mere avocat, while his son Jacques (d. 1659), great-great-grandfather of the minister, was a conseiller in the same parlement. Jacques, however, went on to become intendant of Normandy and to found a dynasty of intendants: the minister was the fourth and last, for he did not marry, in a line broken only by his father, who was prévôt des marchands, then conseiller d'état and finally premier président of the grand conseil. Turgot's mother, Madeleine Martineau, was the daughter of a chevalier of the order of Saint-Lazare.[30]

The fall of Maupeou and Terray

The fall of Maupeou and Terray resulted from a struggle between the new king's official advisers, the departmental ministers, and his unofficial adviser, or his minister-without-portfolio, Maurepas. This structural struggle was predicated on a division from top to bottom within the country on the question of Maupeou's remodelling of the parlements. The issue divided the philosophes, with Diderot against

30 Bluche, *Origine*, 404–6; F. Bluche, *Les magistrats du grand conseil au XVIIIe siècle*, 1966, 141–2; Jougla de Morénas, *Grand Armorial*, VI, 370–; La Chesnay des Bois, *Dictionnaire*, XIX, 266 (for Turgot's maternal grandfather).

the measures, and Voltaire, who wrote an *Éloge de Maupeou*, in favour; the ruling house, with the immediate royal family (with the exception of Marie-Antoinette) for, and the princes of the blood (with the exception of the Comte de la Marche) against; and every talking-shop in the land. Recent scholarship suggests that such a head of steam had built up that if Louis XVI had not restored the parlement there might have been an explosion then and there. Yet the unitary nature of public opinion should be questioned, as it was by Vergennes, as also how this force, inevitably more vocal against government than for, can and could be adequately gauged.[31] One might add that if Louis XVI was determined to listen to public opinion it was desirable that it should be expressed in a formal way, that is through provincial or national assemblies.

Maurepas was aware that his advice to reconstitute the old parlement went against what he himself called the 'principles of [the king's] education' and it caused Mesdames Tantes to regret recommending him. Maurepas must have believed that he had the skill to manage what many considered to be the only legitimate parlement and thus to secure for the young king smooth government without the imputation of despotism. He also thought that what had become in effect a hereditary parlement was a force for stability in a changing world when the self-recruiting ministries of the palmy days of the Phélypeaux had come to an end and the day of the grand seigneur minister was at hand. Véri notes:

Venality of office is regarded by many people and even by M. de Maurepas as an institution which is worth bringing back with the aim of instilling the mentality of the Magistrature in the families destined for it.[32]

It took Maurepas months to bring the king round.[33] Finally he yielded after Maurepas arrived for his travail without his portfolio, refusing to discuss affairs until the king had decided on the fate of the two ministers. Since La Vrillière could not be in two places at once, Maurepas undertook to inform Terray of his dismissal himself. The king told Maurepas, 'I'm sorry; I really would have liked to have been able to keep him, but he is too great a knave. It's a pity, a pity'; and Maurepas himself was to observe ruefully in 1780, 'we are still living off his resources'.[34]

There was question of making him hand back the insignia of the Saint Esprit but this was rejected, not on humanitarian grounds, but lest 'it suggest too great a disorder in the finances'. The only way a robin could become a member of a military order was by becoming an

31 Notably, D. Echeverria, *The Maupeou Revolution*, Baton Rouge, La., 1985; on Vergennes and public opinion, see Hardman, *Louis XVI*, 67–8.
32 Véri, *Journal*, I, 120–3.
33 For details see below, 238–4.
34 Véri, *Journal*, I, 83.

official in it such as treasurer or secretary. The diplomat Bombelles thought this device fooled no one and should be discontinued, 'so as to limit the number of cordons bleus that the sovereign and the people are often obliged to behold festooning the bodies of men dismissed from office'.[35]

La Vrillière, having endured Praslin's repining, now had to face Maupeou's blank refusal to resign the chancelerie. This was his legal right because Louis XIV and Louis XV had not wanted to incur the odium of abolishing this medieval office, political encumbrance though its survival was. Thus Maupeou marked his belief in his policies and the sacrifices he had made for the crown: his son, for example, René Augustin, a président à mortier in the parlement, had had to change to a military career, becoming a maréchal de camp and a chevalier de Saint-Louis in 1788. Since there was no question of putting him on trial, Maupeou, who lived until 1792, remained chancellor until the office was abolished during the Revolution. He was exiled to Normandy and his duties were performed by a keeper of the seals, Miromesnil. Miromesnil told Véri that ministerial exiles were unfair:

From the beginning of this reign, I told M. de Maurepas that he must thoroughly instil this principle into the king: that, as regards the ministers, the king could withdraw his confidence from them and dismiss them but that he should not inflict any other form of punishment on them unless they were guilty of malversation, and that their exile was an injustice.

If Maupeou had asked for his exile to be ended, 'I would not hesitate to satisfy him', but added, 'if it lay in my department. But I believe that it is in that of the secretary of state for the maison du roi'. Véri was surprised:

'I always understood that if the chancellor was at Paris, he would automatically resume his functions'; 'A misconception', Miromesnil replied. 'Can any minister or important functionary in France perform his duties when he does not have the king's ear? The presence of the chancellor would no more embarrass me at Paris than on his estates. I would allow him to to put on all the ceremonial that he liked. We attend the same parish church. If he wanted a ceremonial appearance on Easter Day, I would let him take precedence over me in the most solemn mass'.[36]

Armand Thomas Hue de Miromesnil (1732–96), Marquis de Miromesnil, was the candidate of Maurepas, his 'ami de tout temps', for whom he supplied the plan for a conditional restoration of the exiled parlement (see pp. 219–20). His career had been somewhat unusual. Up to the age of 25 he seemed to be pursuing a classical career within the royal administration – conseiller au grand conseil

35 Marquis de Bombelles, *Journal*, ed. J. Grassion and F. Durif, Geneva, 1978–93, 3 vols, I, 327.
36 Véri, MSS *Journal*, cahier 109.

(1745), maître des requêtes (1751) – but in 1757 he was appointed premier président of the parlement of Rouen, married the daughter of the président à mortier in that body and generally identified himself with his *corps* rather than with the king, an attitude for which he once received a personal rebuke from Louis XV.[37] In 1771, Miromesnil had thrown in his lot with his colleagues when Louis XV, considering the parlement of Rouen incorrigible, had suppressed rather than merely remodelled it.

Many considered that Miromesnil did not have sufficient breeding to be keeper: Véri even said that he had a bourgeois demeanour! Yet the following genealogy shows that his ancestry was quite distinguished within the administrative robe:

*I   Pierre Hue, président in the élection of Saint-Lo; ennobled by lettres patentes of 1590.

II   Michel Hue (Pierre's third son), écuyer, Seigneur de Miromesnil; conseiller in the parlement of Rouen, then conseiller d'état.

III   Thomas Hue de Miromesnil, intendant of Champagne (1675); président in grand conseil.

IV   Thomas Hue de Miromesnil (d. 1749), Marquis de Miromesnil, captain in the Régiment de Quercy; married (1721) Anne, daughter of Claude-Joseph Lambert, auditeur in the chambre des comptes.

V   Armand Thomas, fifth-generation noble; married (1) in 1750 Marie-Louise, daughter of Louis-Marie du Hamel, président à mortier in the parlement of Rouen; (2) in 1762 Blanche, daughter of Armand Jérôme Bignon, conseiller d'état and prévôt des marchands (1762), from a distinguished robe family ennobled by *charge de parlement* starting in 1620.

Miromesnil's children were

I   François Thomas (b. 1768), son of the minister's second marriage; chevalier de Malte de minorité, admitted to the école militaire in 1789 and died young.

II   A daughter of the first marriage married Le Bret, avocat-général of the parlement of Rouen.

III   Marie, daughter of the second marriage, married the Marquis de Bérulle, premier président of the parlement of Grenoble and died the day after her father was dismissed.[38]

Thus the family had been ennobled by lettres patentes rather than the office of secrétaire du roi (which was a straight purchase) and boasted

---

37 Miromesnil, *Correspondance politique*, ed. P. Le Verdier, 1889–, 4 vols, I, 171.
38 For Miromesnil's ancestry and career, see Bluche, *Grand Conseil*, 89–90; Jougla de Morénas, *Grand Armorial*, IV, 315; La Chesnay des Bois, *Dictionnaire*, X, 843.

a conseiller d'état as well as an intendant. The minister's father, it is true, had not progressed far in his military career, nor had he married well, and the minister himself was not well off.

Miromesnil was the most conservative influence on the king during the first thirteen years of his reign. The following letter to the king, dated 20 December 1786, justifying his delaying tactics in according an *état civil* to the Protestants, illustrates how he managed to retain the king's confidence for so long and also why Louis finally became exasperated by his subtlety. Indeed, if this letter does not describe the man, he is indescribable:

From the moment when Your Majesty deigned to summon me to his service, I made myself a rule to open my heart to you in every situation with the most complete abandon. I have never had occasion to regret my decision and I have always met with kindness at your hands; I will never alter my conduct.

I fear that people have tried to persuade Your Majesty that the difficulty I have hitherto experienced in proposing a plan relating to the marriage of Protestants and of those who do not profess the Catholic and apostolic religion, is based on prejudice, pusillanimous fears, superstition or wavering principles.

I can assure Your Majesty that though my family was formerly Protestant and my forefathers only embraced the Roman Catholic religion at the same time as Henri IV embraced it, I am sincerely attached to this religion which I believe to be the only true one but that I do not have any prejudices against the Protestants.

I have as a guiding principle that in great affairs of state one must exercise the greatest circumspection before undertaking anything and that one must firmly maintain a course of action that one has decided after mature reflection and after having weighed all the circumstances and foreseen all possible consequences. I think that changes of policy weaken the effectiveness of government and are the inevitable consequence of taking decisions too lightly.[39]

Bombelles, who knew them both, drew a comparison between Miromesnil and Vergennes. Miromesnil had a fine intellect and was 'one of the wittiest men at court'; on one occasion he 'had [Bombelles] in stitches'. Vergennes, in contrast, was pedestrian. But the king and the state were better served by Vergennes than by Miromesnil, because Vergennes sought to uphold the royal authority whereas Miromesnil, 'confounding prudence with weakness', delivered it piecemeal to the parlement.[40]

Many thought that Malesherbes, an even better conversationalist than Miromesnil, should have been made chancellor instead of him, ignoring the fact that Malesherbes himself did not want the job (on the grounds that any parlementaire would lack the necessary

39 A.N. K163 no. 8. 20.
40 Bombelles, *Journal*, II, 110.

objectivity),[41] nor did the king want him to have it. Maurepas had brought his name up with the king in July but had received the sharp rejoinder: 'Don't mention him for anything; he is too dangerous an *encyclopédiste*'; when Maurepas returned to the charge in August, the king had to remind him, 'I find him unsuitable as I've already told you'. Malesherbes was, according to Véri, 'the only candidate whom the king rejected out of hand'.[42] When Turgot persisted in pressing Malesherbes's claims, Véri comments:

He is unaware of the *décision précise* that the king had pronounced against him and he believed that the king merely has a *simple prévention* against him.

This distinction between a 'décision précise' – a formal and fundamental objection – and a 'simple prévention' – an ordinary prejudice – indicated the limits of the pressure that it was considered legitimate, within the ministerial milieu, to put on the king in the matter of ministerial appointments. Malesherbes was beyond the pale: he was a philosophe, an atheist and, as premier président of the cour des aides he had protested against the suppression of the parlement.

The replacement of Terray

Turgot was the only candidate but there was a problem which Véri defines as follows:

If he quits the position of secretary of state for that of contrôleur-général, it is, according to received wisdom, to take a drop in rank. It also means leaving a stable, quiet and agreeable department in order to take on one that is stormy, subject to constant pressure and very difficult to discharge.

Accordingly before accepting the drop in rank and security of tenure involved, Turgot asked for an audience of the king, a request which Maurepas seconded, 'because he is making a big sacrifice in accepting which you ought to appreciate'. At the audience, Turgot asked 'to put in writing my general ideas and I venture to say my conditions on the way in which you should help me run this department'.[43] Ultimately this approach would prove too much for the king; but on one thing the two men were in perfect accord: Terray's was to be the last bankruptcy.

Turgot was replaced at the marine by Antoine Raymond Jean Gualbert Gabriel de Sartine (1729–1801), who since 1759 had been lieutenant-général de police. Before that he had been conseiller (1752)

41 Véri, *Journal*, I, 175.
42 ibid., I, 156.
43 ibid., I, 186–7.

then lieutenant-criminel (1755) in the châtelet; maître des requêtes (1759). In 1767 he had been made a conseiller d'état and in 1775 was to be made a ministre d'état.

His abundance of Christian names could not conceal the fact that Sartine was one of only two born commoners to be appointed by Louis XVI before the Revolution: he was ennobled by lettres patentes on his appointment as lieutenant-criminel in 1755. Perhaps, as Bombelles observed, this was why 'alone of the secretaries of state and ministres taken from the robe, [Sartine] had the moderation or self-respect (properly understood) not to have himself given one of those offices [in the military orders]'.[44]

Sartine's father, Antoine de Sartine, was born in Lyon but entered the service of Philip V of Spain, became a councillor in the council of finance, and later an intendant des armées. These posts brought him nobility in Spain. He married Catherine Wills, Comtesse d'Alby, lady-in-waiting to the Queen of Spain and daughter of the Jacobite secretary of state for Ireland, Charles Wills. Their son became a naturalized Frenchman and married (1759) Marie-Anne, daughter of Étienne Hardy du Plessis, chevalier de Saint-Louis, a former captain of infantry. Their son became a maître des requêtes and a debauchee. He married the daughter of the courtesan Madame de Sainte-Amaranthe and the three were guillotined together in 1794. Sartine retired to his native Spain.[45]

As lieutenant-général de police, Sartine had been the subordinate of the minister for the maison, though the police minister often had direct relations and a separate travail with the king. Marie-Antoinette, who 'openly protected' Sartine as a protégé of Choiseul's, regretted his appointment to a post so far removed from his talents and experience: in her opinion, the maison was 'effectively the only one which would have suited M. de Sartine'.[46] The debate about the necessity for prior experience relevant to the work of a department continues in all regimes but at the end of the ancien régime there was a notion, possibly deriving from Choiseul and continued by Marie-Antoinette that the marine and war departments ought to be filled by men from the services, who had the requisite birth and training, and that the protean ex-maître des requêtes, such as Sartine, could no longer take on any ministry. This was a novel doctrine: before the mid-century grand seigneurs had considered the post of secrétaire as degrading, as had the Maréchal-Duc de Belle-Îsle, who in 1758 had to be persuaded by a deputation of his peers that acceptance of the war ministry would

44 Bombelles, *Journal*, I, 327.
45 For Sartine's ancestry and career, see B.N. Nouveau d'Hozier, 301; Jougla de Morénas, *Grand Armorial*, VI, 173; Granges, *Répertoire*, IV, 226–7; La Chesnay des Bois, *Dictionnaire*, XVIII, 293; Michaud, *Biographie universelle*, XXXVII, 252.
46 Arneth and Geffroy, *Marie-Antoinette*, II, 237.

not entail dérogeance.[47] He was the last to have such qualms, and the transition from grand seigneurs despising ministerial office to demanding a monopoly of at least the service ministries was rapid and not without consequences for the royal authority which had benefited from their self-exclusion.

1775

The completion of Maurepas's ministry

The two ministerial changes of 1775 were occasioned by La Vrillière's retirement in July, having celebrated fifty years at the maison, and du Muy's sudden death in October. Maurepas profited from them to complete the formation of his 'ministère harmonieux' but not without a struggle (which he was bound to win but which he over-dramatized) with Marie-Antoinette and what was loosely termed le parti Choiseul.

The Duc de Choiseul may have cast a long shadow from his exile at Chanteloup, but equally the battles that were fought in his name were largely shadow-boxing. We know that there was never the least chance of Louis XVI allowing Choiseul to return to office: he disliked him for his enmity with his father, his dominance of his grandfather and his identification with the old parlement. Unfortunately he did not make this sufficiently clear either to Maurepas or to Marie-Antoinette, though Choiseul himself got the message. On 12 June 1774, Marie-Antoinette procured Choiseul's return to court without Maurepas being consulted, but the king said he had permitted this only after Choiseul's old departments of war and foreign affairs had been filled; he added that 'if his friends make too much fuss about his return to Paris he would, as king, be offended'.[48]

On 13 July 1775, Marie-Antoinette wrote to a confidant:

At last we are going to get rid of M. de la Vrillière. Although he is hard of hearing he has finally got the message that it was time for him to go if he didn't want to get his nose trapped in the door.[49]

She had planned to have Sartine moved to the maison, filling his place at the marine with a *Choiseuliste*, d'Ennery. The Maurepas ministry wanted to block this move by having Malesherbes succeed La Vrillière. Unfortunately, neither side had consulted their respective candidates: Malesherbes, who had no administrative ability, thought that a ministerial appointment was 'after a fatal illness . . . the worst thing

---

47 Duc de Luynes, *Mémoires sur la cour de Louis XV, 1735–58*, ed. Dussieux and Soulié, 1860–65, 17 vols, XVI, 390; Cardinal de Bernis, François Joachim de Pierre, *Mémoires et lettres*, ed. F. Masson, 1878, 2 vols, II, 61.
48 Véri, *Journal*, I, 110.
49 Arneth and Geffroy, *Marie-Antoinette*, II, 362.

which could befall him',[50] while Besenval spent two hours trying to persuade Sartine to change jobs:

Having entered into the greatest detail on the dangers and disadvantages of the ministry of the marine, I depicted in as rosy light as I could, the situation of the minister for the maison, on whom everything which related immediately to the king and a large part of the court seemed to depend. I demonstrated that this post, without being exposed to those great affairs of state which often brought about the fall of a minister, nevertheless had a day-to-day importance which made the minister for the maison a person of consequence. Many people depended on him but he depended on no one, and the best proof I could give him was the immense time M. de la Vrillière had been there despite everything which had been done to attack him and despite everything he had done himself to be sacked. . . . M. de Sartine appeared astonished by my words and very attached to the department of the marine, of which he made a thoroughgoing defence.[51]

Years later Sartine told Véri why he so much disliked the maison:

In the first place the court is a hornets' nest of jumped up valets whose insolence or crawling by turns is revolting. It would be the secretary of state who had to carry out the plans for economical reform which the finance ministry has to demand of them; and this reform would be a Hell. . . . As for the department of Paris, it seems in truth . . . that the minister's job is restricted to surveillance of prostitutes and the writers for the Opera. But does he not also have a role in matters relating to the parlement? Do not the affairs of the clergy end up on his desk? And the precautions taken to prevent disorders in the capital, lettres de cachet, orders for the Bastille and Vincennes? Has he not also in his department several [provincial] parlements and the pays d'états?[52]

Nor was Malesherbes more amenable when the king swallowed his décision précise and agreed to appoint him: 'Louis XVI', Véri notes disingenuously, 'is disabused of his false assumptions'. On Malesherbes's refusal, Marie-Antoinette again pressed her candidates. Véri called it 'the moment of battle on whose outcome depends the consolidation of the present ministry or its resignation'.[53] His friends confronted Malesherbes with the spectre of Choiseul's return and war with England within six months; and the king wrote to him: 'Je crois que cela est absolument nécessaire pour le bien de l'État'. Véri sat with Malesherbes's curious reply to the king before him as he made the entry in his diary: 'It contains his acceptance for a while but reserves the right to mention his resignation frequently'.[54]

Chrétien Guillaume de Lamoignon de Malesherbes (1721–94), Seigneur de Malesherbes, had been premier président of the cour des

50 Véri, *Journal*, I, 317.
51 Besenval, *Mémoires*, I, 320–1.
52 Véri, MSS *Journal*, de Witte's copy, cahier 100.
53 Véri, *Journal*, I, 315.
54 ibid., I, 317.

aides since 1749 and in this capacity had prepared the famous *grandes remontrances*. Son of the Chancellor Lamoignon de Blancmesnil, Malesherbes belonged to the most distinguished family in the parlement. The Lamoignon family claimed chevaleresque origins though these were not accepted by Chérin. The descent of Malesherbes and of his cousin Lamoignon de Bâville, who succeeded Miromesnil as keeper of the seals in 1787, can most conveniently be presented as a genealogy:

I	Jean Lamoignon (married 1477), contrôleur de la dépense of the Duc de Nivernais.
II	François de Lamoignon (b. 1480) held a similar post.
*III	Charles de Lamoignon (d. 1572), ennobled by charge de robe (conseiller au parlement, maître des requêtes, conseiller d'état), the process starting in 1557.
IV	Chrétien de Lamoignon (d. 1636), président à mortier (1633).
V	Guillaume de Lamoignon (d. 1677), Marquis de Basville (1670), premier président of the parlement.
VI	Chrétien François de Lamoignon (d. 1709), président à mortier.
VII (1)	Chrétien de Lamoignon, third Marquis de Bâville (d. 1729), président à mortier, grandfather of the keeper of the seals.
VII (2)	Guillaume de Lamoignon de Blancmesnil, chancellor of France (1750–68); married (2) Anne, daughter of Nicolas Étienne Roujault, intendant of Bourges in 1699, whose family was ennobled by the office of secrétaire du roi in 1607.
VIII	Chrétien Guillaume de Lamoignon de Malesherbes, married (1749) Marie-Françoise, daughter of Antoine-Gaspard Grimod de la Reynière, farmer-general, whose father had been ennobled by the office of secrétaire du roi. They had two daughters:

1. Marguérite married (1769) Louis Lepeltier de Rosambo, président à mortier, whose family, one of the most powerful in the parlement, had been ennobled by the office of secrétaire du roi in 1637.
2. Françoise Pauline, married (1775) Charles de Montboissier-Beaufort-Canillac, maître de camp in the Régiment d'Orléans. The nobility of his family was chevaleresque and La Chesnay de Bois characterizes it as 'une des plus illustres maisons du Royaume'.[55]

The appointment of Malesherbes completed the replacement of Louis

55 For Malesherbes's ancestry and career, see Bluche, *Origine*, 234–6; La Chesnay des Bois, *Dictionnaire*, XI, 388.

XV's last ministry. All were to an extent Maurepas's appointments, with the possible exception of du Muy, who had a different outlook and showed more independence than the others; in particular he resisted the tendency of the other ministers to seek unity under Maurepas by performing their weekly travail with the king in his presence. Another characteristic of this ministry was its robin complexion (even du Muy had trained as a lawyer and started his career as a provincial parlementaire). This represented a temporary reversal of the trend of aristocratic influx into the ministry which had started during the Seven Years War. Thus the advantages for Maurepas of Malesherbes's appointment, as presented by Besenval, could equally be applied to the others:

isolated, without a connection, without one of those names which impresses at Versailles and which necessarily carries in its wake a numerous and powerful family; . . . in addition an *homme de robe*, a title which always had claims on M. de Maurepas.[56]

Choiseul, too, in the audience which Marie-Antoinette granted him at the time of the coronation,

disparaged the present ministry with pleasantries. He did his best to ridicule the *gens de robe* and I [Mercy-Argenteau] noticed subsequently that this part of the audience had made an impression on the queen.[57]

The death and replacement of du Muy

Du Muy died in office, during an operation to remove a gallstone, on 10 October, having achieved his ambition of being made a marshal of France earlier that year. His reservations about accepting ministerial office had proved groundless. His replacement went more smoothly for Maurepas than had that of La Vrillière. On hearing of du Muy's death, Besenval went boldly up to Maurepas:

I told him that I had too much respect for him to believe the rumours from Paris that he wanted to give us [the military] an homme de robe; that he was too long in the tooth not to realize that a bigwig was not at all suitable as head of the French army; that we needed a man from our own class.[58]

He recommended Castries, a protégé of Choiseul's who had gained the victory of Klösterseven in the Seven Years War. The queen, according to Véri, also 'wanted Castries to get the job, who assuredly wanted it more than she did'. However, she had come to an arrangement with Maurepas which defined her sphere of influence as court rather than ministerial appointments and as a token of his intent he had allowed the creation of the surintendance de la maison de la reine in favour of

56 Besenval, *Mémoires*, I, 329–30.
57 Arneth and Geffroy, *Marie-Antoinette*, II, 356–7.
58 Besenval, *Mémoires*, II, 11.

her current favourite, the Princess de Lamballe. Indeed Marie-Antoinette was to have no further influence in ministerial appointments for another five years. Accordingly when tackled by Besenval about du Muy's successor, she replied evasively: 'Our business is going well; we are unlikely to have an homme de robe'.[59]

She knew that Maurepas had chosen Charles Louis de Saint-Germain (1707–78), Baron (called Comte) de Saint-Germain; he came of 'an ancient and noble family but very poor and without distinction', originally from Savoy, where Guillaume de Saint-Germain was juge-masse de Bresse (c. 1290). About 1600 the family established itself at Lons-le-Saunier in Franche-Comté. An unconventional man and an unconventional appointment, Saint-Germain trained to be a Jesuit until 1726 (hence Besenval's quip 'he was just an old de-frocked monk totally out of place at court'); in 1733 he left France after killing a man in a duel and sought service with the emperor, becoming a general in 1745 and marrying into the ancient and well-connected Osten family. Returning to France, he quarrelled with his superior officers during the Seven Years War and in 1762 became Danish commander-in-chief.[60] Vergennes considered that his international experience was invaluable, as he told the king at one critical juncture:

the great affairs which he has witnessed and conducted in the course of his life, and the reflective and resourceful mind with which he is endowed can only make his opinion very valuable.[61]

Saint-Germain's disassociation from the disasters of the Seven Years War made him the ideal instrument for the reform of the army which that war had seemed to render necessary. Turgot recommended him to Maurepas and regarded him as a fellow-reformer. Véri observed:

This choice is not the most pleasing to the courtier soldiers but it is to the professionals and to public opinion both in Paris and the provinces

and added that his appointment was

calculated to give the ministry a unity which the character of M. du Muy rendered impossible despite his honesty.[62]

Several sources note Saint-Germain's assiduity in inviting Maurepas to attend his travail with the king;[63] Madame de Maurepas told Véri that Saint-Germain had been appointed as an 'homme sans parti', a characteristic of all Maurepas's appointments, for instance Malesherbes,

59 ibid., II, 12.
60 For Saint-Germain's ancestry and career, see *Correspondance particulière du Comte de Saint-Germain avec M. Pâris-Duverney, conseiller d'état*, London, 1789, 1–3; P. Guichenon, *Histoire du Bresse et du Bugey*, Lyon, 1650, 3me. partie, 343–5; R. Lurion, *Nobiliaire de Franche-Comté*, Besançon, 1890–, 706–7; Michaud, *Biographie universelle*, XXXVII, 321–3.
61 A.N. K163 no. 4, undated.
62 Véri, *Journal*, I, 359
63 Prince de Montbarey, *Mémoires*, 1826–7, 3 vols, 248.

'isolé et sans entours' and Vergennes, whom Mercy rightly considered to lack 'solid backing' at court.[64]

1776

The year saw a resignation (Malesherbes), a dismissal, indeed a *disgrâce* (Turgot), a revival (of the post of chef du conseil royal des finances in favour of Maurepas), a death (of Clugny, Turgot's successor) and a highly unconventional appointment at the finance ministry (Necker).

The replacement of Malesherbes

Notwithstanding Malesherbes's insistence on the right to make frequent reference to his resignation, when at the beginning of 1776 he gave two months' notice, the king was offended: during this period, though he saw Malesherbes twice a week in the conseil d'état, he granted him only one tête-à-tête travail at which he indicated that he would find it disagreeable if the minister raised the subject of his resignation: we know all this from a letter which Malesherbes, unable to communicate with the king orally, was forced to write him.[65] Finally, in May, he obtained his release. He had been made a ministre d'état in 1775 and was to resume his seat on the council in 1787.

Maurepas chose as his successor at the maison Jean Antoine Amelot (1732–95), Seigneur de Chaillou, the son of a close friend and colleague during his first ministry who had been foreign secretary. Prior to his appointment, Amelot had been maître des requêtes (1753); président in the grand conseil (1754); intendant of Dijon (1764) and intendant des finances (1774).[66]

The Amelots, who had been ennobled by lettres patentes in 1580, were a dynasty of noblesse d'état like the Phélypeaux, only less grand, being (with the exception of Amelot's father) intendants rather than ministers. Amelot's descent was as follows:

I   Denis Amelot (d. 1655), Seigneur de Chaillou, intendant of province, intendant des finances, conseiller d'état.

II   Jacques A. de C., doyen of the maître des requêtes (1699).

III   Denis A. de C. (b. 1666), intendant du commerce (1708).

64 Besenval, *Mémoires*, I, 329; Arneth and Geffroy, *Marie-Antoinette*, II, 288.
65 P. Grosclaude, *Malesherbes*, 1961, 117–18.
66 For Amelot's ancestry and career, see Bluche, *Origine*, 60–1, 261 and 410; Bluche, *Grand Conseil*, 44–5; *Dictionnaire de biographie française* (D.B.F.) II, 603–15; Granges, *Histoire nobiliaire*, 4; La Chesnay des Bois, *Dictionnaire*, III, 300–3 and VII, 969–70; N.V. de Saint-Allais, *Nobiliaire universelle de France*, 1872–6, 21 vols, 2, 157–9.

IV   Jean-Jacques A. de C., foreign secretary (1737–44). Our minister was the child of his second wife Anne, daughter of Jean de Vougny, intendant des finances, who was ennobled by the purchase of the office of secrétaire du roi in 1703.

V   Jean Antoine A. de C., sixth-generation noble. He married (1759) Jeanne, daughter of Paul Legendre, président in the chambre des comptes.

VI   Antoine A. (1760–1824), Marquis de Chaillou; intendant de Dijon (1783); married into the family of de Bire, whose nobility was recognized as chevaleresque by an *arrêté* of the parlement of Rennes in 1748.

To this undistinguished functionary, Malesherbes and Turgot would have preferred the Abbé de Véri, who assures us that he would not have declined and even that he regarded his diary as a substitute for political power. But it was none of Turgot's business and his letters to the king criticizing Maurepas alienated them both.

The fall and replacement of Turgot

The conventional view of Turgot's fall is that it was determined by the parlement's opposition to his Six Edicts but this is unconvincing in view of the fact that two months elapsed between their registration by lit de justice on 12 March and Turgot's dismissal. Rather, Turgot fell because his relations with his colleagues and ultimately with the king had deteriorated. This was partly a question of policy; Miromesnil considered that his reforms, however modest, were the thin end of the wedge and would have led to a dissolution of the social structure of the ancien régime;[67] Turgot told the king that Amelot was 'sold to M. de Miromesnil'. Vergennes disliked Turgot's policies less for their content than for their doctrinaire packaging; he also knew that Turgot was opposed to France's involvement in England's quarrel with her North American colonies.

However, the heart of the problem was Turgot's interference in the running of his colleagues' departments. Coordination between the departments was essentially the task of a prime minister or ultimately of the king: this is the force of Louis's celebrated *boutade*, 'M. Turgot wants to be me and I don't want him to be me'. However, neither Louis nor Maurepas was performing this task adequately, at least in the financial sphere, as Véri recognized:

Only the king or M. de Maurepas can force departmental reductions and that is what they are not doing. M. Turgot wanted to carry out their function and has made himself odious even to M. de Saint-Germain whom he got appointed.

67 Véri, MSS *Journal*, cahier 109.

Turgot even went further: through wanting 'the cooperation of his equals' and 'colleagues who shared his views' he was unconsciously moving in the direction of an English-style prime minister. Small wonder that every time he interfered in the other departments, 'a drop of distaste was added to the others so that in their innermost soul there was not one of his ministerial colleagues who did not have a secret wish to be rid of him'.[68]

Turgot felt his dismissal keenly, more, Madame de Maurepas told Véri, than his friend realized. Turgot had been planning to submit to the king his memorandum on reforming the household: 'It will almost certainly be rejected and I will ask for my freedom'. However, the king avoided seeing him and he was dismissed by 'your [Véri's] old friend [Maurepas] without waiting for me to ask to go'.[69] Amelot being new at the maison, the letter of dismissal was delivered by the doyen of the secrétaires d'état, Bertin.[70]

Turgot was succeeded by Maurepas's candidate Jean Étienne Bernard de Clugny (1729–76), Baron de Nuits-sur-Armancon, whose tenure of the contrôle was short (May–October) even by the standards of the reign and unique in being ended by death rather than dismissal. Nevertheless, he had time to repeal most of Turgot's measures. Clugny, who had followed his father and grandfather as a conseiller in the parlement of Dijon, was probably descended from Pierre de Clugny, who was ennobled by lettres patentes in 1380 and whose son was chancellor to the Duke of Burgundy. Clugny's mother was of the powerful robin dynasty of Gilbert de Voisins, ennobled by charge de robe from 1482; he married Charlotte Tardieu de Maleyssie, daughter of the fourth Marquis de Maleyssie, lieutenant du roi at Compiègne, from a family ennobled in the sixteenth century which had provided the army with lieutenant-générals. After leaving Dijon, Clugny had become a maître des requêtes (1764), intendant-général de la marine (1770), intendant of Roussilon (1774) and of Bordeaux (1775).[71]

Turgot's fall revealed that he had been a rival centre of power to Maurepas. Shortly afterwards, the king appointed Maurepas chef du conseil royal des finances. This was not a departmental appointment and the conseil des finances no longer met. Maurepas had revived it in 1774 (it met at Marly on 19 July for the first time in many years)[72] but this was a ploy to circumscribe Terray, whose fall the conseil des finances did not long survive. This seigneurial, remunerative, honorific title, 'as often left vacant as filled', was sometimes held by the leading minister (though it had been held by Choiseul-Praslin rather than by

68 Véri, *Journal*, I, 416 and 424–58, for the details of Turgot's fall and his letters to the king.
69 Véri, *Journal*, I, 431.
70 Croÿ, *Journal*, III, 264.
71 For Clugny's ancestry and career, see Bluche, *Honneurs de la cour*; Jougla de Morénas, *Grand Armorial*, II, 466, IV, 152, and VI, 265; Woëlmont, *Notices généalogiques*, III, 216–24.
72 Véri, *Journal*, I, 134.

Choiseul himself); Chapter 6, on prime ministers, will consider the extent to which Maurepas and his successors turned it into something analogous to the English first lord of the treasury.

The appointment of Necker

Clugny's sudden death led to a division of the finance ministry which, according to Augeard, Maurepas had planned to make in any case.[73] Its titular head, with the title contrôleur-général, became Louis Gabriel Taboureau (1718–82), Seigneur des Réaux. Taboureau was a transfuge, that is he had been a conseiller in the parlement for eighteen years from 1740 before transferring to the conseil d'état, becoming successively maître des requêtes (1757), intendant of Hainault (1764–75) and conseiller d'état (1775).

Taboureau's ancestry cannot be traced back beyond his great-grandfather Louis, a silk merchant at Tours. His son Louis II, merchant and receveur des tailles at Angoulême, purchased nobility through the office of secrétaire du roi in 1713. The minister's father was grande maître des eaux et forêts du Lyonnais and his mother Catherine Bazin, who was descended from Louis XIII's premier médecin who obtained 'lettres de réhabilitation de noblesse' in 1611 and subsequently furnished bishops, lieutenants-général and intendants. In 1773 Taboureau married the daughter of the premier président of the chambre des comptes of Blois, Jean-Amadée Desnoyers, Seigneur de Lorme.[74]

Direction of the trésor royal was given to Jacques Necker (1732–1817). Necker was descended from a line of Protestant pastors established in Brandenburg, though his father Charles Frédéric was professor of German law at Geneva and qualified as 'bourgeois de Genève'. Necker married Suzanne Curchod, woman of letters, in 1764. Their only child, Germaine, married in 1786 Eric Magnus, Baron de Staël-Holstein, the Swedish ambassador to France.[75]

Having made a fortune as a banker, Necker had retired in 1772, and had achieved celebrity the following year with his neo-mercantilist *Éloge de Colbert*. Necker was put in contact with both the king and Maurepas through Alexandre Masson, Marquis de Pezay who, in Véri's phrase, 'had carved out for himself a sort of ministry by writing letters to the king and receiving replies'. Pezay's father, Masson, was an important naval contractor and had had many dealings with Maurepas

73 Augeard, *Mémoires secrètes*, 52ff.
74 For Taboureau's ancestry and career, see Bluche, *Origine*, 391; Bluche, *Grand Conseil*, 139; A.P. Dutertre, 'Notice sur la famille Taboureau', *Nouvelle Revue Héraldique*, Yssingeaux, 1935; Jougla de Morénas, *Grand Armorial*, II, 24; *Société des études de Cambrai*, recueil, XIV (1924).
75 For Necker's ancestry and career, see Granges, *Répertoire*, III, 723; Michaud, *Biographie universelle*, XL, 115–25; Dr Robinet, *Dictionnaire historique et biographique de la Révolution et de l'Empire*, 1898, 2 vols, II, 606–7.

when he was minister for the marine. Maurepas stood godfather to Masson's son, who later wrote a book on the *Campagnes de Maillebois* and became tutor in military tactics to Louis XVI when dauphin. He may even have contributed to Maurepas's own appointment. Through Pezay, Necker sent financial projects to both the king and Maurepas: in August or September 1776 he refers in a letter to Maurepas to 'the analysis of the financial situation which I have made and of which the king approves'.[76] This may have been a bluff; however, the king, having rejected bankruptcy and further taxation of the peasantry, knew that the war with England that seemed to be approaching would have to be fought on credit and Necker plausibly observed that this could more easily be obtained by an ex-banker than an ex-intendant. The ex-intendant, Taboureau, finding his curious position insupportable, resigned in June 1777, taking as his pretext Necker's abolition of the intendants des finances.[77] Necker became directeur-général des finances; as a Protestant he could not be contrôleur-général.

1777

The appointment of Montbarey

In 1776, with Maurepas's encouragement, Saint-Germain had taken as his *adjoint* and *survivancier* his friend and fellow franc-comtois Alexandre Léonore de Saint-Maurice (1732–96), Brigadier, Comte de Montbarey. In 1774 he had been made a prince of the Holy Roman Empire (he was known as the Prince de Montbarey) and in 1780 he became a grandee of Spain. Saint-Germain, who retired through illness in 1777 and died soon after, wanted Montbarey to succeed him to preserve his reforms, which he did though labelling them in his memoirs as a 'slavish imitation of Germanic forms'.

The Saint-Maurice family had been ennobled by charge de robe in the sixteenth century through Jean de Saint-Maurice, who was a conseiller in what was to become the Parlement of Besançon when Spain ceded the Franche-Comté to France. Jean, who became Spanish ambassador to France, had managed to persuade the Habsburgs that his origins were chevaleresque but Chérin was not fooled: 'This proof which needs to go back to 1400 only begins in the year 1547'; nor did Montbarey's exotic foreign titles – and he even managed to marry his daughter to the sovereign prince of Nassau-Saarbruck – impress the court nobility. The title 'prince' conferred no rank at court and though a grandee of Spain enjoyed the privileges of a duc, this was conferred on him because he had already achieved ministerial status.

---

76 A.N. K163 no. 13. 8, unsigned and undated, but Necker to Maurepas, August or September 1776.
77 J.F.X. Droz, *Histoire du règne de Louis XVI*, Brussels, 1839, 168.

Nevertheless by the eighteenth century the family had shaken off their robe origins and enjoyed the honneurs de la cour. The minister's father, a lieutenant-général, married Thérèse, daughter of Eléonor du Maine, Marquis du Bourg, an inspector-general of cavalry, and grand-daughter of a marshal of France. Montbarey himself, who became a brigadier in 1758, married Françoise, daughter of Louis, Comte de Mailly, lieutenant-général.[78] Madame de Maurepas's mother was a Mailly and Maurepas, Montbarey tells us, regarded him 'comme son fils et son ouvrage'. Maurepas was present at Montbarey's first travail with the king.[79]

1778–79

The still-centre of the reign: there were no changes in the ministerial departments; the American war against England was fought without fuss if, at first, without success; the parlements were quiet and made only token protests at Necker's extension of the duration of the two vingtièmes.

1780

The decline of Maurepas and the fall of Sartine and Montbarey

Sartine was enjoying life at the marine. The naval war, which colleagues suspected he had hastened by 'des tournures . . . à sa disposition' had made him 'l'homme important du ministère'.[80] He had built up the navy to near-parity with England's and Véri considered that, of all the departments, his presented 'le meilleur ordre'.[81] Two criticisms were, however, levelled at him. First, the public blamed him for the stalemate in the war, 'the fate', as Véri observed, 'of every minister whose department is put into action but doesn't obtain the success the public wants'.[82] This was unfair because naval strategy was decided by a comité of the king, Maurepas and Vergennes as well as Sartine, whose plans were in particular hampered by Vergennes's insistence on deferring to France's Spanish ally. Second, Sartine was considered to be prodigal and here his robe background continued to haunt him: perversely it was considered that his bourgeois attention to

78 For Montbarey's ancestry and career, see Bluche, *Honneurs de la cour*; Jougla de Morénas, *Grand Armorial*, VI, 135; Granges, *Répertoire*, IV, 175–6; Michaud, *Biographie universelle*, XXIX, 47–8; La Chesnay des Bois, *Dictionnaire*, XII, 903–7.
79 Montbarey, *Mémoires*, II, 250 and 248.
80 Véri, *Journal*, II, 41; Montbarey, *Mémoires*, II, 310–12.
81 Véri, *Journal*, II, 62
82 ibid., II, 314.

detail and his lack of military training led him into unnecessary expenditure. This accusation was made despite the fact that he favoured the nobility in the running of the navy: Croÿ for instance refers to 'sa grande ordonnance de marine qui avait presqu'anéanti la plume, au grande triomphe de la marine noble'.[83]

This notion that technicians made better ministers than the generalist ex-maître des requêtes was much affected by Necker, who engineered Sartine's downfall. In 1779 he had allocated Sartine 120 million livres for the campaign of 1780; considering this to be inadequate, he responded to Necker's bald statement: 'je n'ai ni crédit ni argent à vous donner', by secretly opening a loan of 20 million livres on the treasury of the marine, in violation of the arrêt du conseil of 18 October 1778 providing that departmental treasuries should issue 'ni avances ni billets à terme' without authorization from the finance minister. When in 1780 Sartine claimed that he could put only sixty of the eighty ships-of-the-line to sea for the funds allocated, Necker threatened to resign unless Sartine were replaced.

This placed Maurepas in a dilemma: he was beginning to find Necker's demands insupportable, but England had the funds for the next campaign and he did not. The other ministers, 'disgusted with M. Necker', supported Sartine: Montbarey, for instance, who had opposed Sartine over the declaration of war, now defended him before Maurepas; he explained 'I did this out of self-interest which led me to regard as highly desirable the harmony between all the ministers which had obtained for the last four years'.[84] Vergennes had been pressing Maurepas to dismiss Necker for some time, accusing him of having secret relations with the English to end the war and profit his bank. The ministers were worried about what would happen when Maurepas died: his health had deteriorated and he spent this crisis in bed in Paris with a dangerous attack of gout. Maurepas sought disinterested advice from a group of informal advisers, his wife, his brother-in-law, Nivernais and Véri. They also advised him to let Necker go. However, the king, who spent three days at Compiègne, sent Maurepas the following note which, though not conclusive, pointed in the opposite direction:

Shall we sack Necker? Shall we sack Sartine? I am not displeased with the latter. I *think that Necker is more useful to us.*[85]

A further dimension to the crisis was provided by relations with France's Spanish ally. On 12 September Vergennes received a communication from the Spanish prime minister, Florida Blanca, announcing that Spain had funds for only one more campaign and that

83 Croÿ, *Journal*, III, 293.
84 Montbarey, *Mémoires*, III, 267.
85 Véri, *Journal*, II, 393–4 and 388–90.

unless France would give massive (and expensive) assistance for a conquest of Jamaica which, he hoped, would force England to sue for peace, Spain would be obliged to sue for peace herself forthwith. Vergennes and Sartine were ready to accede to Spain's demands but were overruled by Maurepas:

'You absolutely insist', M. de Vergennes said to [Maurepas] after much useless resistance; 'I shall obey you because you are the prime minister and the king himself; but under protest'.[86]

Not content with this, Maurepas, who agreed with Necker to the extent that he shared his belief that France herself could not afford a further campaign, took the alternative Spanish proposal a stage further: France should ask Spain to sue for peace with England on behalf of both Bourbon powers. Vergennes was not prepared to see his life's work destroyed. He did not threaten resignation, as was his wont: the matter was too important for bluff. Instead he coolly told the king that he was not prepared, by writing to Spain, to 'compromise [the king's] reputation and *gloire*' unless the king 'gave him the order in writing'. Vergennes was thinking partly about legal responsibility but more, perhaps, about his place in history, for he concluded his letter

The circumstances [i.e. financial] which dictate unfortunate measures are soon forgotten but the disastrous consequences stemming from them become more sensible the further they are removed from their original cause.[87]

Louis could not resist this appeal and this threat. Spain was fobbed off with the promise of extra help in the West Indies and the war comité – Louis, Vergennes, Sartine and Maurepas – sat down to plan the campaign which would culminate in the decisive and brilliant victory of Yorktown. Sartine and Maurepas were destined only to glimpse the promised land, Sartine from the political desert, Maurepas from the blur of the deathbed. When Lauzun informed Maurepas of the prizes and trophies captured, the old minister, having sagaciously muttered 'bon, bon' after each item, confessed: 'I am dying and I don't even know whom I have the honour of addressing'. And the unity of the war comité, which had undermined Turgot and contained Necker, was shattered. Resentful and desperately ill, Maurepas was ready to be out-manoeuvred by Necker: having already accepted Necker's analysis of the financial situation (and presented it to the king with his endorsement) he was less inclined to resist its application to a colleague, Sartine, who was considered extravagant and who had shown too much independence.

Meanwhile, pressure was being brought to bear on the queen by

86 ibid., II, 379.
87 Vergennes to the king, 27 September 1780; A.N. K164 no. 3, 1780 no. 3; J. Dull, *The French Navy and American Independence . . . 1774–1787*, Princeton, NJ, 1975, 194–202. Dull considers that Sartine was sacrificed to appease Spain.

her société intime, the Polignac group, to re-enter the political arena by adopting Necker's candidate for the marine, Charles Gabriel de la Croix (1727–1801), fifth Marquis de Castries. Castries, who had become a lieutenant-général in 1758, had become acquainted with Necker when they had been fellow directors of the Compagnie des Indes. Now, apart from his appointment auguring economy as a professional, he more specifically had promised Necker to hand over the treasury of the marine. The queen was embarrassed by these pressures. She did not want to risk Maurepas's resignation at this juncture (see pp. 206–7) and in any case she regarded Sartine as her protégé. Maurepas indeed suspected Sartine of seeking an audience with her to bolster his position.

Necker was able to profit from this confusion to dupe everyone. Just as, in the prelude to his appointment in 1776, he had told Maurepas that the king had already approved his financial projects, so now he profited from Maurepas's isolation to tell him that the queen had obtained the king's positive word to replace Sartine with Castries. When finally Maurepas had recovered sufficiently for Louis to come to Paris to see him (by convention the king did not visit sick ministers) Maurepas applauded what he mistakenly believed to be a fait accompli.[88] Subsequently it suited both Marie-Antoinette and Castries to preserve the fiction that her patronage had secured him the marine.

Castries accepted the marine only on a condition which served to draw a distinction between himself and his robe predecessors:

It is not fitting for me to enter the ministry like a maître des requêtes; I warn you [Necker] that I will accept nothing unless it is agreed in advance that the same day I enter the conseil d'état [i.e. be made a ministre].[89]

It is ironical that the family of the Marquis de Castries, who at this juncture and throughout his career saw himself as the champion of the sword against the robe, should have been ennobled by charge de robe, his ancestor Guillaume de la Croix having been a président in the cour des aides of Montpellier. That, however, had been in the fifteenth century and all the intervening generations had been soldiers. Guillaume had also been governor of Montpellier and this gouvernement remained in the family until our minister exchanged it for that of Flanders on his retirement in 1787. Castries's grandfather became a lieutenant-général and his father Joseph-François had made a brilliant marriage to Marie-François de Lévis-Charlus, daughter of the Duc de Lévis, pair de France, and of Marie-Françoise d'Albert de Luynes, also of ducal family. The future minister in turn married Gabrielle-Thérèse de Rosset de Fleury, daughter of Cardinal Fleury's

88 Arneth and Geffroy, *Marie-Antoinette*, II, 488 *et seq.*
89 Castries, *Journal*, I, fos 36–7.

heir Jean-Hercule, Duc de Fleury and pair de France. Castries's son, Armand-Charles-Augustin, made Duc de Castries (*par brevet*) in 1784, married (1778) Marie-Louise de Bonnières de Guines, daughter of Adrien, Comte then Duc de Guines (1776), the eponymous hero of the affair (see pp. 205–6). When the younger Castries was made a duc, 'the old ducs were a little affronted to see this great dignity given to such a "mince gentilhomme".[90]

These events served only to confirm Sartine in his belief that no reliance should be placed on the king or the queen. Louis, as was his wont when a minister was about to be dismissed, was embarrassed by Sartine's presence in the conseil and sedulously avoided a travail with him. However, Sartine was not exiled. Indeed the generous arrangements for his *retraite*, which became the yardstick by which his colleagues measured their own, led Mercy to speculate that he was being held in reserve to head the ministry on Maurepas's death. He was wrong; the king acted out of shame; nor did this prevent the iron from entering Sartine's soul: 'Everyone', he said bitterly, 'has now had time to judge the king'.[91]

The queen had not brought Sartine down; on this Castries is explicit: 'everything had been arranged with M. Necker before telling the queen'.[92] Nevertheless, Maurepas was so weakened by that event that he was unable to resist the queen's pressure to sacrifice Montbarey. Montbarey had become so wearied of the sniping that he gave his resignation to Maurepas as his patron to give to the king. At first Maurepas refused it, saying that the attack was really on himself and he would retire to Pontchartrain.[93] In December, however, he let him go, hoping thereby at least to influence the succession. Montbarey wanted his wife to have the reversion to his ministerial pension and he asked Vergennes (and this is a measure of Vergennes's growing influence) to intercede for him with the king.[94] Montbarey blamed his fall on the Polignacs, who had told the queen she ought to have her own ministers. However, she took their advice literally, refusing to support their candidate, the Comte d'Adhémar, and putting forward her own, Ségur, who was appointed over Maurepas's candidate, Puységur, as well.

Philippe Henri de Ségur (1724–1801), Marquis de Ségur, was a lieutenant-général in the army, a rank which had been attained by his father and grandfather before him. Chérin says of the family:

la maison de Ségur en Guyenne . . . tient un rang distingué dans l'ordre de

90 For Castries's ancestry and career, see Jougla de Morénas, *Grand Armorial*, III, 114, and II, 185; Michaud, *Biographie universelle*, VII, 190–1; Bombelles, *Journal*, I, 300.
91 Arneth and Geffroy, *Marie-Antoinette*, III, 483; Véri, *Journal*, de Witte's copy, cahier 100.
92 Castries, *Journal*, I, fo. 42.
93 ibid., I, fo. 51.
94 B.N. nouv. ac. franc. 22901 fo. 180.

la noblesse de cette province par son ancienneté, ses services, ses alliances et ses possessions.

Chérin implies provincial rather than national distinction. Ségur's mother was a natural daughter of the Regent Orléans and he married the daughter of a Norman gentleman with large possessions in Sainte-Domingue: Louise de Vernon brought him a dowry of 50,000 livres a year in rent. Their elder son married Antoinette Elizabeth d'Aguesseau, the granddaughter of the chancellor.[95]

Maurepas felt Ségur's appointment as the deadliest blow he had ever received, compounded as it had been by the role that the queen had played in it. In the twilight of his life he had lost control over the composition of the ministry. Véri was quick to signal his decline:

as soon as it was believed that he no longer had the same influence in decisions and in the choice of the men he had to work with. It seemed to me moreover that he could not expect from the newcomers, appointed against his wishes, the same agreement and harmony he had found in their predecessors.[96]

And he was right; Castries did not invite Maurepas to attend his travail with the king; when, as a matter of courtesy, he informed Maurepas of the changes he had made in his secretariat (the subject of his first travail), 'he replied drily that he was already aware of them'.[97] And the balance of power within the ministry had tilted in favour of Necker.

There was one final ministerial change in 1780: when Bertin retired, the department which had been specially created for him was broken up, with most of the provinces he administered going to Vergennes – a further sign of Vergennes's favour.

1781

Necker's resignation and his replacement by Joly de Fleury

In 1781 Necker, feeling himself under attack, made further demands to bolster his position. In February, perhaps sensing that the idea of new loans without the collateral of new taxation was wearing thin, he published his *Compte rendu au roi* in which, with the legerdemain he had displayed on previous occasions, he suggested that, despite three years of war, royal finances were in surplus by some 10 million livres in 1781. Most people were fooled, but there were attacks, notably from those associated with the Polignac group: Montyon, chancellor to the king's youngest brother, the Comte d'Artois, and Bourboulon, his

95 For Ségur's ancestry and career, see Bluche, *Honneurs de la cour*; Jougla de Morénas, *Grand Armorial*, VI, 198–9; La Chesnay des Bois, *Dictionnaire*, XVIII, 493; Comte de Ségur, *Le Maréchal de Ségur*, 1895, 158–61; V. de Ségur-Cabanac, *Histoire de la maison de Ségur*, Brunn, 1908, 64.
96 Besenval, *Mémoires*, II, 113; Véri, *Journal*, II, 417.
97 Castries, *Journal*, I, fos 46–7.

treasurer, attacked the *Compte* while the Marquis de Vaudreuil, one of the set, told Castries that he did not believe a word of it.[98] Calonne, the Intendant of Flanders, who was about to begin his lifetime association with the group, attacked the *Compte* anonymously in *Les comments* and the *Lettre du Marquis de Caraccioli à M. D'Alembert.*[99]

In April, Necker's confidential and highly controversial 1777 memorandum on provincial administrations was leaked through the treachery of the king's second brother, the Comte de Provence. This sensitive document threatened to make two rival authorities, the intendants and the parlements, patch up their differences as the memorandum envisaged that one day the provincial administrations would replace both. There was a question in the parlement of burning the memorandum as an anonymous work and Castries tried to get Maurepas to forbid the parlement to discuss the matter. Maurepas, however, offered no assistance.

Necker also quite reasonably complained that he was treated as a mere ramasseur d'argent and denied a say in framing the general policies he was asked to finance. Accordingly his original demand, presented at Marly, was to become a ministre d'état and it is likely that he envisaged restoring to the conseil d'état the decision-making powers of which Maurepas had deprived it in 1774 (see pp. 170–5). Maurepas objected that the Fundamental Laws of the kingdom barred a Protestant, even perhaps a foreigner from entering the conseil d'état; he told him, 'with a smile, "il faudrait faire la saut d'Henri IV"', which, intended as a joke, Necker chose to interpret as a vile attempt to convert him.[100] The queen, who supported Necker's general position, did not, given her sketchy knowledge of the Fundamental Laws, support him in this particular demand, which he made through her twice (twice also through Maurepas).

On Wednesday 15 May, Necker presented the king through Maurepas with an alternative *grâce d'éclat* which would demonstrate his confidence: a memorandum requesting that the control of the treasuries of the marine and war be entrusted to him, at least for the duration of the war. Next day Necker's ally, Castries, went to Marly and told the king that he was ready to relinquish the treasury of the marine. The initial reaction of the king, who had to consider the long-term integrity of the department, was 'but this separation is impossible'; then he added

M. de Maurepas talked to me about all that; he showed me a memorandum of Necker's; I will read it carefully and decide what I have to do in two or three days.

---

98 ibid., I, fo. 64.
99 For a fuller analysis of Calonne's attack, see Hardman, *Louis XVI*, 65–6.
100 Véri, MSS *Journal*, cahier 130.

Castries then went to see the queen but was told that she was in bed, though Maurepas was present and in the half-hour that Castries waited outside, the king entered three times. When he finally saw the queen, she employed with him an argument designed to win him over: Necker would become 'the most powerful man in Versailles' and

It is pretty certain that you will not keep your place and, once degraded, it will have to be given to an homme de robe and you are against that.[101]

Finally, Maurepas offered Necker the *grandes entrées* (which conferred the right to sit in the king's *cabinet* rather than having to stand in the ante-chamber), entry to all the comités of the secretaries of state and the king's assurance that all the provincial administrations would be set up. According to Castries, Necker was tempted to accept when Maurepas, 'desperately wanting a refusal which he would not fail to distort', diluted and belittled the concessions. Necker then gave his letter of resignation to Maurepas but he, as if to emphasize the withdrawal of any residual element of protection, refused to hand it to the king, telling him to hand it to the queen (which he did on 19 May) 'if he did not want to address himself to the king directly'. Had the king refused to accept Necker's resignation, Maurepas would have resigned himself, though he did not put pressure on the king by telling him this.[102] In fact the king, weary of Necker's demanding conditional marks of confidence like an English minister, did not press Necker to stay, though he blamed him for going.

Necker was ill for weeks afterwards. He had seriously miscalculated: his wife had warned him not to wreck his career for a seat on the conseil d'état.[103] Maurepas clearly did not have long to live and his death would have left Necker supreme.

Necker's subsequent conduct was such as to justify or at least explain the practice of exile. D'Angiviller, the directeur des bâtiments du roi, contrasted Necker's conduct with that which La Vrillière had been wont to prescribe:

Up till then and up to him a disgraced or disgruntled minister, so far from meddling in affairs, prescribed for himself the duty of keeping aloof from them, of living in seclusion, even for a long time of abstaining from seeing those of his friends who might have been so involved, and seemed to want to make himself forgotten.[104]

Necker, however, did none of these things: he kept himself in the public eye and kept his faction at the centre of things, with the assistance of Castries. Vergennes let Castries know through a third

101 Castries, *Journal*, I, fos 72–5.
102 D'Angiviller, *Mémoires*, Copenhagen, 1933, 101.
103 Castries, *Journal*, I, fo. 76.
104 D'Angiviller, *Mémoires*, 114.

party that he could not give him his entire trust since he spent several hours a week in Necker's company, and that it was

almost inevitable . . . that he would entrust to his friend secrets which were no longer his business; and I [Vergennes] feel so strongly that one should not authorize such a suspicion that I stopped seeing *my* friend M. de Sartine the moment he left the ministry.[105]

Necker was succeeded by Jean François Joly de Fleury (1718–1802), Seigneur de la Valette. Joly had followed a classical career within the royal administration, becoming maître des requêtes in 1743, intendant (1749–60) of Dijon (whence the family originated), and conseiller d'état in 1760. However, Joly's immediate family occupied key positions in the parlement, as can be seen from the following genealogy:

I	Barthélemy Joly (d. 1526), avocat in the parlement of Dijon.
II	Barthélemy J. (d. 1590), greffier-en-chef, parlement of Dijon.
III	François J., Seigneur de Fleury, settled in Paris, famous avocat.
*IV	Jean J., écuyer, conseiller in the grand' chambre, ennobled by charge de robe.
V	Jean J., conseiller in the parlement; married a daughter of the avocat-général, Omer Talon.
VI	Guillaume François J. de F., procureur-général in the parlement, married Marie, daughter of Nicolas Le Maistre, substitut du procureur-général in the cour des aides.
VII (1)	Guillaume François Louis J., procureur-général in parlement (1746–71).
VII (2)	Jean Omer J. président à mortier in parlement.
VII (3)	Jean François Joly de Fleury, d. unmarried.
VIII	Armand Guillaume J. de F., son of Jean Omer, avocat-général in the parlement (1775).[106]

These alliances would have recommended Joly to Maurepas since the parlement would be required to register the new taxation which the departure of Necker had made almost inevitable and indeed the parlement entreating Joly to accept 'lui promet pour ses opérations une grande condescendance'. However, according to Montyon, Miromesnil suggested Joly to Maurepas in 1781 with the ulterior motive of keeping him out of his own job, which he was generally regarded as coveting, by promoting him to one from which he was likely to be disgraced. Be

105 Castries, *Journal*, I, fo. 170.
106 For Joly's ancestry and career, see Bluche, *Origine*, 220–1; Bluche, *Grand conseil*, 91; Jougla de Morénas, *Grand Armorial*, IV, 350.

that as it may, Maurepas afforded Joly his protection and regarded him as his nominee.[107]

Joly did not revive the title of contrôleur-général, which had lain vacant since Taboureau's resignation, but coined instead that of ministre d'état et des finances, a modification which registered with commentators; for example, Croÿ noted that he was '*comme* contrôleur-général'.[108] The change was not accidental, for Joly considered that the responsibilities of a contrôleur-général were too great both for the good of his own health and that of the country, fragile alike, in his opinion. In consequence, Joly delegated the management of the *domaine* to Moreau de Beaumont, most of the taxation side of the finance ministry to d'Ormesson, the former intendant des finances avec le département des impositions, who had lost his job when Necker abolished the intendants des finance, and the loan-floating side, with the title intendant du trésor royal, to Bourgade, a close friend whom he paid out of his own salary,[109] though d'Ormesson did not consider that Bourgade had mastered the new techniques introduced by Necker. These changes assisted Joly to live for another twenty years; but he considered such personal arrangements as preliminaries to an institutional change which he hoped would outlast him, the creation of a comité des finances to which he would delegate a power which both he and the public considered too great and too arbitrary and yet which had been insufficient to coordinate departmental expenditure. The comité will be considered at greater length in Chapter 8.

At eleven o'clock on the morning of 21 November, Maurepas died. On 22 November, Castries notes,

The king summoned a comité where he spoke more than usual, as one who was saying to himself, 'I intend to reign'.

---

107 Auget de Montyon, *Particularités . . . sur les ministres des finances les plus célèbres*, 1812, 247 n. a.
108 Croÿ, *Journal*, III, 248.
109 D'Ormesson, *Journal*, A.N. 144 A.P. 130.

CHAPTER THREE

The appointment and dismissal of ministers:
from the death of Maurepas to the Assembly of Notables

1782

There were no ministerial changes in this year.

1783

The last ministerial changes before the convocation of the Assembly of Notables

At the beginning of the year there were two ministerial changes associated with the conclusion of peace with England (preliminaries were signed on 20 January). As a reward for concluding a peace which, if it did not bring substantial territorial gains, achieved the original objectives of the war, Vergennes chose the post of chef du conseil royal des finances which had remained vacant after Maurepas's death. For his part, Joly de Fleury had for some time had the king's consent to his resignation once he had seen the financing of the war to a conclusion. Privately, Joly considered this relatively easy in comparison with 'the embarrassments of peace' without the traditional resource of bankruptcy. In the spring of 1782, he had confided to Véri that

already he foresaw the embarrassments of peace. He confessed that it was this prospect which made him talk about his resignation on the pretext of his age and health.[1]

Vergennes's knowledge and involvement in financial matters had progressed since his confession to the king in 1775 that he knew something about the navy but nothing about the state of the royal treasury.[2] In 1781, the king had asked him for a written opinion of the

---

1 Abbé de Véri, MSS *Journal*, Archives départementales de la Drôme, Valence, unclassified, cahier 105.
2 A.N. K164 no. 3, 1775, Vergennes to the king, 4 May.

Compte rendu and the following year he had played an important part in the negotiations with the parlement leading to the registration of the third vingtième.[3] In December 1782 Castries notes that he raised eyebrows by attending a comité to discuss raising a loan of 40 million livres and concluded from this 'that he had the peace in his pocket and expected to be made président [*sic*] of the conseil royal'. It seems likely that Joly was the guiding force behind Vergennes's choice of the title chef du conseil rather than the more banal one of a dukedom, which he was rumoured to have been offered.[4] On 29 January Joly sent the king a memorandum outlining the functions, such as they were, of the chef du conseil and this is clearly linked with the creation of his brainchild, the comité des finances, instituted by the *règlement* of 26 February, which gave the chef the conseil which had hitherto been lacking.[5]

Joly's resignation had been long meditated but its timing was forced. He had completed the financing of the war and was able to declare to the war comité in December 1782 that the funds for a further year's campaign were assured and the king could give what orders he pleased; and he had set up his institutional reforms.[6] However his departure was actually occasioned by a personal and professional vendetta with Castries, who declared: 'I scorn M. de Fleury; all discussion with him has become difficult'.[7] Each minister attempted, and each nearly succeeded in bringing the other down.

In May 1782, Joly had written 'une lettre impertinente' – the first of many – to Castries accusing him of administrative incompetence and suggesting the appointment of a second trésorier de la marine. In June, profiting from the dipping of Castries's prestige after the Battle of the Saints (which Joly said 'had cost 24 millions'),[8] he got his way. This left the substantive issue between them: Castries, who had been appointed to economize, was spending some 200 million livres a year, or nearly half the royal revenue after the payment of interest charges: apart from the sums which Castries had already spent (Joly indicated to Véri 'by his gestures and his eyes' that they greatly exceeded Sartine's, 'for which he was dismissed'),[9] Joly calculated that there were some 50 million livres of unregistered *lettres de change* which had been issued by the marine to fund the military expeditions in the colonies and which were now winging their way back to France for redemption. As

3 *Observations remises à Louis XVI et par ses ordres le 3 mai 1781*, published by J.L. Soulavie, *Mémoires historiques et politiques du règne de Louis XVI*, 1801, 6 vols, IV, 153; Castries, *Journal*, Archives de la Marine, MS 182/7964 1–2, I, fo. 119.
4 Castries, *Journal*, I, fo. 154; Marquis de Bombelles, *Journal*, ed. J. Grassion and F. Durif, Geneva, 1978, 2 vols, I, 191.
5 B.N. fonds Joly de Fleury, 1442 fo. 9 and 1441 fo. 168.
6 Castries, *Journal*, I, fo. 144.
7 ibid., I, fo. 163.
8 B.N. fonds Joly de Fleury, 1432 fo. 163.
9 Véri, MSS *Journal*, cahier 107.

Joly told Bourgade on 21 February 1783 it was a violation as clear as Sartine's of the arrêt du conseil of 18 October 1778.[10]

On 19 February 1783 Castries precipitated a crisis by obtaining the king's consent to register a token lettre de change. Joly believed that this was designed by Castries and Necker (his old bank Haller's had presented the lettre) to cause his fall by encouraging a flood of similar demands which he could not meet.[11] Joly responded by obtaining from the king an arrêt du conseil on 22 February suspending unregistered lettres de change for a year. This arrêt was read to Castries in the king's presence; the next day Joly sent him the arrêt to sign and when he refused sent him the arrêt already printed above his signature.[12]

On 3 March Joly followed up this advantage by sending Castries a letter requiring him to submit his accounts to the comité des finances. For Castries this was not only a personal humiliation but also that of his ministry: it would have impaired the direct relationship of the secrétaires d'état with the king and made them second-class ministers; he did not accept that this was a necessary sacrifice to an emerging concept of ministerial unity as expressed most urgently in the form of a budget, believing instead that the king was undermining both the person of his ministers – he told Madame de Polignac of 'minimal marks of esteem that the king gives his ministers and the multifarious disadvantages of serving him' – and their departments: a memorandum of his states that 'the offices of secretary of state have lost prestige as a result of the règlement of 26 February'; to the extent that he could no longer serve with advantage.[13]

There is no doubt that Castries intended to resign, as Joly had calculated. On 7 March he handed his resignation to the queen to give to the king but she persuaded him to wait for a week lest he seem to criticize the king's new governmental arrangements and to give her time to hasten Joly's own departure. The king, who did not like open quarrels among his ministers, agreed that both men should depart. Marie-Antoinette arranged the staging of a comedy to clash with the second meeting of the comité des finances due on Saturday 22 March and when the king greeted Joly's request for an alternative date with silence, Joly, concluding that he was out of favour, resigned (29 March), declaring that his job was *infaisable*. The arrangements to sweeten Castries's retraite with the baton of a maréchal became so protracted that he stayed on in the ministry for another four years, continuing his spending unabated and maintaining the navy almost on a war-footing. In 1784, he told the queen that the only way out of the

10 B.N. fonds Joly de Fleury, 1441 fo. 158.
11 M. Price, 'The Comte de Vergennes and the Baron de Breteuil: French politics and reform in the reign of Louis XVI', PhD thesis, Cambridge University, 1988, 179–80.
12 Castries, *Journal*, I, fo. 159.
13 ibid., I, fo. 161; A.N. 306 A.P. 24.

impasse was for the contrôle and the marine to be fused! The queen replied that the king would never consent to amalgamate two departments.[14]

The manner of Joly's departure prevented the implementation of some singular arrangements at the finance ministry which he had suggested to the king in January when the latter had 'ordered' him to remain in some capacity. In the *reductio ad absurdum* of his policy of divestment, Joly proposed that the *place* of contrôleur-général be revived only in order that the new incumbent act as his *assistant*.[15] What that would have left Joly to do – he mentions specifically being rapporteur of the comité des finances – is left unclear, but he devotes another memorandum to the rubric which should be employed on finance arrêts when the finance minister was also a ministre, though that had been his position from the start.[16]

As a parting shot Joly presented the king with a memorandum which, though general in the extreme, laid the foundations for government policy over the next six years. Joly writes in the margin of this memorandum:

I placed this sketch before the king on 26 January 1782 [*sic* for 1783]; it was my first travail after the signature of peace; at the same time I asked for my retraite which had constantly been deferred until this event.

The first section deals with pressing needs; the second, entitled 'Objets d'administration', includes:

1   The Commercial Treaty [presumably with England; Calonne and Vergennes finally concluded this in 1786].

3   Restore a little more equality between the different provinces in respect of taxation.

4   Revise the way in which the vingtième, the taille, the *capitation* and others are levied.

6   Establish a new, simpler and less onerous method of collecting the *gabelle*, the *traites*, the *aides* and the *entrées de Paris*.[17]

When Joly had asked to be assisted by a contrôleur-général he had suggested Vergennes's cousin, Thiroux de Crosne, though he had been grooming d'Ormesson for the job. Nevertheless, when Joly finally departed, the king, perhaps as Price has suggested to circumscribe Vergennes's growing influence, opted for the original candidate.[18] D'Ormesson, who had a *travail particulier* with the king as intendant of the charitable foundation of Saint-Cyr, had also been giving the king

14 Castries, *Journal*, I, fo. 256.
15 B.N. fonds Joly de Fleury, 1442 fo. 10.
16 ibid., fo. 15.
17 B.N. fonds Joly de Fleury, 1442 fo. 39.
18 Price, 'Vergennes and Breteuil', 200.

a six-monthly report on the 'état de ses finances'.[19] D'Ormesson, the first ministerial appointment since the death of Maurepas, was the king's personal choice.

Henri François-de-Paule Lefèvre d'Ormesson (1751–1807), second Marquis d'Ormesson, came of a distinguished family of noblesse d'état, ennobled by charge de robe in the sixteenth century through Olivier Lefèvre, Seigneur d'Ormesson, who had married the great-niece of Saint François-de-Paule. His son had been an intendant des finances and our minister represented the fourth generation of his family to occupy this important position. His father, Marie François-de-Paule, had been created Marquis d'Ormesson in 1758 and had married into one of the oldest families in the parlement, the du Tillet, ennobled by lettres patentes in 1484. D'Ormesson married Louise Charlotte, daughter of Louis Le Peletier, intendant of Soissons, scion of what has been described as a 'leading family both in the Courts and on the Council'.[20]

D'Ormesson, who had become a maître des requêtes at the age of 19 in 1770, was appointed intendant des finances and conseiller d'état in 1777.[21] In 1777 Necker had abolished the intendants des finances but Joly had reinstated d'Ormesson at the département des impositions, though without title or remuneration.[22] D'Ormesson, then, was an expert in taxation and father and son had been in charge of the vingtième, the most dynamic of the regime's taxes, since its inception in 1749. D'Ormesson planned to make the vingtième the basis of a total overhaul of the system of taxation.

D'Ormesson's tenure of the hôtel de la contrôle-générale was brief but his approach was radical and his fall is worth examining in some detail because it isolates many of the problems confronting a radical minister at the end of the ancien régime. For the operation of the comité des finances meant that no one could accuse d'Ormesson of overstepping the bounds of his department.

The fall of d'Ormesson

Three factors contributed to this event: the major operation of d'Ormesson's ministry, the rescinding of the lease of the general farm, and the precipitate withdrawal of the measure; increasingly strained relations with Vergennes; finally, a powerful movement to place the intendant of Flanders, Charles Alexandre de Calonne, at the contrôle.

19 A.N. 144 A.P. 131 dossier 4. 3.
20 V.R. Gruder, *The Royal Provincial Intendants*, Ithaca, NY, 1968, 143.
21 For d'Ormesson's ancestry and career, see M. Antoine, *Les archives d'Ormesson*, 1960; F. Bluche, *L'origine des magistrats du parlement de Paris au XVIIIe siècle*, 1956, 259–61; Jougla de Morénas, *Grand Armorial de France*, 1934–52, 7 vols, III, 386; F. Bluche, *Les Honneurs de la cour*, 1957; F.A. de La Chesnay des Bois, *Dictionnaire de la noblesse*, 3rd edn, 1863–76, 19 vols, VIII, 13.
22 D'Ormesson, *Journal*, A.N. 144 A.P. 130, section 39.

D'Ormesson, if only because of his youth, had more of the outlook of a modern functionary than the majority of his colleagues (he was to find no difficulties in accepting the Revolution and was even elected mayor of Paris in 1792, though he declined the honour). In particular he disliked *la finance*,[23] and supported Necker's moves to replace the venal element in the administration of royal finances with salaried employees (though even he did not have sufficient objectivity to welcome the abolition of the hereditary elite of intendants des finances to which his family belonged). D'Ormesson had long preferred a *régie* (where the *régisseurs* received a salary) or a *régie intéressée* (where, as an incentive, they kept a proportion of the receipts over a certain figure) to a farm, where the crown sold the right to collect a tax for an advance. Now he proposed that the last three years of the *bail salzard*, the contract making over the collection of the indirect taxes to the *fermiers-généraux*, be converted into a régie intéressée with effect from 1 January 1784.

The details of d'Ormesson's measure and the implacable opposition to them from the farmers (who demanded the impossible repayment of their advances to the crown) will be considered in Chapter 7 on finance ministers. To stem the tide of opposition, a meeting of the comité des finances was scheduled for 30 October, at which d'Ormesson intended to read a favourable *rapport* on public opinion, but he expressed to Vergennes his 'anxiety . . . at not having received the king's orders for the Committé'.[24] Instead, the king wrote a nervous letter to Vergennes on 1 November. The farmers seemed to want an accommodation and the government would have to deal with them (a deputation was coming to Fontainebleau next day), though

it would be very annoying to seem to give way to them; it was the letter of M. d'Harvélai [garde de trésor royal] which really scared me. . . . I do not doubt M. d'Ormesson's zeal for my service but if credit should run out, his good intentions will be no substitute.[25]

Vergennes had asked d'Ormesson to resign but he refused: on 31 October Vergennes told the king

He has not concealed from us [Vergennes and Miromesnil] that, confident as he is of the soundness of a measure which has received Your Majesty's sanction in his Committé, he would consider himself blameworthy if he yielded to the efforts of intrigue which sought to decry it and if he abandoned Your Majesty's service in the moment of crisis. He added that he could not resign with honour unless Your Majesty deigned to give him the order directly, whether orally or in writing.[26]

23 D'Ormesson, *Journal*, section 54.
24 A.N. K164 no. 3, 1783, Vergennes to the king, 31 October; note Vergennes's use of the English form Committé.
25 Archives de Vergennes, *Lettres de Louis XVI*.
26 A.N. K164 no. 3, 1783, Vergennes to the king, 31 October.

The king was *peiné* by d'Ormesson's obduracy. Nevertheless, on 2 November, d'Ormesson received the letter he required: 'the state of affairs obliges me to ask you to hand in your resignation but you retain my estime and my protection';[27] the word 'estime' had also been demanded as satisfaction by d'Ormesson.[28]

D'Ormesson had twice, during his brief ministry, declined to be made a ministre, hoping that by avoiding this permanent honour he could return to his work as a conseiller d'état after he had suffered the fate common to most contrôleurs. He was deceived in this hope, and though he was not exiled he suffered a fate as bad: his successor, Calonne, placed spies in his household, 'mêmes dans les campagnes'. Some were unpleasant, like a hideous beggar who hung around the courtyard at Ormesson, but eventually, through the intercession of the lieutenant-général de police, Lenoir, they were replaced by two young apprentice wig-makers, 'fort poli' who attended to the wigs of d'Ormesson's household virtually for nothing and were kept on in his employ when their espionage ended on Calonne's fall in 1787.[29]

D'Ormesson attributed the failure of his operation not to any intrinsic defects but to the treachery of Vergennes, motivated by d'Ormesson's objections to his lining his pockets at the expense of the crown, and to the orchestration of powerful vested interests by Calonne. Further friction developed both with Vergennes and the king over the latter's propensity to buy palaces. D'Ormesson had been mystified to find no reference in the accounts of the trésor royal to the purchase by the king of Rambouillet from the Duc de Penthièvre in Joly de Fleury's time. When d'Ormesson arrived at Fontainebleau he discovered the explanation: Vergennes had bought and was running it out of the funds of the foreign office and was about to buy L'Isle d'Adam from the Prince de Conti and Saint-Cloud from the Duc d'Orléans in the same way. D'Ormesson informed Vergennes that the *exigible* (unfunded) debt would consume all the revenue for the next three years and went to the king, resignation in hand. The king's promise that nothing would be finally decided without consulting him forced d'Ormesson to put his resignation back in his pocket, saying 'coldly to the king that since His Majesty would be giving him further orders on the subject, he would await them'.[30]

A further dispute with Vergennes also came to a head during the voyage de Fontainebleau. Vergennes had been rewarded handsomely for the conclusion of peace; the sleeves of two dossiers (now lost) in the Joly papers are headed *rapports* on increasing the salary of Vergennes's nephew, the intendant of Auch, and on granting

27 Castries, *Journal*, I, 20–4.
28 D'Ormesson, *Journal*, section 72.
29 ibid., section 122.
30 ibid., section 64.

Vergennes himself a 'somme en contrats sur le domaine de la ville'.[31] Even better he had been granted two estates, one at Wesserding, in Alsace, the other at Fravemberg in Lorraine. Not content with this, he wanted to sell back to the crown the regalian rights belonging to these estates at an exorbitant price. D'Ormesson grudgingly acquiesced in the sale of the rights belonging to Wesserding but drew the line when Vergennes proposed a contract similarly ruinous for the crown for Fravemberg. D'Ormesson proposed that the whole matter be discussed before the comité des finances which had been instituted to prevent precisely such transactions. Miromesnil, privately, agreed that the comité was the appropriate place to discuss the matter, while Castries accepted that Vergennes was rapacious in wanting sixty years' purchase for the regalian rights.[32] D'Ormesson was a rich man (we shall see him pitying the Polignacs their poverty) and financial purity was a luxury he could well afford whereas Vergennes was a *novus homo* with a family to advance and none to support him. Moreover, d'Ormesson belonged to a younger generation than Vergennes and one which applied a stricter standard in matters of public finance. (This tendency was also present in English public life.) Nevertheless the integrity of the family d'Ormesson was proverbial – 'probe comme d'Ormesson' – and the king happened to share his concept of public morality.

Accordingly, Vergennes was gravely damaged in the king's eyes by d'Ormesson's accusations. He wrote the king three desperate letters, in one of which he acknowledges that the accusation is 'of having abused the credit of my office', and in another he asks for the matter to be investigated by the new contrôleur or a member of the conseil.[33] The king selected an expert, Moreau de Beaumont, who had run the domaine for Joly. Moreau found against Vergennes, who was reduced to telling the king that he had only wanted to alienate the exclusive right to sell salt belonging to the *seigneurie* of Wesserding, to prevent smuggling from Alsace into France proper and remove the imputation that he was profiting from it! Eventually, Miromesnil told d'Ormesson that the king had finally accepted Vergennes's explanations and d'Ormesson and Vergennes, realizing the damage they were causing each other by their counter-accusations, agreed on mutual silence.[34] Nevertheless, Vergennes's prestige never recovered; he gave up what d'Ormesson called the attempt to 'commander en finance comme un ministre à talon rouge' and confined himself to his departmental duties.

Nevertheless it is hard to credit d'Ormesson's accusation that Vergennes performed a volte-face over the farm just to rid himself of

---

31 B.N. fonds Joly de Fleury, 1440 dossiers 126 and 135.
32 Castries, *Journal*, I, fo. 208.
33 A.N. K164 no. 3 1783 nos. 4 and 5, letters of 10 November, 12 December and undated.
34 D'Ormesson, *Journal*, section 120.

d'Ormesson's embarrassing scrutiny. A more likely explanation lies in Vergennes's propensity to put others forward and jettison them if they met with resistance. Vergennes may well have been the originator of the plan to end tax-farming but he readily, perhaps too readily, accepted the view of the king that its timing was bad.

D'Ormesson was on firmer ground when he stressed the role that Calonne had played in his downfall. On 3 November, the king had written to Vergennes:

You have only to summon M. de Calonne to Fontainebleau, explain our plans for him and report back when you have seen him. I don't know whether he is at Paris or in Flanders.[35]

The king's ignorance of whether Calonne was in Flanders (performing his job) or in Paris (lobbying for promotion) was a little naive. In 1781, immediately after the death of Joly de Fleury's patron, Maurepas, Calonne had come to Paris to observe the finance minister, whose job he coveted, and he had returned to the capital whenever there was a ministerial crisis from which he might profit – and he was strong enough to profit from most. His association with the Polignac group had strengthened, particularly with Vaudreuil and Artois. In addition, he had strong links with la finance through his uncle Bourgade (whose papers he inherited on his death in 1784),[36] and d'Harvélai, the garde du trésor, whose wife he shared and later married. This strength is reflected in the fact that in 1783 he was the second most highly paid intendant.[37] Some sources have him persuading Vergennes to use his new title to make himself prime minister through the comité des finances;[38] though the institution of a body which he was to suppress and which was opposed by the Polignacs as the 'tombeau des grâces' may seem an oblique way of proceeding, the destruction of Joly or Castries or both could not be without advantage to him. At all events d'Ormesson says the argument by which Vergennes overcame his genuine reluctance to become contrôleur was that Calonne

supported at court by a powerful movement had found thereby the secret of prejudicing the king against all the competitors he could think of except me alone whom he did not suspect on account of my age of only 31 . . . so that by my refusal he would be appointed almost inevitably.[39]

Such inevitability is partly explained by the paucity of genuine

35 Archives de Vergennes, *Lettres de Louis XVI.*
36 B.N. fonds Joly de Fleury, 1432 fo. 132.
37 D'Ormesson papers, A.N. 144 A.P. 131 dossier 4.7.
38 Comte de Ségur, *Mémoires ou souvenirs et anecdotes*, 1827, 3 vols, II, 7–8; Besenval, *Mémoires*, II, 118–19.
39 D'Ormesson, *Journal*, section 43.

candidates for the contrôle. The king would have called Necker's bluff when he threatened to resign in 1780, but

scanning the Almanach Royal with M. de Maurepas he did not find anyone suitable in public employment. It was not that he could not find people who wanted the job. Just that, as M. de Maurepas said, only a fool or a knave could want it.[40]

And Maurepas told Véri to which category he thought Calonne belonged:

I have heard M. de Maurepas dozens of times show impatience or ridicule at M. de Calonne's importunities to be contrôleur-général. I also seem to recall that it was with M. de Maurepas that the king formally ruled M. de Calonne out on account of his suspect integrity.[41]

But the choice of beggars is restricted: the king's letter of 3 November to Vergennes about Calonne's appointment concludes with the words:

but the capital point is the support of credit, so that we can service the rest of the year and without any emergency measures.

And Louis told Marie-Antoinette, realistically,

There is not much to choose between all the contenders and at least he has la finance on his side.

Marie-Antoinette, incidentally, was intriguing for Necker: Bourgade reported to Vergennes 'Last Thursday, after the show, there was a "comité de la Reine" about M. Necker'. And Louis had to give Castries a décision précise concerning him:

Considering the generous way I treated M. Necker, and the way in which he left me voluntarily, he must think no more of a return to office.[42]

Vergennes may well have allowed himself to be used by the Polignacs and financiers to propose Calonne to the king but he would once again have preferred his cousin Thiroux de Crosne. Thus Calonne was in no sense Vergennes's nominee and he told Vergennes that he could not be his subordinate.[43]

Calonne's ancestry and antecedents

Charles Alexandre de Calonne (1734–1802), Comte d'Hannonville, came of a long line of Flemish échevins stretching back to Jacques de Calonne (born c.1500), who built the family tomb in the church of Saint-Pierre at Douai. His great-grandfather purchased the seigneurie

40 D'Angiviller, *Mémoires*, 118.
41 Véri, *Journal*, II, 383; MSS *Journal*, cahier 118.
42 Castries, *Journal*, I, fos 204–5; Archives des Affaires Étrangères, Mémoires et Documents 1395 fo. 158, cited in Price, 'Vergennes and Breteuil', 250–1.
43 Castries, *Journal*, I, fos 204 and 209.

of Quesne, but the family was finally ennobled, by charge de robe, through the future minister's father, Louis Joseph Dominique, who rose through the parlement of Flanders to become its premier président in 1767. He married Anne, daughter of Jacques de Franqueville, chevalier, conseiller in the parlement of Flanders. Calonne's first wife was Josephine Marquet, daughter of Louis Marquet, receveur-général at Bordeaux, and Michelle Pâris du Verney, natural daughter of the celebrated financier; his wife's uncle, Jacques Marquet de Bourgade, was intendant du trésor royal (1781–3). Calonne's links with la finance are further underlined by his second marriage, at Bath (1788), to Anne de Nettine, daughter to the imperial banker at Brussels and widow of Bourgade's successor, Micault d'Harvélai. Many of Calonne's loans were to be sourced in the Low Countries.

In 1759, Calonne was appointed procureur-général in the parlement of Flanders but in 1763 became a maître des requêtes. In this capacity he prepared the rapport which served as the basis for Louis XV's speech to the parlement known as the 'séance de flagellation'. This, quite as much as his useful contacts with la finance, would have recommended him to Louis XVI; at the time (1766) it won him the intendance de Metz. In 1778 he returned to Flanders as intendant. In 1784 he was made a ministre d'état and grand trésorier des ordres du roi.[44]

The last of the ministerial changes of 1783 was the appointment to the maison of Louis Auguste Le Tonnelier (1730–1807), Baron de Breteuil. Breteuil's descent was:

I	Jean Le Tonnelier, Seigneur de Breteuil, conseiller au grand conseil (1554).
*II	Claude Le T., ennobled by purchasing the office of secrétaire de roi in 1572.
III	Claude Le T., conseiller d'état.
IV	Louis Le T., conseiller d'état.
V	Louis Nicolas Le T., Baron de Preuilly, introducteur des ambassadeurs, fourth son of preceding.
VI	Charles Auguste Le T., Baron de Preuilly, army officer. He married Marie-Anne, daughter of Jean-Prosper Goujon de Gasville, intendant of Rouen.
VII	Louis Auguste, sixth-generation noble. Breteuil married Françoise, daughter of Jérôme Louis Parat de Mongeron, receveur-général des finances of Lorraine. Their only

44 For Calonne's career and ancestry, see D.B.F., VII, 922–4; Y. Durand, *Les Fermiers-généraux au XVIIIe siècle*, 1971, 80 and 84; V.R. Gruder, *The Royal Provincial Intendants*, Ithaca, NY, 1968, 156; Michaud, *Biographie universelle*, VI, 424–7; Lenoir MS 1423, mélanges, 28. The standard genealogical works have no information on Calonne's ancestors beyond his father. However, the Archives Nationales have genealogical material on microfilm of Calonne papers possessed by the Comte de Franqueville, descended from Calonne's brother, A.N. 263 MI 1. 1–2.

daughter married Louis-Charles de Goyon, Comte de Matignon, son of a lieutenant-général in the army whose nobility was chevaleresque.

Other branches of the Le Tonnelier family had provided a secretary of state for war, a general, two bishops and the blue-stocking Émilie Le Tonnelier, Marquise du Châtelet, Voltaire's 'belle Émilie'.

Breteuil originally chose to follow his father in the profession of arms, becoming a colonel in the cavalry (1759), before transferring to the diplomatic service in which his grandfather had preceded him. He was successively ambassador to Stockholm (1763), The Hague (1767), Naples (1772) and finally Vienna (1774).[45]

Breteuil had been the protégé of Choiseul and he participated in Choiseul's disgrace to the extent that his original appointment as ambassador to Vienna had been cancelled; but he had been the first of the Choiseulistes to comprehend that the future lay not with the duc but with Marie-Antoinette (before whom the duc, in his audience of 1775, ironically called Breteuil his 'ancien et fidèle ami').[46] This fact is the clue to his – often tortuous – conduct throughout her life. To this end he sought the approval not only of the queen, but also of her sister, the Queen of Naples and of her mother the Empress Maria-Theresa.

Breteuil's long-standing ministerial ambitions naturally centred on the foreign office and this, as naturally, brought him into conflict with Vergennes, the incumbent. Vergennes was obsessed with the threat from Breteuil, even though Louis's letters to Vergennes make it abundantly clear that, though the king was pleased with Breteuil's conduct as an ambassador and the quality of his dispatches, there was never any question of his replacing Vergennes. The king was aware of Vergennes's jealousy of Breteuil and sought to assuage it.[47]

Nevertheless, as with Calonne, it was difficult to prevent Breteuil's appointment to the ministry at least in some capacity; especially when, in 1783, already possessed of the queen's support, he gained that of her société intime by promising the hand of his 9-year-old grand-daughter Mlle de Matignon to the son of Madame de Polignac. Mlle de Matignon was a considerable heiress (some said the richest in Paris): the only child of his only child, she would inherit the wealth of the Le Tonneliers and that of Breteuil's wife, the daughter of a rich receveur-général.

This match was a cynical manoeuvre, not only because Breteuil

45 For Breteuil's ancestry and career, see D.B.F. VII, 239–40; Jougla de Morénas, *Grand Armorial*, VI, 323; Granges, *Répertoire*, III, 379–80; Granges, *Histoire nobiliaire*, 339 and 446; La Chesnay des Bois, *Dictionnaire*, III, 828, and IX, 575–625.
46 A. d'Arneth and M.A. Geffroy, *Marie-Antoinette: Correspondance secrète entre Marie-Thérèse et le Comte de Mercy-Argenteau*, 2nd edn, 1875, 3 vols, II, 356–7.
47 See e.g. Archives de Vergennes, *Letters de Louis XVI*, 27 May 1776.

pulled out of the arrangement as soon as he had secured the maison but also because he had nothing whatever in common with the objectives of the Polignacs: whereas they were concerned to win wealth through their connection with the queen but to lend their support to those ministers who wished to restrict her political role,[48] Breteuil, who did not need any more money, intended 'faire régner la reine'.[49]

Breteuil, again like Calonne, spent most of 1783 in Paris. Vergennes abandoned the attempt to block his promotion, seeking instead to guide his footsteps to the portfolio for which he showed the least aptitude: he planned that Breteuil should replace Castries at the marine. This presented several advantages for Vergennes: the queen could not possibly object since she regarded Breteuil as her protégé in a way that Castries had never been (after Breteuil's appointment, Castries notes that he saw much less of the queen); he would be rid of a minister for whom he felt deep hostility; even if Breteuil were to run the marine successfully, its political importance was secondary in time of peace.[50] Unfortunately, the messy arrangements for Castries's departure prevented this solution: Bombelles notes that 'the king, little satisfied with [Castries's] services, lacks the strength to dismiss him'. From June, the queen indicated a desire that Breteuil become minister for the maison.[51] To forestall this, Vergennes offered d'Ormesson Amelot's job at the maison. Many would have jumped at this but d'Ormesson, though he was well aware that the maison was more stable than the contrôle, refused because he disliked the use of lettres de cachet and because his expertise lay in financial matters.[52] Vergennes then came up with the ingenious solution of offering Breteuil a seat in the conseil: he became a ministre d'état on 27 July. Mercy, who believed that it was difficult to move from being a minister-without-portfolio to being a departmental minister (it was certainly unusual) added:

M. de Vergennes will keep him as long as possible in the honourable nullity of the conseil d'état.[53]

But 'as long as possible' was not to be for as long as he wished. In November, Calonne and Breteuil stormed the ministry together, both relying principally on the Polignac group, both profiting from the weakness of Vergennes after the débâcle of the comité des finances, and intending, if not to overthrow him, at least to end his extra-

48 See pp. 202–5.
49 Arneth and Geffroy, *Marie-Antoinette*, III, 36.
50 A. d'Arneth and J. Flammermont, *Correspondance secrète du Comte de Mercy-Argenteau avec l'Empereur Joseph II et le Prince de Kaunitz*, 1891, 2 vols, I, 193.
51 ibid., I, 193 and 200.
52 D'Ormesson, *Journal*, section 55.
53 Arneth and Flammermont, *Correspondance secrète*, I, 200.

departmental excursions. On 18 November, Breteuil was finally appointed to the maison. A final obstacle had been the incumbent, Amelot. Calonne asked Lenoir, who was Amelot's junior minister and enjoyed his 'confiance particulière', to approach him with the offer of a good pension and the intendance of Bourgogone (Amelot's old job) for his son. Lenoir refused the commission. A minister for the maison, whose department 'was not judged by the public', was hard to dislodge; moreover, 'at court people still respected the memory of M. de Maurepas', who had placed Amelot. Soon, however, Amelot fell ill and accepted the conditions.[54] From the start, his successor intended to realize the potential power of a minister for the maison; when, for instance, Lenoir explained that he had been accustomed to having a 'travail particulier' with the king,

Breteuil replied vehemently that that was all right under dolts like Saint-Florentin [La Vrillière] and Amelot but that with him things would be different.[55]

1784–6

Deceptive calm

A period of apparent stability with no ministerial changes. D'Ormesson writes: 'The ministry at that time [1786] . . . seemed unfortunately to be acquiring more and more *consistancé* – 'consistance' being the favourite word used by those in the ministerial milieu, beset with chronic instability, to describe its opposite.[56] General policy was decided by a comité de gouvernement consisting of the personnel of the disbanded comité des finances, the king, Vergennes, Miromesnil and the new contrôleur, Calonne. Peace diminished the role of Ségur and Castries, though the ending of the comité des finances restored their independence. Breteuil's ambitions of realizing the full potential of the maison were ended when he quarrelled irrevocably with Calonne over his purchase of Saint-Cloud for the queen in 1784 without informing the finance minister. In any case there was not sufficient room for two vigorous ministers in the jurisdictionally overlapping departments of the contrôle and the maison. Denied a role in the framing of general policy, Breteuil transferred his undoubted energies from Versailles to the second branch of his ministry, Paris, where he sought to bring about the fall of Calonne by his intrigues in the parlement. In the process, he destroyed the crown's ability to manage the parlement.

Throughout the period, the comité de gouvernement retained a

---

54 Lenoir MS 1423, résidus, 85.
55 ibid., mélanges, 4.
56 D'Ormesson, *Journal*, 121.

perspective which focused on 1787, when a uniform land tax would be introduced to eliminate tax evasion by the nobility and tax avoidance by the clergy and regional variation in the tax take. The exact contours of the plan were framed by the course of Calonne's ministry. Dupont de Nemours, the official who best symbolized the continuity of this period, had told d'Ormesson that an understanding with the parlements would have to be sought for a replacement for the vingtièmes but that some form of national consultation would be necessary for the indirect taxes, 'which we do not think can be touched unless there is a way found to consult and come to an understanding with the Nation for their replacements'.[57] The crown's loss of control of the parlement in 1786 led to the wholesale adoption of the second approach, in the form of an Assembly of Notables whose endorsement of Calonne's measures, it was hoped, would give the king the authority to have the measures immediately registered in the parlements by lit de justice.

57 A.N. 144 A.P. 131 dossier 4. 11.

CHAPTER FOUR

The appointment and dismissal of ministers:

from the convocation of the Assembly of Notables to the fall of the Bastille

In this period the play of 'pure politics' was arrested, though not eliminated, by external opposition to government.

1787

The death of Vergennes

Vergennes died, of over-work, on 13 February. The king's last letter to him is solicitous:

I was very upset to learn, Monsieur, that you were worse yesterday; I am afraid that despite my request you are still working too hard; I urge you even more strongly to look after yourself. You know your utility to my service. It is for myself that I make the request. You have M. de Rayneval [his premier commis] whom you trust, who can look after the foreign side. As for the great question in home affairs [the Assembly of Notables], I will hold all the comités punctually so that there will be no delay.[1]

Vergennes's death deprived Calonne of his principal ally and the king of what Calonne called 'tous ceux de ses ministres qui étoient vraiment à lui', that is who still believed in the absolute monarchy.[2] That said, when the ride became rough, Vergennes would probably have sacrificed Calonne as he had earlier sacrificed the two previous finance ministers, Joly de Fleury and d'Ormesson. Castries asked for Vergennes's post of chef du conseil, but the king told him that it was being suppressed as an economy measure.[3] The provinces that Vergennes administered were given to Breteuil, so that for the last two years of the ancien régime the maison was a true ministry of the interior, responsible for all but the frontier provinces.

Vergennes was replaced at affaires étrangères by Armand Marc de

---

1 Archives de Vergennes, *Lettres de Louis XVI*, dated January.
2 A.N. 297 A.P. 3. 119.
3 Castries, *Journal*, Archives de la Marine, MS 182/7964 1–2, I, fo. 343–4.

Montmorin de Saint-Hérem (1746–92), Comte de Montmorin. Montmorin, who had been one of his menins, was a personal friend of the king and his personal appointment. Bombelles writes that 'the joy that His Majesty experienced in bringing his favourite closer to his person has already diminished the pain he showed in the first moments of his loss of M. de Vergennes'.[4] A professional diplomat, since 1783 he had been ambassador to Spain. In 1784 he had been appointed commandant-en-chef in Brittany. He was minister for foreign affairs until 1791 and was murdered in the September Massacres.

The family of Montmorin de Saint-Hérem enjoyed the honneurs de la cour and their noble descent can be established from 1187. Montmorin's father, Armand Gabriel, was the second son of the second Marquis de Saint-Hérem and, like most of his family, pursued a military career; he was also menin to the old dauphin. He married Catherine, daughter of Thomas Le Gendre, a maréchal de camp whose father had been ennobled by charge de robe, and Marguerite, daughter of Marc René de Voyer d'Argenson, the garde des sceaux. In 1764 Montmorin married his cousin–german Françoise-Gabrielle de Tane, *dame d'atours* to Madame Sophie.[5] They had two daughters, the elder of whom married the son of Montmorin's future colleague La Luzerne. The couple were guillotined in 1794.

The dismissal of Miromesnil

The king told Malesherbes, who had been made a ministre in 1775 and resumed his place in the conseil in 1787, why he had dismissed the garde des sceaux:

It was not those two [Vergennes and Calonne] who most decided me [to convoke the Notables]. It was M. de Miromesnil who, after this counsel, washed his hands of the affair throughout the meeting of the Notables. That is what made me take the step of parting company with him.[6]

Miromesnil's general disposition to undermine Calonne – what the latter termed the 'perfidie du principal des co-opérateurs' – forced Calonne to tell the king that one or other of them must go;[7] he found the king receptive since he could lay four specific charges of his own to Miromesnil's head. First, Calonne had intended to have two of his projects – the extension of the *timbre* and the *inféodation des domaines* – registered in the parlement before the Notables met so

---

4 Marquis de Bombelles, *Journal*, ed. J. Grassion and F. Durif, Geneva, 1978–93, 3 vols, II, 172.
5 For Montmorin's career and ancestry, see Jougla de Morénas, *Grand Armorial de France*, 1934–52, 7 vols, V, 104, and IV, 137; F.A. de La Chesnay des Bois, *Dictionnaire de la noblesse*, 3rd edn, 1863–76, 19 vols, XIV, 420–36, and IX, 133–4; Bombelles, *Journal*, I, 120.
6 Fragment of the *Journal de l'Abbé de Véri*, ed. Duc de Castries, *Revue de Paris*, November 1953, 84–5.
7 A.N. 297 A.P. 3. 119, letter to d'Angiviller, late July 1787.

that he would have some cash in hand. Miromesnil dissuaded the king from this course on the grounds that there was no chance of success and the king reproached him for this advice, which Calonne presented as 'un tour et une finesse', throughout the Assembly.[8]

Second, Miromesnil wanted his protégé (and, reputedly, natural son) Le Camus de Néville, the intendant of Bordeaux, to supplant Calonne. When the king asked Miromesnil to moderate de Néville's outspoken opposition in the Notables, Miromesnil claimed that such counsel would force de Néville either to remain silent or to absent himself from the Assembly.[9] Louis's reply is lost, but Loménie de Brienne, to whom Miromesnil showed it, says that 'the king did not insist'. Nevertheless he must have felt resentment, especially when de Néville proceeded to boast to the queen that he was 'already contrôleur-général'.[10]

Third, Miromesnil concerted parlementaire opposition in the Assembly, each premier président informing his parlement about decisions taken so that when Calonne's edicts came to be registered, opposition would be uniform. This the king knew from opening the mail of the premier présidents.[11]

Fourth, Miromesnil, who together with Vergennes and the king, had checked Calonne's figures the previous autumn, now chose this moment to inform the king (on 5 April) that they had not been 'competent to check' Calonne's états and asked that the two gardes du trésor doublecheck them. This request was both treacherous and an evasion of responsibility. In this letter Miromesnil also enclosed one from Joly claiming that Necker's *Compte* was accurate. Calonne had asked Joly de Fleury for routine confirmation that Necker's *Compte* was suspect. Though Joly knew full well that this was the case (see pp. 138–42), he not only told Calonne that it was accurate but also sent Miromesnil a copy of his letter to make sure that the king was informed.[12]

The king gave Montmorin a letter of dismissal to give to Miromesnil. The letter is now lost but, again, Brienne gives a précis:

The king's letter mentions that for the past two years [Miromesnil] had been talking of retirement on grounds of health; that since sparkling health was required at the moment he thought it best to relieve him of the seals and invited him to propose whatever retraite he thought appropriate.

In a draft reply, Miromesnil took up the pretext of health:

---

8 A.N. K163 no. 8. 21, Miromesnil to the king, 8 December 1786.
9 A.N. K163 no. 8. 28, Miromesnil to the king, 14 March 1787.
10 Comte de Brienne and Loménie de Brienne, *Journal de l'Assemblée des Notables de 1787*, ed. P. Chevalier, 1960, 47; Baron de Besenval, *Mémoires*, ed. Berville and Barrière, 1821, 2 vols, II, 211 and 261.
11 Besenval, *Mémoires* II, 213–14.
12 See pp. 139–42; A.N. K163 no. 8. 35, Miromesnil's letter.

Sire, it is with a heavy heart that I realize that my health is no longer strong enough to support the work demanded of the post which Your Majesty deigned to confer on me.

In the final version, however, he stripped aside the pretence:

I obey Your Majesty's order. I have just returned the seals to M. de Montmorin and I beg Your Majesty to accept my resignation from the charge of chancelier de France which you joined to that of garde des sceaux when you deigned to honour me with it.

I have served you, Sire, out of attachment to your person and my only concern has been the good of your service. The rest of my life will be devoted to praying for the prosperity of your reign.[13]

Miromesnil's surrender of the *survivance* to the chancelerie had been unsolicited, but as Brienne observed, 'a chancellor who does not resign cannot remain in Paris. M. de Miromesnil went freely off into the country'. This was not strictly true: Miromesnil had to ask the king to accept his choice of residence in the country. Miromesnil did not ask for a pension:

I have been too aware of the state of Your Majesty's affairs to be able to accept favours which you ought not to grant. I entered the ministry a poor man and poor I will leave it.

Brienne comments, 'one cannot love money less; the usual retraite of a keeper of the seals is said to be 100,000 livres'.[14]

Miromesnil was replaced by Calonne's nominee, the président de Lamoignon, who was informed of his elevation by Calonne's personal courier. Chrétien François de Lamoignon (1735–89), fourth Marquis de Bâville, a président à mortier since 1758, had been Calonne's ally for several years and there were rumours that when Calonne had been appointed in 1783 he had sought to press home his advantage by ousting Miromesnil, considered vulnerable after the death of his patron, Maurepas, and gravely damaged by the failure of the comité des finances, in his favour.[15] Though Calonne subsequently established a good working relationship with Miromesnil, as his relations with the parlement deteriorated, the need to have a keeper of the seals of his own persuasion became more imperative.

Miromesnil in turn tried to poison the king's mind in advance against Lamoignon. In a letter of 4 January 1786 he refers to 'M. de Lamoignon, whose taste for intrigue is . . . known to Your Majesty'. So it was, but Miromesnil's insinuation in the same letter that 'M. de

13 A.N. K163 no. 8. 33, letter of 9 April.
14 B.N. n.a.f. 20073 fo. 18, draft letter from Miromesnil to the king; Castries, *Journal*, II, fo. 357; Brienne, *Journal*, 62.
15 Castries, *Journal*, II, fo. 355; Besenval, *Mémoires*, II, 2–6 and 13ff; for Lamoignon's ancestry and career, see F. Bluche, *L'Origine des magistrats du parlement de Paris au XVIIIe siècle*, 1956, 234–6, 56–7, 175, 314; Jougla de Morénas, *Grand Armorial*, IV, 401; F. Bluche, *Les Honneurs de la cour*, 1957; La Chesnay des Bois, *Dictionnaire*, XI, 386.

Lamoignon was secretly stirring up the parlement' against Calonne is ridiculous. The height of absurdity was reached in a letter of 4 January 1787, when Miromesnil claims to have been alerted to a manoeuvre directed by Lamoignon to have the parlement give a mandate to those of its brethren who had been summoned to the Assembly of Notables. While it is true that, during the meeting of the Notables, Lamoignon was circumspect in his support of Calonne (for instance he absented himself from the Conférence chez Monsieur of 2 March), the notion that he should seek to sabotage the measures of his ally is scarcely credible and was not credited by the king: ultimately Miromesnil's behaviour hastened the very appointment he had sought to prevent.[16]

Lamoignon was Malesherbes's second cousin, their common great-grandfather being Chrétien François, second Marquis de Bâville (no. VI in the genealogy given for Malesherbes: see p. 46). The minister's grandfather had been a président à mortier, as was his father, Chrétien Guillaume, the fourth marquis who was also grand prévôt of the Order of Saint-Louis and capitaine and gouverneur of Monthléry. Lamoignon's mother was Louise, daughter of Samuel Bernard, maître des requêtes, and granddaughter of the celebrated financier Samuel Bernard, who had been ennobled by lettres patentes in 1699. Lamoignon married Marie-Elizabeth, daughter of Nicolas Berryer, lieutenant-général de police and later garde des sceaux. On paper, the Lamoignons' descent and family alliances were no better than many in the parlement or the council, than Miromesnil's say, with whom comparisons were made. Nevertheless they enjoyed an additional kudos which is reflected in the offices held by Lamoignon's father and summed up by the Comte d'Artois's comment on Lamoignon's appointment: 'c'est un bon choix et un beau nom'.[17]

The minister for the maison, Breteuil, had not delivered the king's letter to Miromesnil because he was lying low at his château of Dangu during Holy Week and because his own job was on the line. Accounts differ but Lenoir, who was to have succeeded him, says that he was actually dismissed for 'an instant' and Montmorin was given a letter for him too, when the queen intervened to save him. Castries has 'the king's hand raised to write to him', while Loménie de Brienne has the queen saying

that she set no store by any particular minister, neither the keeper of the seals nor even the Baron de Breteuil; that as far as she was concerned he could sack the lot of them, but that it was essential to dismiss the contrôleur-général.[18]

Apart from Breteuil's previous manoeuvres against Calonne in the parlement, of which the king had been fully informed by

16 A.N. K163 no. 8. 22, nos 7 and 7(bis) contain Miromesnil's letters.
17 Brienne, *Journal*, 74.
18 Lenoir MS 1423, mélanges, 39; Castries, *Journal*, II, fo. 354.

Miromesnil,[19] during the Notables, Breteuil supported a bear syndicate of speculators, headed by the Baron de Batz, which undermined Calonne's attempts to support the Bourse during the political crisis.

Calonne wanted not only to replace Miromesnil and Breteuil but also to remodel the entire ministry, Puységur to replace Ségur at the war department and d'Estaing to replace Castries, whose opposition had been the most forthright of all and to the king's face: for instance he had reminded him 'Your monarchy is absolute but not despotic'. Castries saw no further than a personal vendetta on Calonne's part: having rid himself of Miromesnil,

whom he abominated, he attempted to extend his malign influence as far as the Baron de Breteuil and thus proceed to the whole ministry.

However, there was a new principle at stake and though of these changes, only the replacement of Miromesnil by Lamoignon subsisted, the king's acceptance, however temporary, of Calonne's demands marked a constitutional landmark. As the near-contemporary Droz remarks:

Louis XVI had come to recognize that the members of a ministry should be united as to *intérêts* and policies.

He was prepared to subordinate his personal independence, which could often be promoted by disunity within the ministry, to the need to carry on his government in the face of an intractable assembly. As political conditions began to resemble those in England, so did the conventions.[20]

The fall of Calonne

Calonne fell because he was appealing from a position of weakness to men who could only lose by the measures they were being asked to endorse. They would have been hurt in their pockets and their social prestige (being asked to sit next to *roturiers* in the proposed provincial assemblies). Moreover the unquantified, permanent tax which the proposed *impôt territorial* represented and the inevitable decline of *pouvoirs intermédiaires*, such as the clergy (which would lose its corporate existence) and parlements, would have created a modern and truly absolute monarchy, foreshadowing that created by Napoleon. Nor, despite the avertissement, had the minister succeeded in enlisting support from a wider audience. Calonne's weakness stemmed from the fact that the government had waited until the crisis, which had been anticipated for so long, arrived. (Calonne had at least wanted to

19 A.N. K163 no. 8. 21, Miromesnil to the king.
20 Castries, *Journal*, II, fos 346 and 357; J.F.X. Droz, *Histoire du règne de Louis XVI*, Brussels, 1839, 261; Bachaumont, *Mémoires secrètes pour servir à l'histoire de la république des lettres*, London, 1777–89, 36 vols, XXXV, 14.

enact the programme in 1786 but had been held up by the king's desire for a thorough discussion.) Thus weakened, Actaeon-like, Calonne was torn to shreds by his own creatures, by a body he had called into being: 'they fell on him', Castries observes in his diary, 'like a quarry they wanted to devour'.

Calonne was dismissed on Easter Sunday, 8 April, on the same day as his rival, Miromesnil. However, the king had taken the decision on the 6th. On that day, Good Friday, Louis wrote the following letter to Chaumont de la Millière, an intendant des finances:

As the good of my service, Monsieur, requires that I ask M. de Calonne to resign as contrôleur-général, my knowledge of your talents and integrity has prompted me to choose you to replace him. I am fully aware of the weight of responsibility which I am entrusting to you but I also count on your zeal for my service and your devotion to my person. I have absolutely no intention of withdrawing the plans for the amelioration of the finances which I caused to be presented to the Assembly of Notables; I intend to follow through the execution of the measures with firmness, whilst allowing such reasonable changes as [the Notables'] representations may present.

For this purpose, my intention is to assemble a comité of the council over which I will regularly preside. Here the representations will be discussed and here I will decide what reply to make to them and the manner of implementing the plans. Your main concern at this present moment will be examining the state of the funds in the trésor royal and with maintaining funding [*le service*] in the interval before the reforms take effect. Give me your reply, Monsieur, through the same channel and keep my secret until I tell you otherwise.

This important letter reveals Louis' determination to press through with the reforms and his personal identification with them: to save them he was ready to ditch their pilot. (Unfortunately, he was to discover that Calonne was unpopular with the Notables because of the reforms rather than vice versa). The letter also shows that, as in 1783, 1788 and 1789, Louis was haunted by the fear of a credit crisis: Calonne was to talk of 'the false alarm instilled into the king that in eight days' time there would not be a sous left in the trésor royal'.

On the 7th, Chaumont asked for an audience to explain why he could not 'carry out [the king's intentions]' and in a quarter-of-an-hour was able to convince the king that though he 'did his best to run his two departments [Ponts-et-Chaussées and Hospitals], he did not understand the ensemble and indeed had a sort of blind-spot when it came to figures'.[21]

The immediate cause of the king's decision to part with Calonne was a defensive-offensive manoeuvre by the queen on behalf of 'her' minister, Breteuil. According to Castries's account, Calonne having asked for Breteuil's dismissal on the 5th,

21 A.N. K163 no. 7. 1–2; A.N. 297 A.P. 3. 119; Brienne, *Journal,* 60.

the king had his hand poised to write to him, having dispatched the keeper of the seals; then he put off the decision for further consideration and in this interval he spoke to the queen who . . . did not leave him until she had saved the Baron de Breteuil and toppled the contrôleur-général.[22]

However, the queen only tipped the balance. The width of opposition is indicated by Calonne, in a letter to d'Angiviller of the following July:

Let [His Majesty] recall everything which has happened since the convocation of the Assembly of Notables, when my ruin was sworn and when unhappily opposition to everything which I presented in the very name of His Majesty seemed only to guarantee. A combination of every kind of obstacle, a union of all the injured vested interests; the baleful preponderance of the clergy; the manoeuvres of a powerful and fanatical sect [Necker's followers]; the perfidy of my main colleague [Miromesnil]; the best intentions denigrated; a war of sophistry; unseemly railing against the minister; the insinuation that his dismissal was the only way of terminating the business and finally the false alarm instilled in the king by the incredible allegation that in a week there would not be a *sous* left in the royal treasury.[23]

The scale of opposition is put in more measured terms by Miromesnil, who orchestrated it:

I see that he [Calonne] is trying to turn you against the bishops, against the parlementaires, against the ministers. He is making a kind of appeal to the people [the avertissement] which may have dangerous consequences. Finally I foresee alarming consequences for your happiness and for the rest of your reign.[24]

The king, however, did not need any prompting from Calonne. Castries, the blunt soldier, even accuses him of inspiring the avertissement: 'Is it Your Majesty who is causing M. de Calonne to act so imprudently?' This differentiates Calonne's dismissal from all the preceding ones. Indeed, it was arguably the first time that a king of France had been forced to part with a minister in whom he retained confidence since the young Louis XIV had sent Cardinal Mazarin into tactical exile. As Mercy-Argenteau put it in a letter of 19 May to Joseph II:

As Your Majesty deigns to observe, the king's authority is all the more grievously compromised by the abandonment of the former contrôleur-général in that his plans had been so explicitly approved by the monarch that he scarcely left himself any way of disowning them.[25]

This embarrassing constitutional predicament explains many of the

22 Castries, *Journal*, II, fo. 354.
23 A.N. 297 A.P. 3. 119, letter to d'Angiviller, late July 1787.
24 A.N. K163 no. 8. 32, Miromesnil to the king.
25 A. d'Arneth and J. Flammermont (eds) *Correspondance secrète du Comte de Mercy-Argenteau avec l'Empereur Joseph II et le Prince de Kaunitz*, 1891, 2 vols, II, 94.

vicissitudes of Calonne's disgrâce, and in particular the transition from a gentle treatment to one of unprecedented severity.

With uncharacteristic sensitivity, Louis saw to it that the details of Calonne's retraite were handled not by his enemy Breteuil but by the foreign secretary, Montmorin, and the former minister for the maison, Amelot. The king's sister, Madame Elizabeth, put it slightly differently: 'I hope that the Baron de Breteuil did not want to undertake the business; that would do him honour'. When Montmorin told Calonne of his dismissal, he added some 'consolant' words from the king which, according to Loménie de Brienne, were:

I am authorized to tell you that your successor will not be displeasing to you and that you are not the only one being dismissed.[26]

Calonne's successor was Michel Bouvard de Fourqueux (1719–89), Seigneur de Fourqueux. Bouvard was descended from Charles Bouvard, Louis XIII's premier médecin, his great-great-grandfather, who had been ennobled by lettres patentes in 1639. In 1738 Bouvard had become a conseiller in the parlement and in 1743 procureur-général in the chambre des comptes, a post in which his grandfather and father had preceded him. In 1768 Bouvard became a transfuge, when he moved to the conseil d'état as a conseiller. His wife's father, Jean-Baptiste Auget de Montyon, had performed a similar evolution, beginning as a maître in the chambre des comptes but later becoming successively intendant of the Auvergne, Aix and finally of La Rochelle.[27]

Bouvard had collaborated closely with Calonne on the preparation of his projects and had been responsible for the memoranda of the 'Third Division' submitted to the Notables.

Much was made of the fact that Calonne stayed on at Versailles (then at his château of Berni, near Paris); he was accused of being 'the minister behind the curtain';[28] and rumoured to have lavishly entertained his protégés Bouvard and Lamoignon.[29] However, his temporary residence at Versailles was purely a practical matter, as Montmorin makes clear in a letter to him of 15 April arranging the details of his exile:

The king, who knows, Monsieur, that you intend to proceed to Hannonville [Calonne's estate in Lorraine] as soon as you have handed over to your successor the memoranda and explanatory notes that His Majesty has charged you to give him, considers that, having done this, you should no longer defer

26 A.N. 297 A.P. 3. 115, Calonne to Montmorin, 12 June; Brienne, *Journal*, 58; Mme Elizabeth to Mme de Bombelles, 9 April, published by F. Feuillet de Conches, *Correspondance de Madame Elizabeth*, 1865, 95.
27 For Bouvard's career and ancestry, see Bluche, *Origine*, 106–7; La Chesnay des Bois, *Dictionnaire*, III, 90–7.
28 A.N. 297 A.P. 3. 119, letter to d'Angiviller, late July 1787.
29 Brienne, *Journal*, 60.

your plans; and just as at Berni you only wished to receive a few of your relatives and close friends, he counts on your also following this course at Hannonville where you will reside until he gives you further orders.[30]

Though politely formulated, this constituted an exile under strict conditions, and contrasted unfavourably with Miromesnil's treatment. On 4 June, the exile was further defined. The Duc de Gramont, having enquired of Montmorin whether Calonne's friends could go to Hannonville:

I replied that I did not know of any formal prohibition; subsequently . . . the king has spoken on this matter and his intention is that no one should go to Hannonville without his permission – he did me the honour of repeating this yesterday on the occasion of granting such permission to Mme la Vicomtesse de Laval.[31]

When Calonne, who had grown thin and was sleeping badly, desired to take the waters at Bagnières, the king in granting his request stipulated 'that his intention was that you should avoid passing through Paris'. Accordingly, Calonne travelled via Burgundy and Franche-Comté.[32]

As Brienne, who had been appointed chef du conseil royal des finances on 1 May, brought his influence to bear on the ministry, Calonne's treatment became harsher. On 12 June he had written to Montmorin offering to resign his charge of grand trésorier of the Saint-Esprit, though it gave him pain to lose this last occasion 'de pouvoir quelques fois lui [the king] faire ma cour'. But he assumed that he would be allowed to wear the insignia of the order, particularly as it was common knowledge that the Dutch had presented him with the star of the order set in diamonds. He also sought this assurance from the previous minister for the maison, Amelot, whose seven years' experience of handling exiles was being enlisted. Amelot, however, had to inform Calonne that this was not the king's intention, adding:

I cannot adequately express, Monsieur, the pain it gives me to be ordered to convey such devastating news to you.[33]

Such a step, contemplated but rejected on the fall of Terray, was, as Calonne rightly observed, 'unprecedented'. Calonne appealed through Toulouse to the king, who replied through his chef du conseil 'that he had already given his orders and that he did not want to make any alterations to them'. Toulouse grounded the king's *mécontentement* on the fact that 'considerable sums of money have left the royal treasury without the king's authorization': 'he wants to make a crime', Calonne told d'Angiviller, 'out of something practised at all times [i.e. the use of

30 A.N. 297 A.P. 3. 110.
31 A.N. 297 A.P. 3. 111.
32 A.N. 297 A.P. 3. 110 and 115.
33 A.N. 297 A.P. 3. 113, letter of 22 June.

'acquits de comptant']'.[34] An investigating body (Calonne called it a comité des finances) was instituted under d'Ormesson, 'a rapporteur who had thoroughly made up his mind against me in advance and whose inclusion is no accident'. His enemies had to inculpate him in order to justify 'les surprises qu'ils ont fait au roi'. Calonne's use of the conventional 'surpriser la religion du roi' highlights the verbal contortions that one can expect from a minister, such as Brienne, who has 'stormed the closet'.[35]

Hearing that the parlement sought means of proceeding against him, Calonne withdrew to Holland – exile proper. Chastened, the queen sent him assurances through Madame de Polignac that he could 'rest easy'. On 11 August a ministerial comité met to decide whether to quash the parlement's proceedings; Castries and Malesherbes, arguing that 'il faut une justice pour les ministres', thought that either the parlement or the king should try Calonne to establish ministerial responsibility; the discussion was subsumed by that of the conseil on 14 August, which decided on the exile of the parlement to Troyes. Calonne continued his journey to England. In Holland, where he had many supporters, he was an embarrassment to the French government at a time of international tension in the region. Advocating the move, the Princesse de Robecq, one of the Polignac group, told him he could work for a return to power as easily from England. Indeed in London Calonne took up lodgings with his publisher the better to oversee production of his *Requête au roi*. No more than his rival Necker did Calonne accept the finality of disgrâce.[36]

One of Calonne's bitterest detractors, Breteuil's lieutenant, Bombelles, was to recant: 'No doubt M. de Calonne had his faults, but I was greatly mistaken when I rejoiced at his dismissal. . . . When he was toppled by a cabal, he was in the process of saving France'.[37]

The appointment of Loménie de Brienne

On 1 May the king filled the vacant post of chef du conseil with Étienne Charles de Loménie de Brienne (1727–94), who had been Archbishop of Toulouse since 1763, and who had been invested with the cordon bleu in 1780 on the queen's recommendation. Brienne was seventh-generation noble, being descended from Martial de Loménie, who had been ennobled by the office of secrétaire du roi in 1552. The son and grandson of Martial rose to eminence as secrétaires d'état in the reigns of Henri IV and Louis XIII, but their descendants, mostly soldiers, had fallen into a relative obscurity, which Brienne, archbishop

---

34 A.N. 297 A.P. 3. 112, Brienne to Calonne, 17 June.
35 A.N. 297 A.P. 3. 119.
36 Castries, *Journal*, II, 387; P.R.O. P.C. 1/125, Princesse de Robecq to Calonne, 17 July 1787.
37 Bombelles, *Journal*, II, 177.

at 37, aimed to rectify. An interest in public finance may have come from his maternal grandfather, Henri-Clément Chamillart, who was a président in the chambre des comptes and garde du trésor royal.[38]

Joseph II had told Mercy-Argenteau:

If the king weakens and abandons [Calonne] . . . the clergy, the nobility and the parlements will form a kind of coalition such that, as in England, he . . . will eventually be obliged to accept ministers of their choice and dismiss those they dislike.[39]

Joseph's view of the English system was unduly schematic, as was his application of it to France. Though Brienne could say with some justification, 'there is some satisfaction in taking the dismissal of the minister [Calonne] as satisfaction due to the Assembly',[40] the Notables did not force the king to appoint Brienne. Rather, the king had the option of dissolving the Assembly or of abandoning his reform programme, but if he wanted the Assembly to approve the programme, Brienne as chef de l'opposition, but mindful of the ministerial traditions of his family, had the best chance of getting it through.

To this end the king and Brienne exchanged several memoranda which modified Calonne's proposals in the light of the Notables' criticisms.[41] The process was initiated when Marie-Antoinette, in pursuance of her long-held plan to make Brienne prime minister, forwarded to the king an anonymous memorandum of the archbishop's. The king was sufficiently interested to enquire as to the author and continue the correspondence. Louis found Brienne disturbingly obtuse over interest rate possibilities. Nevertheless, they managed to thrash out the basis for a compromise. The présidence of the provincial assemblies would always go to the clergy and the nobility; but the assemblies would remain subordinate to the intendant; the amount of the land tax would be raised from the 54 million livres which the vingtièmes brought in to 80 million livres, which would, however, answer the Notables' objections that the tax was for an indefinite sum; the clergy's contribution would be assessed in the provincial assembly but its collection would be left to the administrative machinery of the clergy. These ideas were embodied in the king's speech of 23 April to the Assembly of Notables reopening its sessions after the adjournment caused by the ministerial crisis. Brienne noted that the speech 'was exceedingly close to my proposals'. Louis delayed a further week before appointing Brienne, having long held the view that a priest should not be made a minister on the grounds that he would necessarily be made a cardinal and would acquire too

---

38 For Brienne's career and ancestry, see B.N. Nouveau d'Hozier, 187; Bluche, *Honneurs de la cour*; Jougla de Morénas, *Grand Armorial*, IV, 470.
39 Arneth and Flammermont, *Correspondance secrète*, II, 78.
40 Brienne, *Journal*, 59.
41 ibid., 79–92.

much weight in the conseil. He was finally brought to it by a deputation of the other ministers and made the best of a bad job by employing a formula which implied that the bounds of constitutional propriety had not been exceeded: 'I had some préventions against him but I've certainly come round'.[42]

That night Marie-Antoinette was 'd'une gaieté folle'.[43] Brienne's appointment marked the beginning of her sustained involvement in politics, from which Louis had hitherto been careful to exclude her. Such application did not agree with her and gave her headaches but she was forced to it not only as the patronne of the chef du conseil but also because the rejection of his cherished reform programme had wrought a profound change in the king: from this time he began to lose his grip on affairs, increased his hunting and eating and his dependence on the queen, in short became the king that many assume he always was.

Bouvard, who had wanted to implement Calonne's measures unchanged, resigned as contrôleur-général and was replaced by Pierre Charles Laurent (1742–1828), Seigneur de Villedeuil. The son of the famous inventor Pierre-Joseph Laurent, ennobled by lettres patentes in 1756 for his services to the mechanical arts (arms: a three-arched bridge over a river, surmounted by a mural crown), Laurent de Villedeuil had pursued a classical career within the royal administration: maître des requêtes (1775); intendant in the régie des aides (1784); intendant of Rouen (1785).[44] He had caught Brienne's attention as a fellow member of Artois's bureau in the Notables. In the words of the Abbé de Morellet, Brienne

chose a contrôleur-général, M. de Villedeuil, who would only have his travail with the king in his presence as did M. Necker under M. de Maurepas. The archbishop will in addition be ordonnateur for all the financial side of the department, which M. de Maurepas neither was nor wished to be. However, he does not have any bureaux under him nor any administrative details. He has installed himself at Versailles in the contrôle-général and leaves the hôtel du contrôle, at Paris, to M. de Villedeuil.[45]

However, neither Brienne's increased authority nor the modifications made to Calonne's programme were sufficient to win acceptance for it by the Notables, even with the lobbying which the king had suggested, 'pour cela on peut tâter le terrain'. The measures were sent without the endorsement of the Assembly before the parlement where

42 Castries, *Journal*, II, fo. 362.
43 ibid.
44 For Laurent's career and ancestry, see B.N. Nouveau d'Hozier, 205 (for Pierre-Joseph's *Lettres de noblesse*); Marquis de Granges de Surgères, *Répertoire historique et biographique de la 'Gazette de France'*, 1902–6, 4 vols, III, 274; M. Michaud, *Biographie universelle ancienne et moderne*, 1843–, 45 vols, IX, 930–1; Dr Robinet, *Dictionnaire historique et biographique de la Révolution et de l'empire*, 1898, 2 vols, II, 345–6.
45 E. Fitzmaurice (ed.) *Lettres de l'Abbé de Morrellet à Lord Shelburne*, 1898.

they encountered insurmountable opposition. Brienne came back for more authority to the king who formally made him a prime minister, or ministre principal, a step he had hitherto always resisted: a circular letter from the king informed each minister that with important matters he must either show Brienne his travail before taking it to the king or let Brienne sit in on the travail itself.

Montmorin, who was not a resigner, wrote to the king next day accepting the arrangement: a common 'centre' desirable in the best of times was doubly so in times of difficulty, 'and it is impossible to blind oneself to the fact that those in which the government finds itself have become so in the highest degree'.[46]

Castries and Ségur, however, took the opportunity to leave. They were already in dispute with Brienne over his refusal to intervene on behalf of the Dutch Patriots threatened with an Anglo-Prussian invasion (an intervention which would at least have justified Castries's armaments). Ségur wrote to the king that the extra work involved in preparing a preliminary *travail* for the ministre principal on top of that for the king would be too much for his health; he had, moreover, 'these seven years been accustomed to receive his orders directly from Your Majesty'. He made the following requests:

1.   A *duché-héréditaire* for his eldest son.
2.   60,000 livres a year until he obtained 'un grand gouvernement' fitting for a maréchal de France.
3.   15,000 livres a year for his two sons after his death.
4.   A sum which may enable the Maréchal de Ségur to arrange his affairs, which at the present moment are mixed up with his payment as a secrétaire d'état since the marshal has to pay off people he only took on when he became a minister . . . He asks to be treated in this respect roughly as was M. de Sartine.[47]

Ségur was replaced by Brienne's younger brother, Louis Marie Athanase de Loménie (1730–94), Comte de Brienne. The younger Brienne had pursued a purely military career, becoming a maréchal de camp in 1762. In 1757 he had married the daughter of the farmer-general Clémont de Fizeau, whose wealth restored the fortunes of the Loménie de Brienne family. Devoted to his brother, with whom he shared the château de Brienne, his probity, as Besenval remarked, was the only quality for which he was praised.

Castries had given the queen the benefit of his unsolicited advice on the choice of his successor:

I told her that if there were any question of an homme de robe succeeding me, I should believe it my duty to tell the king that his navy would be ruined; that it was necessary to have at the head of this department a man who knew

46   A.N. K163 no. 10, letter of 27 August.
47   A.N. K163 no. 11. 2, letter of 29 August.

how to command, who was used to doing it and who had the authority to make himself obeyed and that M. de Bouillé seemed to me head and shoulders above those in his class whom the king might consider.[48]

Castries was not replaced by a robin but by César Henri, Comte de la Luzerne, a military man and currently governor of the Windward Islands (he was not presented to the king until 22 December and his functions were performed *par interim* by Montmorin). One of La Luzerne's brothers was the Évêque-Duc de Langres, Brienne's ally in the Notables; another brother was ambassador to England. The La Luzerne were descended from Géoffroi de La Luzerne, écuyer (*c.*1290), and his great-grandson Jean, chambellan to Louis XI. The nobility of the family was considered to be of chevaleresque origins, though this had been sufficiently challenged for the family to be 'maintenu noble' in 1453 and as recently as 1634. The La Luzerne also had important alliances within the *haute robe*: the minister's mother was Malesherbes's sister, while he himself married the daughter of the lieutenant-civil du Châtelet, Denis François Angran d'Allerai. Angran, another member of Artois's bureau in the Notables, had argued that a percentage tax was illegal and that there could be no permanent tax without privileges: 'It would not be just that while the nobleman fights, the magistrate judges, the minister governs and the priest performs divine service, he should not be accorded some privilege'. His efforts had led to his appointment as a conseiller d'état.[49]

The final casualty of Brienne's advancement was Laurent de Villedeuil. Since Brienne's elevation 'no longer permitted him [Brienne] to give his attention to any of the details of the finance department', Laurent asked the king for 'less stressful functions', given that 'the doctors even threaten me with the necessity of going to take the waters'. Louis replied: 'Your modesty could only add to my confidence [in you] but I yield on the grounds of your health'.[50] Laurent, whose health recovered sufficiently for him to live until 1828, received the king's portrait and a pension. He was made a conseiller d'état and assigned to the newly constituted conseil royal des finances.

To succeed him, Brienne selected Claude Guillaume Lambert (1726–94), Comte d'Auverse (guillotined). A transfuge, Lambert had been a conseiller in the parlement (1748) before becoming a maître des requêtes in 1767 under the influence, as Miromesnil later reminded Louis XVI, of the parlementaire L'Averdy, who had become contrôleur-général in 1765. Lambert was promoted conseiller d'état in 1778. His great-grandfather had been ennobled by charge de robe and in 1772 he had married Marie-Madeleine Beyssier de Pizany, the

48 Castries, *Journal*, II, fo. 374.
49 For La Luzerne's ancestry, see Jougla de Morénas, *Grand Armorial*, IV, 490–1; La Chesnay des Bois, *Dictionnaire*, XII, 623–31.
50 A.N. K163 no. 12.

daughter of a maître ordinaire in the chambre des comptes. His eldest son Augustin followed his career-pattern as a conseiller in the parlement (1782) and a maître des requêtes (1788). Lambert's austerity was legendary and he was a skilled proceduralist, but Besenval considered that he was 'totally incompetent in financial matters'.[51]

1788

The resignation of Breteuil

Curiously Breteuil's political importance was diminished by the fall of his enemy Calonne. Moreover Brienne supplanted him as the queen's special minister. The political *raison d'être* for his ministerial existence had gone, while his colleagues regarded him as an incompetent departmental minister. Nevertheless the precise reasons for Breteuil's resignation on 25 July remain obscure. Price, following Bombelles, sees it as a protest against 'a particularly flagrant act of ministerial despotism': Brienne's imprisonment of a deputation of the noblesse of Brittany, who had come to Versailles to protest about the coup d'état of 8 May which transferred the political functions of the parlements to a cour plénière with similar personnel to the Notables. Breteuil resigned rather than sign the order committing the Breton deputies to the Bastille. This symbolized a profound difference between Brienne and Breteuil, who had ceased to believe in the absolute monarchy and wished to endow France with a written aristocratic constitution.[52]

Egret, however, who says remarkably little about Breteuil's resignation and nothing at its chronological place, considers that Brienne forced the resignation of Breteuil, 'who was showing signs of opposition'.[53] Egret also, following Bachaumont's *Mémoires secrètes* and the *Correspondance secrète*, differs *toto caelo* on Breteuil's general position, suggesting that Brienne 'avait contenu longtemps les impatiences autoritaires du Garde des Sceaux et du baron de Breteuil' before finally agreeing to the coup of 8 May. Bachaumont notes in September 1787 that Breteuil proposed the suppression of all the parlements and the fusion of the parlement and the council for the promulgation of laws. Brienne supposedly vetoed this measure.[54]

It is certainly the case that Breteuil, who as minister for Paris was responsible for public order during the coup, took vigorous measures.

51 A.N. K161, no. 28(bis), Miromesnil to the king, 27 May 1785; for Lambert's career and ancestry, see J. Félix, *Les Magistrats du parlement de Paris, 1771–90*, 1990, 189.
52 M. Price, 'The Comte de Vergennes and the Baron de Breteuil: French politics and reform in the reign of Louis XVI', PhD thesis, Cambridge University, 1988, 363–9; Bombelles, *Journal*, II, 213.
53 J. Egret, *La Pré-révolution française*, 1962, 67.
54 ibid., 246; Bachaumont, *Mémoires secrètes pour servir à l'histoire de la république des lettres*, London, 1777–89, XXXVI, September 1787.

In particular the colonel of the gardes françaises, the Duc de Biron, criticized him on 5 May for requiring too many troops for the operation and on 26 May for maintaining too many on alert two weeks after the coup, 'considering the calm that obtains at the Palais [de justice], the Châtelet and throughout Paris'.[55] Breteuil also sedulously prevented groups of the disbanded parlement from meeting in private houses.[56] Thus it is hard to believe that, after managing the coup in a thorough, even heavy-handed manner, Breteuil would resign rather than imprison a deputation protesting against it.

A more credible explanation is that noting the unpopularity of the coup, and nursing a grievance against Brienne for becoming chef du conseil, a post to which he aspired (and briefly, in 1789, attained), he was involved in a manoeuvre to topple Brienne. The marriage of his granddaughter, Mlle de Matignon, into the *frondeur* House of Montmorency on 2 June and the pretext provided by his refusal to arrest the Breton deputies aided a modulation towards opposition which did not compromise him in the eyes of the king. The influence of the Montmorency is suggested in Montmorency-Luxembourg's own account: 'he [Breteuil] had not easily been forgiven for having approved of the cour plénière in the form it took'.[57] The queen was furious with Breteuil and refused to grant him an audience before he resigned. The king asked him to continue attending the council, but he declined.[58]

Laurent de Villedeuil came back into the ministry to replace Breteuil at the maison. He was a 'hardliner'. The last minister to have pursued his previous career solely within the royal administration, he was an uncompromising defender of the royal authority, the last to advocate not summoning the Estates-General (see pp. 163–4).

The fall of Loménie de Brienne and the reappointment of Necker

The occasion of Brienne's fall was a credit crisis; specifically 240 million livres of *anticipations* against the tax revenues of 1789, scheduled to be negotiated in August, were not taken up. Anticipations were a regular part of royal finance and provision for them had been made in the budget which Brienne had published in April. But, as Necker was to put it in his opening speech to the Estates-General:

The ability to negotiate and renew anticipations depends absolutely on the maintenance of credit. . . . one can never take the renewal of anticipations for granted.

55 A.N. O^1 354 nos 54 and 102, Biron to Breteuil.
56 ibid., nos 80 and 89, Breteuil to Crosne, 9 and 10 May.
57 Price, 'Vergennes and Breteuil', 366–7; Duc de Montmorency-Luxembourg, *Mémoires*, ed. P. Filleul, 1939, 271.
58 Bombelles, *Journal*, II, 215.

The failure of the anticipations reduced Brienne to issuing, by the arrêt of 16 August, what was in effect a 'forced loan' of 140 million livres at 5 per cent.

Egret, following Brienne himself, presents this crisis much as d'Ormesson presents those of 1783: in part technical, in part the result of intrigue (the latter element being provided in both cases by Artois and the Polignacs).[59] The usual, and most convincing, view is that the treasury crisis was merely a reflection of the general political one caused by widespread if unquantifiable provincial resistance to the May coup. At all events, as a result of the crisis, Brienne attempted to enlist Necker's services as contrôleur-général.

Brienne had made the same request of the king when he had been appointed chef du conseil, but the king had said that he had been appointed only to spare him Necker. Necker had displeased the king by his resignation in 1781 and by the publication of his *Administration des finances* in 1785 which was calculated to embarrass Calonne. On that occasion, the king had told Necker through his friend Castries to keep away from Paris. Castries asked the king whether that was an order: 'No', he replied. 'If I wanted to give M. Necker an order, it would be the minister for Paris who would dispatch it; nevertheless, I think that the counsels that I give ought to be regarded as orders'. In 1787 he had defied the king's warning by publishing a defence of the compte rendu against Calonne's implied attack on it in the Notables. 'He has let me down', the king told Castries, and exiled Necker sixty leagues from Paris, subsequently reduced to thirty.[60] Brienne now approached Necker through a common friend, Mercy-Argenteau, underlining Marie-Antoinette's central role in the proceedings:

I have come . . . to ask you to sound out M. Necker on his intentions so that I can myself ascertain those of the king. I am pretty sure that I shall find opposition from that quarter but I cannot attempt to overcome it until I know what M. Necker thinks.[61]

Necker refused to co-operate:

I would be without strength and resources if I were to be associated with someone whose reputation with the public is unfortunately ruined and who nevertheless is believed still to enjoy the greatest credit [at court].[62]

Since Brienne, in turn, refused to cede – 'I certainly wished to resign; but I did not want M. Necker to dismiss me'[63] – the king and queen were obliged, the latter with great reluctance, to withdraw their 'credit' from him. The king did not adopt his usual practice of refusing the

59 Egret, *Pré-révolution française*, 311–15.
60 Bombelles, *Journal*, II, 31; Castries, *Journal*, II, fo. 361.
61 Arneth and Flammermont, *Correspondance secrète*, II, 199.
62 ibid., II, 203, Necker to Mercy, 21 August.
63 J.L. Soulavie, *Mémoires historiques et politiques du règne de Louis XVI*, 1801, 6 vols, VI, 248.

threatened minister a travail, but the latter did not experience 'the same cordiality and ease'.[64]

On 25 August, Brienne resigned. He went to his new see of Sens for a few days, then to his château at Brienne, finally, in October, to Italy. Also on 25 August, Necker was reappointed directeur-général des finances, replacing the contrôleur-général Lambert. On the 27th, he finally obtained the grâce d'éclat he had been denied in 1781: he became a ministre d'état. After Mercy-Argenteau's soundings, the king had entered as a principal in the negotiations for Necker's return. On 23 August, Mercy-Argenteau told Marie-Antoinette:

I forgot to say yesterday . . . that M. Necker has no [fixed] ideas on the parlements, that he has no objection to the conseil des finances.

Next day, Marie-Antoinette replied that 'the king has just given me a paper written in his own hand containing his ideas'. This document has not survived, but from Marie-Antoinette's précis of it, it is obviously similar in format to the one he had sent Brienne in April 1787, though substantively, the concessions are greater:

the king desires to put M. Necker once more in charge of the finances; he will enter the conseil and will have an absolutely free hand in his department; the king thinks that after an operation [the coup of 8 May] which was disagreeable but necessary in the circumstances, whatever M. Necker proposes can only be approved by the public and that it will restore confidence; the king is steadfastly determined to hold the Estates-General at the time stated and to seek together with them ways of bridging the déficit and of preventing its recurrence; the king could not make any prior commitment to restore the parlements, but he is working on this for the end of the [parliamentary] vacation, while retaining the benefit conferred on the people by more accessible courts [Lamoignon's grands baillages].[65]

Louis appointed him with the worst of grace, reputedly telling people that he would do everything he told him and they would see what happened. This sulking detachment, this refusal to give Necker the benefit of his experience, was doubly unfortunate because Necker was gravely out of touch – witness his over-reaction to the parlement's September declaration on the organization of the Estates – as indeed was intended by the system for the treatment of ex-ministers, designed as it was to render them unfit to hold office again.

The fall of Lamoignon

Brienne's view of the crisis as a technical one is at least reinforced by the fact that the technician who replaced him, Necker, quickly restored credit. Necker himself, however, did not take this narrow view of the

64 ibid., VI, 250.
65 A. d'Arneth Marie-Antoinette, Joseph II und Leopold II, Vienna, 1866, 206–9.

crisis. Believing that the disturbances in the summer had approached the proportions of civil war, he advanced the meeting of the Estates to 1 January and prepared for the immediate and unconditional restoration of the parlement. The latter move flew in the face of Brienne's parting advice to the king:

Sire, be sure to avoid an unconditional recall of the parlements or your authority will be destroyed and the monarchy with it.[66]

In the spirit of this advice, Lamoignon had opened negotiations with the parlementaires Saint-Vincent, Talon and Sémonville through an intermediary, the conseiller d'état Foulon, who had a strong faction in the parlement.[67] Lamoignon offered two concessions: the limits of competence between the new grands baillages and the parlements could be negotiated and the planned reduction in the number of offices in the parlement would be achieved by natural wastage. It was assumed that the cour plénière, which had not yet been fully staffed, would be quietly dropped. The negotiation was sufficiently encouraging for a conditional restoration of the parlement to have been scheduled for 15 September: Louis's diary for that date runs: 'there was to have been a lit de justice'. The parlement had been summoned to Versailles and the usual orders given to the troops; then the lit was suddenly cancelled.

The most likely explanation of this is the intervention of Necker, who after all had been carried to power on the back of the révolte nobiliare and who was envious of the king's support for Lamoignon, the appointee of his rival Calonne. He may have inspired the parlement's arrêt of 13 September declaring that the cour des pairs would not have anything to do with Lamoignon. Opportunely, Castries had sent Louis a memorandum on 1 September arguing that it was impossible to reconcile the positions of Lamoignon and the parlement and that any negotiations should be abandoned. The Estates-General should deal with judicial reform – exactly Necker's position.[68]

The king sacrificed Lamoignon, who was forced to resign on 14 September, but gave him a brilliant retraite: 400,000 livres to discharge his debts and the promise of a duché-héréditaire and an important embassy for his eldest son at the age of 25. Lamoignon was obliged to keep these details secret lest there be an outcry from a public who would not consider what Lamoignon had sacrificed in the king's service: the impossibility of his children becoming magistrates (hence the embassy) and a marriage worth 1.4 million livres for his second

66 Reported in the *Gazette de Leyde* of 5 September and cited in Egret, *Pré-révolution française*, 319.
67 AAE MDF fos 108–10: a memorandum dictated by Lamoignon for Foulon together with the parlementaires' conciliatory reply, cited in Price, 'Vergennes and Breteuil', 381–2.
68 A.N. 306 A.P. 24.

son to the daughter of a provincial parlementaire, whose brethren threatened to expel him if the marriage went ahead.

When Necker told Lamoignon that he would have to resign, 'he heard him with extreme *chagrin*'; the weather-vane Montmorin also 'told him he would have to drain the bitter cup'. At the prospect of the public rejoicing in Paris, he was 'as upset as a child would have been'. On 15 September, Lamoignon withdrew to his château at Bâville, a mile-and-a-half from the Marais district of Paris. Unfortunately major rebuilding caused the ancient roof to cave in. Bombelles compared Lamoignon's rebuilding, 'prodigious operations doubtless directed imprudently', with his tampering with the political edifice and could not resist the observation that 'one fall involves another'.[69] When, as a parlementaire, Lamoignon had been exiled to Bâville after the Maupeou coup he had told the tax-farmer Augeard that he did not have the resources to withstand a long exile. The resources he lacked were primarily financial (in 1788 he had debts of 1 million livres) but also one feels emotional. At all events on 23 May 1789, Lamoignon shot himself in the grounds of Bâville, destroyed, according to his friend Marmontel, by 'le chagrin de l'exil'.[70] The parlement was restored without conditions.

The king decided to hold the seals himself for a while (that is to be his own keeper as Louis XIV and Louis XV had on occasion been). But the physical delivery of the seals from Lamoignon to Louis degenerated into farce:

I had forgotten to relate [writes Bombelles] a remarkable circumstance and one which proves just how far M. de Lamoigon had lost his head. He sent the seals in a blue sedan chair via a municipal officer. He, arriving at M. de Montmorin's, asked him what he had to do. M. de Montmorin, just as inexperienced in these matters as the young officer, sent him straight round to the king. Happily, as he was about to barge into His Majesty's cabinet, flouting every rule of etiquette, M. de Villedeuil was just leaving and went back in to take the king's orders. These were to the effect that the seals should remain with M. de Montmorin until the hour appointed for the council, when they should be brought in and handed over to His Majesty.[71]

The way in which the seals were shunted around in a sedan chair symbolized the utter dissolution of the state they represented. It will be readily appreciated why it was 'not done' for just anyone to barge into the king's cabinet, that, more than a major breach of etiquette, gaining access to the king was a political act. Some difficulty, however, may be experienced in understanding Laurent's failure simply to take the seals in to the king himself. He obviously did the right thing because the

69 Bombelles, *Journal*, II, 234–5.
70 J.M. Augeard, *Mémoires secrètes*, ed. E. Bavou, 1866, 46; Marmontel, *Mémoires*, 1804, 4 vols, III, 154.
71 Bombelles, *Journal*, II, 236.

king did not tell him to go and retrieve them. No, the seals were not like some stray dog, they had to be delivered to the king in his council. Protocol was made on the hoof and in this at least Louis did not exhibit his customary indecision.

After living with the seals for a week (and offering them in vain to Malesherbes) on 19 September, Louis conferred them on Charles de Paule de Barentin (1736–1819), who after having been avocat-général in the parlement had succeeded Malesherbes as premier président of the cour des aides in 1775. Barentin's previous career was spent entirely in the sovereign courts, for which his appointment represented a triumph. His ancestors, however, who had moved from Blois to Paris in about 1595, had all spent their lives in the council, as can be seen from their genealogy:

I	Claude Barentin married Marie Joret.
*II	Charles Barentin, maître des requêtes (1605), conseiller d'état (1613), ennobled through these offices; married Marie Carré, daughter of the trésorier des bâtiments du roi.
III	Claude Barentin.
IV	Honoré Barentin, maître des requêtes, président in the grand conseil.
V	Charles Honoré de Barentin, intendant of Flanders, married Marie-Renée de Montchal, daughter of a conseiller in the parlement.
VI	Charles Amable Honoré de Barentin, conseiller d'état, married Marie Catherine Lefèvre d'Ormesson, daughter of Henri d'Ormesson, conseiller d'état.
VII	Charles Louis François-de-Paule Honoré de Barentin, Seigneur d'Hardivilliers. Barentin, a former protégé of Miromesnil's, quickly established himself as the spokesman of reaction in the council.[72]

The Comte de Brienne remained at the war ministry until 27 November; curiously it was only after his brother's dismissal that he was made a ministre. He was finally succeeded on 30 November by Pierre Louis de Chastenet, Comte de Puységur, aged 62, a lieutenant-général, an ex-Notable and the member of the new conseil de guerre with responsibility for military hospitals. His appointment was a case of third time lucky for Puységur: he had been Maurepas's candidate for the war ministry in 1780 and Calonne's in 1787. His family, an ancient and many ramified one from the Armagnac, was accepted as being of chevaleresque extraction though the requisite documentation was lacking.[73]

72 For Barentin's ancestry, see Bluche, *Origine ;* Courcelles, *Dictionnaire universelle de la noblesse de la France*, 1820, 3 vols, I, 374.
73 La Chesnay des Bois, *Dictionnaire*, V, 318–33; *Nouvelle biographie générale*, 1968, XLI, 218.

1789

The dismissal of Necker, Montmorin and Puységur, and the resignation of La Luzerne

The departure of these ministers on 12 July was accompanied by the tactical resignation of Barentin and Laurent de Villedeuil to give the king carte blanche to form a new administration (they also thought that their move would placate the National Assembly).[74] The changes were intended to be the prelude to a reassertion of royal authority in the face of the incursions by the National Assembly. Beyond that, one cannot speak with precision. The reaffirmation of the programme outlined in the séance royale of 23 June can be presumed, and this was underlined by the reappointment of Barentin and Laurent de Villedeuil. As garde des sceaux and minister for the maison, they had been able to promulgate the articles of the séance throughout the kingdom even after the king had ordered the union of the orders on 27 June. Troops were summoned, but this was not integrated with the change of ministers: the first orders had been signed by the king on 22 June, while the troop concentration was not expected to be completed until 18 July. Elsewhere I have emphasized the purely defensive role the troops were to play,[75] but the limits even to the defence can be summarized by the following orders of the minister-general, the Duc de Broglie, to the Baron de Besenval, his field commander in Paris:

If there is a general insurrection, we cannot defend the whole of Paris and you must confine yourself to the plan for the defence of the Bourse, the Royal Treasury, the Bastille and the Invalides.[76]

In general, the aims behind the ministerial reshuffle (coup would suggest a decisiveness wholly lacking) were as confused as its timing was unfortunate; the implementation of the changes before the troop concentrations had been completed can best be explained by the Artois-Polignac group's seizing on a momentary vacillation in their favour by the king. How little they could count on the king is shown by the fact that when the Archbishop of Vienne came to support the Assembly's demand that the troops be withdrawn, Broglie 'felt himself obliged to enter the king's cabinet to fortify His Majesty against so scandalous an attack on his dignity and authority'.[77]

The details of Necker's exile, to Switzerland, are instructive. The king did not serve Necker with a lettre de cachet because he apparently

---

74 Barentin, *Mémoire autographe sur les derniers Conseils du Roi Louis XVI*, ed. M. Champion, 1844, 257.
75 J. Hardman, *Louis XVI*, New Haven, Conn., 1993, 155–8.
76 Published in P. Caron, 'La Tentative de contre-révolution de juin–juillet 1789', *Revue d'Histoire Moderne*, 1906, VIII: 27–8.
77 Bombelles, *Journal*, II, 344, entry for 8 July 1789.

believed that he no longer had the legal right to issue one.[78] Instead, on 11 July he sent Necker a gentle letter:

When I engaged you, Monsieur, to remain in place [after the séance royale], you asked me to adopt a plan of conduct towards the Estates-General and you have shown me on several occasions that a plan of extreme complaisance was the one you preferred. Since you did not believe you would be of use in executing other plans, you asked for permission to resign if I adopted a different course of action. I accept your offer to leave the kingdom during this moment of crisis and I count on your departure being, as you promised, swift, and in secret. It behoves your reputation for integrity not to give rise to any disturbances. I hope that when things have calmed down I will be able to give you proof of my sentiments towards you.

The last sentence preserved the king's option to recall Necker. Necker obeyed the king's request for a 'swift and secret' departure to the letter (he had already promised that if he left that would be his mode) and was twenty leagues from Paris before the news of it leaked out.[79]

At the same time Montmorin was exiled and La Luzerne resigned, Barentin having tried to persuade him to stay on.[80] The ministre d'état, Saint-Priest, who had been appointed in 1788 and who had sent the king an eloquent memorandum in favour of Necker's stance on the séance royale, was also exiled.[81] Puységur was asked to make way for Broglie, but was promised the cordon bleu and the governorship of the Calaisis.

On 12 July new ministers were appointed, though there is doubt about exactly which of the portfolios in this 'ministry of the hundred hours' were actually filled (La Porte, for example, may or may not have been appointed to the marine). Certainly Breteuil achieved his long-standing ambition of being made chef du conseil; the Duc de Broglie was made minister for war and finally the Duc de La Vauguyon got foreign affairs. Barentin and Villedeuil resumed their portfolios.

The inclusion of Broglie and La Vauguyon made this, the last ministry of the ancien régime, also the most aristocratic (though it would be ridiculous to build too many conclusions on such insubstantial foundations). Prior to his appointment Paul François de Quélen (1746–1828) Duc de La Vauguyon, had been successively ambassador to the United Provinces and to Madrid. The de Quélen were an ancient Breton family which additionally represented several lines extinct on the male side: the de Stuer, the de Caussade and the La Vauguyon. The minister's great-grandfather had been a lieutenant-général and a conseiller d'état d'épéé, while his grandfather, Nicolas, had married

78 J. Necker, De la Révolution française, 1797, 3 vols, II, 5.
79 A.N. C185 (123) 9; Bombelles, Journal, II, 338.
80 Mémoire pour M. de Barentin . . . , 1790, 254–5.
81 États-généraux, recueil des documents relatifs au états-généraux de 1789, ed. G. Lefebvre, 1953–70, 4 vols, 1(2), 196–9.

into the Bourbon-Bussy family. The family's real break, however, came when his son Antoine became menin to Louis XVI's father, the dauphin son of Louis XV, with whom he shared a certain gloomy pedantry. As we have seen, this position of menin was so often a passport to ministerial preferment. A lieutenant-général, in 1758 Antoine was made governor of Louis XVI's elder brother, the Duc de Bourgogne, and later of the future king; he was also created a duc. This black-biled and (according to Marie-Antoinette) 'black-hearted' man was blamed by the queen for nurturing in Louis XVI an inderadicable suspicion of the House of Austria.[82]

Victor François, 1718–1804, Duc de Broglie, had been made a maréchal de France in 1762 and a Prince of the Holy Roman Empire in 1759. Further honours had not come the way of the Broglie under Louis XVI, who had curtly dismissed the claims of Victor's brother, the Comte de Broglie, to a dukedom for his services to Louis XV's secret diplomacy.[83] Nevertheless on 1 July 1789 Louis had appointed the duc to the command of all the troops round Versailles and Paris, including his own bodyguard – an exceptional abdication of a treasured royal prerogative. According to their subsequent accounts, this appointment was made without the knowledge of either of the ministerial protagonists, Necker and Barentin.[84] The Broglie family were of Piedmontese origin, François Broglia, grandfather of our minister, having become a naturalized Frenchman in 1654. His son, also François, was ambassador to England, maréchal de France, and was created Duc de Broglie by lettres patentes of 1742. Our minister married into la finance, in the person of Louise-Augustine de Crozat de Thiers and under the Restoration, his grandson was to repeat the exercise by marrying Necker's granddaughter.[85]

The ministerial changes had been brought about by a temporary alliance between the queen and the Polignacs. Whatever their social links, their political objectives had been divergent throughout the reign and acutely so after 1787. After the fall of the Bastille, their paths were to diverge once more: Artois and the Polignacs, intransigent in exile (and with Calonne back as their 'prime minister') were a thorn in the flesh of Marie-Antoinette's more moderate secret diplomacy. However, during the last week of June and the first two of July, the two groups were in alliance or rather coalition, for their aims remained different and the compromise between them played a crucial part in the failure of the venture. The position of Breteuil explains much of this.

Breteuil's was one of Louis XVI's most inexplicable appointments, in view of his merited if brief dismissal in 1787 and his equivocal

82 La Chesnay des Bois, *Dictionnaire*, XVI, 579–83.
83 Hardman, *Louis XVI*, 90–1.
84 Though Barentin made the assertion in the course of his published defence to the charge of lèse-nation, *Mémoire pour M. de Barentin*, 20.
85 For the Broglie family see La Chesnay des Bois, *Dictionnaire* IV, 216–98.

resignation the following year. His relations with Artois and the Polignacs had been bad during the Notables and would be worse during the emigration. Nor, when an accommodation had been sought the previous April, could his plan of action, or rather of inaction, have reassured them: when asked what should be done he replied 'nothing'; it was too late and they would have to 'trust to the tutelary genius of France'.[86]

No, Breteuil headed the ministry as the price of the queen's adherence to the countermeasures. Moreover, the new ministers were essentially of his choosing. The foreign secretary, La Vauguyon, was his confidant; d'Amécourt, Breteuil's ally in the parlement, was expected to be appointed contrôleur-général, and in addition Foulon, another of Breteuil's allies from the days of his opposition to Calonne, was offered the administrative side of the war ministry .

Many considered that these ministers regarded their promotion as an end in itself. Breteuil busied himself with organizing his secretariat, as he had during his first ministry, making sure that all the bureaux of the maison were under one roof. In the days preceding Breteuil's appointment, the king, who still considered the crisis primarily a financial one, asked him to devise a way of raising a loan. Breteuil, whom the king wanted to remain at his château of Dangu, left the details to his factotum, the Baron de Batz, Hamelin, former premier commis at the contrôle, La Vauguyon and Bombelles, who was to get the Constantinople embassy if the enterprise succeeded. They concocted a plan to raise 150 million livres at 7.3 per cent and thought they had pledges from 'the best banking houses in Paris' – perhaps they too had misread the political market. La Vauguyon also drew up a general plan upon which Bombelles made a reflection which could serve as the epitaph of the Breteuil minstry:

It is well presented but does not indicate with sufficient precision what would have to be done in this major crisis. . . . I count more on the faults . . . of [the King's] enemies than on the adequacy of the means employed for the restoration of peace and of the royal authority.[87]

The fall of the Breteuil ministry

The resignation of the Breteuil ministry and the recall of Necker was not only a response to the logic of the situation after the fall of the Bastille but also the subject of a specific demand by the National Assembly. The demand for the dismissals was made on 15 July; the motion was adjourned on the proposal of Clermont-Tonnerre (the cousin of Breteuil, who may have been in negotiation with him for a

86 Bombelles, *Journal*, II, 30–3.
87 ibid., 330–1.

peaceful resolution of the crisis) but renewed the next day, when the président informed the Assembly that Barentin and Broglie had tendered their resignations. Barentin was not revealing undue perspicacity when he concluded that the king had lost the power to appoint and dismiss ministers : 'It was there [in these ministerial changes] . . ., that the intention to subjugate the king ceased to be a mystery'. For Barentin, the illegality was symbolized when, according to his account, Louis told him to join him at Montmédy in 1791 to resume his tenure of the seals.[88]

The renewed demand by the Assembly for the resignation of the other ministers and the recall of Necker coincided with news that this had already been effected. The king, in his letter to Necker of 16 July availed himself of the loop-hole he had left himself when dismissing him: 'I wrote that when things had calmed down, I would give proof of my sentiments towards you'.[89] Necker's ministerial colleagues resumed their portfolios, and Saint-Priest was appointed to the maison.

The subsequent history of the 'ministers of the hundred hours' is of some interest and no little curiosity. Breteuil himself, who was still in the king's cabinet at 6.30 on the evening of the 16th,[90] perhaps profiting from the nebulous nature of his post, never resigned, though he emigrated, or more accurately was exiled. This was not, however, how he put it himself. In a remarkable letter to the king in December, he writes:

I feel that I owe Your Majesty an account of how I have employed the permission that he has been kind enough to grant me to travel outside the kingdom for as long as the state of my health required. I took the waters at Spa and then at Aix-la-Chapelle. [This not availing, he sought the Swiss air which had made the 'Genevan Heads' such an attractive proposition for *rentiers*.] I have been here [at Soleure] since the 4th of last month and I plan to winter there.

We have seen several cases of 'diplomatic' 'flu' among our ministers: Joly de Fleury divesting himself of nearly every duty on these grounds, Villedeuil similarly resigning the finance ministry and proceeding to live to 90 and Ségur claiming that his health could not stand the strain of a travail with Brienne as well as one with the king, but as a sustained flight of fancy Breteuil's must take the biscuit.

The demand for crumbs was in fact the real point of Breteuil's letter. 'My fortune', he continues,

was far from the riches people supposed simply because thanks to careful planning and a little domestic economy I have lived unencumbered with

---

88 Barentin, *Mémoire autographe*, 266 and 269.
89 A.N. C185 (123) 9.
90 Letter of Salmour to Stutterheim, cited in J. Flammermont, *La Correspondance des agents diplomatiques Étrangers en France avant la Révolution*, 1896, 240.

debts despite keeping up the grand state required by the different posts with which Your Majesty has honoured me.

Gone were the days when Breteuil entertained with what Bombelles called 'solid magnificence', his guests dining off silver by the greatest goldsmiths, the Auguste – 'the son really just as good as the father' – and sitting on furniture by the royal *ébénistes*. Now Breteuil asked the king for an embassy – an impossible request at the end of 1789, and one indicating that the Revolution had destroyed his judgement as well as his fortune. Louis, without making any enquiries about the state of Breteuil's health, simply told him :

I am distressed to see that you should be suffering as a consequence of the choice I made of you and from your zeal for my service, but in the present circumstances it is impossible for me to do anything for you whatsoever.[91]

That, however, was not the end of the story. Breteuil indeed was never to receive a sous from Louis, but a year later he was made not only an ambassador but also his minister plenipotentiary to all the powers and before the flight to Varennes was busy constructing his second cabinet.

Breteuil may have been prompted to make his original request by the fact that after his dismissal, La Vauguyon returned (briefly) to Madrid as minister plenipotentiary. Under the Restoration, he was made a duc et pair, in 1818.

Barentin continued his functions *par intérim* until 3 August, before emigrating. During an interval in the crisis meeting of the council on the night of 15/16 July, he had told the royal historiographer, Moreau, 'that it would be necessary to have recourse to a new dynasty'.[92] The following December he was indicted *in absentia* for the new crime of *lèse nation*, the first of several such moves deemed necessary to appease the blood lust of the people.[93] Receiving a garbled version of the charges, he leapt into print with a defence which, coming from the former head of the judiciary, sheds much light on the rapidly evolving notions of ministerial responsibility brought about by the Revolutionary crisis.

Discussing responsibility for the articles of the séance royale of 23 June, he roundly declared:

His Majesty approved them in his council. That is enough to place the ministers above all charges. To what wretched condition would they not be reduced if, sandwiched between their obligation in the secrecy of the king's councils to speak what their conscience demands and the fear of criminal prosecution, they were held responsible before the tribunal of the nation for

91 P. and P. Girault de Coursac, *Louis XVI et Marie-Antoinette*, 1990, 586.
92 Hardman, *Louis XVI*, 158.
93 This argument is advanced by B.M. Schapiro, *Revolutionary Justice in Paris, 1789–1790*, Cambridge, 1993.

their own opinions? No, since the responsibility of ministers did not even exist then, whatever may be its extent today, its limits should not be carried that far. A minister can [i.e. could] be held responsible for malversation of funds; likewise for a matter relating to his department, for an order emanating from him; but never for an opinion given in the council.[94]

Barentin also made the point that, even if his advice had been mistaken, 'there is a great chasm between error and crime' and that many of the charges were incapable either of proof or of disproof; such as that of his wanting to 'beseige Paris': 'do I need to enter into an epistemological discussion [of the meaning of the word "seige"] to demolish this assertion?' Whether his defence was considered valid, or whether, as Schapiro considers, Lafayette was pursuing a policy of calculated leniency, Barentin was acquitted, as he had been tried, *in absentia*, a rare occurrence at any time and unique in the annals of the Revolution.[95]

Barentin also drew attention to a curious feature of the accusation:

It names the Comte de Puységur and myself, despite the fact that all the matters relative to the Estates-General were debated either in the king's councils, composed of all his ministers, or in the comités where a majority and often the totality of them assembled.

Puységur, it will be remembered, had not formed part of the Breteuil ministry, having been asked to step down in favour of Broglie. Indeed the National Assembly had declared on 12 July that he 'carried with him the regrets of the nation'. He had not emigrated. It seems that the Revolutionary authorities were more interested in prosecuting those who had given reactionary advice to the king in May and June than the Breteuil ministry which was supposed to have given it practical effect. Nevertheless, though he was indicted, Puységur was never brought to trial. On 10 August 1792 he led the tiny band of 300 nobles who offered their services to the king for the defence of the Tuileries. The two other ministers who so distinguished themselves were Malesherbes (wearing a sword for the first time in his life) and Montmorin, so that the three elements of Louis's ministries, robe, sword and diplomatic service, had one, but only one, representative each.

Finally Broglie, having famously advised Louis against flight at the council of 15/16 July – 'We can certainly go to Metz, but what do we do when we get there?' – fled himself, dying at Munster at the ripe old age of 86.

94 *Mémoire pour M. de Barentin*, 38.
95 ibid., 40 and 50; Schapiro, *Revolutionary Justice*, 163.

CHAPTER FIVE

Conclusion to Part One

An account of the appointment and dismissal of ministers under Louis XIV would have been a relatively short business. Ministers were more or less appointed because they found favour with the king and dismissed because they lost it. When Louis XVI, however, made a personal appointment, we have seen fit to remark upon the fact. Such appointments numbered only Maurepas, du Muy, possibly Vergennes, probably Necker, d'Ormesson and Montmorin. The prime ministers Maurepas and Brienne were responsible for almost as many; Maurepas for the appointment of Turgot, Miromesnil, Malesherbes, Clugny, Saint-Germain, Montbarey and Joly de Fleury; and Brienne for those of Laurent de Villedeuil, the Comte de Brienne, La Luzerne and Lambert. Breteuil, we have suggested, was responsible for the appointment of most of the ministers in his ill-fated second ministry. The queen played a part in the appointment of Castries and Ségur and was determinant in those of Breteuil and Brienne (probably also in Breteuil's return in 1789). A court grouping of the Polignacs in alliance with the king's youngest brother, the Comte d'Artois, played an important role in the appointment of Calonne and in the changes of July 1789. Other influences were public opinion, to which, however defined, Louis XVI paid great attention (the reappointment of Necker springs to mind), la finance (Calonne), and other members of the royal family: Mesdames Tantes guided Louis's initial choice of Maurepas but played little part thereafter. Finally, Miromesnil and Joly de Fleury were selected by Maurepas because of their connections in the parlement.

A similar variety of forces contributed to the dismissal of ministers. Dismissals through loss of the king's confidence were scarce: only Turgot and Miromesnil. They were equalled by those who resigned against the king's wishes: Malesherbes and Necker. The pre-Revolutionary crisis ushered in a period when the king was forced to dismiss ministers in whom he retained personal confidence – Calonne and Lamoignon – or official confidence, what was called his *estime*, Brienne and the second Breteuil ministry. The only instance before

1787 was when Necker forced him to sacrifice Sartine in 1780. The queen was directly responsible for the dismissal of d'Aiguillon and gave La Vrillière and Calonne the final shove. The Polignac-Artois faction contributed to the fall of Sartine and Montbarey and to that of Brienne.

It can thus be seen that an examination of the appointment and dismissal of ministers gives a crude approximation to the balance of forces working in politics. It gives a context within which to place the king's now limited role. The royal government, of course, had never operated entirely in a vacuum, but as the ancien régime matured, it became increasingly subject to outside pressures. However, since France lacked 'representative institutions', it is sometimes hard to pinpoint them. Talleyrand called such 'pressure groups' *sociétés*:

France gave the impression of being made up of a certain number of sociétés with which the government had to reckon.[1]

The question arises as to whether these individual sociétés, in addition to being 'reckoned with' by the government, played a part in determining its actual composition; and if so, whether the placing of one of their number was a chance occurrence or was consciously sought, and whether a balance of such interests was a necessary ingredient of political stability. As one would expect, the appointment of courtier ministers from the mid-century led to closer links between the government and the court; there is evidence that the various interests came to regard it as desirable that they should be represented in government – the Polignacs' attempt to place d'Adhémar at the war ministry in 1780 springs to mind. Again, as an archbishop complained to Véri in 1785:

Do you know why . . . we have these difficulties with ministers who do not favour us? It is because the clergy does not have any minister *auprès du roi*.[2]

Likewise, though parlementaire influence was not determinant in the appointment of Joly de Fleury, the parlementaires urged him to accept as belonging to the conciliar branch of a prominent parlementaire family and promised him 'une grande condescendance' for his operations. Similarly, the queen's advisers urged her to have 'her' ministers. In 1777 Breteuil advised the queen to influence the choice of ministers, only admitting men who 'crussent ne pouvoir remplir leur administration qu'autant qu'il feraient régner la reine'.[3]

It must be stressed, though, that there were no formal arrangements:

1 Prince de Talleyrand, *Mémoires*, ed. Duc de Broglie, 1891–2, 5 vols, I, 63.
2 Abbé de Véri, MSS *Journal*, Archives départementales de la Drôme, Valence, unclassified, cahier 133.
3 A. d'Arneth and M.A. Geffroy (eds) *Marie-Antoinette: Correspondance secrète entre Marie-Thérèse et le Comte de Mercy-Argenteau*, 2nd edn, 1875, 3 vols, III, 36.

the composition of a ministry was partly a chance configuration; yet the sheer persistence of certain interests and their ministerial candidates is striking. Some appointments, the best examples being those of Calonne and Breteuil, have a quality of inevitability about them, though this can partly be explained by the small number of genuine candidates: one can picture Louis and Maurepas poring over the *almanach royal*, trying to weed out the 'fools' and the 'knaves'.

The case of Calonne's appointment is illustrative of the conflicting pressures on the king. His appointment was clearly the price that the king had to pay to la finance for the failed coup against the farmers-general. Louis was well aware of this: 'le premier point', as he told Vergennes when making the appointment, 'est le soutien du crédit'. Not everyone, however, was satisfied; Calonne's appointment was anathema to the parlement and it was probably only a matter of time before they came to their mutually destructive blows. A contrôleur's backing determined the nature of his funding: Necker and Calonne, lacking parlementaire support, relied on loans; Calonne further relied on traditional finance, Necker on newer procedures. Joly and d'Ormesson, who both had powerful relatives in the parlement, enjoyed the favour of that body. Accordingly, Joly increased direct taxation, as would have d'Ormesson had he survived longer.[4]

In a sense all ministries, through the backing and background of their members, were coalitions and each minister had his constituency. Thus in 1786, the last year in which the ancien régime functioned normally, the departmental ministers owed their positions to the following interests: Vergennes, a career diplomat, to the king; Breteuil, a career diplomat of grander background, to the queen; Miromesnil, the ex-premier président, to his links with the parlements; Calonne (ex-intendant, the only one in the ministry) owed his appointment to the Polignacs and finance but had additionally earned the king's trust; Castries and Ségur, military aristocrats, looked to the queen.

The background of the men who became ministers, as between robe and sword, was not subject to any laws but nevertheless there are discernible patterns. Maurepas favoured hommes de robe, taking them mainly from the royal administration but also from the sovereign courts (Miromesnil and Malesherbes). His preference for robins even extended to the service ministries (he had himself been a successful minister for the marine): before his appointment to the marine, Sartine had been the lieutenant-général de police; even du Muy had started his career in a parlement. Other things being equal, a man trained up in the royal administration could be expected to have a conciliar viewpoint and one trained in a parlement a parlementaire one: an obvious point which Malesherbes articulated when he said that 'neither he nor anyone from his class should be made chancellor'. The

4 See e.g. A.N. 144 A.P. 131 dossier 4. 4, d'Ormesson's August memorandum to the king.

cases of Maupeou and Lamoignon – men from leading parlementaire families who attacked the parlement – seem at first to refute Malesherbes's argument. On closer examination however, they serve to reinforce it: Maupeou and Lamoignon had been divisive forces within their corps and Maupeou in particular used his coup to settle old scores. What these two and Miromesnil lacked was objectivity in dealing with the parlement. That was why Malesherbes, Turgot and Véri begged Maurepas to become chancellor himself to reconcile 'royal authority' with the 'liberty of the citizen' because 'in short we recognized in him the mixture of parlementaire rules and a sense of royal authority which is necessary to suppress misplaced opposition'.[5]

There is a certain sameness about the ancestry of those members of the robe (whether administrative or parlementaire) who attained ministerial office. The families of the vast majority had risen from obscurity on a ladder of legal offices, obtaining nobility on the way. A handful of families had risen through la finance: Terray's father was a farmer-general, Bourgeois de Boynes's was the treasurer of John Law's bank, Taboureau des Réaux's grandfather had graduated from being a silk merchant to being a receveur des tailles. He is the only merchant in our genealogies. There were no manufacturers, though Laurent de Villedeuil's father was a construction engineer, symbolized by the bridge in his grant of arms. This is saying no more than that the ancien régime was essentially a lawyers' regime: even the king's functions were seen as essentially judicial; the ministers were performing in large what their ancestors had performed in small.

All Parisians are still said to have two homes, Paris and their province of origin. (Often they have two houses as well.) But except in this romantic sense, most of our robe ministers (and their fathers) came from Paris or the Île-de-France. Again the exceptions form a handful: Bertin's father came from Bordeaux, du Muy began his career in the parlement of Aix (the only example of the fusion in one person of robe and sword), Vergennes grew up in Dijon, Sartine in Spain, though his father came from Lyon. Calonne began his career in the parlement of Flanders, returned there as intendant (something Louis XIV would never have countenanced) and built up a political machine. These are the exceptions; the high robe tended to have their seats in the Île-de-France: Pontchartrain, Ormesson, Bâville. They had no status or traditions outside the service of the Capetian dynasty.

For the nobility of the sword it was different. They had an existence independent of the crown; they had a status even if they never attained to office or an office. This was especially true of the *noblesse de race* since their nobility had not been conferred by the dynasty or by anyone. That was why Maurepas favoured the *noblesse de robe*: the preponderance of his own family, the Phélypeaux, began and ended

5 Abbé de Véri, *Journal, 1774–80*, ed. J. de Witte, 1928–30, 2 vols, I, 175–6.

with the Bourbons; the history of the twelve Phélypeaux ministers is virtually the history of royal absolutism. Maurepas arrested and even reversed the incursion of grand seigneurs into the ministry which had begun in 1747 and reached a climax under Choiseul. However, his dam began to crumble in his last, humiliating year, with the appointment of the soldiers Castries and Ségur, so that by the end of our period, ex-maîtres des requêtes were in a minority in the ministry. The revival of grand seigneur ministers must be attributed in part to the patronage of the queen. As a general rule they gravitated towards the 'queen's party', whereas the robins formed the king's.

There was, however, a limit to how far the grands seigneurs could go in taking over the ministry, despite what Calonne said about their 'all being seized by ministerial mania' and his sarcastic comment that they were 'all equally entitled to believe that they have the same degree of aptitude to fill any [department]'.[6] For they lacked the technical expertise to run the contrôle, and really the maison, as the incompetent tenure of Breteuil with his military and diplomatic background demonstrated. However, the very limits to the ministerial ambitions of the grands seigneurs reinforced the divisions within the ministry, the social divide being reinforced by the functional, so that Ségur could say that the policies of the comité des finances represented a 'war to the finish between the hommes de robe and gens de notre espèce'.[7]

In terms of outlook and attitude towards the exercise of royal authority, the distinction between a robe minister and a sword one was important. In terms of ancestry and alliances it was often blurred. Indeed a male-line descent from a minister often partially explains why a soldier (or a prelate) took ministerial office. It is no accident that the first two soldier ministers, Puysieux, who became foreign secretary in 1747, and Belle-Îsle, who became war secretary in 1758, were so descended; the Marquis de Puysieux from the chancellor, Brûlart de Sillery, and his son the war secretary, both of whom were disgraced in 1622, and the Maréchal-Duc de Belle-Îsle from the last surintendant des finances, Foucquet. The Duc d'Aiguillon was descended from Richelieu's heir and the Duc de Nivernais from Mazarin's. The Loménie de Brienne brothers had not forgotten the ministerial traditions of the Loménie family under Henri IV and Louis XIII.

Family alliances between our ministers, whether of robe or of sword, were also fairly common. Maurepas, Malesherbes and La Luzerne participated in this process in large measure. Thus Maurepas's half-sister married Nivernais and, through the Mailly, Maurepas's wife was related to Montbarey, whom Maurepas 'regarded as a son'. Maurepas told Louis XVI that of the ministers he inherited, 'some are

6 C.A. de Calonne (attrib.) *Lettre du Marquis de Caraccioli à M. d'Alembert*, 1781, 19 and 21.
7 Baron de Besenval, *Mémoires*, ed. Berville and Barrière, 1821, 2 vols, II, 125.

our close relatives [La Vrillière, d'Aiguillon, Maupeou], others are known to us only through repute'. Malesherbes, the son of a chancellor, was also the cousin of another, Lamoignon de Bâville. Malesherbes's sister married La Luzerne's father. La Luzerne's son married Montmorin's elder daughter. Montmorin was descended from the Comte d'Argenson, Louis XV's war secretary. Breteuil and Bourgeois de Boynes were brothers-in-law, each having married one of the wealthy Parat de Mongeron sisters; Barentin's mother was a d'Ormesson – he adopted the d'Ormesson family name of Vincent-de-Paule. Finally, the lines of Broglie and Necker, antagonists in July 1789, were later united when the grandson of Broglie married the granddaughter of Necker.

These links were far from restoring ministerial government to the oligarchy that it had largely been for most of the Bourbon period. The office of secretary of state continued to be venal (the chancellor and contrôleur's offices had never been), the incoming minister reimbursing the outgoing, usually with financial help from the king. But a secretary was no longer succeeded by his survivancier. Between 1615 and 1660 secretaries were sometimes succeeded by their sons or nephews; between 1660 and 1740 usually so; after 1758 never. A practice withered away as mysteriously as it had sprung up but its passing must have removed a great element of stability.

Instability was the hallmark of ministerial politics under Louis XVI – instability and division. Ministerial instability was Miromesnil's excuse for doing nothing: 'It takes a king', he told Véri, 'and even one of talent and strong character to produce dramatic changes. The rest of us, ministers, unsafe in our jobs, can only prepare modifications and plan obsolescence'.[8] Division was not only between robe and sword but also between the various 'constituencies' of the ministers, of which first and foremost were the king and the queen. Consequently it is seldom useful to talk of the policies of 'le gouvernement' or 'le ministère', although contemporaries did. The question of ministerial unity underlies many of the themes of Part Two of this book, affecting as it does the roles of prime ministers and contrôleurs, the king and the queen, and the whole process of decision-making.

8 Véri, MSS *Journal*, cahier 109.

PART TWO

SEPARATE COUNCILS

MESSENGER: Besides, he says there are two councils kept;
And that may be determined at the one,
Which may make you and him to rue at th'other.
  . . .

LORD HASTINGS: Go, fellow, go, return unto thy lord;
Bid him not fear the separated councils.

(Richard III, Act III, scene 2).

CHAPTER SIX

Prime and principal ministers

PRECEDENTS

There were French prime ministers long before there were English ones; unlike their English counterparts, these also had the official title, created by lettres patentes registered in the parlement. The provisions of Cardinal Dubois, ministre principal to Louis XV, dated 22 August 1722, affect great precision: Dubois was to

jouir de tous les honneurs, rang, prééminence, prérogatives, gages . . . y attachés, tels et semblables qu'en ont joui *ou du jouir* [!] les précédents principaux ministres de notre État.[1]

However, the official premiers of the eighteenth century had short or unsuccessful ministries, often both. They were Dubois (1722–3), the former Regent Orléans (1723), the Duc de Bourbon (1723–6) and finally Loménie de Brienne (1787–8). Brienne and Dubois were styled principal rather than premier ministre but on 22 February 1723, the day after Louis XV attained his majority, Dubois became premier ministre, a post which presumably enjoyed a higher status;[2] it was certainly understood that Brienne's status was somehow less than that of a premier ministre.

The minister who had the longest and most successful premiership, Cardinal Fleury, enjoyed neither of these titles. Nor does the official title or its provisions sufficiently define the attributes of a premier, which were in any case under constant renewal, the reign of Louis XVI being especially fertile in this respect.

These examples from the beginning of the reign of Louis XV were important, however, because they were a formative influence on the young Maurepas (a secretary of state from 1718). In particular, he was

1 My italics; published in Comte de Luçay, *Les Secrétaires d'état en France depuis les origines jusqu'à 1774*, 1881, 246–7.
2 On the grounds that only a major king could appoint a premier ministre; on the other hand, the responsibility of the first minister of a minor king was greater.

impressed by one aspect of their influence: the right to be present at all the king's political encounters. Strictly speaking this right did not reside exclusively with the premier, but when it did not it often led to trouble. Thus in 1721, the Regent Orléans exiled the young king's governor, the Duc de Villeroy, for not allowing Orléans to speak to the king tête-à-tête. In the scene which had preceded this event, the king's preceptor, Fleury, had discreetly remained present himself. When the Duc de Bourbon was made prime minister in 1723, Fleury was always present at his travail with the king. Indeed Bourbon's complaint at this procedure occasioned his disgrace in 1726, when Louis XV told the conseil d'état: 'I will fix the time for [the ministers'] individual travail at which the former Bishop of Fréjus will always be present'.[3] Thus it seems that Fleury invented this way of monitoring the king's political relations or rather that it stemmed naturally from his original, official role, in the king's education as preceptor. Maurepas himself was recalled in 1774 to teach the 19-year-old Louis XVI his métier. During the period when Fleury had been grooming the keeper of the seals, Chauvelin, to succeed him, Chauvelin had been present at the king's travail with the other ministers, in addition to Fleury or instead of him during his retreats to Issy. His main role was one of liaison between the government departments. This also was to have its influence on Maurepas.[4]

MAUREPAS

Louis XVI sought to model himself on Louis XIV – a view of himself in which his flatterers, such as Vergennes and even Joly de Fleury, were prepared to indulge him. Accordingly he did not intend to have a prime minister. Nevertheless, in his first audience Maurepas bluntly stated that Louis XV had been most successful during the premiership of Fleury. He further defined what the role of a premier should be, essentially one of coordination between the departmental ministers; there must be a 'centre': 'if you won't or can't be one, you must necessarily choose someone else'.[5]

Louis did neither, which was arguably the fundamental weakness of his reign. It also provided the framework within which Maurepas had to operate. He had less power than if the king had appointed him prime minister, but more than if the king had been his own.

The restrictions on Maurepas's power were considerable. In the first place, Maurepas was not a viceroy, did not enjoy the delegated

3 M. Antoine, *Louis XV*, 1990, 161.
4 ibid., 112–15, 143, 161, 270.
5 Abbé de Véri, *Journal, 1774–80*, ed. J. de Witte, 1928–30, 2 vols, I, 93–8.

authority which Louis XV had conferred on Fleury in the following instruction:

We order. . . to have his travail and despatch all matters under the direction of the bishop of Fréjus [Fleury] and to carry out everything he tells him, *as if we had said it ourselves.*[6]

Nor did Maurepas enjoy the power of independent decision-making. Every decision of any importance had to be argued over with the king, a process which could take weeks or months or end inconclusively. Véri writes on 9 August 1774:

If [the king's 'lassitude'] gains the upper hand and his spirit of indecisiveness, M. de Maurepas would be forced to usurp, so to speak, the function of prime minister for decisions;[7]

and, a year later:

I see . . . M. de Maurepas pretty exhausted with always having to force out decisions. It would be quicker to give them himself. I think [Véri adds optimistically] that he could do it without displeasing the king and that he should for the public good.[8]

Mercy-Argenteau joins in the chorus:

the moral organization of the king . . . makes any decision infinitely difficult for him.[9]

The charge is that the king will not or cannot govern and that he is preventing other people from doing so. However, it can be argued that the two decisions in question here, the recall of the parlement and Joseph's request for French support over the Bavarian exchange, revealed, on the part of the king, not pusillanimity but principled and sensible resistance to unwarranted pressure, and, on the part of those who were exerting it, merely their sense of frustration.

Maurepas possessed the king's confidence but not in its entirety: 'Souvent il m'échappe', Maurepas complained, 'par son silence indécis sur des affaires importantes'. Moreover, Maurepas believed that the king's confidence must be given spontaneously: 'Je ne vaux rien pour arracher toujours la confiance et pour usurper la décision'. However, Louis XVI, like his grandfather, was naturally distrustful, and this quality must have been reinforced by the way in which Maurepas had manipulated him over the recall of the parlement. In addition, Louis had a variety of extra-ministerial sources of information, the chief of which was d'Ogny, the intendant des postes, who had a travail with

6 My italics; Lucay, *Les Secrétaires*, 265.
7 Véri, *Journal*, I, 159.
8 ibid., 243.
9 A. d'Arneth and J. Flammermont (eds) *Correspondance secrète du Comte de Mercy-Argenteau avec l'Empereur Joseph II et le Prince de Kaunitz*, 1891, 2 vols, I, 79, Mercy to Joseph II, 16 December 1781.

the king on Sundays when he read him extracts from intercepted private mail. Even Maurepas's wife censored her own private correspondence in the belief that d'Ogny read the king extracts from it.[10]

Nevertheless, within these limitations Maurepas managed to become what he himself described as an 'ombre de point de réunion', and what many colloquially called a prime minister, by his skilful use of his own access to the king and by controlling the access of others. The one tangible advantage that Louis gave to Maurepas on his recall – he was already a ministre, he did not want a département – was Madame du Barry's former apartments, crammed between the king's and the eaves of Versailles. They were so incommodious that Necker was to say that they represented 'un extrait, et un extrait superfin de toutes les vanités et toutes les ambitions';[11] they were, however, connected to the king's by a 'secret' staircase, though Maurepas apparently did not make use of it until he was granted the grandes entrées in 1776. The passage enabled Maurepas to see the king without being seen by the courtiers who thronged the public rooms; it also secured informality of access – the system of Maurepas was based entirely on informality – and enabled Maurepas to know who was seeing the king.

The essence of Maurepas's power was that he acted as screen or filter interposed between the king and those who wanted to talk politics with him (d'Ogny's travail was the most obvious haemorrhage of the system). In the case of the other ministers, this screening took the form of Maurepas's coming down the staircase to the king's apartments to sit in on a minister's weekly travail with the king; as Maurepas's gout and favour increased, the king and the minister might climb the staircase to see him. This system evolved over the space of two years, being naturally resisted by Louis XV's old ministers but voluntarily adopted by the new, at least in times of crisis. Thus during the Choiseuliste manoeuvres at the time of the Guerre des farines in 1775 Véri notes:

In this situation the ministers have felt the necessity of being more united and of having an internal central force. M. de Vergennes, M. de Miromesnil and M. Turgot decided in the last few days to invite M. de Maurepas to their individual travail with the king and to give him thereby the role of being the only centre.[12]

This system became general after the fall of Turgot, which revealed that he had been a rival centre of power. On Turgot's fall, Véri noted:

The supreme direction of affairs is going to be found in [Maurepas's] hands.

10 Véri, *Journal*, I, 251; II, 66–8, 149 and 245.
11 Quoted in E. Lever, *Louis XVI*, 1985, 255.
12 Véri, *Journal*, I, 112 and 312.

The king wants him to be present at the ministers' travail with him when anything concerning the overall view of their departments arises.[13]

This arrangement was facilitated by the fact that most of the new ministers owed their appointment to Maurepas: du Muy, who owed his directly to the king, refused to let Maurepas attend his travail. After Maurepas lost the power of appointment in 1780, Castries and Ségur refused to let him attend their travail on the grounds that this would constitute an infringement of the right of a secretary of state to have direct, untrammelled relations with the king.

After Turgot's fall, again, Maurepas was made chef du conseil royal des finances, the only governmental post ever conferred on him by Louis XVI. The post had great prestige – and 60,000 livres a year – attached to it. But since the conseil royal had fallen into abeyance, its chef had nothing over which to preside, and it is difficult to see what, if any, function he performed. Lenoir states that the chef had the right to present the king with new contrôleurs;[14] d'Ormesson says that it was in virtue of this right that Vergennes presented him to the king.[15] However, on this occasion, the king had made the choice himself. On Vergennes's appointment as chef du conseil in 1783, Castries says that he had been accorded

all the attributions which M. de Maurepas possessed, which makes the place very important and that it is not restricted to a vain title such as it was under M. de Praslin.[16]

However, he gives no indication what 'all the attributions' might have been. Joly de Fleury, however, in a memorandum to the king of 29 January 1783 does, and at some length:

The place of chef du conseil royal des finances was created by the règlement of 15 September 1661 of which I gave Your Majesty a copy.

This règlement and the provisions of M. de Maurepas (of which I enclose a copy) do not confer on the titular any authority over finance.

They only give him a seat of honour at the conseil royal and at the grande and petite direction des finances. In these three councils, the chef takes the first place after the chancellor or keeper of the seals; in the other councils, he only has his ordinary rank of seniority [as a ministre].

M. de Charost and M. de Praslin had no authority, nor influence over the administration of finance. The contrôleurs-généraux have enjoyed the same functions and the same authority whether the place of chef du conseil royal was vacant or occupied.

M. de Maurepas himself had no influence over the administration of finance save only what came from the confidence with which Your Majesty honoured him and he only began to countersign the edicts and lettres

---

13 ibid., 439–40.
14 Lenoir Papers, Bibliothèque municipale d'Orléans, MSS 1421–3, 1423, *Résidus*, 263.
15 D'Ormesson, *Journal*, A.N. 144 A.P. 130, section 43.
16 Castries, *Journal*, Archives de la Marine, MS 182/7964 1–2, I, fo. 158.

patentes when M. Necker was in office because M. Necker [as a Protestant] could neither countersign edicts nor sign arrêts and again because Your Majesty only had the travail with M. Necker in the presence of M. de Maurepas.

It is the confidence of Your Majesty which gives more or less influence and *you are always able to increase or diminish it at will* [the italicized portion is added in Joly's hand].[17]

This is the best 'job description' of this nebulous post that we possess. It gave Maurepas no 'attributions'. His precedence in the conseil d'état was in virtue of his having been a ministre since 1738. The arrangement made with Necker arose because of Necker's religion, not because of Maurepas's post as chef du conseil royal. Everything depended on the king's fluctuating confidence. Nevertheless, after Maurepas's death, all but the clear-sighted Joly invested the post with powers it had never conferred, arguing fallaciously that since Maurepas was the leading minister and since he was also the chef du conseil royal, this post must have conferred primacy.

Was Maurepas, then, a prime minister? Many in the ministerial milieu assumed that he was. As Maurepas lay dying, Mercy called him 'le vieux principal ministre'.[18] In 1780, when Maurepas overruled Vergennes's plan for a Franco-Spanish invasion of Jamaica, the latter replied: 'I will obey you because you are the prime minister, but under protest'.[19] It is perhaps pedantic to quarrel with their view. For though Maurepas did not possess the powers of previous prime ministers – in particular delegated authority or that to take decisions – he invented a system of premiership which could work within the constraints imposed by Louis XVI. Moreover, though his system was highly innovative, elaborate, slowly evolved, even artificial, such was his finesse that people came to assume that his was the natural way in which prime ministers had always exercised their power. Like Maurepas, aspirant premiers must needs be chef du conseil royal, and regulate the royal travail.

Maurepas died without leaving or designating a successor. Véri sees this as an example of the corrupting nature of power. Earlier, in 1775, Maurepas had introduced Malesherbes to the king in the following terms:

I am giving you a man with whom to replace me and you will do well to put your confidence in him . . . he will coordinate policies and ministers.[20]

However, by 1780 Maurepas would have been 'very embarrassed if he

17 B.N. fonds Joly de Fleury, 1442 fo. 9
18 Arneth and Flammermont, *Correspondance secrète*, II, 175.
19 Véri, *Journal*, II, 354.
20 ibid, I, 317.

had been asked to designate a successor from among those whom he has chosen for the ministry'.[21]

VERGENNES

Nevertheless, Maurepas and the king had increasingly been reposing their confidence in the foreign secretary, Vergennes. Louis, for example, had turned to him for a private evaluation of Necker at the time when the Genevan had been making his exorbitant demands in 1781.[22] A portion of Maurepas's mantle fell on Vergennes. Indeed he has recently been described as a prime minister himself.[23]

Vergennes modelled himself on Maurepas, most obviously in becoming chef du conseil royal. However, there were significant differences in the way he exercised his much more limited power. In particular, Vergennes did not possess the dominance in ministerial appointments enjoyed by Maurepas until 1780: it is difficult to think of a single such appointment over which his influence was even decisive. We have seen that in 1783, at the height of his power, he was unable to obtain the finance ministry for his cousin, Thiroux de Crosne, who had to content himself with the lieutenance de police.[24] Nor, in that year, were the combined forces of Vergennes and Joly sufficient to break Castries; nor was Vergennes able to prevent Breteuil, a feared and secretly detested rival, first from entering the conseil and then obtaining the maison.

Vergennes's lack of influence on the composition of the ministry also made it unlikely that ministers would invite him to sit in on their travail with the king: the panoply of the comité des finances can be seen as the only way in which Vergennes could interpose himself between the king and Castries and Ségur, something which those ministers were not slow to grasp. The only case of Vergennes's not indeed attending the travail but of casting a preliminary eye over it was that of d'Ormesson: when d'Ormesson's successor Calonne observed that he could not be Vergennes' subordinate, the latter replied

Monsieur, that is only fair. . . . I did not ask M. d'Ormesson to bring me his portfolio as he did and it was likewise without informing me that he withdrew the facility.[25]

21 ibid, II, 322.
22 *Observations remises à Louis XVI et par ses ordres le 3 mai 1781*, published by J.L. Soulavie, *Mémoires historiques et politiques du règne de Louis XVI*, 1801, 6 vols, IV, 137–53.
23 J. Labourdette, *Vergennes*, 1990; M. Price, 'The Comte de Vergennes and the Baron de Breteuil: French politics and reform in the reign of Louis XVI', PhD thesis, Cambridge University, 1988.
24 Price, 'Vergennes and Breteuil', 198–201.
25 Castries, *Journal*, I, fo. 209.

It would also have been more difficult for Vergennes to attend ministers' travail as he possessed no advantage of physical access to the king. At the most, the king would sometimes invite him round for an informal chat in the early evening.[26] Maurepas's apartments, however, were given to simple courtiers, as Castries notes:

The apartment of M. de Maurepas is divided between M. de Cossé and M. d'Aumont, thus the whole edifice of the premier ministre is destroyed.[27]

Vergennes did, however, possess a source of influence that Maurepas had neither sought nor exercised: departmental. In addition to foreign affairs, in 1780 Vergennes was given the bundle of provinces which Bertin had administered. They included Normandy, Guyenne, and the *généralité* of Lyon. Vergennes exercised a patronage network in these provinces, one man for example sending him a request to be made Intendant of Rousillon,[28] though such appointments normally fell to the contrôleur. These provinces included the great mercantile cities of Marseilles, Rouen, Bordeaux and Lyon, and Vergennes carved out for himself what has been described as a 'sort of ministry of commerce',[29] in the firm belief that commerce should be handled by the foreign secretary rather than the minister for the marine. This viewpoint naturally added to his difficulties with Castries. In 1783, when the re-establishment of the East India Company was being considered, Vergennes stated quite baldly:

the most widely held view is that the company should be under the eyes of the finance ministry, which should direct its operations in concert with the department of foreign affairs.[30]

It was into this departmental influence that Vergennes retreated when the débâcle of the comité des finances and d'Ormesson's damaging accusations of abusing his position for financial gain reduced (without, however, ending) the king's confidence in him. Bombelles, his insight heightened by his bias, gives a good if spiteful explanation of the failure of Vergennes's larger ambitions: 'From the moment he emerged from the apparent modesty which had served him so well with the king and with the public, he mined the edifice of his own consideration'.[31] If indeed Vergennes was ever a prime minister, his premiership lasted at most from February to November 1783. Admittedly Lenoir, who had sent Maurepas police reports, continued to send them to Vergennes until 1785 'on account of the more or less extended

26 E.g. the king's letter of 30 November 1784, Archives de Vergennes, *Lettres de Louis XVI.*
27 Castries, *Journal*, I, fo. 96.
28 P.N. Ardaschef, *Les Intendants de province sous Louis XVI*, 1909, 61.
29 Labourdette, *Vergennes*, 95.
30 ibid., 96.
31 Marquis de Bombelles, *Journal*, ed. J. Grassion and F. Durif, Geneva, 1978–1993, 3 vols, I, 205.

degree of authority possessed by M. de Vergennes', a cautious estimation of Vergennes's power which can serve for our own.[32]

LOMÉNIE DE BRIENNE

Louis did not intend to appoint another chef du conseil: when Castries asked for the post he told him he was suppressing it as an economy measure. Circumstances forced him to appoint Loménie de Brienne first chef du conseil (1 May) and then ministre principal (26 August). The period between the death of Maurepas and the débâcle of the Assembly of Notables leading to Brienne's appointment may be said to be that of Louis XVI's personal rule. This period and the preceding one of Maurepas's dominance were both characterized by extreme informality. Brienne, however, inaugurated one of institutional formality to deflect accusations of 'ministerial despotism', that is ministerial power uncontrolled by the council and also to introduce a greater degree of 'ensemble' into government. On 5 June, he gave himself a real conseil des finances over which to preside and used it to institute a radical reorganization of royal finances.

However, the political situation continued to deteriorate and Marie-Antoinette prevailed on the king to invest Brienne with further authority. The manner of Brienne's appointment to the premiership on 26 August was somewhat unusual. It was said that he was made principal rather than premier ministre because the latter appointment would have required lettres patentes registered by the parlement which happened to be in exile at Troyes. This variant may also have enabled the king, who had said he would never have a premier ministre, to save face. Another unusual feature was that Brienne was not given a 'brevet d'appointment'. Instead, each minister received the following circular letter from the king which was practical and explanatory rather than a list of Brienne's *attributs* :

Since the present situation requires a common centre in the ministry to which all the various parts relate, I have chosen M. l'Archevêque de Toulouse as my principal minister and I am writing you this letter to inform you about it. My intention is that consequently you warn him of all the *affaires principales* whose importance requires that I be informed either by you and him together or in your travail with me and I am writing you this letter to notify you. For the rest, this arrangement, whose sole purpose is to create more ensemble in government, in no way diminishes my confidence in the ministers charged with the departments and in particular that which I have always shown you.[33]

---

32 Lenoir MS 1423, résidus, 95.
33 Castries, *Journal*, II, 393.

The system for regulating the ministers' travail which had evolved under Maurepas is thus given formal definition in a very complicated sentence. Brienne, as principal ministre, would be informed only of affaires principales, and this would be achieved either by Brienne and the relevant minister arriving together at the king's cabinet, or by Brienne's performing a preliminary inspection of the minister's travail. Louis's use of the word 'principal' seems to relate to the kind of matter with which Brienne will be concerned as much as to his precedence over his colleagues. The indebtedness to Maurepas is evident, both in the mechanism – supervising the travail – and in the central, indeed 'sole purpose' of creating 'more ensemble in government'. The premier is distinguished from the ministers with departments, and as if further to emphasize that Maurepas was his model, on becoming principal minister, Brienne gave up his collaborative supervision of the contrôleur. He no longer had time to spend on 'any of the details of the finance ministry'.

The one innovation is the preliminary inspection by the premier of his colleagues' travail, a variant of Maurepas's system which Vergennes had applied in the sole case of d'Ormesson. This was a refinement because it meant that the premier could not only know what the king was being told but also, if he wanted, prevent him from being told.

NECKER'S SECOND MINISTRY

The preliminary inspection would seem to have been also employed by Necker in his second ministry. Thus in June 1789 Bertrand de Molleville, former intendant of Brittanny and future minister for the marine, asked Montmorin to read to the council a memorandum on dissolving the Estates-General. Montmorin, however, replied:

M. Necker would stop me and demand that first the memorandum should be communicated to him and the king would order me to give it to him.[34]

Marie-Antoinette, who was primarily responsible for Necker's recall, intended to prevent such a situation arising by having a principal minister appointed over him. She told Mercy-Argenteau on 18 August:

We need a [principal minister], above all with M. Necker. He needs reining in and the person above me is in no state to do it. . . . M. du Châtelet could perhaps represent the prime minister. He is an honourable man and the one that the Archbishop [Brienne] would prefer. He would get on well with M. Necker and leave him alone in his department.[35]

---

34 A.F. Bertrand de Molleville, *Mémoires secrètes pour servir à l'histoire de la dernière année du règne de Louis XVI, Roi de France*, London, 1797, 3 vols, I, 123.
35 A. d'Arneth, *Marie-Antoinette, Joseph II und Leopold II*, 2nd. edn, Vienna, 1866, 198.

Apart from the fact that the Duc du Châtelet refused the job,[36] Necker had no intention of having a prime minister over him. On 24 August he told Mercy-Argenteau,

I presume that there is no intention of replacing [Brienne's] title of principal [minister] before we have seen what ordinary reason can achieve.[37]

The absence of a formal prime minister ensured that Necker would acquire many of the characteristics of an informal one. Indeed, the memorandum which the king gave Marie-Antoinette as the basis for Necker's return discussed the general situation amd made promises that one would not make to a mere directeur-général des finances. Necker was clearly more than that. Barentin, for example, claims that after the séance royale of 23 June 1789 he advised the king to retain Necker as finance minister but

to restrict him to his department alone, to deprive him of all influence over the Estates-General and [even] to restrict his dealings with them on financial matters.[38]

After the séance royale, however, Necker himself intended to demand the dismissal of those who had opposed him in the conseil, a request similar to that made by Calonne during the Notables and akin to an English style of premiership. In particular he informed Saint-Priest that he was to replace Laurent de Villedeuil at the maison. Necker had no time to make these demands because a popular movement in his favour made it difficult for him to put pressure on the king by threatening resignation.[39]

During his third ministry, from 16 July 1789, Necker enjoyed the curious but descriptive title 'premier ministre des finances'.[40]

We do not know whether Breteuil, during the hundred hours that he enjoyed the honour of being the last chef du conseil royal, planned any extension to the attributs of that protean office. The Revolution arrested such developments. Article XXVII of the constitution of 1791 stipulated that there should be no prime minister. The constituent assembly was not mindful of any of our concerns but was uniquely preoccupied with locating individual responsibility, conceived of as criminal rather than political. 'By responsibility we mean death', proclaimed the Girondin Isnard with no more than his customary exaggeration. Prime ministers were proscribed because they did not have a portfolio and their guilt would be more difficult to determine. In the same spirit, two of Montmorin's colleagues objected when he

36 Soulavie, *Mémoires historiques*, VI, 253.
37 Arneth, *Marie-Antoinette, Joseph II und Leopold II*, 210.
38 Barentin, *Mémoire pour M. de Barentin. . .*, 1790, 58–9; Barentin, *Mémoire autographe sur les derniers conseils du Roi Louis XVI*, ed. M. Champion, 1844, 256 *et seq.*
39 *Études biographiques*, 223 and 24.
40 P. Viollet, *Le Roi et ses ministres pendant les trois derniers siècles de la monarchie*, 1912, 238.

wanted to continue attending the conseil as a minister-without-portfolio after his resignation as foreign secretary.[41]

CONCLUSION

What did it mean to be a first minister under Louis XVI? To have the chief, though not exclusive, confidence of a king who was now only the principal source of power. The king could, as Joly de Fleury reminded him, increase or diminish this confidence at will. The minister's power then was totally informal; the title chef du conseil conferred nothing tangible. Even when Brienne was made ministre principal it was done by means of an ordinary letter whose content has survived only because Castries's mistress copied it into his diary. There were no attributs or prerogatives; premiership under Louis XVI was a very workaday experience. But though there was no formality, the premier's function was very specific: coordination. Alone of the ministers his influence outside his department was challenged, if at all, only in amount, not in principle. This was necessarily so in the cases of Maurepas and Brienne since they had no department; they were the only true premiers. The application of this rule makes clear exactly what Vergennes's position was: we have plotted the moves he made towards an extra-departmental goal and the strenuous and ultimately successful resistance he met from the other ministers, notably Castries and Calonne. For this to work it was desirable and probably necessary that the premier should have the principal say in the appointment of his colleagues. This was true in the cases of Maurepas and Brienne, and also it would seem in the case of Breteuil's 1789 ministry.

---

41 Bertrand de Molleville, *Mémoires secrètes*, I, 205.

CHAPTER SEVEN

The 'embarrassments of peace' and the paradoxes of power:
contrôleurs, directeurs and ministres des finances

There is something admirable, something almost gravity-defying in the facility with which the [English] nation or rather its representatives embark on such terrifying [naval] expenditure. Assuredly we have more solid resources than England but we are far from being able to call them into play so easily. This is the result of [public] opinion, which cannot develop in an absolute monarchy to the extent that it can in a mixed monarchy.

(Vergennes to Noailles, French ambassador to England, 15 November 1776)

INTRODUCTION

Colbert assumed the title contrôleur-général des finances in 1665, and his successors used the title unchanged for over a hundred years. In the thirteen years following the dismissal of Turgot in 1776, however, four different titles were employed: some used the old title but Necker was 'directeur-général', Joly de Fleury, 'ministre d'état et des finances', and Brienne was 'chef du conseil royal des finances'. In the period between his appointment as chef du conseil in April 1787 and his elevation to ministre principal the following August, Brienne was the financial supremo (in a detailed way to which Vergennes and especially Maurepas had never aspired). The contrôleur-général Laurent de Villedeuil was his subordinate and glad to be so: on Brienne's elevation he resigned, since Brienne's new dignities 'no longer permitted him to give his attention to any of the details of the finance department'.[1] The other finance ministers, Clugny, d'Ormesson, Calonne, and Lambert reverted to the style 'contrôleur-général'. After the fall of the Bastille, Necker returned to office with the title 'premier ministre des finances' but his successor was given the mealy-mouthed title 'ministre des contributions publics' – as if in a democratic system people paid their taxes voluntarily!

1 A.N. K163 no. 12.

The instability of title mirrored the instability of the office: fifteen months was the average span for Louis XVI's finance ministers. In Part One we have suggested some of the reasons why this should have been the case: the junior status of the post within the ministry and the unresolved ambivalence of his role: was he a mere 'ramasseur d'argent' or the man without whose consent 'nul département ne peut aller'? The problem was put succinctly by the lucid Joly de Fleury; on 4 October 1782 Véri notes:

M. Joly de Fleury . . . told me that in a comité presided over by the king, M. de Ségur had presented a plan [for an invasion of England] which required an additional eight millions and that he, as minister of finance, without entering into a discussion of the merits of the plan had said to the king that in his first travail with him he would demonstrate the impossibility of finding the eight millions. 'I do not claim', said M. de Fleury, 'to discuss the operations of the other ministers. I confine myself to saying whether I have or do not have the money that is being asked of me. But as, by the same token, I do not want them interfering with my administration, I will only show the details to the king alone'.[2]

Joly's logic was impeccable, but it led to the inescapable conclusion that the finance minister should decide matters of peace and war and military operations. Maurepas, however, had thus qualified his defence of Turgot's leading role: 'he believed that *in time of peace* a contrôleur-général should have principal influence'.[3] Peace and war was a question for the king, and the finance minister's job was to find the money. Unfortunately for him, our entire period was dominated by the American War: the shadow of war (rearmament, American subsidies), financing the campaigns, and, after the conclusion of peace, discharging the 'war debt' and Castries' maintenance of a wartime establishment. One of the reasons for Turgot's dismissal had been his reluctance not only to go to war, but also to prepare for the contingency. Sartine wanted to double his spending for 1776 from 29 million livres to 62 million. A transitional stage is indicated by the instructions for large-scale naval manoeuvres in March 1776: 'the ships [were to be] armed as for war, with a crew a little less than for a time of war but larger than for a time of peace'.[4] During the war itself, the government was determined that in this 'guerre des écus', as Vergennes termed it, France would not run out of them first. Joly's papers contain a large dossier on the comparative state of English and French finances.[5] In a real sense, though, the financing of the war was easier than what Joly termed 'les embarras de la paix'. It was then that

2 Abbé de Véri, MSS *Journal*, Archives départementales de la Drôme, Valence, unclassified, cahier 108.
3 My italics; Abbé de Véri, *Journal, 1774–80*, ed. J. de Witte, 1928–30, 2 vols, I, 338.
4 Archives de la Marine, B4 126 fo. 79, cited in L. Laugier, *Turgot ou le mythe des réformes*, 1979, 196.
5 B.N. fonds Joly de Fleury, 1436.

the 'war debt' had to be discharged. The war debt consisted principally in supplies purchased overseas by the promissory notes (lettres de change) issued by the treasury of the marine. Interest was not paid on them during the war, but after it capital and accrued interest were paid off together.

Naval wars were much more expensive than land wars because of the capital expenditure on the ships. In the eighteenth century the cost of the navy in relation to that of the army rose exponentially. Louis XV wept at the loss of life he witnessed at the Battle of Fontenoy; Joly de Fleury coolly calculated that the defeat at the Battle of the Saints had cost 26 million livres of capital expenditure lying at the bottom of the sea.[6] A problem which perplexed the French government was how the English, with one-third of the population and only slightly greater per capita wealth (these things were known in this great age of statistics) could finance their wars better. Their public debt was similar but they paid lower rates of interest. The reason for this was not only that the debt had wider backing, being national rather than royal, but also that the tax-basis providing the collateral for loans was also wider, since the nobility paid a larger proportion of their wealth in taxation than their French counterparts. The French government could not adequately exploit the growing prosperity of the country in the eighteenth century, a problem which is sometimes summed up in the phrase 'a poor state in a rich country'.

A precondition for the general economic prosperity in the eighteenth century was the stability of the currency. After Louis XIV's *réformations* (devaluations), the value of the *livre tournois* (whose name was changed to the *franc* by Bonaparte) remained constant from 1726 until 1932 (except during the Revolution). There were twenty-four to the pound sterling. There was, however, the question of bi-metallism, which was of more immediate concern to Louis XVI's finance ministers. France operated under a gold and silver standard, though there was a prejudice against the yellow metal (which was largely used for trade with Asia), so the Mint paid too little for it. England, however, was virtually on a gold standard from 1774: England paid too much for gold and had captured the trade of Portugal's colony Brazil, the main source of the yellow metal. Naturally there was a glut of gold in England and a dearth in France. This situation was at the heart of the crisis at the Caisse d'escompte in 1783. Calonne remedied it by his 1785 re-coinage, when the Mint raised its gold:silver ratio to 15½:1, midway between that paid by England and that paid by Spain. No longer did the government need to hang on the arrival of bullion wagons and ships.

For most of the long reign of Louis XV, France, after centuries of stagnation, experienced solid growth: the population expanded

6 ibid., 1432 fo. 163.

without causing people to die of famine. The economic growth was largely agricultural, because France was largely agrarian; but within the agricultural sector, the growth in agricultural rents outstripped that of agricultural prices and wages. It was precisely these rents, the *produit net* or clear profit from the land that François Quesnay, who published his *Tableau économique* in 1758, thought should provide the basis for royal taxation (this consideration was uppermost in a work shown first to Louis XV in the middle of the Seven Years War). In truth, each age devises economic theories appropriate to it: the mistakes come when economists (or more often their disciples) come to believe that their theories are of universal application. Quesnay, if not all of his 'sect', the *Économistes* or Physiocrats, addressed practical problems and his influence on government was immense: most of our finance ministers (the exceptions being Terray and Necker) were consciously or subconsciously influenced by him.[7]

Quesnay, then, argued that the recipients of the produit net should alone bear the burden of royal taxation. The subsistence farmer and the agricultural labourer should not pay anything; nor should the merchant or artisan in the towns or the professional classes, because they were not creating wealth, only consuming it. This was consistent both with current practicalities and with a fundamental law of royal taxation, that the peasant should not be taxed to the point where his ability to earn (and therefore pay taxes) was diminished, for instance he must be left enough to pay for seed corn. As regards the towns, the fact was that movable wealth was difficult to detect and assess. Therefore since the landowners were to bear the entire burden of direct taxation, it was a cardinal point that they be rigorously assessed.

Unfortunately, it was easier to tax the peasants than the landowners. The amount levied on them could be raised at will and in secret without registration in the parlement, until Necker voluntarily (and in Joly de Fleury's view irresponsibly) surrendered this right in 1780; whereas the recipients of the produit net were also the privileged orders of the ancien régime, the nobility and clergy. The physiocratic imperative of ending the tax evasion of the former and the tax avoidance (through the inadequate *don gratuit*) of the latter would be met with the cry of France's American ally: 'no taxation without representation', which ultimately meant the Estates-General. In view of Quesnay's distinction, Herbert Lüthy has made the point that the king's rule over the peasants was 'absolute', in the sense that they offered neither resistance nor support; but over the landed orders who constituted the polity of the ancien régime, constitutional tax increases had to be bargained for but, one might add, in the last analysis they would defend the monarchy, or at least their conception of it.

It would also seem that the landowners suffered disproportionately

---

7 H. Lüthy, *La Banque Protestante en France*, 1959–61, 2 vols, II, 9–45.

from the relative economic decline which the reign of Louis XVI witnessed. This decline should not be exaggerated. R. Mandrou concludes that under Louis XVI increasing prosperity was interrupted by a series of 'meteorological accidents' and that the pain was harder to bear because of the contrast with fifty years of unbroken prosperity and the impact of the seigneurial reaction.[8] Without going into the intensity of the latter, it would seem that it was prompted by indebtedness among the landowners caused in part by their investment in the new industries: 'it was a question', Lüthy argues, 'of extracting from an agricultural country the resources necessary for industrialization'.[9] They paid the price of Calonne's drive towards industrialization, but only those at the very pinnacle of society were bailed out by him. At all events they had less left over to pay for the crown's increasing demands on them and called for the Estates-General perhaps as a mechanism of self-defence.

Such concerns came to dominate the thinking of most of the finance ministers with whom we are concerned – notably Joly de Fleury, d'Ormesson and Calonne. The one great exception was Necker. He did not come to the finance ministry with a background in French government administration nor was his approach conditioned by it. He relied on loans rather than taxation and believed in any case that the yield of taxation depended more on how it was collected (or who collected it) than on how it was assessed. The rest of this chapter will be concerned with these differences between Necker and all his successors in the six years between his resignation in 1781 and the ending of the independence of the contrôle-générale after the débâcle of the 1787 Assembly of Notables.

NECKER'S FIRST MINISTRY

Necker made three important changes to the way in which French public finances were conducted: a reliance on loans, and loans of a different nature, rather than increased taxes, even in time of war; a tendency to replace venal office-holders with salaried officials; finally to divulge the *arcana imperii* of royal finances to the public in his celebrated *Compte rendu* of 1781. This is regarded by Robert Harris as a good example of Necker's 'liberal' approach to reform as opposed to the 'enlightened despotism' of native-born reformers – a tradition from which 'physiocracy' sprang and which it in turn reinforced.[10]

On 25 August 1774 the new contrôleur-général, Turgot, is said to have admonished the king: 'no bankruptcy, no new taxation, no

8 R. Mandrou, *La France aux XVIIe et XVIIIe siècles*, 1974, 144–5.
9 Lüthy, *Banque Protestante*, II, 689.
10 R.D. Harris, *Necker: Reform Statesman of the Ancien Régime*, Berkeley, Calif., 1979, 71.

loans'. As regards the first and third prohibition, Louis had little choice. Terray's 1770 bankruptcy (or forced conversion as we should say) had made loans all but impossible, as Terray himself had discovered. His loan of 1771 was a complete failure. Turning to the Dutch from his fleeced flock (whom the cold had made more alert), he attempted to raise 25 million livres in Amsterdam. He gave every guarantee: payment of interest would take precedence over every obligation and would not be interrupted even if France and Holland went to war; all to no avail – only a quarter of the loan was subscribed. In the seven years prior to Necker's appointment, the royal government had either been unable or unwilling to borrow. For Necker to finance the American war with loans, something else had to be tried: the techniques devised by his own and other Swiss banks. The traditional French loan had been a perpetual loan, with no repayment of the capital but with interest at only 5 per cent (4 per cent when the crown's credit was good). Until the Seven Years War, this had sufficed the French government nor had it needed to borrow abroad. Terray killed off the perpetual loan and it could not be resuscitated. This 'was the most evident symptom of the deterioration of public credit'.[11]

Necker did not invent life annuities; Louis XIV had issued them with six rates of interest from 7 per cent to 14 per cent depending on the age of the holder. An average life was considered to be some 20 years. Necker, however, not only issued annuities of 9–10 per cent without age distinction but also allowed the income to be paid to the last survivor of up to thirty people: investors would choose groups of young girls from Switzerland who had passed the age of infant mortality and breathed the clean mountain air above Geneva. Actuaries calculated that the last survivor of the batch would live for another sixty years, hence 'les trente immortelles de Genève'. In the four-and-a-half years of his first ministry, Necker raised 470 million livres in this way, contracting the treasury to pay 44 million a year for 60 years. When his successor Joly de Fleury attempted to float a loan of conventional *rentes perpetuelles*, he met with even less success than had Terray.[12]

In his *Éloge de Colbert* of 1773, which paved the way to his ministry, Necker had argued that if the government needed to borrow, say, 100 million livres, rather than increasing taxes by that amount, it should levy merely sufficient to cover the interest, leaving inflation to erode the capital. Necker, however, did not even do this, though he did prolong the life of the second vingtième, due to expire in 1781, for another ten years. And because he did not increase taxation, he did not see the need to reform it either. By freezing in 1780 the amount raised by the taille unless the increase were registered by the

11 Lüthy, *Banque Protestant*, II, 470.
12 ibid., II, 467.

parlement, he recognized that the peasantry could pay no more – an assumption which was becoming a commonplace (except for the unsentimental Joly de Fleury). His successors all drew the logical conclusion, reinforced by physiocratic tenets, that any increase of revenue would have to come from a stricter assessment of the clergy and nobility. Necker differed from them in concluding that this was not the primary problem and turned his attentions instead to reducing the take of the venal officers in charge of collecting and spending royal revenues, known collectively as la finance. If one had to put the difference between Necker and his successors in a word, it would be the relative importance that Necker placed on the collection and the others placed on the assessment of taxation.

La finance was one of the most characteristic institutions of the ancien régime. These officers bought their offices, which represented a loan to the state on which they received 5 per cent interest. In addition they were paid a salary and a commission on the funds which passed through their hands. Sometimes, as with the treasuries of the departments of marine and of war, these funds simply came from the royal treasury. In 1778, Necker abolished twenty-nine such offices in the two service ministries, leaving a treasurer-general at the head of each. However, the receivers-general of the direct taxes and the farmers-general of the indirect taxes were advancing their own money to the king in respect of taxes which were uncertain in amount and slow (two years in the case of the taille) in collection. Necker reduced the forty-eight receivers to twelve salaried ones, though these did have to put up 1 million livres on which they received the customary 5 per cent.

In collecting the indirect taxes there was considerable debate over the rival merits of a régie (where the régisseurs received a salary) or a farm, where the crown sold the right to collect a tax for an advance against estimated future receipts. A halfway-house was the régie intéressée (where as an incentive the régisseurs kept a proportion of receipts above an agreed figure). When Necker negotiated the lease of 1780 with the farmers-general, he employed a further variant: the king would keep everything over a fixed sum. He later claimed that there was not a lot of difference between the two:

The King says to the *régisseurs*: 'you can have a certain proportion of the revenue which surpasses a certain sum'. He says to the *fermiers*: 'The King will have a certain proportion of the revenue which surpasses the fixed sum of the lease'.[13]

It was a moot point whether the régie or the farm yielded more for the crown, for the farmers had an obvious incentive to collect as much as possible. Indeed Necker may well have reached this conclusion

13 R. D. Harris, *Necker: Reform Statesman of the Ancien Régime*, Berkeley, Calif., 1979, 140.

himself since he considered that the régisseurs were less vexatious to the population.

One aspect of Necker's first ministry which has received little comment is his symbiotic relationship with the high nobility and clergy. This may seem a surprising statement in view of his celebrated reduction of court pensions, a task facilitated by his subjugation of Amelot's ministry of the maison du roi and by what Besenval described as

the degradation into which the grands seigneurs have fallen, which is such that assuredly they are not to be feared and that there is no need to take their views into account in any political calculation.[14]

Besenval was commenting on Necker's depriving the great officers of the maison of their spending powers and conferring them on a commission of bureaucrats in 1779.

Nevertheless, though he reduced what he would have regarded as their parasitical pensions, Necker favoured a positive political role for the nobility and clergy both at provincial and national level. The pilot provincial administrations which he set up in Berry and Haute-Guyenne were presided over by a bishop, that of Berry by the Archbishop of Bourges, Maurepas's cousin, Phélypeaux de La Vrilliere. Calonne, then intendant of Flanders, pointed out the incongruity of Catholic bishops consorting with the Protestant minister, but concluded that 'the clergy was sold to anyone who increased their power'. Brissot called these administrations 'aristocratic intendants', and as Necker's leaked memorandum on the subject made clear, he intended that these bodies should gradually eclipse both the intendants and the parlements. The provincial assemblies which Calonne was to propose to the king were to leave the powers of the intendant intact. Moreover Necker's administrations, in contrast with Calonne's original proposals for assemblies, were to be based on social orders for, as Necker's daughter Madame de Staël observed, her father wanted to 'give the grands seigneurs of France a *consistance politique*'.[15]

At the national level, Necker was responsible for bringing the grands seigneurs, as represented by Castries and Ségur, back into the ministry. Calonne in his *Lettre du Marquis de Caraccioli à M. D'Alembert*, published anonymously in 1781, is particularly scathing about this development. While Necker was still a banker, the affairs of the Compagnie des Indes 'had put him in contact with several grand seigneurs; he gave them suppers'. At first they doubted what he could do for them, 'but the displacement [of Sartine] and even more the replacement [by Castries] infinitely raised his stock'. All those loosely

14 Baron de Besenval, *Mémoires*, ed. Berville and Barrière, 1821, 2 vols, I, 429.
15 P. Renouvin, *Les Assemblées provinciales de 1787*, 1921, 48.

termed Choiseulistes lauded Necker in the hope of getting ministerial preferment: the Archbishop of Toulouse, the Duc de Châtelet ('worthy of high office had he not so desperately coveted it'), the Prince de Beaveau, who wanted the maison or a seat on the council, Castries, who wanted still further promotion, for 'pretensions are often in inverse proportion to merit'. Calonne noted: 'the commotion resulting from the conflict of the courtiers' ambitious pretensions and confusion which will follow until each one of them has been placed'. For there was no logical reason why this should not happen, since 'all the grands seigneurs are equally entitled to believe that they have the same degree of aptitude to fill any ministry: their eyes are glued on these posts and they are all consumed with ministerial mania'. Necker was able to 'recruit them to his cause by meting out to each of them larger or smaller degrees of hope'.[16]

This was good knockabout stuff but, as so often with Calonne, his wit concealed a serious purpose. Calonne was to lavish money on individual great families, but sought to make the nobility and clergy pay their share of taxation and to exclude them from the political process. Necker, however, attacked the sinecures of the court nobility, but left their tax exemptions intact and increased their political role. His attempt to formalize the latter (influenced no doubt by his admiration for the English political system) culminated in his disastrous attempt to introduce bicameralism in 1789. Necker's relationship with the aristocracy is the best example (perhaps the only meaningful one in the eighteenth century) of what Harris terms his 'liberalism'. [17] For though in the context of 1789 the phrase 'liberal nobility' implied a contradiction, for most of the century 'liberal' and 'noble' went together and implied opposition to royal 'despotism'.

The Compte rendu

The most lasting legacy of Necker's first ministry was the *Compte rendu au roi*, which he published in February 1781. Publishing an account of royal finances drawn up for the benefit of the king, was in itself a contradiction of the theory and practice of royal government. Not surprisingly, the *Compte* sold extremely well (over 20,000 copies), but it was a *pièce d'occasion* and did not become a classic: there was no edition after 1781. Necker was responding to a particular situation: there had been a lively pamphlet war against him which Maurepas, smarting from the ministerial changes that Necker had sprung on him the previous autumn, encouraged rather than contained. Necker's January loan met with a lukewarm response despite the fact that for the first time he had exempted the interest payments from the *retenue*

---

16 C.A. de Calonne (attrib.) *Lettre du Marquis de Caraccioli à M. d'Alembert*, 1781, 21–4.
17 Harris, *Necker*, 140.

(10 per cent taxation deducted at source). After the *Compte* had proclaimed that there was a surplus on the 'ordinary' account for 1781 of 10 million livres, Necker was able to close this loan and float another in March; the preamble creating this loan acknowledged that publication of the *Compte* had made this possible.[18]

Most historians have taken the line that the short-term advantage gained by Necker's fraudulent statement was overshadowed by the misleading picture of the crown's finances presented to the public; that if they had to be told anything, they might as well have been told the truth. How could any successor plead poverty? And despite Maurepas's quip that 'the irreplaceable man had yet to be born',[19] one is inclined to apply to Necker Mercy's observation that in Calonne France had never had so dangerous a finance minister because he would make the position of any successor untenable.[20] However, Robert Harris has conducted a defence of the veracity of the *Compte rendu*, which must be taken seriously.[21] In particular his claim that what distinguished the accounts termed 'ordinary' from those that were 'extraordinary' was their degree of certainty. Or, as Necker himself put it: 'The ordinary revenues and expenditure are as well known at the beginning of the year as at the end of the fiscal year'.[22] One can accept that his contemporaries found the concept of the ordinary year meaningful and used it widely. Thus Clugny, Necker's predecessor, submitted to the king a *compte* stating that there was a deficit in the 'ordinary' account for 1776 of 24 million livres. Necker thought it was nearer 27 million and Calonne nearer 37 million but they were clearly dealing with the same animal.

The best way, if not the fairest way (since they were his enemies), of controlling Necker's figures for the ordinary account is to discuss the criticism of them made by Calonne, then intendant of Flanders, and his uncle, Jacques Marquet de Bourgade, whom Joly de Fleury appointed intendant du trésor royal and who instituted a thorough investigation into the accuracy of the *Compte*. Calonne's criticisms were published in his anonymous pamphlet of 1781: *Les Comments*, a series of queries about the *Compte rendu*. Harris concedes that the criticisms Calonne made in 1781 were exactly the same as those he made in 1787: Calonne's attacks were not *ex post facto*, he was not merely trying to justify his need for money in 1787.[23] The sort of questions that Calonne asked were why did Necker not include as an item of expenditure the interest charges on his loans? Why include the income from the *Domaine d'occident* which, being overseas, produced nothing in time of war, etc. Calonne further contended that

18 ibid., 133.
19 J.F.X. Droz, *Histoire du règne de Louis XVI. . .*, 1839, 198.
20 A. d'Arneth and J. Flammermont (eds) *Correspondance secrète du Comte de Mercy-Argenteau avec l'Empereur Joseph II et le Prince de Kaunitz*, 1891, 2 vols, II, 40 n. 1.
21 Harris, *Necker*, 217–35.
22 ibid., 122.
23 ibid., 230.

the *Compte* was accurate neither for 1781 'nor for any other time: it is not applicable to any [specific] year'; and again, it presented 'shifting tables, rotating on pivots, depending either on one hypothesis or another according to need'.[24] Nevertheless there are specific points of comparison which can be made and which should provide a path out of the jungle.

Comparing like for like, then, Calonne put the deficit in 1776 at 37 million livres, Necker at 27 million: not an enormous difference. Calonne and Necker were agreed on what the latter's loans would cost to service; indeed Calonne put the cost at slightly less, 44 million as opposed to Necker's 45 million livres per year. So it all comes down to Necker's claims that he saved an annual 84 million livres from his *améliorations* (economies). If he really did save a sum equal to the take from all three vingtièmes together, then he really did square the circle and his policy of financing the war 'without tears and sighs' is fully vindicated. As Calonne ironically observed, 'the words "à l'immortalité" should be inscribed in gold on the blue covers of the work'. The main saving made by Necker had been the suppression of offices on which interest was paid by the crown. In the 'Mémoire d'observations sur le Compte rendu par M. Necker au mois de Janvier 1781', which Bourgade drew up for Joly de Fleury in July, the value of these offices is put at 47,340,000 livres.[25] Necker, who was a fair-minded man, did not simply suppress these offices. He undertook to repay their capital cost (*finance*). Only in the *Compte rendu*, he took credit for the saving in annual interest payments without mentioning the cost of repaying the capital. As Calonne put it:

under the heading repayment of the capital [of offices], *how* can he justify not making provision for [repaying] the *finance* of these offices, given that the king, in suppressing them, solemnly promised to reimburse their holders?[26]

This was also Bourgade's principal objection to Necker's figures. The other was that Necker had failed to mention 150 million livres of *dette arrièrée* (war debt). Payment of the 'debts in arrears' was conventionally suspended for the duration of the war, so Necker was technically justified in omitting them from the *Compte* for 1781, but Calonne maintained that Necker's 'predecessors had always included them in the statements they gave the king'. In any case, as Bourgade concluded,

If peace is signed by 1783 [preliminaries were in fact signed in January of that year], the deficit in the 'ordinary' expenditure will then be 51,855,000 on account of the reimbursement of the suppressed offices and of the 'debt in arrears' which presumably will be commenced with a view to its being

24 C.A. de Calonne (attrib.) *Les Comments*, 1781, 11–12.
25 B.N. fonds Joly de Fleury, 1438 fos 217–35.
26 Calonne, *Les Comments*, 15.

discharged within ten years.[27] [Calonne was to accomplish it sooner, as he boasted: 'J'ai soldé l'arrière'.]

Let it be said in passing that Necker estimated that the peacetime establishment of the marine would be 29 million livres a year, Bourgade putting the figure at 35 million. Both were wildly optimistic: Joly's 'moles' in the marine informed him that Castries would spend 100 million livres in the first six months of 1783 alone.[28]

Bourgade drew up his memorandum for the benefit of Joly and of the king. A year later he briefed his minister to answer questions from the parlement about the need for a third vingtième, given 'the approval . . . which [the parlement] had given the *Compte rendu* of M. Necker'. The parlement assumed that there had been a surplus on the 'ordinary' account but

If, as we can prove and the king knows, there was on the contrary a gaping hole between revenue and expenditure, it follows that it is indispensable to fill it in.[29]

In view of all this, in 1787, Calonne, who had inherited his uncle's papers (many annotated by Joly de Fleury) on Bourgade's death in 1784, wrote to Joly to enlist his support against Necker's faction in the Assembly of Notables. The reply he received (a copy of which Joly also sent to Miromesnil) was a shock; the key passage ran

Since you have asked, I will say frankly that I do not believe that there was a deficit when I was entrusted with the finances. Your uncle may have thought so, but he did not persuade either M. de Maurepas or myself.[30]

Harris, naturally, places great store by this letter, but neglects to set it in context. Joly was in fact nursing a sense of grievance at the way that Calonne had dealt with his administration of the finances during his opening speech to the Assembly of Notables. Calonne was in a difficult situation. Necker had asked him not to attack the *Compte rendu*, and, given the strength in the Assembly of his followers (what he was later to call a 'fanatical sect'),[31] he minced his words, leaving an implication that Joly was responsible for the deficit. Joly sought revenge and, unlike the two protagonists, Calonne and Necker, he was a man who bore grudges. Prudently he sent Miromesnil only the beginning of his vitriolic letter to Calonne, which concludes

You have denounced me to the king, to the Assembly of Notables, nay before the eyes of the whole of Europe as one of the principal authors of the

27 B.N. fonds Joly de Fleury, 1438 fo. 217.
28 ibid., 1441 fo. 139, cited in M. Price, 'The Comte de Vergennes and the Baron de Breteuil: French Politics and Reform in the reign of Louis XVI', PhD thesis, Cambridge University, 1988, 177.
29 B.N. fonds Joly de Fleury, 1438 fo. 211.
30 A.N. K163 no. 8. 35.
31 A.N. 297 A.P. 3. 119, letter to d'Angiviller.

terrifying disorder which you have revealed *and for which you are alone to blame.*[32]

Joly dealt Calonne a devastating blow by sending an extract of this letter to the king via Miromesnil together with Calonne's original letter: 'I made the only use of it I could, which you could have predicted'. But he went one further by furnishing Necker with ammunition for his reply via his associate, Valdec de Lessart (the future finance and foreign minister who was impeached in 1792). 'I do not want to be quoted', Joly adds, 'I do not want anything to trouble my present peace of mind'.[33] De Lessart replied: 'I can assure you in advance of M. Necker's *sensibilité* both for this communication and for the assurance of the sentiments with which you accompany it'.[34]

The 'communication' contained a copy of Bourgade's memoranda, which Joly claimed were written with the sole purpose of bouncing Maurepas and himself into 'proposing to the king to charge his peoples with a new tax, a step for which we felt great repugnance',[35] a demonstrable lie in view of the alacrity with which Joly had seized on the defeat of the Battle of the Saints to bounce the king into imposing a third vingtième (see pp. 216–17). Joly's attempt to align himself with Necker's no increase of taxation school of thought is as distasteful as it is hypocritical. Calonne's reply to Joly concerning the latter's disavowal of Bourgade is surely right:

You cite M. de Maurepas; His Majesty, who has a very good memory, knows better than anyone what he [Maurepas] thought about that [the *Compte rendu* which Maurepas called the *Conte bleu* because blue wrappings were used for fairy tales].

As for the opinion of M. de Bourgade, I could not ignore it, it is borne out by his writings. I had rather supposed that it had influenced your own thinking relative to the administration of the trésor royal with which you had entrusted him. I have the duplicates of the memoranda which you gave to the king [i.e. in 1781], in the form in which he gave them to you, if one can go by the marginal annotations.[36]

Bourgade was Joly's personal friend: he uses the form *mon ami* in letters to him, which is rare between people in the ministerial milieu.[37] Joly, who had no prior knowledge of government finance and whose ministerial aspirations had lain rather in the direction of Miromesnil's job, was personally responsible for Bourgade's appointment and paid him 40,000 livres out of his salary as finance minister. He even

32 B.N. fonds Joly de Fleury, 1432 fo. 136.
33 ibid., fo. 133, undated but April 1787.
34 ibid., fo. 134.
35 ibid., fo. 133, Joly de Fleury to de Lessart.
36 ibid., fo. 139, Calonne to Joly de Fleury, 7 April (A.M.).
37 The only other case I can think of is Calonne writing to d'Angiviller, e.g. A.N. 297 A.P. 3. 119 and 121.

invented Bourgade's title, intendant du trésor royal, as well as his own, ministre d'état et des finances. Bourgade was not a minister but for nearly three years he ran the finance side of the finance ministry. Is it likely that Joly would or even could have formed a technical financial opinion independent of that of his principal adviser? Indeed in memoranda submitted to Joly de Fleury on the organization of the 1783 comité des finances, Bourgade himself was to make the point that magistrates were no longer equipped to understand the increasing complexities of public finance without technical assistance. The preparatory work for meetings of the comité should be performed by a petit comité, consisting of people like himself and d'Harvélai, the garde du trésor royal. Joly de Fleury could only have welcomed this further reduction of his workload, though Bourgade's petit comité was never formally appointed.

It is worth saying something about Bourgade because he had a deep influence not only on Joly but also, though he resigned at the end of 1783, on government policy in the unified period 1781–7. Bourgade was one of an elite group of a dozen or so men at the top of la finance often referred to as the 'faiseurs des services du roi', whom Necker had left largely unscathed. Others included Micault d'Harvélai, the garde du trésor royal and Badaud de Saint-James and Mégret de Sérilly, the trésoriers-généraux for the marine and war department. These men were all extremely rich and apart from the purchase of their offices they advanced considerable sums to the crown: in 1781, for example, Bourgade advanced 4.8 million livres to the treasury. The treasurers to the service ministries, in particular, could make a lot of money at the expense of the crown, by taking a percentage of all the huge sums handled during the wars (but not as much as Henry Fox made in the same way as the English paymaster-general). Equally, however, they lived in constant dread of their own or the crown's bankruptcy, which often came to the same thing: in 1787 it was Mégret de Sérilly who went bankrupt, not the crown.

Necker stressed the advantages to be gained from handling the king's money. Bourgade stressed the symbiotic relationship. They propped the crown up and vice versa depending on their relative credit-worthiness at any one time. They were French, subjects of the crown; they stood or fell with it; they were, as we would say, part of the 'establishment'. Necker and his banker friends could shift their 'hot' funds out of France whenever they saw a better risk:reward ratio in England or Holland. On Bourgade's advice, therefore, Joly de Fleury restored the forty-eight receveurs-généraux which Necker had abolished. Joly's immediate object was financial: to get hold of their finance for the war effort. However, Bourgade's memorandum on the subject had employed almost mystical arguments:

In a monarchical kingdom, where the authority of the sovereign, or even that of one of his ministers, can regulate everything, destroy everything, it is necessary to sustain the illusion of the relationships and distinctions which tie or which separate . . . the relative obligations of sovereign and subject.

It is not as a good economic calculator that one measures the effects of a destructive system, but as a statesman who raises his sights to events to come, etc.[38]

His nephew Calonne shared this almost Montesquieuean idealization of the financial establishment of the ancien régime; Necker had 'destroyed all *crédit intermédiaire* . . . and confined all lending to the banking system'.[39] Such views must seem somewhat old-fashioned in 1781; Bourgade, who was an old man, looked back (like many others) to Cardinal Fleury's time, which he considered as 'le temps le plus heureux de la France'.[40] However, Bourgade could seek inspiration for reform in the past. Thus Bourgade, in search of a land tax which should fall on privileged and non-privileged alike, favoured a revival of the ill-fated *cinquantième* of 1725, because he did not think that the *vingtièmes*, however modified, would ever serve this function (this is perhaps why Joly was prepared to abandon *vérifications*). The cinquantième, Bourgade argued, 'would serve as a pretext and a means to make the pays d'état and the clergy pay [a fair proportion] and would also enable us to know the true product of the kingdom'.[41]

This particular version of a *subvention territorial* came to nothing, but the need for this form of tax as the only way to end tax evasion was seldom forgotten by the post-Necker ministry from 1781 to 1787.

JOLY DE FLEURY

This attempt to put old wine into new bottles (which was to have the result foreseen in the Gospels) provides the best clue to the principles behind the administration of Joly de Fleury. This has generally been considered the embodiment of pure reaction. Droz, Chérest and Bosher all take this line, though they do not all share Droz's view of Joly's importance:

The period of his administration has too often been regarded as insignificant: it was during the two years we have just reviewed that the decline began of a government whose incompetence seemed to increase in proportion to the dangers it faced.[42]

Véri considered that Joly's edict on the regulation of the grain trade

---

38 B.N MS Fr. 8020, fo. 196, cited in Price, 'Vergennes and Breteuil', 209.
39 Calonne, *Lettre . . . à d'Alembert*, 4.
40 B.N. MS Fr. 8020, fo. 31, cited in Price, 'Vergennes and Breteuil', 140.
41 ibid., fo. 33.
42 Droz, *Histoire du règne de Louis XVI*, 205.

was inspired by 'des principes administratifs qui sont ceux des temps les plus reculés'.[43] Véri uses the expression 'temps les plus reculés' for dramatic effect, but it does provide the clue to Joly's outlook, which was that of the antiquarian reformer. This was not an uncommon position in a polity dominated by lawyers: Le Paige had used antiquarian arguments to attack the royal authority, Lamoignon was to use them to defend it. In this spirit Joly de Fleury's memorandum to the king advocating a comité des finances (a body which will be considered in more detail in Chapter 8 on the council) stresses the return to the conciliar principles of 1661. The year 1783 was to be a new start for Louis XVI, but the comparison goes back to the young Louis XIV, the death of Mazarin being compared to that of Maurepas.

In other respects, Joly was more forward-looking. Henri Fréville has ably demonstrated how Joly upheld the rights of the third estate against the nobility in the Breton estates more vigorously than did any of Louis XVI's contrôleurs, even being prepared, in 1781, to dissolve the Breton estates. This policy, continued under the comité des finances, was reversed by Calonne, who felt it necessary to woo the Bretons who had not forgotten his part in the La Chalotais affair.[44]

The bare essence (what he himself called a 'sketch') of Joly's thinking is contained in the memorandum that Joly gave the king when he asked to resign (see pp. 65–8)

1.   The Commercial Treaty [presumably with England; Calonne and Vergennes finally concluded this in 1786].
2.   Revoke [Necker's] declaration concerning the *brevet général* [of the taille]. . . . it is very restricting for the Administration, which cannot tax without *enregistrement.*
3.   *Restore* [my italics] a little more equality between the different provinces in respect of taxation.
4.   Revise the way in which the vingtième, the taille, the capitation and others are levied.
6.   Establish a new, simpler and less onerous method of collecting the gabelle, the traites, the aides and the entrées de Paris.

This was the essence of Calonne's programme, and rather than denouncing Joly should have taken credit for it. Lüthy talks of Calonne's 'disturbing originality', but in his opening speech to the Notables, the minister made a virtue out of *not* being original, saying his projects were a résumé of the best thinking over the past century. The differences between Joly's objectives and those of Necker lie in their attitudes to the reform of taxation. Necker did not think it necessary to increase the tax-take; *a fortiori* there was no need to reform its basis. He surrendered the right to raise the taille; Joly

43 Véri, MSS *Journal*, cahier 101
44 H. Fréville, *L'Intendance de Bretagne, 1689–1790*, Rennes, 1953, 3 vols, III, 57–69.

thought this was a needless concession. As a war-time expedient Joly imposed a third vingtième on the old registers (which will be considered in Chapter 11 on the parlement) but saw the need for reform once the war was out of the way. Necker did not think it necessary to make any provision for the repayment of the royal debt: inflation would take care of that (and with the issue of the *assignats* ten years later it did). Repayment was important to Bourgade, and Joly took the step of finding a sinecure for Isaac Panchaud, the most celebrated advocate of a 'caisse d'amortissement' (sinking fund), which was to be set up by Calonne and receive payment of 8.5 million livres in 1785 and 1786. By the time of his resignation, Joly de Fleury had put in place the nucleus of the ideas and of the team which would lead to the projects Calonne laid before the Notables. By calling the period 1781–7, 'Six Years of Reaction', Bosher at least gives a back-handed recognition of its unity.

D'ORMESSON

In many respects Joly's successor, d'Ormesson, was the most radical of Louis XVI's finance ministers, for he combined Necker's distrust of la finance (a distrust which found expression in his conversion of the general farm into a régie) with Joly's and Bourgade's belief that a radical restructuring of the direct taxes was necessary. Apart from fleshing out Joly's skeletal proposals, he also supplied a date for their implementation – 1787. His papers show that he was in constant communication both with Panchaud and with Dupont de Nemours and thus with the reforming spirit which permeated the bureaux of the contrôle.[45] Dupont's memoranda contain not only many projects but also much pessimism about the chances of implementing them and about the weakness of the position of a contrôleur. Thus he envisages the current lease of the general farms as being the last, 'provided that the administration of M. le contrôleur-général lasts until its expiry [1786] and provided that he retains the *crédit* and authority which his application, intelligence and his virtues deserve'. He thinks that there is no point trying to enforce economies since 'they would perhaps require more authority than a contrôleur-général can possess'. Nor could they 'touch' the *grandes branches* such as the gabelle, aides, and *tabac*, 'except in so far as there was a way of consulting and coming to an understanding with the Nation over their replacements'.[46] This pessimism at the heart of government was to culminate in Calonne's

---

45 A.N. 144 A.P. 131 *dossier* 4. 11, May–August,1783.
46 ibid., Dupont de Nemours, 'Mémoire secret contenant l'aspect de la position des finances . . .', 13 August 1783.

anguished cry to Castries after the convocation of the Notables had been announced: 'There is no one in France strong enough to carry through all that is necessary'.[47]

Dupont provides the link back to Turgot and forward to Calonne. D'Ormesson's own links with Turgot are clear from the dossier entitled 'Memoranda and draft-edict on the establishment of a subvention territorial drawn up in 1775 by M. d'Ormesson at the request of M. Turgot'. A memorandum dated 24 February 1775 is a passionate defence of the vingtièmes which his father administered as intendant des finances (and he would himself administer from 1777) and a plea that the projected subvention should replace not them but the 'absurd' taille or equally 'absurd' capitation.

Unconvinced, Turgot insisted on replacing the vingtièmes and d'Ormesson dutifully drew up the draft edict, leaving the minister to write the preamble. The king explains through d'Ormesson that he could have raised more money by continuing with the vérifications to the vingtième; but this would have 'fatigued' his peoples. So the total would be fixed at the present take and a cadastre instituted simply to achieve a fairer assessment. Henceforth the vingtième

would be collected under the name of subvention . . . this subvention will be called territoriale since it will be imposed solely on land, the only basis of real wealth. The same edict will end the necessarily arbitrary and destructive vingtième on industry.[48]

The young d'Ormesson had framed the edict in the purest physiocratic jargon. The existence of this draft edict, complete with its 'Louis par le grâce de Dieu', would tend to suggest that some of Turgot's more radical proposals were nearer to the surface than has sometimes been supposed.[49]

If Turgot could have entrusted the 23-year-old d'Ormesson with such an important and controversial task, it may seem surprising that the public view of him was that he was dull and incompetent, if honest; indeed his appointment spawned a series of jokes based on this theme. Thus, when invited to dinner, people asked 'Have you got a good cook?', to which the reply was 'No, but I've got an honest one'. Or people might say 'I need to break in a wilful horse' – 'Have you got a good groom?' – 'No, but I've got an honest one'. Also, d'Ormesson was not entirely his own man. Above him was the recently appointed chef du conseil royal, Vergennes, who, without consulting d'Ormesson, asked Bourgade to continue in his functions. This, d'Ormesson considered, 'necessarily made him independent of my choice and my administration'. D'Ormesson reflected on the fate of the 'virtuous and

47 Castries, *Journal*, Archives de la Marine, MS 182/7964 1–2, II, fo. 335.
48 A.N. 144 A.P. 133 *dossier* 3. 2.
49 For instance by the subtitle of Laugier's *Turgot ou le mythe des réformes*.

unfortunate' Taboureau, who had played contrôleur to Necker's directeur du trésor,[50] and who had won d'Ormesson's affection by resigning over Necker's suppression of the intendants des finances. Vergennes explained that Bourgade had been kept on because d'Ormesson lacked experience in raising loans. True as this was, d'Ormesson considered that Bourgade was equally ignorant of the new techniques introduced by Necker. And so it was to prove: on Bourgade's advice, d'Ormesson raised 48 million livres in lotteries, contracting to provide 70 million in prize money over the following eight years.[51] This was one of the few loans that was mostly repaid before the ravages of Revolutionary inflation.

To postpone the need for another such loan, Bourgade persuaded d'Ormesson, against his better judgement, to put pressure on the Caisse d'escompte (discount bank) secretly to lend the crown 24 million livres (24 August 1783). The Caisse d'escompte had been set up by Turgot in 1776 to foster commerce by lending at 4 per cent through a convertible paper currency and to maintain confidence it was obviously desirable that it should remain independent of the government, whose credit was worse than its own. Inevitably the secret arrangement of 24 August leaked out and there was a run on the bank. For reasons entirely unconnected with the loan to the government (which was in paper), the Caisse lacked the gold coins to meet the demand. The Caisse had to suspend payment; d'Ormesson drew up an arrêt making the Caisse's notes legal tender and Vergennes went to Versailles to get the king's signature. Louis had gone to bed, so Vergennes issued the arrêt on his own authority, a necessary step, but one which made a mockery of Joly de Fleury's old-fashioned contention that 'the king promulgates arrêts only in his council'.[52]

The crisis had arisen because of the shortage of specie, resulting from the overseas war and (as we have seen) from the fact that the Mint did not pay enough for gold; the government resolved it temporarily by expensively importing *piastres* from Spain. When these were minted up into gold 'louis', Bourgade, who had arranged the operation, allowed his agents to take the customary 'cut', known as the *sur-achat*. D'Ormesson blamed him for this as well as his bad advice, and Bourgade resigned on 26 October, under a cloud. D'Ormesson, for whom the whole episode had confirmed his distrust of la finance, reminded the hapless banker that he still had some explaining to do. Accepting his resignation, he wrote 'All the same, I expect from you the reply which is necessary to clear up a number of essential facts'.[53] A sad end for a sick man (he died the following year) who had just

---

50 D'Ormesson, *Journal*, A.N. 144 A.P. 130, section 45.
51 Lüthy, *Banque Protestante*, II, 520.
52 Price, 'Vergennes and Breteuil', 124.
53 AAE MDF 1395 fo.207, cited in Price, 'Vergennes and Breteuil', 81.

lent the crown nearly 5 million livres. Apart from the recriminations and despite the fact that it was merely 'a banal banking crisis',[54] the run on the Caisse d'escompte served to undermine d'Ormesson's more ambitious plans and make them even more difficult of execution.

D'Ormesson recognized this himself: over his important August memorandum to the king on reform, he scrawled 'suspendu par l'événement de la Caisse d'escompte'. The tenor of this memorandum can be gleaned from the following extract:

We cannot really get down to reforming internal administration as long as the level of taxation prevents us from working on a better assessment; as long as the disadvantageous form of the farms, according to which several important parts of the king's revenues are still alienated to powerful syndicates, prevents us from modifying the nature of these revenues without compromising the necessary guarantee of their yield and without exposing us to paying considerable compensation.

Luckily, the approaching expiry of the present lease of the general farms and the ending of the third vingtième, both of which fall in 1786, allow us to prepare by this not too distant date a better internal order; as well to replace or modify the consumption taxes that are presently farmed out and which may be harmful to agriculture and trade as to let Your Majesty finally know the relative wealth of his provinces, which is still unknown, by means of a better assessment of the two vingtièmes, the only tax which is uniform throughout the kingdom and consequently the only one susceptible of establishing an exact basis of comparison between the different provinces.[55]

D'Ormesson here recognizes that while the general level of taxation is high, tax evasion will be so also: the third vingtième brought in much less than the other two. When it and Necker's *sols pour livre* ceased in 1787, the government would have not only the need but also the possibility of increasing the yield by a more equitable assessment. There is no mention of a subvention territorial.

It is clear from this memorandum that the king had not yet been informed of d'Ormesson's immediate objective, the reform of the farm, though plans for this were well under way. A related letter from one of d'Ormesson's senior commis to Vergennes is dated 10 May;[56] and d'Ormesson and Vergennes worked on the proposals throughout the summer, planning to have them ready by October, when they could take advantage of the less formal arrangements obtaining at Fontainebleau to closet the king. D'Ormesson's preference for a régie over a farm was longstanding: Turgot's *régie des poudres* of 1775 had been based on d'Ormesson's rapport. Necker's *régie des postes* had in turn been modelled on this and during d'Ormesson's brief ministry its conditions had been tightened since d'Ormesson considered that the personnel of the postes

54 Lüthy, *Banque Protestante*, II, 694.
55 A.N. 144 A.P. 131 dossier 4. 4, 'situation des finances', August.
56 AAE MDF 1394 fo. 192.

chosen for the most part from the former farmers-general and consequently imbued with the principles, the mentality and the customs of the old finance were far removed from the disinterestedness of the new régisseurs des poudres.[57]

D'Ormesson planned to convert the last three years of the bail Salazard, the contract making over the collection of the indirect taxes to the farmers-general, into a régie intéressée with effect from 1 January 1784. In fairness to the farmers, who had three years of their lease left, they would become the régisseurs, their *fonds d'avance* and their *bénéfices* remaining the same, which would also ensure the credit of their notes. The régie would not at first save any money for the crown, but would give the king a free hand when the bail expired in 1787. Then the 'consumption taxes', as d'Ormesson told the king in his August memorandum, would either be 'replaced or modified'.

Most historians miss the cautious nature of the operation (it represented only a shift in emphasis from the lease that Necker had instituted in 1780) and attribute its failure to d'Ormesson's rashness.[58] This is because d'Ormesson's own account, one moreover corroborated by Castries and Véri – 'et M. d'Ormesson n'est pas menteur' – has not been examined. Moreover, d'Ormesson had the support of his two ministerial colleagues in the comité des finances, Miromesnil and Vergennes. Miromesnil's dislike of the farm was longstanding: in 1764, when premier président of the parlement of Rouen, he had denounced their operations,[59] while Vergennes may even have first conceived the measure. Vergennes's principal concern was that American ships were being driven to English ports by agents of the farm coming aboard in connection with tobacco, salt and other duties. Castries, who was not, however, consulted, considered that la politique (foreign policy) was determinant in the decision. D'Ormesson was buoyed up by the support of the chef du conseil: 'No doubt', he wrote to Vergennes on 13 October, 'we shall have to fight pressure groups and prejudice; but we are accustomed to fight them and I feel that with your help I have the strength to overcome them'.[60] Perhaps the weight of the comité would achieve what Dupont had feared the contrôleur could not achieve on his own?

If d'Ormesson made a mistake, it was in not postponing his plans for the farm to allow time for the revival of credit after the crisis of the Caisse d'escompte: after all he had himself recognized that his wider reforms would have to be 'suspended' by that 'event'. However, he pressed on, and on Friday 23 October, at Fontainebleau, presented his rapport on the farms to the king in the comité des finances: 'the king',

---

57 D'Ormesson, *Journal*, section 54.
58 See G.T. Mathews, *The Royal General Farms*, New York, 1958, 260–1.
59 J. Egret, *Louis XV et l'opposition parlementaire*, 1970, 117.
60 AAE MDF 1395 fos. 192–3, cited in Price, 'Vergennes and Breteuil', 239.

he tells us, 'alone of the members of the comité, appeared . . . to hesitate a little before accepting the rapport' but any doubts were dispelled by Vergennes, who stressed 'most forcefully the paramount . . . consideration of American trade'. Next day the decision was embodied in an arrêt du conseil, but during d'Ormesson's travail on the Sunday, the king expressed 'surprise and anxiety at the speed of its publication'. D'Ormesson guessed that the king's doubts centred on his ingrained habit of regarding the farmers as one of the 'columns of the state' through their provision of credit, currently in short supply. Vergennes began to trim while the farmers, according to d'Ormesson, deliberately engineered the collapse of their own notes on the Bourse (a credible interpretation since their collateral had not been affected by the operation) to give them the excuse to demand the impossible repayment of their advances to the Treasury of some 60 million livres.[61]

The details of d'Ormesson's fall have already been considered (see pp. 68–73) but we can add as a postscript the delight of Bourgade, whose role in d'Ormesson's fall and in Calonne's appointment will not be found to have been least. 'Ah mon Dieu,' he wrote to Vergennes, 'my hearty congratulations both to you and the Country on M. d'Ormesson's departure!'[62]

CALONNE

The fascination which Calonne has exercised on his contemporaries and on his historians is not hard to explain, nor is the controversy surrounding the man and his measures. The king was reluctant to appoint him because Maurepas had warned about his 'droiture suspecte', but he was soon won over. His brilliant presentation of financial matters gave intellectual satisfaction to a king who prided himself on his understanding of public finances. Calonne had been a brilliant classical scholar at the École des Quatre-Nations, winning most of the prizes for Latin and Greek; his classical allusions could only have pleased the king, who also loved Latin. His reference to du Châtelet in the *Lettre . . . à D'Alembert* as 'worthy of the highest office had he not so coveted it' must have delighted the king, modelled as it was on the epigram on the Emperor Galba of Louis's favourite Latin author, Tacitus – *capax imperii nisi imperasset.* He was also that *rarissima avis* among the king's ministers, an absolute believer in the absolute Monarchy.

61 D'Ormesson, *Journal*, section 83.
62 AAE MDF 1395 fo. 215, Bourgade to Vergennes, 3 November 1783, cited in Price, 'Vergennes and Breteuil', 234.

Malouet famously called Calonne 'the incarnation of every abuse he sought to eradicate' but was he not also the incarnation of every charm which the Revolution eradicated? Talleyrand, to whom Calonne was related by marriage,[63] and who collaborated with him on the proposals he laid before the Notables, could have been thinking of him when he penned his lines about the 'douceur de vivre' of that vanished age. However, Talleyrand also said that 'the majority of men like to see the qualities of hard work and prudence in ministers; Calonne was not reassuring on either count'.[64] He is said to have greeted everyone who knocked on his door with his full attention, as if relaxing after the day's work. Perhaps he was, for the Duc de Lévis, who knew him well, thought that he trusted too much to his 'extreme facility for work', so that 'at the end of the week there was a déficit of time as difficult to cover as that of the treasury'.[65] Calonne burned both ends of the candle, often, according to Bombelles, gambling until three in the morning, and 'exhausted by this kind of life, of all the ministers, not excepting M. d'Ossun, he was the one who got in most sleep during the meetings of the conseil d'état'.[66] Gomel, however, who was a severe judge of his administration concedes, 'He was not the man to misappropriate the king's money'.[67] Lévis noted that his wit was never at the expense of others.[68]

On his appointment, Calonne's immediate task, as the king had indicated, was 'the support of crédit, so that we can service the rest of the year without any emergency measures'.[69] This Calonne managed with such success that he soon had to stamp on speculation in the shares of the Caisse d'escompte. But did he in addition have a longer view, or were the measures that he submitted to the Notables merely the desperate improvisation of a ministry as bankrupt morally as it was financially? Louis Blanc argues attractively, if ultimately unconvincingly, that Calonne planned through over-spending to confront the nobility and clergy with the stark alternative of bankruptcy or reform: to 'lead them to the abyss on a carpet of flowers', but to give them a good time first: 'ménager pour les grands un moment de bonheur'.[70] Suzanne also insists on a long-term if less colourful plan and makes this thesis the title of his work: *La Tactique financière de Calonne* ('strategy' might have expressed his meaning better).[71] That this was indeed the case seems self-evident from Calonne's inaugural speech to the chambre des comptes of 13 November 1783:

63 Calonne's wife's sister was married to the Baron de Talleyrand.
64 Prince de Talleyrand, *Mémoires*, ed. Duc de Broglie, 1891–2, I, 104.
65 Duc de Lévis, *Portraits et souvenirs*, 1813, 295.
66 Marquis de Bombelles, *Journal*, ed. J. Grassion and F. Durif, Geneva, 1978–93, 3 vols, II, 107.
67 H. Gomel, *Les Causes financières de la Révolution française*, 1892–3, 2 vols, II, 198.
68 Lévis, *Portraits*, 295.
69 Archives de Vergennes, *Lettres de Louis XVI*, the king to Vergennes, 3 November 1783.
70 L. Blanc, *Histoire de la Révolution française*, 1847–63, II, 151.
71 G. Suzanne, *La Tactique financière de Calonne*, 1901.

As soon as I have crossed the desert of discharging the war debt, I will apply my mind to the execution of a plan of general reform which, grounded in the very constitution of the monarchy, embraces all its parts, regenerates rather than squeezes resources and reveals the true secret of lightening taxation in the proportionate equality of its assessment and the simplification of its collection.

This seems clear cut, and all the more plausible because we now know that this had been the plan of the comité de gouvernement since the signature of peace. The year 1787 was the natural date for its implementation.

Herbert Lüthy, however, in his brilliant analysis of Calonne's financial operations, suggests that there were two distinct, indeed contrasting, phases to Calonne's ministry.[72] In the first, Calonne behaved responsibly, clamping down on speculation, banning 'derivative' markets, such as futures trading in politically sensitive stocks, investing in genuinely useful projects, such as giving modest assistance to the Compagnie des eaux. In the second phase, dating from 1786, far from discouraging speculation, Calonne employed government funds to drive it into a manic phase redolent of Law's system. The implication is that the recourse to the Assembly of Notables was born of the desperation of this second phase. Lüthy stressed the haste with which Calonne's 'think-tank' worked on the proposals. We find this thesis all the more attractive because it can be buttressed by a rational explanation for the change which Lüthy himself does not supply. That explanation lies in Calonne's relations with the parlement which will be examined in greater detail in Chapter 11. Suffice it to say for the present that in 1785 Calonne lost control of the parlement and recognized that the loan which was registered with such difficulty in December of that year would be the last. He made a desperate attempt to regain control of the parlement in 1786 and only when that failed did he turn to the Notables.

In a real sense, though, these two views of Calonne's policy are not mutually exclusive. What happened in the parlement merely gave him the courage (of despair) to do what he had all along known was necessary. He tried to pass the chalice by replacing Breteuil at the maison, but failing, decided to drink it to the lees: 'I would indeed have no regrets', he told the king, 'if I were the scapegoat necessary for the success of the enterprise'.[73] But whatever view one takes of Calonne's motivation, the contrast between the two phases of his ministry is worth considering.

The germ for many of Calonne's policies in the first phase of his ministry can be found in his 1781 pamphlet *Les Comments*. He denounces Necker for closing a loan early so that his banker friends

72 Lüthy, *Banque Protestante*, II, 686–711.
73 John Hardman, *Louis XVI*, New Haven, Conn., 1993, 105.

could sell their rentes at a profit, 'giving the impression that he wanted to increase the profit from speculation (*agiotage*), which he should have been preventing'. And for the first two years of his own ministry, Calonne strove manfully against a rising sea of speculation on the Bourse, if only because it diverted funds away from his own loans. In particular he checked speculation in the shares of the Caisse d'escompte by forcing it to pay shareholders a dividend justified by its profits. On several occasions (but in vain) he made futures trading illegal: in England futures contracts were not recognized at law. Equally salutary was his 1785 recoinage: simply by increasing what the Mint paid for gold in relation to silver he ended the *disette de numéraire* which had brought d'Ormesson down. The trade in piastres withered away unbidden: the legislator's pen had ended a traffic which had prospered for two centuries, not by making it illegal, but by making it pointless. Only those who had profited from it had grounds for complaint. Nevertheless, led by the instant opposition from the innumerate parlementaires, there was an outcry against the measure.

In *Les Comments*, Calonne had called France 'a kingdom where resources are increased by the very act of expenditure'. This theory has been seen as a precursor of Keynes's 'multiplier', though it was in fact at the heart of the Physiocrats' teaching. At all events, Calonne inaugurated a policy of 'easy money'. He embarked on a series of great public works, such as embellishment of towns, construction of canals, and improvement of roads. He encouraged the crown's bankers and the departmental treasurers to invest their own money and the crown's (the two often virtually indistinguishable) in commercial and industrial enterprises. He built a fine wall round Paris. In accordance with his adage – 'one must repay infinitely to borrow still more' – he paid off the arrears on the rentes and for the first and last time under the ancien régime, paid current interest on time. Whether the prosperity and sense of well-being these policies engendered were artificial or confined to narrow social and geographic areas, much seemed to justify the contemporary jingle:

> Tout le monde jusqu'à la gent bretonne
> Aime Calonne, Aime Calonne.

During the second, degenerate phase of Calonne's ministry, shortage of money was desperate. The only immediate benefit from his policies had been the extra 12 million livres he got from the farmers when their lease was renewed in 1786 on account of the reduction of smuggling caused by the Paris wall. Meanwhile opposition from the parlement had forced him to abandon all hope of another loan and the third vingtième was due to expire at the end of the year, equally with no hope of an extension. Short-term expedients worthy of the worst days of Louis XIV became the norm, and were compounded by the development of rococo financial instruments. As the Assembly of Notables opened in February 1787, the Caisse d'escompte, which Calonne had protected from itself seemingly for this very purpose, made a substantial 'rights issue' in return for giving the government an enormous surety-bond (*cautionnement*) of 70 million livres. Cautionnements were merely a money-raising device: caution itself was thrown to the winds. The Caisse d'escompte's was only the biggest of many such cautionnements as new companies were floated. But 'with all these cautionnements, it was still only royal paper which returned to the king's treasuries'.[74] And the dividing line between the shares in these companies and royal notes became so thin that Calonne was obliged to intervene on the Bourse. As Lüthy has put it:

In the second phase of Calonne's ministry, it was the treasury itself, unable to borrow normally and to release normal resources, which was speculating through its intermediaries in its own paper and on an indefinite bull market in the shares on the Bourse, carried to double or treble their real value in an infernal gearing.[75]

One way of looking at this second phase of Calonne's ministry is through two of his decisive friendships: one (which turned sour) with Breteuil, the minister for the maison du roi, and the other (which was proof against everything) with the king's youngest brother, the Comte d'Artois.

Calonne and Breteuil had stormed the ministry together, and in the early days, Lenoir, the lieutenant-général de police and Breteuil's subordinate, had 'seen and heard them plotting together, as it were, how they could best govern France'.[76] Later they quarrelled when Breteuil attempted to buy the palace of Saint-Cloud for the queen without telling Calonne, and when Calonne arranged for Lenoir to send him police reports on the Bourse without telling Breteuil. Both these quarrels, let it be said, were functional rather than personal, arising as they did over the overlapping jurisdictions of their respective departments. Thus Breteuil could buy Saint-Cloud out of the funds of the maison because the contrôleur had not established control over the departmental budgets. Similarly the trouble with the police reports arose from the fact that while Breteuil was the minister for Paris, the contrôleur had obvious responsibilities in the capital, recognized in the fact that the intendant of Paris reported to him. Because the overlapping jurisdictions that affected all the six ministries were most acute in the case of the contrôle and the maison, conflict was inevitable when both were run by strong characters. (It had been avoided when Necker and the self-effacing Amelot had been the occupants.)

Though Breteuil was a strong character, he was also an incompetent minister, which exacerbated the problem. Castries (he could talk)

74 Lüthy, *Banque Protestante*, II, 692.
75 ibid., 692.
76 Lenoir Papers, Bibliothèque municipale d'Orléans, MSS 1421–3, 1423, résidus 85.

noted: 'It is possible that he will not be able to retain the easiest ministry to run: his ignorance of every aspect of administration . . . causes him to stumble at every step'.[77] Miromesnil told Véri that this incompetence did not matter, 'now that we [himself, Vergennes and Calonne] have enough credit with the Master to prevent his errors or at least correct them'.[78] He was in effect excluded from central policy decisions. This, however, had the effect only of throwing him back on his Parisian fiefdom.

The parlement of Paris was naturally located in the capital, and because it had police jurisdiction which itself overlapped with Breteuil's, Breteuil had legitimate dealings with the parlement. Because the prévôt des marchands was also the subordinate of the minister for the maison, Breteuil had access to the list of rentes which was deposited at the hôtel de ville. All it took was a little ill-will for him to supply his faction in the parlement with the proof that Calonne had extra-legally taken in 120 million livres after the various loans had been closed. It did not matter that all the finance ministers did this, and that, in proportion to his opportunities, the 'virtuous' Turgot had been the worst offender in this respect.[79] This material became combustible in Breteuil's hands.

These and other developments centring on Breteuil's dealings with the parlement will be considered in Chapter 11 but Breteuil was also concerned with the commercial development of Paris, which directly related to his department. The most famous clash with Calonne occurred over their rival plans to increase the water supply to Paris. Calonne backed the Compagnie des eaux de Paris, which aimed to use the fire-pumps invented by the brothers Périer. Under Calonne, the trésor royal lent them 1.2 million livres in August 1784 in return for 1,000 shares at par; he also encouraged the treasurers of the war and marine, Sérilly and Saint-James, to continue their financial assistance. This was merely supporting a capitally intensive and long-term project of public utility, but when the shares began to slide, in April 1786, Calonne gave the Italian banker Campi 1.5 million livres to intervene on the market, which share-support operation doubled the price of the shares.[80] Breteuil, meanwhile, had given his support to a rival scheme to divert the course of the river Yvette, a project which he claimed (with some reason) was more hygienic. The matter was argued out adversarially in the conseil des dépêches in April 1786, Calonne 'presenting to the king the project of MM. Périer and their shares as state stocks which the government could not cease to support without harming their credit and that of all the other royal bills'.[81] The king

77 Castries, *Journal*, entry for 31 October 1784.
78 Véri, MSS *Journal*, cahiers 124–5.
79 Laugier, *Turgot*, 87–8.
80 Lüthy, *Banque Protestante*, II, 709.
81 Bombelles, *Journal*, II, 133.

came down on Calonne's side, even slapping Breteuil down 'assez nettement et assez durement'.[82]

Breteuil, however, was to have his blundering revenge. In April 1788, with Calonne in exile, he put pressure on the prévôt des marchands to buy out the Compagnie des eaux at three times the real value of the company. The Périer brothers were excluded from the new administration royale des eaux de Paris and made debtors of the new company, which gave rise to litigation which was still continuing under the Consulate.[83]

There was a further twist. In August 1786 the Compagnie des eaux had obtained an arrêt du conseil to set up a fire insurance company. Notwithstanding, the following November, Breteuil procured another arrêt giving the same rights to another company advocated by Clavière and backed by a syndicate of Swiss bankers under the protection of Breteuil's agent d'affaires, Jean, Baron de Batz. The new company had to deposit 8 million livres from the sale of its shares in the bureau of the hôtel de ville. It was seven months before the issue was subscribed, but this did not stop the company applying for another franchise, that of life assurance. The royal privilege for that had already been allocated to another company backed by Calonne's adviser, Panchaud. But after Calonne's fall, it was transferred to Breteuil's syndicate in return (in effect) for taking on the debts of the deceased estate of the Duc de Choiseul.[84]

It is not known whether Calonne and Breteuil had personal links with the rival companies they supported. Breteuil had started his career under the auspices of Choiseul, but the relation had cooled by 1775. The old story that the king had given Calonne 230,000 shares in the Compagnie des eaux to clear his debts seems absurd;[85] for one thing it implies that the king himself was speculating in the shares. However, the princely, grand seigneurial and banking magnates, who were rebuilding Paris in a speculative boom supported directly or indirectly by the government, had links with Calonne and Breteuil. The ubiquitous Bourgade, for example, was responsible for developing the Chaussée d'Antin complex, while Breteuil had obligations to the Duc d'Orléans who had embarked on the commercial exploitation of the Palais-Royal. The Abbé de Breteuil had been the chancellor of the late duc (the father of Égalité) and had left our minister the Pavillon du Mail in the grounds of Saint-Cloud.[86] These examples were probably only the tip of the iceberg.

Breteuil's associates, Étienne Clavière, the future Girondin finance

82 Castries, *Journal*, entry for 1 April 1786.
83 Lüthy, *Banque Protestante*, 710–11.
84 ibid., 711–13.
85 Originating with Auget de Montyon, *Particularités sur les ministres des finances les plus célèbres*, 1812, 279; Lüthy gives it credence, *Banque Protestante*, II, 694.
86 ibid., 697.

minister, and the Baron de Batz, more famous as the counter-revolutionary conspirator, made their everyday living as bear speculators on the Bourse. After the convocation of the Notables (concerning which he had not been consulted), it occurred to Breteuil that the way he could do Calonne maximum damage was to give this bear syndicate every encouragement as a way of undermining royal credit and therefore Calonne's position during the critical period of the meeting of the Assembly. Calonne more than rose to the challenge. By the judicious (or possibly injudicious) use of the 12 million livres Calonne gave them, a bull syndicate headed by the Abbé d'Espagnac bought up on the futures market all the shares in the Compagnie des Indes and operated a 'bear squeeze' on Breteuil's group. Mirabeau and Clavière, renegades from Calonne's 'think-tank', cried foul; perhaps the ensuing outcry was just what Breteuil wanted. Calonne's only too successful coup de Bourse did him damage, though his departure made this and other problems he left behind insoluble.

Calonne's 12 million had been entrusted to what Lüthy terms 'a band of shady speculators for the most part sprung from the stables of the Comte d'Artois':[87] the relationship between Calonne and the prince throws light – and not always a shady light – on many aspects of Calonne's ministry.

Calonne got to know Artois through the Polignac group and in particular through Artois's best friend, the Comte de Vaudreuil, who was appointed governor of the citadel of Lille, the seat of Calonne's intendancy, in 1780. Vaudreuil was a sailor and in 1782 after the Battle of the Saints led a brilliant retreat which restricted the losses to 24 million livres' worth of ships. As most of his property was in the West Indies, Vaudreuil received no income during the war and obtained a pension for the duration, which was not unduly generous, considering how much money his exploit had saved. Calonne became close to two other members of the Polignac group, the Prince and Princesse de Robecq. As commandant-en-chef of Flanders, the prince ran the province in conjunction with the intendant. The princesse corresponded with Calonne in exile,[88] with no ulterior motive, or no political one, since Louis XVI did not permit 'comebacks' to the ministry.

Artois and particularly his treasurer Bourboulon were active in the campaign against Necker in the last year of his ministry. Necker had damaged Artois's financial interests by suppressing the receveurs-généraux in his independent estates (*appanage*). In 1780 a pamphlet appeared with the title *lettre de M. Turgot à M. Necker*; it attacked Necker's suppression of offices of la finance and Bachaumont noted: 'It appears certain that the pamphlet against M. Necker was written under the auspices of the Comte d'Artois, who had it printed at the

87 Lüthy, *Banque Protestante*, II, 627.
88 See P.R.O. P.C. 1/125.103 and A.N. 297 A.P. 3. 114.

Temple and on the day it came out, His Royal Highness himself distributed it.'[89] In 1781 Bourboulon published his *Réponse au conte bleu*, and, alone of the pamphleteers, acknowledged his work. Necker demanded to have a disputation with Bourboulon before a comité of the council; this meeting may or may not have taken place. Calonne's 1781 pamphlets cite Bourboulon with approval. But it is unlikely that there was any liaison. Indeed a solecism in Calonne's *Lettre . . . à d'Alembert* suggests that at this date Calonne was somewhat hazy about the structure of the queen's société intime. For he believed that Adhémar, one of the group for whom Vergennes later procured the London embassy, was defending Necker with the queen.[90] An independent identity of views between Calonne and Artois can be assumed. Was it, on Artois's part, based on any more than his financial needs?

It is well known that on 28 December 1783, a month after Calonne's appointment, the trésor royal undertook to service Artois's debts of 14 million. Under Calonne's predecessors, he had merely been authorized to issue rentes against his appanage. Artois's appanage was tiny in comparison with that which previous brothers of the kings had received, in particular in comparison with the last one to have been instituted, that of the Duc d'Orléans, brother to Louis XIV. Artois had received only 150,000 livres by 1783;[91] he had, as Necker conceded in 1790, been put in charge of a large household at the age of 16;[92] he had been systematically robbed by his surintendant, Radix de Saint-Foix, and sooner or later his affairs had to be put on a satisfactory basis. Harris, brought up in a republican tradition, has not the remotest idea what the Comte d'Artois was 'for'. 'Where', he asks, 'did the money go? The household existed only to maintain the prince in a "state of splendour" befitting the youngest brother of the king; it provided no other useful function for the state or the taxpayers'.[93] There is no arguing with this view, based as it is on a rejection of an assumption of ancien régime society which even the Revolution accepted when it accorded the king a civil list large enough to maintain his 'splendour'.[94]

Artois was not the only one bailed out by the government in the last years of the ancien régime, and some of the most striking examples occur outside the span of Calonne's ministry. We have mentioned the concealed subsidy to Choiseul's heirs (1788). But the start of the sequence of *échanges*, which Calonne may be said to have perfected, antedates his ministry. In a typical échange, a private family sold the

89 Bachaumont, *Mémoires secrètes*, XV, 153–4, cited in Harris, *Necker*, 198.
90 Calonne, *Lettre . . . à d'Alembert*, 15.
91 R. Lacour-Gayet, *Calonne*, 1962, 96.
92 Harris, *Necker*, 195.
93 ibid., 197.
94 For a discussion of such assumptions see N. Elias, *La société de la cour*, Flammarion, 1969.

crown, at an inflated rate, an estate or seigneurial rights pertaining to one. This was the essence of Vergennes's sale of his regalian rights to the crown in 1783. In that year also the Rohan sold their seigneurial rights over l'Orient in Brittany to the crown so that it could be made into one of the free ports set up to trade with the United States. The minutes of the comité des finances make it clear that this was to help the family to get over the spectacular bankruptcy of the Prince de Rohan-Guéméné in 1781.[95]

Lüthy argues that the great court families were at the apex of the constituted society of the ancien régime. Just, he might have said, as Saint-Just was to argue that the nobility were outside the 'sovereign', so before the Revolution the noble landowners alone constituted the sovereign, and the government could not let its leading representatives go under. Louis XVI, one might add, did not entirely agree with this view and this perhaps is why he was unpopular with his courtiers. Though he consented to give the Rohan some relief, he considered that they had been irredeemably dishonoured by their bankruptcy: the Princesse de Guéméné had to surrender her post of gouvernante to the royal children.

Be that as it may, the most interesting question in the relationship between Calonne and Artois is how to square their defence of the offices of la finance and Calonne's subsidies to the high nobility with the radical proposals of 1787: equal taxation of landed wealth made possible by assessment by provincial assemblies organized with regard not to rank but only to the amount of land owned. Having rewarded his backers, was he now about to make them foot the bill? Then again, is not the genuineness of the radical position of Calonne and Artois in 1787 put into question by their subsequent position at the head of the counter-revolution? The depth, even (dare one say of one who was not a great thinker) the ideological depth, of Artois's support for Calonne's 1787 programme is revealed by an examination of the debates of the bureau in the Assembly of Notables over which he presided. Indeed, in these debates, Artois displays a certain brutality towards the nobility. When someone observed that it might arise that there were no nobles in the area of a district assembly, Artois interjected: 'if we reserve the presidency for them, they will crawl out from under the stones!' When the Duc de Guines said that often a provincial nobleman had exhausted his patrimony in the service of the king and it would be nice if he could count his military pension as the equivalent of landed property, Artois replied, somewhat brutally, 'The situation of these worthy soldiers is very unfortunate but having dissipated their own properties [Artois could talk!] is hardly a qualification for administering other people's'. Again, over the

---

95 A.N 144 A.P. 131, 14th and 15th meetings of the comité; see Price, 'Vergennes and Breteuil', 313–16.

presidency of the provincial assemblies, he says, 'It is a question of the happiness of everyone and it is just that all should be able to claim to contribute to it'.[96]

In 1788 and 1789, both Artois and Calonne were to defend the consistency of their position, and with some success. At the time of the *Mémoire des princes* of December 1788, Artois claimed, 'all that was at issue [in 1787] was repairing not destroying'.[97] While Calonne, who in 1781 had castigated Necker for 'insulting then despoiling' the financial officers, said in his *Lettre au roi* of 1789:

I have always shown the same way of thinking and I never proposed to you [the king] a single destruction; because that name should not be given to the proscription of pecuniary privileges, which are not rights.[98]

Only by abolishing tax exemption could the society which Calonne and Artois, Talleyrand and Joly de Fleury loved be preserved.

Calonne's fall entailed the fall of the contrôle-générale. Brienne's early policies were predicated on the assumption that Calonne had misappropriated vast sums of money – the difference between his, Calonne's, compte and that of the 'virtuous' Necker. Only thus could the constitutional scandal of the king's being forced to part with his favourite minister be masked. The new contrôleur, Laurent de Villedeuil, was Brienne's subordinate and Brienne took his position as chef du conseil royal des finances literally. He ascribed to the *désuétude* of the finance council many of the abuses of the preceding period. Vergennes's sale of regalian rights to the crown was singled out by him in a *Mémoire . . . concernant les finances*,[99] while Calonne's destruction of the comité des finances had, in his view, paved the way for Calonne's *gaspillages*.

Accordingly on 5 June 1787, the conseil royal was reconstituted; it was to meet once a month and to include, besides its chef, the contrôleur, the keeper of the seals, six ministres and two conseillers d'état. The finance ministry had become collegiate. In the preamble to the règlement setting up the conseil royal, the king was made to say:

His Majesty hopes to derive from the *consistance* and the energy he will impart to this council, the advantage of preserving himself from the errors, the 'surprises' [to his religion] and the inconsistencies to which a great department is exposed.

Despite the cant, the conseil royal removed all the obstacles which had lain in the path of our finance ministers. Most importantly, it fixed the budget of each department: 'The reform was necessary', wrote one of the conseillers d'état attached to the conseil royal, 'and it was

96 Bibliothèque de l'Arsenal, MS 3978, 147, 148 and 34.
97 J. Hardman, *Louis XVI*, New Haven, Conn., 1993, 140.
98 C.A. de Calonne, *Lettre au Roi*, London, 1789, 106.
99 Calonne Papers, P.R.O. P.C. 1/125. 276.

necessary to adopt drastic measures'.[100] In March 1788 a global budget was published; the departments lost their separate treasuries when they were all amalgamated into a central one.[101] In this way both the power and the frustrations of the contrôleur-général came to an end.

---

100 Vidaud de la Tour to his mother, 9 June 1787, quoted in J. Egret, *La Pre-Révolution française*, 1962, 105.
101 ibid., 104–6.

CHAPTER EIGHT

Decision-making:
councils, comités and conférences

When seeking advice of more than one person, a prince who is not himself wise will never get unanimity in his councils or be able to reconcile their views.

(Machiavelli, *The Prince*)

THE COUNCILS OF NECKER'S SECOND MINISTRY, 1788–9

The procedure for decision-making was in theory straightforward: the king assembled his council and asked his ministers for their individual opinions; a vote was taken and the king abided by the majority decision. If there was a tie, he had the casting vote. Two of the most famous decisions of the reign were indeed taken in this way. However, these are confined to the period of Necker's second ministry (August 1788 to July 1789) and the procedure was dictated both by the gravity of the crisis and the predilections of the minister, who had always set great store by being a ministre and intended to use the council once he had secured entry by becoming one. The first of these decisions related to the representation of the third estate in the forthcoming Estates-General and was embodied in the résultat du conseil of 27 December 1788; the second, relating to the question of royal intervention in the proceedings of the Estates-General/National Assembly, culminated in the séance royale of 23 June 1789.

The background to the decisions embodied in the résultat du conseil is well known. The parlement, restored unconditionally by Necker after the fall of Brienne, had implied by its declaration of 25 September that the representation of the third estate should be based on that obtaining when the Estates had last met in 1614. Necker had sought a second opinion from the Assembly of Notables, which sat again from 6 November until 12 December. Six out of the Notables' seven committees, however, also rejected double representation for the third estate. The memorandum of the princes of the blood had pronounced in a similar sense. The king and Necker favoured doublement, though with some misgiving, the former having been stung by the révolte nobiliaire, the latter worried by the fall of royal stocks on the Bourse which had followed the publication of the *Mémoire des princes*. To go against these weighty pronouncements and also to quell their own doubts they needed all the formality that the council could muster.

Lenoir accused the king of 'despotically' overriding the majority opinion of the council when he pronounced in favour of doublement at the end of the conseil des dépêches.[1] This is strictly incorrect. There were nine ministers present – Necker, Barentin, the keeper of the seals and the four secretaries of state, Montmorin (foreign affairs), Laurent de Villedeuil (maison), Puységur (war) and La Luzerne (marine) – and three ministers-without-portfolio, the Duc de Nivernais, Saint-Priest and Bouvard de Fourqueux. Malesherbes had ceased attending the council some time in the autumn, probably after the fall of Brienne and his cousin Lamoignon. Of these ministers, according to Necker, the basic disposition was eight to one in favour of doublement. Even his principal antagonist, Barentin, who favoured fobbing off the larger towns with some additional seats, concedes that the split was five to four.[2]

Lenoir would have been on surer ground if he had merely accused the king of exploiting the procedures of the council to get the result he desired. As before the convocation of the Notables, the preparatory work was given to a comité of ministers whose views were presumed to be similar to those of the king who presided, that is Necker and his principal supporter, Montmorin. On this occasion, however, the conseil des dépêches was not presented with a fait accompli; instead there was a further series of comités consisting of the king, Necker and Barentin as the two protagonists and two further ministers, each time different, that is twenty pairs, in sessions lasting four or five hours each. Finally the king held a double session of the conseil des dépêches at which he kept taking votes until a consensus had emerged in favour of doublement. The style résultat rather than the more usual arrêt du conseil conveys this emergence of a conclusion. The king did not reveal his hand (apart from not being satisfied with the first vote) but the presence of the queen, who was known to favour doublement, applied pressure. Marie-Antoinette had attended the ministerial comité which sent Rohan before the parlement and had attended them regularly in Brienne's time, but this was the first – and last – time she attended the conseil d'état. In the course of the

1 Lenoir Papers, Bibliothèque municipale d'Orléans, MSS 1421–3, 1423, résidus, 122.
2 Barentin, *Mémoire autographe sur les derniers conseils du Roi Louis XVI*, ed. M. Champion, 1844, 87 ff.

discussion, according to Barentin, several ministers changed their minds: Nivernais moved from being an opponent of doublement to not giving an opinion; Puységur wobbled. Only Laurent de Villedeuil stuck to his guns.

Nevertheless the week-long debate reflected the fact that the ministry was more divided than it had ever been except perhaps at the beginning of the reign during the period of cohabitation between Maurepas and Louis XV's old ministers. The issue of the representation of the third estate cut across existing divisions and would have been difficult to predict at the time of individual ministers' appointment or in terms of their social and career categories. Those initially opposed to the claims of the *tiers* were Barentin, Nivernais, Puységur and Laurent de Villedeuil. Barentin's promotion from the cour des aides coincided with the triumphant return of the parlement and their pronouncement on the Estates. The opinion of this former protégé of Miromesnil's would have been the easiest to predict. Nivernais had given few guides to his future conduct, except perhaps that he had been one of the twelve peers who had protested against the Maupeou coup and as an avid supporter of the parlement, Maurepas had been unable to get him the ministry of foreign affairs. Puységur, a military man whom Maurepas had wanted to succeed Montbarey, had strong views on nothing but the efficacy of Mesmerism: his two-volume work *Mémoires pour servir à l'histoire du magnétisme animal* appeared in 1784–5.

The most interesting case is that of Laurent de Villedeuil, an ex-intendant and virtually the last defender of the old administrative monarchy. He voted against doublement but that was not the ground on which he would have chosen to fight. He would have preferred to cancel the meeting of the Estates altogether on the grounds of general unrest and convoke 'une Assemblée de la Nation sans distinction des ordres' to deal exclusively with the financial crisis. Such an assembly would have been similar to the one advocated by Brienne and Malesherbes, with the important distinction that whereas theirs would have been elected by the provincial assemblies, Villedeuil's would have been nominated by the king, like an Assembly of Notables.

The résultat papered over the cracks, but they reappeared along the same fault-line over the coming six months. Moreover, Necker's opponents occupied the key ministries apart from his own and their importance was further enhanced by the peculiar circumstances of the crisis: Barentin, as keeper of the seals, had special responsibility for the conduct of the Estates-General; Villedeuil had responsibility for the maintenance of order in the capital, while a general insurrection would call on the services of Puységur. Throughout the summer of 1789 these men pressed the king to intervene in the proceedings of the Estates-General. Even old Nivernais asked the king at the beginning of June to intervene; Necker, who was 'unexpectedly' present, told him it was 'still too early'.[3] When Necker finally did decide that it was time, another debate took place to determine the form this séance royale should take.

This debate took as long as the previous one. Necker adumbrated his proposal for a séance royale to the conseil des dépêches on 17 June; this was followed by two meetings of the council at Marly (on 19 and 20 June) and two more at Versailles on 21 and 22 June at which the programme for intervention in the dispute between the orders emerged in its final, perverted form. Death played its part; that of the dauphin, which enabled the Artois-Polignac faction to persuade the king to retire to Marly, where conditions were less formal and ministers did not have automatic right of access to the king; and that of Necker's sister-in-law, which caused him to miss the crucial second meeting of the council at Marly (on the 20 June). Proceedings were less regular than those of the previous December. True, Marie-Antoinette did not actually attend any of the meetings. However, having moved away from supporting the third estate, she attempted to dissuade Necker from reading his rapport to the council at Marly on 19 June. This proposed a compromise whereby matters of general interest, including the organization of future Estates, would be decided by voting in common but matters relating specifically to the nobility (e.g. feudal dues) and those to the clergy (e.g. tithes) would be decided by voting by order. Having failed to alter the agenda of the meeting, Marie-Antoinette interrupted it when, according to Necker, the king was about to adopt his conclusions. An official in attendance entered and whispered something to the king, who adjourned the decision till the next day. 'We are undone', Montmorin whispered to Necker, 'only the queen could have permitted herself to interrupt a meeting of the conseil d'état'.[4]

The absence of Marie-Antoinette, however, was more than made up for by the presence (at the second council at Marly) of the king's brothers Provence and Artois. Otherwise the personnel was as in December, except that Nivernais, residing at Saint-Omer, was to travel in only 'if his health permitted'.[5] He had recently ceased attending the council after his advice that the keeper of the seals should perform the 'vérification des pouvoirs' before the opening of the Estates had been rejected.[6] Symbolically, Necker's ministerial allies Montmorin, La Luzerne and Saint-Priest travelled with him to the first council at Marly in the same coach. Bouvard, another ally, travelled separately. In a memorandum to the king, Saint-Priest made the point that these five were the only ministres d'état, which was scarcely relevant because the

3 États-généraux, recueil de documents relatifs au états-généraux de 1789, ed. G. Lefebure, 1953–70, 4 vols, I (2), 48.
4 J. Necker, De la Révolution française, 1797, 253.
5 Barentin, Lettres et bulletins à Louis XVI, ed. A. Aulard, 1915, 34.
6 Études biographiques (Saint-Priest), 219.

discussions took place in the conseil des dépêches, not the conseil d'état.

Unable to go to Marly on 20 June and sensing that his opponents would turn the séance royale to their own purposes, Necker sent an urgent letter to the king:

Several drawbacks to a séance royale which I had missed have been pointed out to me, and it is thought that a simple letter of invitation [to the orders] would serve better.[7]

To an extent, Necker's fears were justified. The substantive changes made at the second council at Marly were not great but they tipped the balance in Necker's proposals against the tiers. According to Barentin there were four differences. First, Necker wanted the king to *order* the nobility and clergy to join the tiers, whereas Barentin thought that this was beyond the king's authority; curiously, though, Necker's note of the 20 June mentions 'a simple letter of *invitation*'. Second, Necker wanted to pass over in silence the declaration of a National Assembly and the Tennis Court Oath whereas the séance royale actually annulled them. Third, although in the séance voting in common was retained for matters of general interest this was re-defined to exclude the organization of future Estates. Fourth, Necker's article proposing the 'carrière ouverte aux talents' in the army was omitted, not because Barentin disagreed with its principles but because, as the war minister Puységur observed, the king did not need to consult the Estates about the fate of 'le règlement du Maréchal de Ségur'. In the second part of the programme presented at the séance, the déclaration des intentions du roi, the only difference was that whereas Necker wanted to *order* the ending of fiscal privilege, Barentin maintained that this was inappropriate since the first two orders had already expressed their readiness to renounce these, waiting only for their chambers to be formally constituted.[8]

Two further meetings of the council were held at Versailles on 21 and 22 June to finalize the details. The presence once again of Artois and Provence on 21 June convinced Necker that the battle was lost. Nevertheless, the king was still sufficiently undecided to ask Saint-Priest and Montmorin for their views in writing before the meeting on 22 June in the knowledge that they would favour Necker's proposals. However, the honest pessimism with which Saint-Priest concluded his eloquent memorandum may have persuaded the king that there was little to be gained by adopting Necker's plans:

I fear that the third estate in its present state of exaltation will reject those absolutely just restrictions to be imposed on deliberating in common. I even

7 A.N. K163 dossier 13. 1.
8 Barentin, *Mémoire autographe*, 196–9.

fear that they will complain about the sovereign intervention of Your Majesty at this juncture.[9]

If Saint-Priest was right, then the decision was not of the crucial importance usually supposed: Necker's and Barentin's proposals represented merely the obverse and reverse of a coin which the National Assembly no longer regarded as legal tender. Nevertheless, it was a bad decision, and one influenced by the irregular way in which it had been arrived at: the king cut off from his official advisers, the ministers; the council overawed by members of the royal family. If the discussions leading to the résultat were a caricature of the conciliar ideal, those leading to the séance were a corruption. The exotic final flowering of conciliar decision-making at the end of the ancien régime was what one might have expected from an organism given sudden exposure to light after years in the dark.

THE CONSEIL D'ÉTAT AND FOREIGN POLICY

The reasons for this eclipse relate to the particular circumstances of the beginning of the reign. Maurepas had been summoned to be the new king's informal adviser. At the same time Louis XVI had retained all his grandfather's ministers: the last of them, La Vrillière, did not go until July 1775. That this was likely in itself to lead to conflict should perhaps have been foreseen by Louis. What, however, he could not have foreseen was that Maurepas intended to reverse the event upon which the policies of the old ministry were predicated: the Maupeou coup d'état. Consequently, until Maurepas had winkled out Louis XV's ministers, there was no question of the council deciding much, as a glance at the composition of the conseil d'état in July 1774 may serve to demonstrate (under Louis XVI the conseil d'en haut for foreign policy was simply referred to as the conseil d'état). D'Aiguillon had been dismissed, but Vergennes, his successor as foreign secretary, had not yet returned from Stockholm; Maurepas, a ministre since 1738, returned to the conseil, where he encountered Terray, Bourgeois de Boynes and his Phélypeaux cousin, La Vrillière; there was also the Maréchal-Duc de Rohan-Soubise, the vanquished of Rossbach, but the personal friend of Louis XV. Louis XVI retained Soubise for twelve years out of respect for the memory of the old king until the Diamond Necklace Affair caused him to turn against the whole Rohan clan.

The slow procedure for entry and exit from the conseil d'état meant that Maurepas had no desire to consult a body which the 'old gang' could still dominate. Once the ministry had been renewed with

9 A.N. K679 no. 86 (Saint-Priest) and 87–8 (Montmorin).

Maurepas's creatures, the conseil d'état continued to take foreign policy decisions for about two years, that is until the approach of the American War. Sometimes a degree of formality enabled a minister to share responsibility for a difficult decision with his colleagues and this was the main appeal of using the conseil d'état for Vergennes. Thus in February 1776 he read out the intercepted dispatch implicating Guines, though typically, the king partially neutralized the effectiveness of this by pocketing the evidence at the end of the meeting and ignoring the minister's ceremonious hints that he should return it. Vergennes, however, would not accede to Guines's request that the publication of other papers relating to the affair be discussed in council, 'Since Your Majesty does not want the requests of his ambassadors to be placed under the eyes of the council'.[10]

With the approach of the American War, the conseil's role was reduced to a largely formal one. Thus the arrangements with Beaumarchais to subsidize the American colonists were conducted by Vergennes and the king personally. Vergennes's first letter to the king on the subject is dated 2 May 1776;[11] thereafter, the king took charge of the arrangements. Indeed Véri claims that Louis had instructed Beaumarchais to negotiate with the Americans without consulting his ministers, 'or if he did consult them, they are denying it now'.[12] Either way, obviously these crucial negotiations were too secret to be trusted to the conseil. A debate did rage between the ministers about the desirability of entering the war, Vergennes and Sartine being in favour, Montbarey, the war minister, disinterestedly against, Maurepas and the king undecided, but how much of this took place in the conseil d'état is not known.[13] Vergennes gives the following account of how the crucial decision to enter the war without having secured Spanish participation was taken:

First of all we [Vergennes and d'Ossun, the former ambassador to Spain] talked it over together and then with M. le Comte de Maurepas. Next the King heard my personal report, kept the documents and examined the pros and cons. Since [Maurepas] had an attack of gout at this juncture, His Majesty went to his apartments yesterday, M. d'Ossun and myself being also present. The matter was discussed again afresh and minutely debated etc.[14]

Once war had been properly joined, reasons of security meant that there was no question of the conseil having more than a formal role. In 1779, Vergennes told Véri:

10 A.N. K164 no. 3, 1775 no. 5, Vergennes to the king, 23 February (draft).
11 A.N. K164 no. 3, 1776 no. 9.
12 Abbé de Véri, *Journal 1774–80*, ed. J. de Witte, 1928–30, 2 vols, II, 47.
13 J. Hardman, 'Ministerial politics from the accession of Louis XVI to the Assembly of Notables', DPhil thesis, Oxford University, 1972, 195–6.
14 A.A.E. Espagne, vol. 588 no. 11, quoted in H. Doniol, *Histoire de la participation de la France à l'établissment des États-Unis d'Amérique*, 1886–, 5 vols, II, 736–7.

I haven't brought anything secret there since I've been badly caught out several times.[15]

When d'Ossun himself was made a ministre, Véri was scandalized:

I know that an extra seat in the council (such as it is at present) is of no significance. But it is bad for the state that it should be all one whether one appoints an able man or a fool.[16]

Entry to the council had become just another piece of patronage.

That, however, was not quite the end of the story. After the débâcle of the comité des finances, Calonne and Breteuil, still in alliance, sought to force a weakened Vergennes to bring all major foreign-policy decisions before the conseil d'état. This did happen. Castries, who was a ministre, notes in 1784 that the council started discussing matters of substance. However, he also finds Vergennes seeking to use the council to his political advantage. On 18 July he read out a dispatch from d'Adhémar, who in gratitude for the London embassy that Vergennes had procured for him, reported that the English court was worried that Vergennes had lost 'credit'. But the council greeted the news with embarrassed silence. Again, the previous June, the king had asked each ministre for a memorandum on Austro-Russian relations with Turkey but, as Castries correctly guessed, this was because Vergennes did not want to take sole blame from the queen for an anti-Austrian stance.[17] In 1784, the tactic was repeated: on 6 November Louis tells Vergennes: 'You will do well to communicate your important note on the present crisis to each of the other ministres in order to have their advice as we did last year'.[18]

Thus the underlying reason for the revival of the conseil d'état may have been the family politics of the king rather than ministerial politics. Marie-Antoinette was badgering him to support her brother Joseph II in his dispute with the United Provinces and over the Bavarian Exchange. Earlier in his reign, Louis would simply have ignored Marie-Antoinette's clumsy attempts to influence high politics. Now, with the birth of the dauphin in 1781 and with the queen possessing her own ministers, notably Breteuil, he had to adopt a different tactic: strengthening his hand with the written opinions of the ministres. This was done with some subtlety and the stratagem was assisted by Breteuil's peculiar position as a former member of the secret du roi. The council cynically concluded that they would consent to the exchange on the impossible condition that Frederick the Great agreed also.[19] It is likely that this use of the conseil d'état continued to

15 Véri, *Journal*, II, 201.
16 Véri, *Journal*, II, 44.
17 Castries, *Journal*, Archives de la Marine, MS 182/7964 1–2, II, fos 191, 242 and 252.
18 Archives de Vergennes, *Lettres de Louis XVI*.
19 A.N. K164 no. 3 1784 nos. 3 (Breteuil), 4 and 5 (the opinions of the ministres); ibid., 1785 no. 1; Louis XVI to Joseph II, 6 January 1785, quoted in A. d'Arneth, *Marie-Antoinette, Joseph II und Leopold II*, 2nd edn, Vienna, 1866, 65–8; Castries, *Journal*, II, fo. 191.

be exceptional, though Louis remembered the tactic in 1792 when he insisted on the individual written advice of the Girondin ministers before he declared war on Austria.[20]

THE USE OF COMITÉS

The history of the conseil des dépêches dealing with home affairs pursued a rather different course. Louis XV's old ministers also dominated that body in 1774 and home affairs, that is the question of the parlement, were Maurepas's immediate priority. Consequently, politics led to an important institutional change: the transference of decision-making from the council to *comités restreints*. Under Louis XV comités had prepared work for the council but that body had taken the decision.[21] Maurepas's task was probably made easier by the fact that Louis XV had not summoned his grandson to the council, so that he knew little of its importance or its functioning. Moreover those early meetings must have been stilted affairs since the burning issue, the question of the parlement, was, as Alsace-Lorraine was later to be, 'in everyone's heart but on nobody's lips'.

As a result of Maurepas's arrangements, therefore, the conseil des dépêches' role in policy-making became largely formal, or an aspect of public relations. Thus on 17 January 1786, Miromesnil wrote to the king in connection with a jurisdictional dispute with the parlement over the Lemaitre affair:

In accordance with the views which Your Majesty expressed to me on Sunday morning. . . . I wrote the draft arrêt du conseil which I had the honour of sending to Your Majesty.

Should you approve it I will have the honour of expounding the matter to you in the next conseil des dépêches and of proposing this arrêt. The fact that it has been given by Your Majesty in your council will remove the impression of haste or of being suggested by me alone.[22]

Véri's first reference to the use of comités was 14 August, though they had been in existence long enough for the public to make 'a hundred conjectures about this new procedure'.[23] Maurepas met the complaints of the excluded ministers with a circular letter telling them 'I cannot teach a young man his métier of king in councils of eight to ten people where everyone gives his opinion in order of rank and often *extempore* without having been notified of the subject', and concluding disingenuously,

20 J. Hardman, *Louis XVI*, New Haven, Conn., 1993, 215.
21 M. Antoine, 'Les Comités des ministres sous Louis XV', *Revue Historique de Droit français et étranger*, 1951, 228.
22 A.N. K163 no. 8, 8.
23 Véri, *Journal*, I, 170.

I am not claiming that comités should take all the decisions. Their results are often taken either to the conseil d'état or the conseil des dépêches to receive their final forms, because I have no desire to deprive any member of the ministry of the consideration which is his due.[24]

Though Maurepas's motives were largely political, the practical considerations he sets forth in his circular were not without point. Meetings of the council not only were formal, but also had become formalized. Ministres delivered their opinions in order of a rank derived from a combination of the precedence of the post they occupied and their personal seniority as a ministre. Thus Joly de Fleury could inform the king that the chef du conseil's rank came after the chancellor's in the conseil royal but in the other councils 'he only had his rank based on seniority'.[25] By the time Joly made these observations in 1783 his points were largely academic but Maurepas, who had made them so, as a young ministre could remember heated debates on the subject.[26]

The ministerial opinions tended either to be delivered extempore or to be the subject of elaborate preparation; they did not lead to a general conversation or even to a formal debate. The surviving memoranda, as those for the 1784 Dutch crisis, in a sense constitute the minutes of the council, provided they are arranged in order of precedence. In his circular on comités, Maurepas seems to be unfamiliar with the concept or pattern of a debate, to be labouring to describe what a general discussion might be, as if having witnessed one for the first time: 'comités are lost conversations in which the right to speak comes and goes as the other participants see fit' – a sign perhaps that he is innovating. One can see why Maurepas did not consider that meetings of the council would help him to teach the young king his métier; they do not teach historians much about decision-making either. And though the minutes of the comités would, none were taken, since they were, as defined by Maurepas, 'conversations perdues'.

Maurepas's real objections to the council, however, were largely political. Véri transcribes the above circular letter in his diary entry for 14 September, that is after the fall of Maupeou and Terray, special circumstances continuing to make Maurepas disinclined to use the council. For two of the new ministers, Vergennes and du Muy, the king's personal appointments, did not see why Maupeou's reforms should not survive the fall of their author. Ordinarily, this would not have mattered: they would have been outvoted in the council and the king would have gone along with the majority decision. However, for

24 ibid., 188.
25 B.N. fonds Joly de Fleury, 1442 fo. 9.
26 See e.g. Duc de Luynes, *Mémoires sur la cour de Louis XV, 1735–58*, ed. Dussieux and Soulié, 1860–5, 17 vols; I, 187–8.

this particular operation, the restoration of the parlement, the king's passive acceptance was not sufficient. It was necessary, as Véri puts it, that the king 'should be made to regard the plan that has been decided as his own and to be able to spread this idea among the public'. 'The important point is that the decision should spring from his mind and not from the council of his ministers'. Since this was literally not the case it was essential that the task of re-education should be conducted by a unified comité. It consisted of Maurepas, Miromesnil, Turgot and Sartine and achieved its purpose to the extent that the king did not apppear to recite his lines like an automaton at the lit de justice of 13 November.[27]

By the time the lit took place on 13 November, government by comité was firmly established. It was easily grafted on to the procedure of Maurepas's sitting in on a minister's travail with the king. Indeed at times the two were indistinguishable: his attendance on Necker's travail constituted the finance comité, and on Vergennes's that for foreign policy. With the creation of the 'ministère harmonieux', membership of comités was decided along functional rather than political lines. However, the presence of Necker, who was never fully accepted by his colleagues, ensured that these should be narrrowly drawn. Necker complained at his exclusion from all but the comités dealing specifically with raising money. Vergennes, in particular, who suspected Necker of being in treasonable correspondence with England, was careful to exclude him from the war cabinet, which consisted of Maurepas, Vergennes and Sartine. In a conversation with Vergennes in February 1779, Véri, while applauding the use of comités 'where you only invite people who are necessary, maintain secrecy and are united', added, inconsequentially, 'but I regret not seeing the man of finance present'. Vergennes conceded that Necker would be less troublesome if he had helped to make the policy he was asked to finance and this over-exclusivity led to the ministerial crisis of 1780, culminating in the fall of Sartine and Montbarey.

Comités, then, were presided over by the king but differed from councils in being restricted in numbers and ad hoc – the king would assemble a comité or a minister would ask the king for one – whereas the conseil d'état met regularly on Sundays and Wednesdays and the conseil des dépêches on Tuesdays and Saturdays. The only recorded instance of Louis XVI not presiding over what was termed a comité was a continuation in his absence of the extraordinary session of the conseil d'état which discussed relations with Austria in November 1784: on the 12th, Vergennes wrote to the king: 'I have the honour of sending Your Majesty the draft of the Declaration to be made to the Emperor which was drawn up yesterday in a committee [sic] in which all the members of your council took part'. The king then made

27 Véri, *Journal*, I, 204–5.

several changes to the text.[28] Louis XV had not presided over ministerial comités. They were instituted by Cardinal Fleury after Chauvelin's disgrâce, to provide the function of liaison that the disgraced minister had fulfilled. In 1747 Louis XV, feeling that they could threaten his independence of action, stipulated that these ministerial comités, still held in his absence, could convene only on his orders. In 1755, one such, called a comité secret, met to discuss the 'renversement des alliances'.[29]

Under Louis XVI, in contrast, when small groups of ministers met among themselves or with the parti ministériel of the Paris parlement (or its provincial equivalents) or with the representatives of France's Dutch or Austrian allies, the gathering was distinguished from the comité, where the king presided, by being called a conférence. Thus on 28 December 1786, Miromesnil wrote to the king:

All these crucial matters [relating to the forthcoming Assembly of Notables] have only been treated very superficially in our conférences [i.e. of himself, Calonne and Vergennes] and very little in the comités where Your Majesty has been good enough to listen to us.[30]

In the period 1785–7, Miromesnil informs the king of twelve such conférences, either using the form 'j'ai conféré avec' or 'j'ai eu une conférence'.

To modern ears, the word 'conférence' connotes a grand, often formal, seldom useful and always well-attended function. There were only two conférences in our period which remotely approached this level. One was a marathon meeting on 25 July 1786 to sort out all the outstanding difficulties between the government and the parlement of Bordeaux: alluvial rights, payment in lieu of the corvée, internal disputes dating back to Maupeou's time, and so on.[31] Miromesnil tells the king:

After examining (in conformity with Your Majesty's orders) the registers and documents brought by the parlement of Bordeaux, I thought that it was necessary that M. le contrôleur-général should be informed of the results. Consequently I invited him together with M. de Vergennes to come to my place at 5.30 p.m.; also MM. de Sauvigny, de La Tour [conseillers d'état] and [representing the parlement of Bordeaux] MM. Le Berthon, Dudon and the Greffier. The first items were read out, M. le contrôleur-général conferred with M. Le Berthon and Dudon and discussed the most essential points very well. The conférence did not finish until nine o'clock.[32]

The other weighty conférence also involved Calonne speaking

28 Archives de Vergennes, *Lettres de Louis XVI.*
29 M. Antoine, *Louis XV*, 1989, 676.
30 A.N. K163 no. 8. 22.
31 W. Doyle, *The Parlement of Bordeaux and the End of the Old Regime, 1771–1790*, 1974, 260.
32 A.N. K163 no. 8. 12.

brilliantly but without total success over a period of hours: it was the 'Conférence chez Monsieur' of 2 March 1787 where he made a desperate effort to salvage his measures before representatives of the seven bureaux of the Assembly of Notables.

The other conférences were smaller affairs. Indeed, they sometimes involved just Miromesnil and the premier président of the parlement, d'Aligre. Usually, though, they were informal gatherings of ministers and usually, in the last years of the regime, the same three, Miromesnil, Vergennes and the contrôleurs-généraux, Joly, d'Ormesson and especially Calonne. The service ministers, Castries and Ségur, do not figure; nor perhaps would one expect them to in general operations of government, particularly after the conclusion of peace in 1783. Vergennes's correspondence with the king refers to conférences sparingly and then mostly with diplomatic representatives. This is simply because whereas the king never aimed to handle the technical details, say of relations with the parlements, he regarded foreign policy as his métier. The independent and often rival foreign policies of Castries and Breteuil, if they were fully recognized, were overlooked.

The frequent occurrence of the name of Calonne and the absence of Castries and Ségur can partly be explained in terms of their ministerial functions. However, it would be straining credulity to explain the omnipresence of Vergennes in terms of his responsibility (after 1780) for Bordeaux, which features heavily in Miromesnil's correspondence. No, he was there because he enjoyed the king's confidence and continued to have some extra-departmental role. If function were the main criterion, one would expect copious references to the minister for the maison, the proto-minister for the interior. Miromesnil does mention a conférence which included Breteuil to meet delegates from the parlement of Dijon in January 1787 but that is the extent of it.[33] Breteuil was considered by his colleagues to be incompetent. Moreover, Miromesnil talks quite openly to the king of 'the animosity which reigns between [Calonne] and M. de Breteuil', so cooperation with him would in any case have been difficult.

The divisions, however, were more than personal, more even than functional. During the six-year period between the death of Maurepas and the meeting of the Notables, the ministry was divided between on the one hand Maurepas's or the king's old robin appointees, Vergennes and Miromesnil, plus the contrôleur of the day, and on the other hand between the grand seigneurial newcomers Castries and Ségur plus, after 1783, Breteuil. All owed their appointment more or less to the queen, or at least looked to her for protection. This was clearly an important development: Maurepas must have turned in his grave. However, the queen's ministers could be ignored at least in the day-to-day running of the country; when the 'king's ministers' were

---

33 A.N. K163 no. 8. 25.

presided over by the king, it was as a comité de gouvernement that they sat. The comité des finances of 1783 was an attempt to formalize its role and subordinate the other ministers to it. It was also an attempt to provide the ensemble in government lacking because of the king's reluctance to appoint a prime minister; indeed Mercy-Argenteau thought that it 'could become a three-man prime minister'.

THE COMITÉ DES FINANCES

It is instructive to compare the comité des finances with another short-lived comité from the previous reign, devised by the foreign secretary, Bernis, in 1758. This also aimed to provide a 'centre' and thus obviate the problems caused by the king's reluctance to appoint a prime minister: Bernis actually called his comité a 'premier ministre collégial'. It was to consist of the personnel of the conseil d'en haut plus the contrôleur-général. Departmental ministers 'could not propose new expenditure without [its] consent'. During the second half of 1758 it met three times a week and submitted its proposals, decided by majority voting and signed by everyone, to the king for acceptance or refusal. The king did not attend the comité 'lest ministers conceal their real opinions'. The comité came to a singular end: in October Bernis's cardinal's hat came through and since precedence dictated that the meetings of the comité should be held in his apartments, he asked the king for more commodious ones: 'a cardinal-ministre hosting the comité', he told Madame de Pompadour, 'must be suitably accommodated'. Louis XV, however, already feeling that the comité was encroaching on his authority, exiled Bernis on grounds of ingratitude: 'I felt that you did not respond . . . to the extraordinary favours I have heaped upon you in so short a time'.

Nevertheless, the comité did have time to reveal the deplorable financial management of the marine. 'The ministers charged with this department', Bernis notes,

have for a long time decided everything in their travail with the king and always kept the king's council in the dark. . . . [Everyone in the comité] groaned at an administration so vicious on the financial side: no accountability, no order, lettres de change drawn on the treasury to pay expenditure whose amount is not finalized for many years afterwards.[34]

The debts for the marine from the Seven Years War were not liquidated until 1768. A similar task confronted the comité des finances of 1783.

Short though its life was, the comité des finances illustrates many of

34 Antoine, *Louis XV*, 745–50.

the themes of this study. Its objectives, as outlined by Joly de Fleury in his letter proposing it to the king, were straightforward:

Your Majesty can only . . . procure a real and lasting reduction in taxes for his subjects when he knows the size of previous debt and when he has definitively regulated the expenses of all the ordonnateurs on the basis of the most severe economy.[35]

Miromesnil claimed that the comité des finances was not 'concerned with criticism but with coordination'. Its members were not concerned with discovering how much had been spent during the late war in order to apportion blame (though its figures enable us to conclude that the American War had cost 850 million livres)[36] but with discovering the amount which was owed and whether it was 'constitué' or 'exigible', that is funded or not.

Nevertheless, the fact remains that the root of the problem lay in Castries's refusal to let Joly de Fleury 'definitively regulate' the expenses of his department even though he had been happy to let Necker do this. Joly told the king reasonably that the comité would want to know 'l'état des dépenses que [chaque ordonnateur] croirait nécessaire en temps de paix' but for several months Castries refused to give the comité this information; he is reported to have had the following conversation with the king:

'Your Majesty . . . led me to hope, some time ago, that I could present my accounts to the conseil d'état. I am now in a position to do so'. – 'Yes I consent to that: but first they must be brought before the comité'. – 'I have already represented to Your Majesty the disadvantages which can result from thus dividing your ministry, from rendering one portion of it subordinate to the other and the obstacles which your own authority could suffer in the departments that are entrusted to us. We should lose the respect of the soldiers under us'.[37]

If the comité had lasted it would, as Castries claimed, have led to the formal creation of two levels of minister and ended the autonomy of the travail.

Joly, however, also saw the comité as limiting the power of the finance minister himself. As a conseiller d'état, he had, in 1777, lamented the abeyance of the conseil royal des finances and the fact that arrêts nominally issued by that body were usually issued by the contrôleur or the weekly council of the intendants des finances, 'n'ayant aucune espèce de forme'.[38] This theme was stressed by Joly in

35 B.N. fonds Joly de Fleury, 2487 no. 139. For the definitive treatment of the comité des finances, see M. Price, 'Vergennes and Breteuil', Ph.D. thesis, Cambridge, 1988, 153–261.
36 Hardman, 'Ministerial politics', appendix 1.
37 Abbé de Véri, MSS *Journal*, Archives départementales de la Drôme, Valence, unclassified, cahier 114.
38 M. Antoine, 'Les Conseils des Finances sous le règne de Louis XV', *Revue d'Histoire Moderne et Contemporaine*, 1958, **5**: 161–200, esp. 198–200.

his letter to the king proposing the comité, which he liked to think of as a comité intérieur of the conseil royal, which had become 'trop nombreux' (in fact it had ceased to meet). The king also appeared to countenance this fiction; at least on 19 April he told Vergennes testily:

M. d'Ormesson hasn't asked me for a conseil royal [des finances] for this week . . . I don't know what's put this idea into his head except perhaps that they don't usually meet in Holy Week.[39]

In fact this council, which had 'become too congested' and 'didn't usually meet in Holy Week', had met only once in the entire reign, on 19 July 1774. Its meeting had been a ploy of Maurepas's to restrict Terray, who seemed to be gaining in the king's favour, though he gave as his motive 'the use of a council removes the shadow of despotism, that is to say the arbitrary decisions of one man'.[40]

Joly's actual motives were similar to Maurepas's avowed ones. By setting up the comité, Joly saw himself as divesting himself of a power which he as well as the public believed to be arbitrary. Thus d'Ormesson's travail with the king would be reduced to a report on the state of the trésor royal. Joly believed that the new formality would reassure the public,[41] whom Besenval considered 'thereby safeguarded from a contrôleur-général and the often faulty calculations of one man'.[42]

The comité was the only decision-making body of the reign to keep minutes. Joly de Fleury, the antiquarian who spent the first session examining the archives of Louis XIV's conseil royal des finances, saw to that. The *procès-verbal*, duly signed by the king, has survived in d'Ormesson's papers.[43] However, it is not an exciting survival: there is very little discussion and normally the contrôleur-rapporteur's proposals were automatically adopted in the form: 'Le Roy a marqua . . . sa satisfaction'; or 'le Roy ordonne'; or 'le Roy a annoncé que M. de Castries devoit remettre incessament à Sa Majesté les états [de son département]', etc. If there were arguments between the members of the comité des finances, the comité was the last place where they were resolved. Vergennes refused to let his differences with d'Ormesson over the sale of his regalian rights to the crown be thrashed out before the king in the comité, though Miromesnil assured d'Ormesson that this was the correct procedure.[44] Similarly the drama concerning the lease of the farm was not played out before the members of the comité. Rather it was when the king declined to give d'Ormesson (as Joly before him) a date for the next comité that he knew that his ministerial days were numbered.

39 Archives de Vergennes, *Lettres de Louis XVI*.
40 Véri, *Journal*, I, 134.
41 B.N. fonds Joly de Fleury, 2487 no. 139.
42 Baron de Besenval, *Mémoires*, ed. Berville and Barrière, 1821, 2 vols, II, 121.
43 A.N. 144 A.P. 131 dossier 5.
44 D'Ormesson, A.N. 144 A.P. 130, *Journal*, section 44.

The débâcle of the operation concerning the farm and d'Ormesson's allegations led to the collapse of the comité, though it had succeeded in its original purpose of making the ordonnateurs submit their accounts, Ségur submitting his on 31 May and Castries on 6 June. Nevertheless, the comité des finances never formally decided the peacetime establishment of the marine, though d'Ormesson was ready to present this at the time of his fall. The new contrôleur, Calonne, took advantage of the diminished prestige of Vergennes to reassert the independence of the contrôle. In his *visite de début* he informed Castries and Ségur that the comité was over.[45]

THE COMITÉ DE GOUVERNEMENT, 1783–7

Nevertheless, in the remaining four years during which the ancien régime functioned normally, that is until 1786, it was the old members of the comité des finances, plus the new contrôleur, who continued to take most of the key decisions, with the informal title of comité de gouvernement. This was partly a question of the king's confidence (the other ministers had the queen's), partly simply of the relative importance of their departments in time of peace.

These ministers also met together on a social basis. Vergennes made a point of dining with Calonne whenever the contrôleur was most embattled with the parlement. Bombelles attended a ghoulish evening of amateur theatricals put on by the children of Vergennes and Miromesnil at the latter's house, with Calonne and d'Angiviller, 'les intimes de M. de Vergennes', being also in the audience. Bombelles thought that they had no talent and (with the exception of Vergennes's second daughter-in-law) were ugly and slovenly to boot. Bombelles could not explain how a man of Miromesnil's wit could spend so much time in Vergennes's company except by the desire to cling to office. Breteuil had confided to Bombelles that the acquisition of office was a 'dessicating' business; so, Bombelles thought, was its retention. The division in the ministry even extended to opposing views on the merits of Mesmer's animal magnetism, Vergennes and Calonne being taken in, Ségur agnostic, and Breteuil against 'tooth and nail'.[46]

It was the comité de gouvernement which took what was arguably the most important decision of the reign, that to convoke the Assembly of Notables. This operation made virtue of a necessity: the breakdown in relations between crown and parlement (see Chapter 11) gave the comité de gouvernement little option but to implement the programme

45 Besenval, *Mémoires*, II, 149.
46 Marquis de Bombelles, *Journal*, ed. J. Grassion and F. Durif, Geneva, 1978–93, 3 vols, II, 62 and 52.

adumbrated by Joly de Fleury and developed by d'Ormesson. D'Ormesson himself, blinded to this continuity by his hatred of Calonne, wrote scathingly of this measure, 'proposed by M. de Calonne with his customary levity and adopted by the king who all too often acted likewise, on the sole advice, it is said, of M. de Miromesnil and M. de Vergennes, without consulting his other ministers'.[47] He was right, however, to stress the narrow ministerial basis of the decision. Castries, one of those excluded from the discussion, commented: 'The king, who likes unanimity so that he can sleep peacefully, prefers this agreement to the resistance which leads to a better course of action'.[48] Unanimity, however, was not what the king found even in the restricted comité that discussed the proposals. Vergennes, it is true, favoured the measures and may even have been their originator.[49]

Miromesnil, however, criticized every aspect of the proceedings. He told the king that 'in an operation as important for your gloire as for the safety of the state' the other secretaries of state should be included, if not in the main comité at least in the conférences which would be necessary to draft the legislation.[50] He persisted in this view to the end. In his last travail with the king the following April he advised that the concluding opinions of the Notables should be discussed in a joint session of the conseil des dépêches and that of finances, whereas Calonne 'wanted only his comité of himself and the keeper of the seals with the king'. Miromesnil implicitly objected to being surrounded in the comité when he told the king that he would voice his doubts in letters rather than in the comité 'so as to avoid dissensions which are disrespectful in Your Majesty's presence'.[51] Above all his substantive objections to a uniform land tax anticipate the line that would be taken by the Notables and which he would himself endorse. When the king accused Miromesnil of 'disavowing the enterprise', and when Calonne talked about the 'perfidy of my main collaborator', they were blinding themselves to the fact that Miromesnil had made his position clear.

Miromesnil stressed that Calonne's uniform land tax violated corporate and provincial agreements and customs, and was therefore illegal. (He pretended that Calonne had merely overlooked this fact.)[52] He continued this line during the Notables and put it eloquently in a letter of 4 April shortly before his dismissal:

[The Notables] beg for your kindness in beseeching you to respect established forms, approved by the kings your ancestors, for the different corps and provinces of your kingdom, provided only that these forms and usages do

47 D'Ormesson *Journal* section 90.
48 Castries, *Journal*, II, fo. 335.
49 See Hardman, *Louis XVI*, 105.
50 A.N. K163 no. 8. 22, letter of 28 December 1786.
51 ibid.
52 ibid.

not thwart your intention that each landowner of no matter what order should pay the tax in proportion to his property.[53]

Louis should also have been prepared for Miromesnil's defence of the Notables' right to raise objections, which ran counter to Calonne's idea of a puppet assembly restricted by the king's personal endorsement of the measures, and further limited by the *supplément d'instruction* of 24 February. Miromesnil told the king that he had to decide

whether he wants to convoke this assembly merely to communicate his *volontés* to it, without permitting any *représentations* or whether he is resolved to consult it and consequently to see fit for it to present him with *de très humbles représentations.*

He concluded: 'in the former case the usefulness of the assembly will not be great'.[54] It is true that the use of the phrase 'de très humbles représentations' was unfortunate, redolent as it was of the 'très humbles remontrances' in which the parlements expressed their resistance to royal legislation. For by convoking the Notables, Calonne specifically intended to spare the king the kind of protests with which the parlements 'treated everything that did not meet with their immediate approval as surprises to the king's religion'.[55]

Nevertheless the manner in which the king sought advice before what Castries called 'the most remarkable event of your reign' meant that he was assured of the active support of only two ministers, one of whom, Vergennes, was to die before the opening of the Assembly.

Reducing the numbers of those who took the decision did not, however, mean that it was reached speedily, though in a letter to the king of 20 August Calonne had stressed that timing was of the essence: 'Unless the projects are adopted during the court's removal to Fontainebleau [9 October to 15 November] to be announced and concluded in November, the difficulties would be extreme, perhaps the harm irreparable'.[56] By this Calonne meant simply that the loan from the new National Bank and the new taxes must be in place before the third vingtième expired in December. In his letter of 20 August he had made a distinction between urgent (i.e. financial) measures which would have to be implemented in 1786, and what one might call constitutional ones, such as the provincial assemblies, which could be 'trailed'. Louis, however, ruined this schedule by insisting on a discussion by the comité de gouvernement which lasted until the end of December. It was this delay which made Calonne contemplate sending the timbre and the inféodation des domaines before the parlement in December so that he would have something under his belt when he faced the Notables.

53 A.N. K163 no. 8. 30.
54 ibid.
55 A.N. K677. 103.
56 A.N. K164. 104.

What was the king doing with these months? Artois told his bureau in the Notables that he had spent six months examining Calonne's figures.[57] Miromesnil and Vergennes also examined them, though Miromesnil later told the king that they had lacked the necessary expertise. Delay would also be caused by the original intention that (for reasons of secrecy?) all the legislation would be drafted by the three members of the comité. Miromesnil's complaint that it was too much for them was certainly justified.[58] However, the main cause of the delay must have been Miromesnil's subtle rearguard action and perhaps Louis's belief that he had to convince him. Miromesnil's longest letter, that of 28 December, may have finally convinced the king that this was an impossibility: he summoned the conseil des dépêches the next day and presented the convocation of the Notables as a fait accompli. This and a sense of shock pre-empted discussion but the forces which had been ignored, notably the queen's ministers and the parlement, joined forces with Necker's powerful faction and the threatened vested interests to defeat the measures in the Assembly. Miromesnil was their apologist with the king.

CONCLUSION

Many of the decisions we have examined were ill judged or at least all contributed to the fall of the ancien régime. The recall of the parlement, decided against the young king's better judgement; the convocation of the Notables without assuring adequate support; the résultat du conseil, which can be criticized for being too timid, and the séance royale, for being too little, too late. It could even be argued that American independence could have been achieved without incurring the expenditure of war and that the prolongation of the struggle would have further weakened England. Yet the people who took these decisions were not fools. The king himself was intelligent and hard-working and his talents lay in the most appropriate fields, foreign policy and finance. In Maurepas and Miromesnil he possessed two consummate politicians; in Vergennes a master of the old diplomacy; in Turgot and Calonne gifted administrators; in Necker an innovative financier; finally in Malesherbes one of the greatest political theorists of the day who, moreover, in his second ministry (1787–8) was specifically relieved of departmental duties that he might be the freer to give the king advice on the general situation. This he did for instance in his now lost memorandum suggesting that the Estates-

---

57 Bibliothèque de l'Arsenal MS 3978 pp. 196–7.
58 A.N. K163 no. 8. 22.

General should not be convoked in the old form but that instead the provincial assemblies should co-opt a National Assembly.[59]

Was then a deficient observance of the formal decision-making procedures to blame, a departure from the role assigned to the council by the founding fathers of the ancien régime? Most decisions were taken by comités consisting of the king and at most three ministers; sometimes by one minister alone in his weekly travail with the king. Generally, however, though they were taken informally, they were not taken quickly. On the contrary, all the decisions we have examined were protracted. All were decided by the king 'en connaissance de cause'. It does not follow that if d'Ossun or old Soubise could have chipped in with his two penn'orth the régime could have been saved. If, though, as Louis had written in his Réflexions, 'counsel is of the essence of the monarchy', it is preferable to receive it in an orderly way.[60] To receive it from 'favourites' would pertain to 'arbitrary' government. Louis was not swayed by favourites, but the advice he took before the séance royale of 1789 was unusual to say the least.

Again, ruling through comités might be sensible if, as Maurepas's circular letter implied, it were a question merely of establishing an efficient inner cabinet. That may have been how the system worked during his lifetime, for Maurepas had a large measure of control over the composition of the council. By 1786 Louis XVI had partially lost this. To that extent the monarchy was already weaker even before the convocation of the Notables. We have suggested that the convocation was a response to that weakness: to exclude ministers for the sake of efficiency is one thing, to exclude them because they are powerful (or represented powerful interests) is another. It may, as Castries observed, have 'enabled the king to sleep peacefully' but before long it was bound to lead to a rude awakening.[61]

Perhaps it did not make any difference whether the council was properly consulted (as before the résultat), or abused (as before the séance royal), or ignored (as in the recall of the parlement and the convocation of the Notables). Perhaps, even, the decisions were the best that could be obtained. It is at least arguable that if the old parlement had not been recalled in 1774, expectations of change ran so high that there might well have been a general insurrection. If the Notables had not been convoked the crown would probably have relapsed into the grinding tutelage to the parlement Louis XV experienced in the 1760s. Better to go out into battle with one's programme fully unfurled. The résultat was perhaps the one decision that might have made the difference: a clearer lead from the crown might have saved the day; by 23 June things had deteriorated so far

59 J. Egret, La Pré-Révolution française, 1962, 322 n. 1.
60 Quoted by P. Girault de Coursac, L'Éducation d'un roi, Louis XVI, 1972, 98.
61 Castries, Journal, II, fo. 335.

that, as Saint-Priest observed, the third estate in its 'exalted' mood might well have objected to even Necker's version.[62]

62 A.N. K679 no. 86.

CHAPTER NINE

Louis XVI and the politicians

Louis XVI's role in government was important: as we have seen in Chapter 6 on prime ministers, every decision of any weight had to be argued over with the king. Nor can it any longer seriously be maintained that Louis had little interest in or comprehension of the issues of government. (His role in the Assembly of Notables provides the best refutation of this myth.) Yet beyond this it is hard to speak with precision, to improve on Véri's almost impressionistic description of a government decision: 'Louis XVI . . . prend . . . des informations de toutes mains et les décisions partent de sa personne'.[1] For Louis rarely emerges from the shadows imposed by the recesses of his own personality and the stylized conventions of Bourbon kingship, which are epitomized by the elaborate responses to illness and death. If a minister were merely ill, the king would not see him, but if he were dying he might; a minister dying in office had to be removed from the château as soon as possible, though an exception was made in the case of Maurepas – 'a high favour', as Castries notes.[2] When the king himself died, his alter-ego, the chancellor, did not go into mourning, to emphasize the continuity of monarchy. Such conventions served to rob the king of his individual personality.

One would not expect, in a study such as this largely of 'pure' politics, that the king would have a large role. For in a theoretically absolute monarchy, 'politics' was deemed not to exist: 'la politique' meant foreign policy and nine-tenths of Louis XVI's surviving correspondence is devoted to this topic, the true métier of a king. If, as Miromesnil claimed, managing the parlement was no task for a chancellor, still less was it for a king. (That was perhaps why George III created such a stir – and was so inevitably successful – when he decided to be his own political agent and take personal control of the distribution of crown patronage.)

---

1 Abbé de Véri, *Journal 1774–80*, ed. J. de Witte, 1928–30, 2 vols, I, 111.
2 Castries, *Journal*, Archives de la Marine, MS 182/7964 1–2, I, fo. 93.

Nobody really wanted a personal monarch, and this was as true of an 'absolute' monarchy, such as France in some ways still was, as of a constitutional one. One of the most striking things about the Assembly of Notables, which reveals the core of the regime through the cracks it showed up, is the deep embarrassment caused to the politicians by Louis's personal identification with Calonne's projects. At the same time the ministers did not want the king to act as a dummy; though the lines and often the ideas he uttered were often theirs, they wanted him to deliver them as if they were his own. The aim of the comité which prepared him for the lit de justice restoring the parlement in 1774 was

to persuade this prince that the result would be his own doing, so that he could apply the degree of warmth and interest which is necessary to all general operations of this kind. The volonté of the master, known and reputed to be constant, is the final court of appeal in internal troubles. It is necessary to give him this in reality and not be content with clothing it with the appearance.[3]

Similarly, Sartine complained:

The statement that the ministers are carrying out the king's volonté is no longer an effective weapon in their hands. People will treat this merely as their personal volonté which they can expect to overcome.[4]

This had always been a problem. It had sometimes been necessary for Louis XIII to appear in person before a rebellious town to ensure submission. Miromesnil, as premier président of the parlement of Rouen, had to expend much energy disabusing his colleagues of the idea that Louis XV did not even know what a vingtième was, let alone how many were currently being collected. Sometimes the king was in fact ill informed about a case, as with the dispute in the 1780s between the government and the parlement of Bordeaux over the *alluvions*. The crown claimed that alluvial deposits bordering rivers and islands which had formed in their midst belonged to the royal domain; the parlement that the domain's rights extended only to the river bed and, near the coast, to land exposed at low tide. As minister for the province, Vergennes had the parlement of Bordeaux summoned to the vicinity of Versailles 'to suffer interminable boredom in the [outlying] villages' and 'learn respect for their master' while the case was being minutely examined by two conseillers d'état. In fact this examination led to an unexpected result. The king took an interest in the details of the examination and concluded that he had been misled. Louis was an expert in geography, would have followed the technical discussions and concluded that the alluvions had been created not from deposits

3 Véri, I, 204.
4 Abbé de Véri, MSS *Journal*, Archives départementales de la Drôme, Valence, unclassified, 1974, de Witte's copy, cahier 100.

from the river bed but from private land upstream. When the magistrates returned to Bordeaux they wrote to the king, thanking him for his 'patience infatiguable dans sa recherche'.[5] Louis's diary entry for 29 July 1786 presents the matter in a slightly different light; 'second audience of the parlement of Bordeaux. Its length prevented me from hunting the roe-buck'.

If it was believed that the king was informed about and personally supported a measure then obedience would be more easily enforced and the criticism of 'ministerial despotism' or of 'surprising the king's religion' deflected. When Louis XV or his grandson actually lost his temper at a lit de justice this accusation was harder to sustain. Véri told Miromesnil that he had a great advantage in dealing with the parlements in that the king's anger against them was always smouldering and could be ignited at will.

In truth the ministers wanted to have their cake and eat it, as if a modern monarch were expected to deliver an impassioned 'speech from the throne'. For though the ministers wanted the king's support to seem spontaneous, many of the conventions governing the relations not only between the crown and the parlement but also between the king and his ministers were based on a distinction between the king's personal volition (often treated as whim and the basis of arbitrary government) and the abiding values of the monarchy. This was the basis of the parlement's persistent claim to be more royalist than the king but it was also the assumption on which his ministers often acted in their relations with the king.

When Maurepas set up the system of government by comités at the start of the reign, the meetings were held in the king's apartments, but he was encouraged to go away if he became bored, only returning when the discussion was over 'whether to be informed of straight decisions or to reconcile conflicting opinions'.[6] This procedure admittedly was designed to make his course of instruction more palatable to the youthful king, but it does suggest a *roi fainéant* or rather a chairman or referee: if there was a clear majority he should abide by it; only if there was not should he try to produce one. This passive role was that of any judge in an adversarial rather than inquisitional judicial system, conciliar decisions being akin to judgements. In his letter to the king proposing the comité des finances, Joly had envisaged discussion in front of the king prior to a session '*afin qu'en cas de diversité des avis* votre Majesté fut en état de décider en connaissance de cause'.[7] It is noteworthy that Joly is not embarrassed to tell the king that it is only when he is required to reconcile ministerial differences that he needs to be fully informed.

5 W. Doyle, *The Parlement of Bordeaux and the End of the Old Regime, 1771–1790*, 249–61.
6 Véri, *Journal*, I, 186.
7 My italics; B.N. fonds Joly de Fleury, 24876 fo. 139.

This way of proceeding permeated matters big and small. Thus in November 1774 a comité was arranged to regulate whether a man chosen by lot to serve in the militia could pay for a replacement. The voting was likely to be three to three and the king would have to decide for himself.[8] Thus also Barentin justifies the decision to modify Necker's plans for a séance royale on the grounds that Necker had been supported in council only by Montmorin, La Luzerne and Saint-Priest, and the king was adopting the advice of the majority.

The only dissentient from this view was Marie-Antoinette: telling Joseph of the séance royale in the parlement of 19 November 1787, she claimed: 'the king presides over his parlement as he presides over his council, i.e. without being bound by the majority opinion'.[9] However, her opinion was based on ignorance rather than principle. It may be the case that Louis's use of the restricted comité de gouvernement in the period 1781–6, restricted that is to men who shared his general views, was his way of asserting his independence from the tyranny of majority decisions, so that government by comité would not be the same as government by committee.

Even the manner in which councils were conducted served to present the king as a distant, hieratic character and one with little power. The key word was 'respect'. Showing respect actually mattered to Louis himself: he showed respect for the memory of his father, of Louis XV and of Maurepas. When, during the Revolution, he was asked why he tolerated the espionage of Chauvelin at his court, he is said to have replied 'out of respect for the memory of his father'. Castries tells us that Louis was distressed that Loménie de Brienne rested his elbows on the council table because this showed lack of respect and augured that the king had an overmighty prelate on his hands.[10] Barentin was always at great pains to conceal his hatred of Necker 'and above all in council, given the respect that was due to the presence of the king'.[11] When Castries and Vergennes shouted at each other in the council over the peace preliminaries in 1782, the king blushed with embarrassment because this showed a lack of respect not so much for his person (he was quite without personal pomposity) but for his position.[12] During the discussions leading to the convocation of the Notables, Miromesnil sent the king

a few observations which I intended to make to you yesterday in the comité but which I could not develop without causing dissensions which a sense of respect did not permit me to tolerate in your presence and which sometimes

8 Véri, *Journal*, I, 217.
9 Marie-Antoinette, *Lettres*, ed. La Rocheterie and Beaucourt, 1895–6, 2 vols, II, 108–9.
10 Castries, *Journal*, II, fo. 365.
11 Barentin, *Mémoire autographe sur les derniers conseils du Roi Louis XVI*, ed. M. Champion, 1844, 235.
12 Castries, *Journal*, I, fo. 98.

serve only to make matters more difficult since the discussion should be cool, calm and collected.[13]

Here, however, as we have suggested, Miromesnil's main concern was that he should have a chance to present his views without fear of contradiction.

Often indeed ministers exploited the sense of respect due to the king's presence to their own advantage. The best example of this is the way in which Vergennes liked to present the king with a united front in the comité des finances. The preliminary meetings envisaged by Joly de Fleury never took place, or not in the king's presence. As d'Ormesson observes, 'the decisions concerted in advance between M. de Miromesnil, M. de Vergennes and myself . . . were nearly always adopted without discussion'.[14]

Even when there had been a disagreement in the preliminary discussions, the ministers concealed their differences from the king in the comité. Thus when d'Ormesson proposed the continuance of Necker's régie des postes, Vergennes supported him in the comité even though in preliminary discussions he had favoured either a farm or higher salaries for the régisseurs. Afterwards, Vergennes explained that there should not be

divergences of opinion in the king's presence – a principle [d'Ormesson considered] which could indeed be useful to the personal credit of the ministers but which must often have been harmful to the good of the country.[15]

D'Ormesson was correct in accusing Vergennes of bending the conventions to his own advantage, for Louis did not mind disagreements among his ministers provided they were not heated. (Indeed the adversarial system was the way in which government decisions were supposed to be reached.) Thus when Castries told Louis in November 1782 that he was concerned that his open quarrel with Joly over the funding of his department showed lack of respect to the king, Louis told him not to worry, that there were procedures for adjusting their differences: 'Il faut plaider contradictoirement cette affair devant moi'.[16] The two ministers had a formal disputation before the king-judge, and though nothing was resolved, no offence was caused either.

It was understood that the various restrictions on the king's personal activity did not lessen his absolutism because the ministers concerned were his choice to the extent that they had not been imposed on him by external forces. Those in the ministerial milieu were also mindful of

13 A.N. K163 no. 8. 22, 28 December 1786.
14 D'Ormesson, *Journal*, A.N. 144 A.P. 130, section 55.
15 ibid.
16 Castries, *Journal*, I, fo. 140.

the pressure that it was legitimate to put on the king both in the matter of appointments (the distinction between a 'simple prévention' and a 'décision précise' on the king's part) and in the exercise of their power. Lenoir was scandalized that Brienne and Necker should have been appointed against the personal wishes of the king and surprised that they should have been able to run the country without his confidence.[17] Maurepas believed that the king's confidence must be given spontaneously: 'je ne vaux rien pour arracher toujours la confiance et pour usurper la décision'.[18]

Yet even with this intimate question of confidence the tension between the king's actual and conventional feelings was never far from the surface. Nowhere is this more so than in the terms on which the king parted with a minister. D'Ormesson placed great emphasis on the insertion in his letter of dismissal that he retained the king's 'estime'. Yet we know, from the king's letter to Vergennes about d'Ormesson's good intentions being no substitute for credit, that he did not esteem d'Ormesson, and we know from d'Ormesson's diary that he was perfectly aware of the king's feelings and indeed reciprocated them. Obviously d'Ormesson did not have the king's esteem in the modern English or contemporary French acceptance of the word. 'Estime' in this context meant that d'Ormesson's dismissal did not amount to a disgrâce and he would not suffer exile; he could keep his decorations and could hope – such *was* his hope – to be re-employed, though of course in a different capacity.

Estime was not the same as *confiance*, which referred to the actual state of the king's mind and could not, as Maurepas said, be *arraché*. Confiance was voluntary. Louis's valet de chambre, Thierry, said that Maurepas did not receive 'a voluntary token of confidence' from the king until 1780.[19] Necker caused Louis a lot of embarrassment in 1781 by demanding 'conditional marks of confidence' (conditional meaning that if he did not obtain them he would resign). Louis actually offered him the grandes entrées, which was a personal gift from the king since it offered intimate access to his person. But Necker overstepped the mark: he should have learned from Maurepas that confiance could not be arraché. Necker, then, was either trying to change the constitutional conventions or (more likely) was still ignorant of them. In 1788 Lamoignon took with him, even into exile, 'l'estime et en secret la confiance du Roi'. Calonne's retention of the king's confidence – or in Castries's words, an 'attachement secret' – meant that he was treated as a 'ministre derrière le rideau' in the days after his fall. Confiance can also be distinguished from crédit. Because confiance was secret it was practically less effective, though more enduring, than crédit. Necker

---

17 Lenoir Papers, Bibliothèque municipale d'Orléans, MS 1421–3, 1423, mélanges, 32.
18 Véri, *Journal*, I, 251.
19 Castries, *Journal*, I, fo. 110.

would not cooperate with Brienne in August 1788 because the latter was known still to possess crédit with the king and queen. He did not, however, worry that this would survive Brienne's fall. Brienne continued to write Marie-Antoinette letters, he continued to have her confiance, but without office he had lost his crédit.

The relations between the king and his ministers were often as strained as the conventional language which described them. They were often far from harmonious; in many cases the 'respect' felt was purely conventional: contempt would better describe the feelings of Castries and d'Ormesson and Sartine towards the king. Often their relations were characterized by a sense of malaise which is expressed most forcefully by Sartine in an outburst to Véri in 1782:

You will not see any class of citizen, among those in public life, for whom the king and his family display the slightest partiality. They will allow the different groups to fight each other if they want and the king will sacrifice them one to the others beginning with the ministers of whatever party.[20]

Sartine after two years was still smarting from his unfair dismissal, but most of the ministers who have left a record of their relations with the king – Castries, d'Ormesson, Calonne (after his fall), Vergennes, Turgot and Malesherbes – were hurt by his treatment of them.

In 1780 Véri called Maurepas 'the only minister whom the king treats with any consideration', yet even he was exhausted with having constantly to 'arracher sa confiance'; in 1782 the king's valet de chambre, Thierry, elaborated on Maurepas's difficulties, telling Castries:

[The king] never expressed his feelings and until the last year of his life, that is for over six years, M. de Maurepas never obtained from him either a token of friendship or a voluntary token of confidence, but in the last year he possessed it completely; what will surprise you is that but for me he would never have had the *entrées familières* [grandes entrées]; the king always let him go the long way round even though his apartments gave on to [M. de Maurepas's] and he was often too gouty to walk; on my representations to the king he told me to get him [Maurepas] to ask for the entrées via the premier gentilhomme de la chambre and he would him grant them.[21]

Maurepas's successor in what passed for the king's confidence, Vergennes, constantly believed that he was about to be dismissed. In 1783 he wrote to the king, 'My misfortune is extreme because I have caused Your Majesty a moment of pain' and in 1785, 'Various indications make me only too aware that Your Majesty's kindness towards me is no longer the same'.[22] In Vergennes's case, however, it should be added that his fears of disgrace were neurotic, that the 'moment of pain' he caused the king related to the sale of his regalian

20 Véri, MSS *Journal*, de Witte's copy, cahier 100.
21 Castries, *Journal*, I, fo. 110.
22 A.N. K164 no. 3, 1783 no. 4 and 1785 no. 5.

rights (see pp. 70–2) and that he was possibly the only minister to whom the king did display kindness and consideration. He even sought to allay his fears, on one occasion writing: 'I tell you this to dissipate your fears (if you could ever have had any) and to demonstrate my confidence in you.'[23] Louis wept at his grave because, though he did not always respect him, he always trusted him.

The other ministers fared worse; in 1783 Véri wrote that the king 'sets . . . the example of contempt for his ministers'.[24] D'Ormesson and Castries took their revenge through their diaries. D'Ormesson confides that it was *pénible* to have dealings with 'a king who treats me and all too often the most important public affairs with such indifference'. His weekly travail with the king consisted merely in authorizing payments by the trésor royal: 'the king through the natural brusquerie of his rather uncouth character never engaging in or tolerating any other conversation or discussion in the course of it'.[25] When the king ended Necker's exile in 1787 without informing his friend Castries, the latter noted on 4 June, 'It would be too distasteful to serve such a master if one were serving him alone and not the state at the same time'.[26]

This malaise in the relations between the king and the politicians was no doubt partly due to the king's character, 'un peu sauvage' as d'Ormesson observes,[27] and to his insensitivity, as does Thierry in the case of Maurepas. However, it also went deeper since it often took the form of a lack of trust, and the question arises as to whether the king and the majority of his ministers did in fact have the same conception of the role of the monarchy. We have seen how the noblesse d'état's dominance of the ministry was increasingly contested by the military aristocracy. Louis himself was undoubtedly most comfortable with the former group to which the three men who most enjoyed his confidence – Maurepas, Vergennes and Calonne – belonged. They (and particularly Vergennes and Calonne) shared his conception of the absolute monarchy. Castries complained in 1787 that after six years in office he had no more of the king's confidence than on the first day;[28] given his views of Louis in particular and the way in which he wanted the monarchy to develop in general one is not surprised. Men like Castries and Breteuil wanted a decentralized government based on estates dominated by the landed nobility; Miromesnil, the ex-premier président, wanted to maintain the status quo but let the balance tilt back in favour of the parlement.

Louis, however, did not consider that the maintenance of the status

23 Archives de Vergennes, *Lettres de Louis XVI*, letter of 27 May 1776.
24 Véri, *Journal*, II, 322; MSS *Journal*, cahier 112.
25 D'Ormesson, *Journal*, sections 59 and 60.
26 Castries, *Journal*, II, fo. 371.
27 ibid., fo. 374.
28 D'Ormesson, *Journal*, section 58, A.N. 144 A.P. 130.

quo was any longer an option. Radical change was necessary. He warns Brienne when he is negotiating his entry to the ministry, 'Remember what is said at the beginning of the [Calonne's] Mémoire, that palliatives would be worse than the disease'.[29] The twin planks of Louis's policy are expressed clearly and passionately during the crisis of the Notables: first, the absolute monarchy must be maintained intact without any devolution of power; second, the extra money it needed to enable it to survive in a modern form must come from the privileged classes not the peasantry.

Thus Louis makes clear to Brienne that the new provincial assemblies must not impair the authority of the intendant, the key official of the absolute monarchy and considered by Louis 'the best part of my system':

[The Assemblies] will only have the authority to see to the execution of what has already been determined and to establish fairness in the assessment [of taxation] but they will not even have the power of 'simulated consent' enjoyed by the estates of the other provinces.[30]

In the Notables, the intendants came under heavy attack and were scarcely defended, even by the noblesse d'état, even by former and present intendants. Afterwards, one of their number, La Bourdonnaye de Blossac, wrote to Brienne complaining that 'in a memorable assembly, the administration of the intendants . . . had been as fiercely attacked as it had been feebly defended'. He made the same point to his cousin d'Ormesson, who merely conceded that 'a few intendants might have made good use of the powers entrusted to them'.[31] Even in the heart of the royal administration, then, Louis was in an increasingly small minority in his uncompromising belief in the future of absolutism.

The king's isolation on the second plank of his platform, reform of taxation, is just as marked and comes over clearly in his cri de coeur during his last travail with Miromesnil,

The king said [Miromesnil told Brienne] that they [the nobility and clergy] were opposing everything; that they paid nothing; that the people paid everything . . . the minister replied that he begged the king not to be prejudiced against any order or any corps.[32]

The king's isolation also took the form of attempts by his ministers to shift responsibility for major decisions directly on to his shoulders. During the crisis of the Guerre des farines in 1775, Véri comments that Maurepas 'is averse by character . . . to facing obstacles himself,

---

29 Comte de Brienne and Loménie de Brienne, *Journal de l'Assemblée des Notables de 1787*, ed. P. Chevallier, 1960, 81.
30 ibid., 79.
31 A.N. (fonds d'Ormesson) 144 A.P. 133.6.4.
32 Brienne, *Journal*, 63.

preferring to let his prince do it on his own'.[33] In 1780 the financial situation was so parlous that there was question of a forced peace with England which, before the victory at Yorktown, could have been only on very bad terms. Fearing to take responsibility for it, and also hoping to stiffen the king's warlike resolve, Vergennes asked him for written orders if he were to open negotiations.[34] It was of course also open to the king to pass the buck. Thus during the last three years of the Seven Years War, Louis XV consistently met Choiseul's request for a decision on whether peace initiatives were to be pursued with characteristic late-Bourbon silence:

was this incompetence, [mused Véri] or was it a secret intention to make his minister take sole responsibility for the continuation of war or the conclusion of a mediocre peace?[35]

As the crisis of the regime developed, responsibility involved more than merely the risk of disgrace for a minister; it could lead to criminal prosecution, as Barentin found to his cost in 1789 when he was tried in absentia for the new crime of lèse nation for the advice he gave the king in the summer of that year. In the *mémoire* he published in 1790 as his defence, Barentin throws the responsibility squarely on to the shoulders of the king:

The king deigns to summon his ministers to [the council]; he consults them; he makes them argue in his presence; he listens to their observations; he decides. What proceeds from the council proceeds from the king alone.

Are we censuring the speeches pronounced by the king in this séance [of 23 June 1789]? . . . no matter whether the king took the trouble to draft them all himself, whether he charged someone honoured with his confidence to furnish him with material, whether, even, he adopted them in the form in which they had been presented to him, from the moment when His Majesty pronounced them, they became his own; and the king's acceptance is the most perfect guarantee that the mandatory of his authority can receive.

Barentin neatly avoids the imputation of sheltering behind the king by observing that 'the National Assembly had recently pronounced the king to be inviolable'. Louis was to use this defence at his own trial, with the results that we know.

In his later *Mémoire autographe*, Barentin also develops the related doctrine of collective responsibility. A minister should not be held responsible for collective government action with which he might have disagreed in the council but which disagreement the 'obligation sainte' of silence prevented him from revealing. If a minister was responsible for 'a measure adopted or ordered by the king . . . the government

33 Véri, *Journal*, I, 308.
34 AAE MDF 1897 fo. 103, Vergennes to the king, 27 May 1780, quoted in M. Price, 'The Comte de Vergennes and the Baron de Breteuil: French politics and reform in the reign of Louis XVI', PhD thesis, Cambridge University, 1988, 156.
35 Véri, *Journal*, I, 221.

would display lack of nerve and energy in a decisive moment during which the administration would be reduced to acting with timidity and lack of resolve'; yet he knew that royal or collective responsibility had not fully been established and one can readily see that in talking about a 'government without nerve and energy' he is precisely describing the conduct of the Breteuil ministry.[36]

In fact the paralysis had begun to affect the government the previous summer, at the time of the Lamoignon coup. Breteuil, then minister for the maison, wanted the French Guards to supply him with 'such detachments as he felt necessary'. The Duc de Biron, colonel of the Regiment of Guards, told him that he could not give him such an 'open-ended commitment' without the king's direct orders:

if there are ugly incidents, the parlement could take me to task and I could only defend myself by exhibiting the orders I had received from the king. . . . It is necessary in such situations that the Colonel of the Guards know the king's personal intentions [avoir le secret du roi] in order to carry out His Majesty's orders to best effect.

If things became more serious, he would go to Versailles himself despite the poor state of his health to see what the king really wanted.[37] Nor was Biron's an idle fear: when the parlement returned in triumph in September, it summoned him to explain his conduct during Lamoignon's coup. In the same crisis, Breteuil himself told the king that he wanted him to make out an entire lettre de cachet in his own handwriting (rather than the normal procedure of giving him a pro forma signed Louis).[38] What we do not know is the king's response to these attempts to place responsibility directly on to him. Did Biron leave his sick-bed to travel to Versailles? Did Louis write Breteuil out a holographic lettre de cachet? Or, as is most likely, were both of them met with evasion or silence?

Silence was the characteristic weapon employed by both Louis XV and his grandson to cope with unwarranted pressure or embarrassment or an unfair question. In a similar situation, lesser mortals resort to a lie. The pressure came either from the court or from the ministers. Louis XIV had not had to face pressure from the court because he lived an entirely public life. Louis XV moved out of Louis XIV's bed-chamber and had private apartments constructed in a side wing of the Cour de Marbre.[39] Nevertheless he was preserved from embarrassment by the self-censorship of his intimates. As Calonne observed, even Louis XV's 'most cherished courtiers' did not discuss matters of state with the king: *They would not have dared*. Nor would

36 Barentin, *Mémoire pour M. de Barentin* . . ., 1790, 38–40; Barentin, *Mémoire autographe*, 57–9.

37 A.N. O¹ 354 no. 54.

38 ibid., no. 51.

39 N. Elias, *La Société de la cour*, Flammarion, 1985, 145.

his queen, Maria Lesczinska. Marie-Antoinette, however, constantly 'talked shop' to Louis, asking him for impossible things like going to war to further her brother Joseph's territorial ambitions. Louis, who did not like 'scenes', raised a stone wall of silence. Once, however, in 1778, he spoke his mind:

'The ambition of your relatives is going to overturn everything. They began with Poland; now Bavaria will form the second volume: I am sorry for it on your account'. – 'But you cannot deny, Monsieur, that you were informed and in agreement on this Bavarian matter.' [Marie-Antoinette had taken Louis's silence for assent.] – 'So little was I in agreement that we have just given orders to the French ambassadors to make it known in all the courts that the dismemberment of Bavaria is being carried out against our wishes and that we disapprove of it.'[40]

Like Marie-Antoinette, Turgot often took Louis's silence for assent. 'Divining [the king's] silence', to use Véri's phrase, became a necessary skill for Louis XVI's ministers. Maurepas was better at it than Turgot, but even he had not been able to divine why the king was silent about the claims of Nivernais to be foreign minister and his own to be prime minister. 'Souvent', he lamented, 'il m'échappe par son silence indécis sur des affaires importantes.'[41]

Silence was the first stage in the king's denial of familiar access to his ministers; exile was the last; in between fell the king's unavailability. When the disgrace of a minister was being considered the minister was unable to see the king, though he always tried. We have evidence of enough cases to state this as a general rule, as Brienne did in the case of Calonne:

Since last Thursday, the king has not wanted to see the contrôleur-général, in accordance with his practice of avoiding a travail with or even seeing those whom he is determined to remove.[42]

In addition to Calonne, Sartine,[43] Joly de Fleury,[44] and d'Ormesson[45] received exactly the same treatment. When his own turn came Brienne *was* permitted to see the king, but Louis became less affable. When Terray asked the king if he was satisfied with his services, he was met with a wall of silence, as was Turgot in similar circumstances.[46] Finally, when Malesherbes wanted to resign, Louis would not grant him a travail, though he continued to see him across the table of the conseil d'état (see pp. 49–50). This case, where Louis wanted to retain

40 Mercy to Maria-Theresa, 18 February 1778, A. d'Arneth and M.A. Geffroy (eds), *Marie-Antoinette: Correspondance secrète entre Marie-Thérèse et le Comte de Mercy-Argenteau*, 2nd edn, 1875, 3 vols, III, 168–9.
41 Véri, *Journal*, II, 66–8.
42 Brienne, *Journal*, 57.
43 Véri, *Journal*, II, 392.
44 Brienne, *Journal*, 57.
45 D'Ormesson, *Journal*, sections 70–3.
46 Véri, *Journal*, I, 185 and 450–7.

Malesherbes, was not entirely different from those of Calonne, Sartine and Brienne, all of whom retained a measure of the king's confidence. In all the above cases, Louis wanted to resist being manoeuvred by personal pleading.

Another step Louis took to secure his independence from his official advisers was to seek extra-ministerial advice, the sense of Véri's 'le roi prend des informations de toutes mains'. Louis XIV had frankly told his son that the ministers, 'though they often hate each other, have common interests and can gang up to deceive the master. He, therefore, must gather information outside the narrow circle of the council'.[47] Louis XVI continued the tradition and was bombarded with letters – from cranks, men with projects, and informers. To some he replied: Pezay was one and we have seen how Necker was worked into the ministry through his agency. In addition, Louis inherited from the previous reign d'Ogny, the intendant des postes, with his secret bureau of twelve clerks, the cabinet noir, employed to open intercepted correspondence. D'Ogny had a travail with the king every Sunday when he read him extracts from his discoveries. Even Madame de Maurepas censored her own private correspondence in the belief that d'Ogny read extracts to the king.[48]

Lenoir informs us that he had a direct travail with the king which was unbeknown to his superior, the minister for the maison. In 1785, as divisions within the ministry intensified, Vergennes and Calonne asked Lenoir to send key reports direct to the king without informing Breteuil. (They assumed that having them sent to the king was tantamount to having them sent to themselves.) Lenoir replied correctly that all reports had to go to his superior, Breteuil. In fact, unbeknown to all the ministers, the king who 'sans avoir de l'éloignement pour le Baron de Breteuil, n'avait pas en lui beaucoup de confiance', was in the habit of asking Lenoir to observe people at court and 'expressly asked him to say nothing to the Baron de Breteuil'. Breteuil discovered some of this when a royal messenger gave Lenoir a letter from the king when he was in Breteuil's cabinet. Lenoir defended himself by saying that he did not regard it as any 'usurpation sur son département' and that it was not the first time that he had had a 'correspondance particulière avec le roi'.

Lenoir concludes his account of this episode with some reflections which touch on the nature of ministerial power.

A lieutenant-général de police could be well ensconced in his job and better so perhaps than the ministers his superiors if, during a long exercise of the duties and functions attached to the job, he had been in a position, through relations which could be useful but could also be dangerous, to receive the orders of his sovereign directly and secretly.

47 Elias, *Société de la cour*, 133.
48 Véri, *Journal*, II, 149.

Lenoir's influence (which he equates with security of tenure) comes from receiving 'direct and secret orders from the king'. This was the basis of ministry: did it matter what one's nominal department was or even if, as in the case of Maurepas, one had none? Apparently not, for Lenoir's secret correspondence with the king went on for eighteen months after he ceased to be lieutenant-général de police in August 1785.[49]

One does not have to agree with Véri's contention that opening private correspondence made Louis indecisive, to see that the steps which he took to secure his independence within the government all tended to undermine the efficacy of that government. This is as true of the small measures we have just looked at as of the major ones that have figured in previous chapters: maintaining the barbarous practice of exile for ex-ministers until he himself recognized its illegality during the Revolution; not appointing a prime minister until he had to, and discouraging ministerial unity, again until he had no choice, when the forces of resistance to government itself became of more pressing importance than his individual position within it. His conduct stemmed from jealousy of his position and lack of trust for his ministers; the former from a belief that he should model himself on Louis XIV, which was misconceived because kings of strong character were the exceptions in French history and were not in any case always the most successful rulers. His lack of trust was innate but was also reinforced by his awareness that many of his ministers no longer believed in the system they were operating.

---

49 Lenoir MS 1423, mélanges, 3–5 and 39.

CHAPTER TEN

The political role of Marie-Antoinette[1]

Marie-Antoinette was placed in a false position almost from the start. The alliance of 1756 between France and her hereditary enemy Austria was unpopular, involving as it did such an abrupt change that it is often referred to as the 'diplomatic revolution'. The doubts that many entertained had been confirmed by the French defeats during the Seven Years War and within six months of Marie-Antoinette's arrival in France, the pro-parlementaire, pro-philosophe and above all pro-Austrian faction which had arranged her marriage to the Dauphin had fallen from power, Choiseul and his cousin Praslin being ordered into exile by Louis XV on Christmas Eve 1770. This faction was replaced by one which was anti-parlementaire, dévôt and anti-Austrian, whose titular head, after the death of the old dauphin, was her husband. In a move that was to weigh heavily on her future, in 1771 Choiseul's nomination of the Baron de Breteuil to the Vienna embassy was cancelled in favour of Prince Louis de Rohan, whose family were bastions of the anti-Austrian faction. Thus to many in France, before as during the Revolution, at court as in the country, Marie-Antoinette was above all L'Autrichienne.

She had to be on the defensive; there was constant pressure on her to act out a political role to which she was not suited. Mercy-Argenteau , the Austrian ambassador, had summed her up by 1780, when he told her mother the Empress Maria-Theresa that the queen 'acts less through her own volition than through instigation'.[2] Perceiving her to be malleable, Mercy-Argenteau and her Habsburg relatives intended to forge her into a tool of Austrian foreign policy. For her own part, she did not really have the intelligence or, to be fair to her, the ambition, to do much more than to reward those whom she

---

1 The title of this chapter is of course a translation of that of Jeanne Arnaud-Boutloup's study of 1924.
2 A. d'Arneth and M.A. Geffroy (eds) *Marie-Antoinette: Correspondance secrète entre Marie-Thérèse et le Comte de Mercy-Argenteau*, 2nd edn, 1875, 3 vols, III, 449.

liked and punish those whom she disliked. She confessed as much to Madame Campan, when she had been forced on to the political stage:

there has been no happiness for me since they turned me into an intriguer . . . the Queens of France are only happy when they meddle with nothing, just keeping enough 'crédit' to set up their friends and a few devoted servants.[3]

She was in any case incapable of pursuing a consistent policy based on concepts rather than on personalities: her personal vendettas, ranging from that against d'Aiguillon at the beginning of the reign to that against La Fayette at the end, were indeed pursued consistently.

Marie-Antoinette's depiction of the proper role of a Queen of France corresponded to the ones played by Louis XIV's queen, Marie-Thérèse, and Louis XV's, Maria Lesczinska. It also corresponded to the one Louis XVI intended to assign to his queen. This was doubly necessary because Marie-Antoinette's mother Maria-Theresa and (more blatantly) her brother Joseph II intended her to be a tool of Austrian foreign policy. Moreover the main aim of Louis's foreign policy, in which he succeeded, was that Austria should not exploit her alliance with France in the way she had under Louis XV. Louis was largely successful in excluding Marie-Antoinette from affairs until 1787 when, after the rejection by the Notables of the reform programme on which he had set his heart, Louis underwent a form of 'nervous breakdown' from which he never fully recovered. Thereafter he consulted his queen as readily as he had hitherto excluded her from decision-making, so that there were two distinct, indeed contrasting phases, to Marie-Antoinette's political role: before and after 1787.

In both phases, the Austrian interest was active. In the first its principal objective was to obtain French assistance for the cardinal plank of Joseph's foreign policy, exchanging the Austrian Netherlands for Bavaria to round off his territories and increase his consequence in Germany; in the second phase, quite simply to shore up the French monarchy through support of Brienne and, when his fall became inevitable, through the recall of Necker, who had always enjoyed the support of the House of Austria. The Austrian agents on the spot were the Comte de Mercy-Argenteau, the ambassador, a native of the Austrian Netherlands, and the Abbé de Vermond, who was the queen's *lecteur*, and directed both her conscience and her education (rudimentary when she had left Vienna). Joseph and Mercy had rather different roles in mind for Marie-Antoinette. Joseph wanted her to maintain a low profile, to keep her prestige intact to help him in foreign policy; she should not dissipate it by seeking pensions for her personal friends; nor should she meddle in ministerial politics.

Mercy, however, thought that she should play an active role in

3 Madame Campan, *Mémoires sur la vie privée de Marie-Antoinette, Reine de France et de Navarre*, London, 1823, 2 vols, II, 29.

politics, even urging that the prime minister, if there had to be one, should be dependent on her. Indeed in jottings of 1788 he muses: 'Reflections on the advantages and the disadvantages of having a prime minister . . . she [the queen] ought to retain this office for herself'.[4] In less extreme form, Mercy-Argenteau continues this theme throughout the reign. In 1780 he tells Maria-Theresa that when Maurepas dies or retires, 'it is of the utmost importance that [his successor] be chosen by the queen alone and become her creature'.[5] In 1783 he opines: 'it is certain that the comité des finances could become a three-man prime minister, none of whom is the queen's creature, and that consequently its authority would be . . . a sort of barrier to the influence of this princess'.[6] In 1787 he finally achieved his goal when the only prime minister to possess the official title, Loménie de Brienne, was appointed through her influence and became indeed her 'creature'.

Mercy believed that a queen and a prime minister were natural antagonists, alternative sources of power: 'The métier of a prime minister in France has ever been to intercept and destroy the "crédit" of the queens'.[7] Since no Queen of France had exercised political power for over a hundred years, one might ask how Mercy-Argenteau could have come to this perverse conclusion. The answer lies in the particular circumstances of the new reign. Marie-Antoinette was different from the colourless queens, her predecessors. Louis, who did not take a mistress, came to love his queen as one; although previous queens had had little political influence, previous mistresses often had. In particular, Madame de Pompadour had been in many respects a prime minister. The comparison is particularly apt because Maurepas's first ministerial career had been ended by Madame de Pompadour and he was determined that his second should not be ended by another woman. Moreover, like Madame de Pompadour and like Marie-Antoinette, Maurepas's own power depended not on formal position but on confidence and above all intimate access. Marie-Antoinette and Maurepas were in this sense direct competitors. This is why Mercy could talk of a prime minister 'intercepting' or 'acting as a barrier' to the queen's influence: as we have seen, Maurepas based his system on 'intercepting' those who wanted a political relationship with the king. It also explains why Mercy was even led to instigate a modification to the physical layout of the royal apartments.

Mercy felt that Maurepas had an advantage in access to the king which Marie-Antoinette did not possess: whereas his apartments were connected to the king's by a 'secret' connecting staircase, the queen

---

4 A. d'Arneth and J. Flammermont (eds) *Correspondance secrète du Comte de Mercy-Argenteau avec l'Empereur Joseph II et le Prince de Kaunitz*, 1891, 2 vols, II, 195.
5 Arneth and Geffroy, *Marie-Antoinette*, III, 449.
6 Arneth and Flammermont, *Correspondance secrète*, I, 169.
7 Arneth and Geffroy, *Marie-Antoinette*, II, 147.

had to pass through a crowded room to get from her apartments to the king's (unless she took the back way through those of the king's inquisitive and generally hostile aunts). In 1775, therefore, Mercy arranged for the construction of a special connecting passage between the queen's apartments and the king's.[8] That would put her at least on a par with Maurepas.

Mercy, however, complained that Marie-Antoinette was not making sufficient use of this passage and the question arises whether this might not also have been true of the advice she received from the Austrian quarter in general, be it from her relatives or from Mercy. Maria-Theresa's view was that Louis XV's last ministry had been ideal (it had allowed her to share in the Partition of Poland). The disgrace of Maupeou was 'incomprehensible', while Joseph castigated Marie-Antoinette for her role in d'Aiguillon's dismissal and exile. Nor did Austria want the return of Choiseul, Lorrainer and pro-Austrian though he was. Maria-Theresa thought that his exile should be ended – she even extended her solicitude to Choiseul's sister, who had been included in the proscription – but the idea of his return to office filled her with alarm.[9] Indeed she believed that had Choiseul still been in office at the time of the Partition of Poland, he would have profited from the occasion to grab a slice of the Austrian Netherlands. Her daughter, however, favoured not only Choiseul but also all his connections. It was through Marie-Antoinette that Choiseul and the Choiseulistes had mounted their challenge to Maurepas in 1775–6. We have, however, suggested that this struggle over ministerial appointments was a largely artificial contest. Louis XVI had no intention of allowing Choiseul to return to power: his return would have upset the delicate balance in parlementaire relations which he sought to maintain: the return of the parlement must not be accompanied by that of its outspoken adherents.

Nevertheless, during this struggle several steps were taken to stabilize the queen's influence, and they came both from the Austrian quarter and from Maurepas himself. Joseph delivered his sister a stinging rebuke:

My dear sister, what do you think you are doing, ousting ministers [La Vrillière], dispatching another to his estates [d'Aiguillon], giving this département to one and that to another, helping yet another to win his suit [Guines], creating a new and ruinous *charge* at your court [surintendant de la maison de la reine]?[10]

On the question of Malesherbes's appointment to the maison,

8 ibid., II, 356.
9 ibid., II, 153.
10 ibid., II, 364.

Vermond told Turgot: 'M. de Maurepas must not give way to her on this occasion. The issue is of too great consequence for the state'.[11]

At the same time Mercy and Vermond sought to detach the Choiseulistes from the unacceptable Choiseul and forge them for the future into a genuinely queen's party of ministerial calibre numbering Breteuil, Castries, and Vermond's close friend Loménie de Brienne. This group had a definite 'tone', a synthesis or amalgam of the various forces which had made it. From Choiseul himself they inherited a pro-philosophe stance though, with the exception of Vermond and Brienne, without the intellectual pretensions of the man who had corresponded with Voltaire. Breteuil's education was limited, while as a minister Castries employed other pens for his memoranda. The deeper reaches of Philosophie were obviously beyond Marie-Antoinette, though she may have caught a whiff of the 'enlightened despotism' of her brothers Joseph and Leopold. From Choiseul also they inherited a penchant for the parlement, which began to show itself as soon as government relations with that body became difficult (Castries from 1787, Breteuil as early as 1785). Like Choiseul also they believed that the old aristocracy should have a place in the ministry: Choiseul's views on this impressed Marie-Antoinette;[12] many of them, however, were later to advocate an extension of aristocratic power through revived provincial estates and estates-general which, as we shall see, was less attractive to her.

Few if any of them supported her attempts to further Austrian foreign policy, least of all the Bavarian exchange. This is clearest in the case of Breteuil, whose training in the secret du roi had left him with an indelible suspicion of Austria. This could have been predicted before his appointment when, in 1779, at the Congress of Teschen, he had fobbed Joseph off with a few scraps of territory. Indeed, Maria-Theresa would have dearly liked to have had him recalled but having got rid of one ambassador (Rohan), feared that to lose two might seem like carelessness.[13] During the second phase of the Bavarian crisis, Breteuil was, as a ministre, to deliver the strongest opinion in the conseil d'état against the exchange, an opinion which included a scathing attack on Joseph: 'he seems to think that the prince who will go down as the greatest in history will be the one who conquers the most territory'.[14] All this without losing the queen's favour.

Meanwhile in 1775/6 Maurepas took two steps of his own which helped to keep Marie-Antoinette out of ministerial politics for another five years: the planting of his niece, the Comtesse de Polignac, in the queen's intimate society, and the recall of her protégé the Comte de Guines, as ambassador to England.

11 Abbé de Véri, *Journal, 1774–80*, ed. J. de Witte, 1928–30, 2 vols, I, 316.
12 Arneth and Geffroy, *Marie-Antoinette*, II, 356–7.
13 ibid., III, 308 n. 1.
14 A.N. K164 no. 3 1784 no. 4. 3.

The appointment of a surintendant of her household – Joseph's 'charge dispendieuse' – was the result of a concordat between Maurepas and Marie-Antoinette which had been conducted on the queen's behalf by the Comtesse Jules de Polignac. She represented the queen but was in fact, as Mercy observed, 'manifestly bribed and conducted by the Comte de Maurepas' and had even suggested to the queen 'that it would be in her [the queen's] interest to persuade the king to appoint [Maurepas] premier ministre'. Madame de Polignac was a country-relation of Maurepas's, rescued by him from provincial obscurity and launched in the salon of his ally the Princesse de Rohan-Guémené which was much frequented by the queen. She soon won the queen's notice and became her exclusive favourite after she quarrelled with the Princesse de Lamballe in 1777.[15]

The negotiations which Madame de Polignac conducted were, moreover, ones in which she had a direct interest: the appointment of a surintendant symbolized the definition of the queen's sphere of influence as court rather than ministerial appointments. From these the Polignacs could hope to benefit, particularly as the appointment of the Princesse de Lamballe and the replacement of the Comtesse de Noailles, 'Madame Étiquette', by the Princesse de Chimay as the queen's dame d'honneur, led to a relaxation of old ways and the replacement of old personnel: the Noailles were gradually replaced by the Polignacs as the main recipients of court pensions.

This did not happen immediately, nor was it as extensive as is often supposed. Until 1780 the Polignacs only enjoyed two court offices: Madame de Polignac had a place as dame d'honneur to the Comtesse d'Artois and in 1776, Maurepas obtained for her husband the survivance as premier écuyer to the queen, braving the opposition of the incumbent's in-laws, the Noailles. Another example of Maurepas rather than the queen promoting their interests occurred in 1779. In December of that year, the queen and Necker worked out the size of the Polignacs' pension. Judging this inadequate, they went direct to Maurepas, 'who lent his support to the full range of their greed': the modest arrangement of the queen and Necker was torn up.[16] In 1780 the fortunes of the family improved dramatically: Madame de Polignac was made gouvernante des enfants de France, her husband a duc and directeur-général des postes and their daughter was given a dowry of 800,000 livres.

It has been argued that by allowing Marie-Antoinette a major share in the distribution of court patronage (embassies, colonelcies and ecclesiastical appointments) in return for her abstention from interfering in ministerial ones, Maurepas in fact allowed her to build

15 Arneth and Geffroy, *Marie-Antoinette*, II, 437, 367 and 402.
16 ibid., III, 381–2 and 391.

up a power base from which she could later attack these too.[17] However, the fact that his own political supporters, the Polignacs, were the main beneficiaries of the transaction lessens the concession of what was in any case the queen's natural right of patronage. By neutralizing the queen's political influence, the Polignacs earned their corn and the king's favour. Thus in April 1780, Mercy reports: 'the main support of the Comtesse de Polignac's position is that the king seems to have contracted a sort of friendship for her'. The following June he visited her at home in Paris – the first time he ever entered a private house.[18] The Polignacs may, as Wick has argued, have alienated the court by monopolizing favours,[19] but the court, as its historian Phillip Mansell observes, was not the centre of political power.[20]

The king and queen were at the point of intersection between two spheres, the court and the government. The relationship between these two spheres has never been better analysed than by Calonne:

Formerly [he was writing in 1781], the royal family, surrounded by an austere etiquette, did not discuss affairs of state with those who formed the court. Even in the most intimate recesses of their society, there was no discussion of anything relating to the administration. The late king and the late queen did not permit even their most cherished courtiers to address them on affairs of state nor to give their views on the performance of ministers: none of them would have dared.

The gentle charm which today tempers the harsh brilliance of the throne has rendered it more accessible. . . . [the rulers] are no longer strangers to the delights of society, and certainly there can result from this much that is beneficial to the happiness of the peoples. But it also has the consequence that when the people who have the most access to the royal family concert action to make a view prevail, they flatter themselves that they can carry their influence even to the operations of the government and that society judges the ministers.[21]

Calonne was writing not about the influence of the court in general (though he argued that this did increase with the advent of the courtier-ministers whom the queen elevated) but of the queen's société intime, the Polignacs. And, as he stood on the threshold of power, he realized that the best way of achieving and retaining it would be to join the group. To that extent he became a courtier himself: the Duc de Lévis remarked that he was the only robin to have court manners. However, in alliance with Artois, he made sure that the

17 M. Price, 'The Comte de Vergennes and the Baron de Breteuil: French politics and reform in the reign of Louis XVI', PhD thesis, Cambridge University, 1988, 34–5.
18 Arneth and Geffroy, Marie-Antoinette, III, 420–1 and 437.
19 D. Wick, 'The court nobility and the French Revolution: the example of the society of thirty', Eighteenth-century studies, 1980, XIII: 263–84.
20 P. Mansell, The Court of France, 1789–1830, Cambridge, 1988.
21 C.A. de Calonne (attrib.) Lettre du Marquis de Caraccioli à M. d'Alembert, 1781, 15.

Polignac group reflected the king's policies rather than the queen's and became in effect a cordon sanitaire against infection from the rest of the court. In this way he built on the foundations laid by Maurepas, to whom we now return.

Maurepas's second device for checking the influence of the queen was employed in what has come to be known as the Affaire de Guines, which reached its twin climax in 1775 and 1776. Since 1770 the Comte de Guines, ambassador to the Court of St James, had been engaged in a lawsuit with his secretary, Tort. Tort had been speculating on the London futures market, gambling that if war broke out between England and France over the latter's support of Spain's claims to the Falkland Islands, government stocks would fall. The *disgrâce* of Choiseul ensured that peace was maintained, stocks rose and when Tort was asked to honour his contract, he claimed that he had been acting as Guines's agent. Guines denied the connection and sued Tort. He also accused the former foreign secretary, d'Aiguillon, of displaying bias in the case and asked Marie-Antoinette to help him recover letters in the possession of the lieutenant-général de police which tended to prove this assertion. Marie-Antoinette was only too happy to oblige a man who was at once the protégé of Choiseul and the enemy of d'Aiguillon. But her meddling infuriated the new ministry and in particular its foreign secretary, Vergennes, who wrote angrily to the king: 'I was really astounded that [Guines] should have had recourse to the queen's protection for something which I could have procured for him without troubling Your Majesty'.[22] On 7 June, Guines duly won his case, which Joseph II for one attributed to the queen's intervention. Marie-Antoinette herself wrote exultantly to Rosenberg: '[D'Aiguillon] had sought to brave my wrath more than once in M. de Guines's affair; as soon as the judgment had been delivered I asked the king to exile him'.[23]

Guines resumed his embassy in triumph but the ministry sought a pretext to cashier him and at the same time deliver a warning to the queen not to meddle in affairs. Guines soon obliged by proposing to England mutual neutrality in the Spanish–Portuguese dispute over the boundaries of Brazil. He made this proposal without authorization and Vergennes found out about it only when a letter from the Spanish ambassador to London was intercepted. Fearful of 'braving the wrath' of the queen, like d'Aiguillon, Vergennes then put up Turgot, 'who was not afraid to affront the queen and importune the king' until Guines had been recalled.[24] Louis further told the queen that Guines's diplomatic career must be considered at an end: 'I have made it abundantly clear to the queen', he told Vergennes, 'that he [Guines]

22 A.N. K164 no. 3, 1775, Vergennes to the king, 12 April.
23 Letter of 13 July, Arneth and Geffroy, *Marie-Antoinette*, III, 362.
24 Véri, *Journal*, I, 389–90.

could not serve either in England nor in another embassy'.[25] When, however, the queen counterattacked and attempted to arrange a disputation before Their Majesties between Maurepas and himself on the one hand and Guines on the other, Vergennes threatened resignation and starkly exposed the issues to the king:

If Your Majesty deigns to recall that it was at his direct command that I informed [Guines] of his recall, he will realize that the only explanation I can give him is to tell him quite frankly that he was dismissed because Your Majesty ordered me to dismiss him. There would be no harm in Your Majesty's informing the queen of the reasons for your decision, but to submit them for discussion with Guines would not so much compromise the character of your ministry as undermine your own supreme authority.[26]

That ended the matter, though an angry Marie-Antoinette boasted that she would have Guines made a duke and Turgot thrown in the Bastille on the same day. A year later, she succeeded in her first objective. Turgot considered that this rendered Guines 'blanc comme neige',[27] but this reflected his feeling that he had been made the scapegoat of the affair. It is true that the queen's activity in the two phases of the Guines Affair had formed a counterpoint to the two most critical moments in Turgot's ministerial career, the Guerre des farines and the lit de justice enforcing his Six Edicts. Nevertheless, as we have seen, the queen did not bring Turgot down, the king did; and Guines's dukedom should be seen as the queen's consolation prize for political defeat.

Things remained like that for the next five years until the strains of war and old age brought about the decline of Maurepas's bodily and political system. The queen had stuck to her bargain and the Polignac group, which apart from the Duc and Duchesse numbered the Marquis de Vaudreuil and the Comte d'Adhémar and was increasingly associated with the king's brother Artois, had remained loyal to Maurepas; though it was the queen's 'société intime', it had sided against her in every difficulty she had with Maurepas. By 1780, however, everyone knew that Maurepas could not last much longer: Mercy, for instance, penned some 'reflections on the approaching death or retirement of the Comte de Maurepas, whose career at the age of more than 80 will soon be terminated one way or another'.[28]

The Polignacs, like everyone else, had to look to the future. Whereas Mercy concluded that the next prime minister must be the queen's 'creature', the Polignacs concluded that if their own career were not to come to an end, they needed supporters in the ministry.

25 Archives de Vergennes, *Lettres de Louis XVI*, letter of 6 February.
26 A.N. K164 no. 3. 1776, undated.
27 Véri, *Journal*, I, 431.
28 Arneth and Geffroy, *Marie-Antoinette*, III, 449.

To this end they had formed an alliance with Necker to bring down Sartine and replace him with Castries. Castries was a long-standing member of the queen's party, so Madame de Polignac and Vaudreuil thought they were doing the right thing when they suggested to her that she summon Castries, 'to inform him that she was taking him under her protection and to make him aware that he would owe his appointment to Her Majesty'.[29]

This tempting suggestion placed her in a quandary, because her position in 1780 was still insecure. In 1778 she had given birth to a daughter but this had been followed by a miscarriage and it was thought unlikely that she would ever bear a dauphin. Mercy and Vermond advised her that to provoke the resignation of Maurepas at this juncture would be disastrous since she would have little prospect of influencing the choice of his successor. Indeed that successor was likely to be the Duc de Nivernais, Maurepas's Prussophile brother-in-law. Accordingly Marie-Antoinette confined her attention to procuring the cordon bleu of the order of the Saint-Esprit for the man she ultimately wanted to head the ministry, Loménie de Brienne (14 October). A year later, after the death of Maurepas and after the birth of the dauphin, she apparently proposed that Brienne enter the council as a ministre, but the king angrily scotched this idea.[30] With her head full of such schemes, she merely told Madame de Polignac that she would mention the matter of Castries to the king. Necker and the Polignacs, as we have seen, duped them all and Castries was appointed. It was a subtle manoeuvre and even that astute observer, the Abbé de Véri, was taken in: 'Here is the first step we have seen the queen take to meddle, with the king's consent, in ministerial appointments'.[31]

Marie-Antoinette, however, soon had her revenge on her favourite. When the position of the war minister, Montbarey, became untenable, the Polignacs aimed to go one better and place one of their number, d'Adhémar, in the ministry as his successor. To have got their hands on military promotions would indeed have been a major coup. Marie-Antoinette blocked d'Adhémar, and her own candidate, Ségur, was appointed instead. Suddenly and unexpectedly, Marie-Antoinette was in a very strong political position. Ségur was her appointment and he was to display an exaggerated deference to her in making military promotions. Castries may not have been her appointment, but it suited them both to act as if he had been. Furthermore, Necker himself, who favoured the aristocratic decentralization advocated by many in the queen's party, often sought her protection. In 1780 Mercy told Maria-Theresa: 'Of all the king's ministers, the directeur Necker is the

---

29 ibid., III, 488–9.
30 Lenoir Papers, Bibliothèque municipale d'Orléans, MSS 1421–3, 1423, mélanges, 39.
31 Véri, *Journal*, II, 392.

one of whom the queen has the best opinion and who has the most of her esteem'.[32]

Necker's ill-judged resignation the following year deferred for several years not only his chance of being de facto prime minister but also Marie-Antoinette's of playing a central role. She vainly strove to prevent Necker's resignation and, unlike the king, she did not blame him for it, believing that he had been brought down by a 'machination infernale'.[33]

After Maurepas's death, the parties regrouped. His old lieutenants, Vergennes and Miromesnil, together with the new finance minister, Joly de Fleury, stood against the queen's ministers, Castries and Ségur, shortly to be joined by Breteuil. The Polignacs were rudderless. At the beginning of 1783, Vergennes anchored them firmly to the comité de gouvernement by the key play of obtaining for d'Adhémar the English embassy, which Marie-Antoinette had refused to solicit for him.[34] Artois now headed the group. Calonne was brought by them into the ministry and, according to Augeard, gave Artois 56 million livres to discharge his debts.[35] The group began to acquire a coherent political creed which they were to take into the pre-revolution and the counter-revolution. The acquisition of *redevable* ministers did not bring Marie-Antoinette much joy. Castries was always complaining. Breteuil did not support the Habsburg interest in the council and was spectacularly incompetent at the maison. Moreover, his advice to the queen over the purchase of Saint-Cloud and the Diamond Necklace Affair led to a dangerous increase in her unpopularity.

Both Louis and Marie-Antoinette were personally frugal: Louis quartered his writing paper to save money and Marie-Antoinette spent most days in the company of and at the expense of the Polignacs. The running of the court amounted to no more than 6 per cent of royal expenditure. In one respect, however, they were extravagant: their propensity to buy palaces, so that 'by 1789 the countryside around Paris resembled a vast park dominated by the palaces, *châteaux* and pavilions of the House of Bourbon'.[36] We have seen that in 1783 d'Ormesson had castigated Vergennes for purchasing Rambouillet from the Duc de Penthièvre out of the funds of the foreign ministry without his knowledge and for attempting to buy Saint-Cloud from the Duc d'Orléans in the same way. D'Ormesson's righteous indignation caused the king to shelve the plan, but only for a year. In September 1784 it resurfaced but with two variations: the negotiations were to be carried out by Breteuil rather than Vergennes (and presumably be paid for out

32 Arneth and Flammermont, *Correspondance secrète* II, 189–96; Price, 'Vergennes and Breteuil', 44–5.
33 Arneth and Flammermont, *Correspondance secrète*, II, 210–11.
34 Arneth and Geffroy, *Marie-Antoinette*, III, 486.
35 J.M. Augeard, *Mémoires secrètes*, ed. E. Bavoux, 1866, 248.
36 Mansell, *Court of France*, 9.

of the funds of the maison du roi) and the purchase was to be in the queen's own name. Castries considered this to be unprecedented: 'It is said to be the first time that there has been a question of giving an estate to a queen of France, because it is for herself and not for the dauphin that the queen wants Saint-Cloud'.[37]

We do not know how and why these modifications to the original plan came about. Mercy believed that Louis was trying to divert Marie-Antoinette from supporting Joseph's designs on Bavaria.[38] Price considers that it was part of the plan that Breteuil had outlined to the queen in 1777, to 'faire régner la reine'. In token of this plan, the palace servants at Saint-Cloud wore the queen's livery and orders were issued 'de par la reine'.[39] If that was indeed Breteuil's plan, it served only to make them both look ridiculous.

Moreover the actual purchase caused problems out of all proportion to its object. Calonne, like d'Ormesson before him, was furious at not being consulted and like him managed to defer the purchase, but only for a month, until 24 October. Calonne played a formal part in the second stage of these negotiations but Marie-Antoinette insisted on being present at his travail with the king when the matter was being discussed, playing the prime minister for the nonce. Lenoir, a close friend of Calonne, considered that the open quarrel over this matter, between Calonne on the one hand and the queen and Breteuil on the other, led to the formation of a king's party and a queen's party.[40] Certainly their quarrel, if indeed this was its origin, contributed not only to the collapse of the ancien régime but also to the division of royalist reactions to the Revolution. However, Calonne was not the only dupe: when the negotiations resumed the queen entrusted them not to Breteuil, who also played only a formal role, but to Vermond and Brienne.[41]

The purchase of Saint-Cloud, which cost 6 million livres and whose interior had to be completely reconstructed, satisfied no one. It was too small to house the court, many of whom had to seek accommodation in the village, and too near to Paris for the king's taste, since it attracted a less desirable class of visitor than ventured to Versailles. When after the first visit in September 1785 Louis proposed that they should all leave early for Fontainebleau, everyone breathed a sigh of relief. Even the queen, who on the grounds of her pregnancy travelled there in a magnificent yacht, which had cost 100,000 livres.

Breteuil's miscalculations in the Diamond Necklace Affair were of even greater consequence than in the purchase of Saint-Cloud. For if any one incident may be said to have begun the 'unravelling' of the

37 Castries, *Journal*, Archives de la Marine, MS 182/7964 1–2, I, fo. 256.
38 Arneth and Flammermont, *Correspondance secrète*, I, 314–15, Mercy to Kaunitz, 27 October.
39 Price, 'Vergennes and Breteuil', 283–5; Arneth and Geffroy, *Marie-Antoinette*, III, 36.
40 Lenoir MS 1423, résidus, 287.
41 Castries, *Journal*, II, fo. 256; Price, 'Vergennes and Breteuil', 285–6.

ancien régime, it was this,[42] touching as it did every nerve-centre of the body politic. The facts of the case are well known. A gang of confidence tricksters headed by Madame de la Motte-Valois persuaded Prince Louis de Rohan, Cardinal-Archbishop of Strassbourg and grand almoner, that he could overcome the queen's hostility if he procured for her without the king's knowledge a fabulous diamond necklace in the possession of the court jewellers, Böhmers. Rohan had alienated Maria-Theresa by his personal deportment when ambassador to Vienna. However, the circumstances of his appointment to that embassy had a more direct bearing on the course of the affair: he had been appointed by d'Aiguillon and had supplanted Choiseul's nominee, Breteuil. When Böhmer presented Rohan's promissory notes accompanied by her forged signature to the queen for redemption, Breteuil thought he could exploit the queen's fury to exact a stunning revenge. Since the lieutenant-général de police and the governor of the Bastille were his subordinates, he was in a good position to do this: Rohan was arrested in his full pontificals as he was about to celebrate mass and thrown into the Bastille.

The other ministers, who would have counselled caution, were not consulted. Miromesnil, who was himself attending mass at Paris (it was the Feast of the Assumption), was summoned to Versailles. Not realizing why the minister for the maison was closeted with the king and queen, his first reaction, such was the climate of ministerial instability, was that he was about to be disgraced.[43] The next day, the king wrote to Vergennes:

You will surely have learned, Monsieur, that I had Cardinal Rohan arrested yesterday. From what he confessed and the papers found on him, it is proved only too conclusively that he has employed false signatures to get hold of diamonds worth 1,600,000 from a jeweller.[44]

The king's reference to a confession raises the possibility that Rohan was not a dupe but planned to use the diamonds to restore the ruined finances of his house. Be that as it may, the king at least decided to consult the other ministers on the question of how to try the cardinal. For Rohan wanted to be tried by the parlement: the queen and Breteuil were inclined to accede to this request. Their reasons for doing so and the disastrous consequences of such apparent generosity will be seen in Chapter 11 on the parlement.

---

42 Rather than the Damiens Affair suggested by Dale van Kley in the title of his *The Damiens Affair and the Unravelling of the Ancien Régime in France*, Princeton, NJ, 1975.
43 Véri, MSS *Journal*, cahier 135; Castries, *Journal*, II, fo. 297.
44 Archives de Vergennes, *Lettres du Louis XVI*, letter of 16 August.

THE ASCENDANCY OF MARIE-ANTOINETTE

The darkest hour is before the dawn. At the beginning of 1787, Marie-Antoinette's influence had reached its nadir. She had failed utterly to gain any support for her brother in his quarrels with the Dutch or his Bavarian exchange project and, as Bombelles notes, 'her société [the Polignacs] had an opinion very different from that of the queen on this great question'.[45] She had been humiliated in the Diamond Necklace Affair and had been unable to exercise her vengeance on Calonne and Vergennes for supporting Cardinal Rohan. When Vergennes had died, she had been unable to secure the appointment of her candidate to succeed him: 'I proposed M. de Saint-Priest,' she wrote to Mercy, '. . . I could not insist against the king's inclinations'.[46] Above all, neither she nor 'her' ministers, Breteuil and Castries, had been consulted over the convocation of the Notables. The king's defeat at the hand of the Notables changed everything. In examining the appointment and dismissal of ministers we have seen how she had given Calonne the final shove. Earlier she had been, as she told Besenval, 'neutral', and though this earned her his stinging rebuke 'c'était déjà trop', it was only when she smelt blood that she moved in. On or about 1 April she had given a favourable reception to Castries when he had said 'that it was necessary to get rid of M. de Calonne'.[47]

Thereafter her influence on the appointment and dismissal of the key ministers was decisive. She was instrumental in the appointment of Brienne, and only when she reluctantly withdrew her support did he finally conclude that he would have to go. Likewise she facilitated the reappointment of Necker and, I have suggested, his replacement by Breteuil on 11 July 1789.

Brienne's and Necker's appointments had in common not only Marie-Antoinette's agency but the king's disheartened resentment, his prediction and almost the perverse wish that they should fail. Conversely, Marie-Antoinette became actively involved in politics: she started attending ministerial comités and she became sufficiently informed about affairs for us for the first time to be able to attempt a sketch of her political ideas. The queen's identification with Brienne, whose appointment her political advisers had worked for so patiently, was especially close. As Egret has observed: 'During the entire course of his ministry, she maintained her support for him with a fidelity which never wavered'.[48]

Castries might have disagreed; at least he noted on 23 June 1787, 'Il [Brienne] n'a aucune confiance directe de la reine à lui', and observed

---

45 Bombelles, *Journal*, II, 21.
46 Marie-Antoinette, *Lettres*, ed. La Rocheterie and Beaucourt, 1895–6, 2 vols, II, 102, 14 February 1787.
47 Castries, *Journal*, II, fo. 358.
48 J. Egret, *La Pré-Révolution française*, 1962, 61.

that he was still dependent on Vermond for his information. What caused him to say this was that it took Brienne eight days to learn that Castries was seeking to resign. This, however, can be attributed to delicacy on the queen's part, knowing as she did that Castries, who had himself asked for the post of chef du conseil royal on Vergennes's death, was jealous of this newcomer to the queen's ministerial affections. Jealousy of Brienne must indeed be taken as the principal motive for the resignations of the queen's original ministers, Castries and Breteuil, and the consequent fragmentation of her political party.

However, in addition to personal jealousy, there developed on the part of Castries and (despite the ambiguities of his resignation) to a lesser extent even of Breteuil, a divergence from the constitutional position of Brienne and consequently of the queen, on which Brienne had a formative influence. Castries favoured an aristocratic gloss on the constitution; Breteuil may have moved in that direction under the influence of his granddaughter's in-laws, the Montmorency. Yet when Marie-Antoinette heard the Duc de Montmorency-Luxembourg lamenting that the great families in France did not have the powers of the princes of the Holy Roman Empire, she looked daggers at him.[49] For whatever his claim that he would be a 'notable au ministère', Brienne had been hired to shore up the absolute monarchy and salvage Calonne's reforms. Marie-Antoinette may have opposed Calonne on personal grounds, but Joseph recognized in him a kindred spirit and correctly predicted that if the king relinquished him, his authority would be 'lost forever'.[50] Even if it could have saved Calonne, Joseph's letter arrived too late. Nevertheless Marie-Antoinette came to recognize that her opposition had been a mistake;[51] one may see that, shaking off the Choiseuliste mentality of her original ministers, she was reverting to a Josephan enlightened despotism. Resentment at the révolte nobiliaire obviously hastened this evolution in her thinking and Necker was able to deploy it during her unique attendance of the council before the résultat du conseil when she silently intimidated those ministers who were reluctant to accord double representation to the third estate. At this time the queen was wont to boast: 'je suis la reine du tiers état, moi'.

Another aspect of her divergence from the views of Castries concerned the roles of the Estates-General and of the parlement. Castries's parting shots to the queen, as well as his request that he be succeeded by a grand seigneur, included the words:

As a Frenchman I want the Estates-General; as a minister it is my duty to tell you that they could destroy your authority.[52]

49 Duc de Montmorency-Luxembourg, *Mémoires*, ed. P. Filleul, 1939, 289–90.
50 Joseph II to Mercy, 26 April 1787, Arneth and Flammermont, *Correspondance secrète*, II, 78.
51 In letters of 1791–2 published by Klinckowström in *Le Comte de Fersen et la cour de France*.
52 Castries, II, *Journal*, fo. 395.

In fact, when still a minister he had read the council a memorandum advocating the convocation of the Estates.[53] Marie-Antoinette's position on the Estates, however, was precisely that of Brienne: their convocation should be deferred, preferably until the Greek Calends but certainly until order – financial and civil – had been restored. She concludes a letter to Joseph describing the séance royale of 19 November 1787 with the words:

What causes me a lot of distress is that the king has announced that he will hold the Estates-General five years from now. There is such a demand for the Estates that the king was advised to summon them on his own initiative while he still had the choice. This would also have ensured that they were more manageable than has sometimes been the case.[54]

On 16 July 1788, she wrote again:

What upsets me is that if we were forced to go to war, we would also be forced to hold the Estates-General and that perhaps before order had been entirely restored.[55]

Similarly with the parlements: shortly before his resignation took effect, Castries was summoned from the country to attend the debates of the council which resulted in the decision to exile the parlement to Troyes. Of this decision he notes

I would have preferred not to have to choose between my general position as a Frenchman and my particular one of minister, not that the two are inconsiderable [sic for incompatible] but as a citizen I might come to a conclusion which goes against a duty I have to perform as a minister.[56]

Marie-Antoinette, however, was fully informed of and fully supported Brienne's measures against the parlement. Indeed it is from her pen that we glean the first recognizable picture of the cour plénière. On 24 April she tells Joseph

the idea is to confine [the parlements] to the function of judges and to create another assembly which will have the right to register taxes and general laws for the [whole] kingdom.[57]

Fears about the parlement are uppermost in her mind when she relinquished Brienne, as she tells Mercy:

I fear that it will drag us into many misfortunes vis-à-vis the parlements. I have just written three lines to M. Necker summoning him here tomorrow at ten o'clock to see me. We can hesitate no longer; if he can set to work tomorrow, so much the better. I tremble (forgive this weakness) that it is I who am bringing him back. My fate is to bring misfortune; and if infernal

---

53 A.N. 306 A.P. 23, quoted in Price, 'Vergennes and Breteuil', 374.
54 Marie-Antoinette, Lettres, II, 109.
55 A. d'Arneth, Marie-Antoinette, Joseph II und Leopold II, 2nd edn, Vienna, 1866, 117–18.
56 Castries, Journal, II, fo. 389.
57 Marie-Antoinette, Lettres, II, 117.

plots cause him to fail again or if he makes the king's authority recede, I will be detested even more.[58]

Marie-Antoinette continued to correspond with Brienne, whose parting advice to the king had been: 'Sire, be sure to avoid an unconditional recall of the parlement or your authority will be destroyed and the monarchy with it'.[59] She tried in vain to salvage Lamoignon's grands baillages at the price of jettisoning the cour plénière and on 11 September, 'in a filthy mood, she flew into a passion against all the ministers in a comité when the the way of restoring the parlement to its functions was being debated'.[60]

Yet despite her passionate defence of the royal authority, she also to an extent shared Castries's anguish and inner conflict. After the 1787 séance royale, she tells Joseph, 'I am grieved that we are obliged to employ such authoritarian measures'; before the coup of 8 May, 'It is very irksome to be obliged to institute changes of this nature'; and during the unrest that followed it, 'It is grievous to be obliged to employ the way of force'.[61] She resented the révolte nobiliaire yet disliked taking the harsh measures necessary to suppress it and at the same time had serious doubts about their efficacy. This inner conflict is surely the clue to the volte-face in her conduct towards the third estate, supporting them over doublement but subsequently opposing their demand for voting by head in the Estates. This volte-face is hard to map precisely because of a gap in her correspondence with Joseph during the critical period (May–June 1789) during the early weeks of the Estates-General. In June Necker's son-in-law, the Baron de Staël, writes of Artois's confidence 'now that he has won over the queen' and Mercy says that she had been 'swept along by the infernal plot directed against the finance minister'.[62] Under the influence of Artois and the Polignacs, she played a major part in the proceedings at Marly, weaning the king away from the third estate with the 'emotional blackmail' described by the Comtesse d'Adhémar.[63] After the débâcle of the séance royale, however, the union of the orders on 27 June was, according to Mercy, effected by the 'moderation and wisdom of her counsels'.[64] With a 'severe gesture', she ordered Vaudreuil to leave the room for suggesting that Necker should be put on trial for not attending the séance royale.[65] Her vacillation (or middle position)

---

58 Arneth and Flammermont, *Correspondance secrète* II, 210–11.
59 Reported in the *Gazette de Leyde* of 5 September.
60 Arneth, *Marie-Antoinette, Joseph II und Leopold II*, 206–9; Bombelles, *Journal*, II, 232.
61 Marie-Antoinette, *Lettres*, II, 108–9, 115 and 118–20.
62 *États-généraux, recueil de documents relatifs aux états-généraux de 1789*, 4 vols, 1953–70, I (2), 94.
63 Comtesse d'Adhémar, *Souvenirs sur Marie-Antoinette . . .*, 1836, 4 vols, III, 170–5.
64 Mercy to Joseph II, 4 July 1789, Arneth and Flammermont, *Correspondance secrète*, II, 253.
65 Vaudreuil, *Correspondance intime du Comte de Vaudreuil et du Comte d'Artois*, ed. L. Pingaud, 1889, 2 vols, I, xxvii–xxviii.

drew her back once more to Breteuil and I have suggested was responsible for his appointment on 12 July. Whereas Castries, however, set up camp with the *émigrés* at Coblenz, Breteuil, as the king's plenipotentiary, adopted a line more moderate both in aim and method.

CHAPTER ELEVEN

The crown and the parlement

The relations between the absolute monarchy and the parlement in the last fifteen years of the existence of both presents a paradox for the historian: the mutually destructive crisis of 1785–6, to which I shall devote the bulk of this chapter, was preceded by over ten years of stability. In 1782 this stability was celebrated, rather smugly, by the two men with the main responsibility for securing it, Miromesnil, the keeper of the seals, and Étienne-François d'Aligre, the premier président of the parlement. Miromesnil, while conceding to Véri that people blamed his 'grande complaisance' towards the parlementaires, added 'the magistrature had nevertheless not made any trouble while I have been in office'.[1] D'Aligre likewise told Vergennes, 'Since the king's accession, he had not experienced any difficulties on the part of the parlement of Paris. They have always registered everything immediately'.[2] The context for these self-congratulatory remarks was the registration of the edict establishing the third vingtième, which was generally considered to be the perfect example of harmony between crown and parlement. This edict was indeed registered fairly easily (after one set of remontrances). Nevertheless many aspects of the process betray anxiety on all sides and show why this was in fact the last direct tax to be imposed by the ancien régime.

Admiral Rodney himself could not have rejoiced more at his victory in the Battle of the Saints than the finance minister Joly de Fleury. It gave him the perfect excuse to raise taxation, as he told the king on 23 June: 'The recent naval reverses . . . have already prepared opinion for this tax and it could prove very inconvenient to give it time to cool off'. This letter sets the tone for the negotiations with the parlement to register the tax and in particular furnished the line of argument which

---

1 Abbé de Véri, MSS *Journal*, Archives départementales de la Drôme, Valence, unclassified, cahier 109.
2 AAE MDF 1392 fo. 170, letter of 9 July, cited in M. Price, 'The Comte de Vergennes and the Baron de Breteuil: French politics and reform in the reign of Louis XVI', PhD thesis, Cambridge University, 1988, 165.

Joly's friend Lefebvre d'Amécourt, the *rapporteur* (political agent) of the king in the *parlement*, used with his colleagues. Thus Joly argued that the tax would shorten the war

by making our enemies see that one reverse . . . does not exhaust French financial resources.

Moreover,

The period during which it will be levied, being much shorter than that of the first and second *vingtièmes*, and its completely different character, will reassure people that its life will not be extended beyond the prescribed limit.[3]

The 'prescribed limit' was three years after the signature of peace. Further to emphasize the transitory nature of the third *vingtième*, Joly de Fleury promised, not indeed as has often been said that *vérification* for the other *vingtièmes* would be abandoned, but that the new tax would be collected on the existing rolls. However, such was the *parlement*'s suspicion that even d'Amécourt believed that the government deliberately prolonged the war to secure an extra year's revenue.[4]

These themes resurfaced the following year, 1783. Vergennes believed that Austria and Russia planned a total dismemberment of the Turkish Empire and did not intend that France should stand idly by as she had during the Partition of Poland but should at least mobilize. He confided his fears to Bertin with the request that he suggest sources of additional taxation which would get through the courts. Bertin made the general observation that

There can be no success in the courts if they see [a tax] as the concern of the finance ministry and to disabuse them of this notion and guarantee success it must be presented to them (as indeed it is) as pertaining to the ministry of peace and war, that is to say of foreign affairs. I think that this is truer than ever at the present moment. You have yourself already experienced this as regards the edict of M. de Fleury [the third *vingtième*]. Your presence in the *conférences* with the gentlemen from the *parlement* was, believe me, decisive, and the main theme of the enclosed preamble [i. e. considerations of foreign policy] reinforces the point.

Having observed that there could be no question of further *vingtièmes* or *sols pour livres*, Bertin continued

There are items of luxury which could easily bear a tax but as they would fall on the people who are in the best position to evade them, a progressive tax on saddle and carriage-horses and valets would frankly yield very little and would stir up the most violent storm against their author.

He concluded in favour of a stamp duty on commercial transactions but thought that there should be a promise that it would end at the

---

3 B.N. fonds Joly de Fleury, 1438 fos 204–7.
4 D'Amécourt, *Journal du règne de Louis XVI*, B.N. n.a.f. 22111 fo. 66.

same time as the third vingtième, '*even if it came to war*', since 'this would be an additional reason for the courts to agree to an edict which would calm their anxieties concerning its continuation'.[5]

The war-scare (one of several in the 1780s) receded but the episode further demonstrates that the registration of the third vingtième reveals not harmony between crown and parlement but that for ten years after 1774 the government bought peace by eschewing controversial legislation. The resistance provoked by the only exception, Turgot's Six Edicts, had led their author to tell the king in 1776:

Louis XV at 40 still enjoyed the plenitude of his authority: no corps had chanced its arm. Whereas you, Sire, are 22 and the parlements are already more restless, more audacious, more linked to court cabals than they were in 1770 after twenty years of success.[6]

Turgot implies that conflict was inevitable, that the parlements were like a vigorous perennial weed which had to be cut to the ground every so often but every time would grow up stronger.

Yet the relationship between the absolute monarchy and the parlement should have been a symbiotic one: rule by crown and parlement without reference to representative institutions being the essence of the political system of the ancien régime. At times the parlementaires seemed to recognize this and defended the structures of the post-medieval state. If only out of self-interest they asserted that the country should be run by the 'gent robine' and not by the old military aristocracy. The provincial parlements may have often made the intendant's life a burden to him but they defended his position against local assemblies, whether the old provincial estates or the new-fangled provincial assemblies. This view also extended to the Estates-General: the king and parlement alone were competent to run the country. But the parlement employed paradox in its defence of the king's interests, with its endless (and to the king) wearying variations on the theme that it was more royalist than the king, preventing him, for example, from selling out the interests of the Gallican church to the Pope, preventing 'his religion from being surprised' by evil advisers (i. e. his own ministers, etc.) and its own position was paradoxical. For the parlementaires were themselves noble landowners, juridically and economically indistinguishable from the military nobility that they wanted to exclude from politics and administration and as reluctant to pay the vingtième. Indeed, having an official position, they tended to be more successful than the 'noblesse d'épée' in overawing the tax assessors. Thus, as Bailey Stone has observed, the parlementaires championed the new state but denied it the wherewithal to operate effectively.[7] Another American historian, Durand Echeverria, takes an

---

5 B.N. n.a.f. 6498; one of Bertin's letters is dated 16 July 1783.
6 Transcribed by the Abbé de Véri, *Journal 1774–80*, ed. J. de Witte, 1928–30, 2 vols, I, 452.
7 B. Stone, *The Parlement of Paris, 1774–89*, North Carolina, 1981, 180.

even more pessimistic view of the relations between crown and parlement: 'It would be difficult to conceive of any alternative at this juncture [1770] to Maupeou's absolutist coup except an aristocratic takeover'.[8]

The English historians Doyle[9] and Rogister[10] argue that the parlement was both weaker (especially, Doyle argues, after the 1774 restoration) and less intransigent. In particular it did not intend to starve the monarchy of funds. We find this view less plausible. For the parlementaires could not understand the financial needs of the modern monarchy and out of self-interest they often turned a blind eye to such illumination as came their way. Not that much came from the royal quarter: on the one occasion when the clouds lifted from the arcana of royal finances it was to reveal the rosy light of Necker's *Compte rendu*. The *Compte* made life difficult for Necker's successors. Considering some replies to imagined objections to the third vingtième, Bourgade notes that though the parlement had 'given its approval to this *Compte*' it must nevertheless be made to understand 'that if, as we can prove and as the king has been informed, there were on the contrary a gap between revenue and "ordinary" expenditure, it must follow that it would be indispensable to bridge it'.[11]

However, it was a lost cause. Joly de Fleury was right when he told the king that the conditions for imposing the third vingtième were ideal and never likely to be repeated. This was why he thought that Necker had been ill advised to freeze the level of the taille in 1781. It will be remembered that Joly's parting advice to the king on leaving office in 1783 was 'Revoke the declaration concerning the "brevet général" [of the taille] . . . it is very restricting for the administration which cannot tax without enregistrement'.[12] Necker's measures, combined with Louis's views on bankruptcy and the parlement's attitude to the taxation of the nobility, epitomized by Duval d'Éprémesnil's 'taxation is but a temporary inconvenience',[13] implied that sooner or later there would be a crisis.

Yet Maurepas thought he knew what he was doing in recalling the parlement in 1774 and if anyone could have managed that body it was him, as he had shown during his first ministry, when he had brought 'legal knowledge, foresight, and skill as a negotiator' to the task.[14] The

---

8 D. Echeverria, *The Maupeou Revolution*, Baton Rouge, La., 1985, 11.

9 W. Doyle, 'The Parlements', in K.M. Baker (ed.) *The Political Culture of the Ancien Régime*, Chicago, 1987.

10 J.M.J. Rogister, 'Conflict and harmony in eighteenth-century France: a reappraisal of the pattern of relations between Crown and Parlement under Louis XV', DPhil thesis, Oxford University, 1972.

11 B.N. fonds Joly de Fleury, 1438 fos 211–12.

12 ibid., 1442 fo. 39.

13 B. Stone, *The French Parlements and the Crisis of the Ancien Régime*, North Carolina, 1986, 123.

14 Rogister, 'Conflict and harmony', 36.

1774 restoration was not intended to be of the status quo ante 1771, and discipline was to be reinforced with management, the stick with the carrot. If the parlement engaged in the more extreme tactics it had employed in the previous reign it was to be judged by a cour plénière consisting of various 'notables' and if the parlementaires resorted to a judicial strike it was to be automatically replaced by the grand conseil, as had happened in 1771. Unfortunately Miromesnil undermined the efficacy of this threat from the start by 'cooperating [with the parlement] in the degradation' [of the grand conseil].[15] In 1777 the grand conseil had to ask the king to defer publication of a règlement 'which the keeper of the seals is currently working at' restricting its jurisdiction in conformity with the parlementaires' wishes.[16]

The carrot, in the form of patronage, was employed to better effect. In 1774 the powers of the grand' chambre staffed by senior judges more susceptible to government influence were strengthened at the expense of the junior and traditionally more independent chambers, the *enquêtes*, whose numbers were reduced. Using the *état nominatif* of pensions published by order of the National Assembly in 1789–90, Bailey Stone has shown the extent of pensions paid to leading grand' chambriers. D'Aligre received 80,000 livres in 1768 to defray his installation expenses; in 1775 he was given a pension of 20,000 livres, and his wife one of 8,000 livres in 1779. His deputy, Président d'Ormesson, had long enjoyed a pension of 15,000 livres, while Président Joly de Fleury had three pensions totalling 17,000 livres; Séguier, the avocat-général, enjoyed pensions totalling 16,000 livres, while in 1781 Lefebvre d'Amécourt was granted a pension of 6,000 livres 'in consideration of his services' as the king's political agent.[17].

What the état nominatif does not tell us, however, is the money, favours and promises which the judges received unofficially. These were often more effective because being secret they were also conditional; they could be withdrawn. The government, for instance, in addition to granting d'Aligre his pensions turned a blind eye to two considerable debts of his to the crown. One was of 50,000 livres for the charge of conseiller au parlement for his son and the other was for 200,000 livres, the capital on a life annuity from the loan of 1781 on which by 1786 he had received 81,000 livres interest. Moreover the king, who did not like financial dishonesty in public administration, had not been informed.[18] The potential for blackmail was considerable.

The recipients of crown patronage were often referred to as the parti ministériel, and Stone considers that their numbers were confined

15 Véri, *Journal*, I, 420.
16 Stone, *Parlement of Paris*, 42.
17 ibid., 22–8.
18 A.N. K163 no. 8. 14, Miromesnil to the king, 5 August 1786.

to two handfuls: d'Aligre, d'Ormesson, the Joly de Fleury brothers (a président and a procureur-général – the finance minister was also their brother), Séguier, the avocat-général, the Abbé d'Espagnac and his successor as rapportuer du roi, d'Amécourt.[19] The term parti ministériel implies, however, that the ministry was united, which was not always the case. In any case the patronage was not distributed collectively by the ministry. In 1782 Miromesnil claimed that he had never bought votes, only given money to some magistrates 'à raison de malheurs domestiques'; he added, 'I know that often the finance ministers have adopted this method: it should not be that of a chancellor'.[20]

The contrôleur-général was indeed the largest dispenser of patronage. At the end of the Diamond Necklace Affair, heard before the parlement in 1785/6, d'Aligre supplied Mercy-Argenteau with a list of eleven judges whom Calonne had influenced:

1. Président de Gilbert is listed as being 'sold to the contrôleur-général who has sold his estate at Saint-Étienne for him to the king'.
2. Président de Rosambo was almost ruined and was making many financial requests of Calonne.
3. Président de Lamoignon is described as 'particulièrement lié' with Lenoir, Calonne's âme damnée during this period, and particularly influential with the parlement with whom he had relations as lieutenant-général de police. Calonne of course had his own line to Lamoignon and was suspected of trying to eject Miromesnil in his favour in 1784.[21]
4. Oursin was Le Noir's cousin and devoted to Calonne.
5. Pasquier was dependent on the contrôleur-général whom he was asking to waive the tax on his son's charge.
6. Delpech.
7. Barillon was several years behind on the payment of his capitation and he wanted the contrôleur-général to let him off.

A further four judges were influenced by three of the preceding: Lepelletier de Saint-Fargeau followed Lamoignon and Rosambo; Saron and Glatigny followed Lamoignon; and le Pileur followed Barillon.[22]

The cases of Pasquier and Barillon were similar to d'Aligre's and Calonne developed this form of pressure into a fine art. He did not, however, invent it: d'Aligre's own forgotten debts went back to 1781. In 1782 the publication of Turgot's papers caused great embarrassment when it revealed a list of magistrates secretly pensioned by the former

19 Stone, *Parlement of Paris*, 26.
20 Véri, MSS *Journal*, cahier 109.
21 Baron de Besenval, *Mémoires*, ed. Berville and Barrière, 1821, 2 vols, II, 2–6 and 13 *et seq.*
22 A. d'Arneth and J. Flammermont (eds) *Correspondance secrète du Comte de Mercy-Argenteau avec l'Empereur Joseph II et le Prince de Kaunitz*, 1891, 2 vols, II, 32–6.

contrôleur-général.[23] It should be noted that the judges influenced by Calonne were not the parti ministériel. Indeed, in the case in point, the Diamond Necklace Affair, these parlementaires actually voted on opposite sides to the parti ministériel. A similar situation would have obtained in Turgot's day: one may presume that his following was geared to registering the Six Edicts which Miromesnil was trying to block.

Ironically a constant theme with Miromesnil is that only divisions within the ministry made the parlement dangerous. Véri warned Miromesnil in 1782 that when peace came the parlement was to be feared because it would be difficult for the government to extend the life of taxes.

To be feared [rejoined the Keeper] never! That was one of Louis XV's childish notions; at least a division among his ministers made them seem formidable. Are you having me believe that one should fear three or four thousand unarmed men in black robes?[24]

THE BREAKDOWN IN RELATIONS BETWEEN
CROWN AND PARLEMENT, 1785–6

The rest of this chapter forms a series of variations on the theme that Miromesnil set before the king in 1785:

Nothing disconcerts intrigue like union of the ministers with each other and with the premier président . . . the main thing is that your business gets through and Your Majesty will judge each man by his conduct.[25]

In December 1785 the parlement registered the edict creating the third and last of Calonne's annual loans. With the rejection of bankruptcy by the king and of new taxation by the parlement, Calonne was thrown back on loans to liquidate the war debts and pay for Castries's naval expenditure which continued unchecked after the failure of the comité des finances. The parlement showed little understanding of and less sympathy for Calonne's predicament. Calonne's quarrels with the parlement went back to the previous reign when as a young maître des requêtes he had been rapporteur in the La Chalotais affair. However, the decisive event was his quarrel with Breteuil over the purchase of Saint-Cloud and over the king's decision that Calonne should receive police reports concerning financial operations direct from Le Noir rather than through Le Noir's superior, Breteuil.[26] Not only did Breteuil as minister for Paris have legitimate concerns with

23 Véri, MSS *Journal*, cahier 109.
24 ibid.
25 A.N. K163 no. 8. 4, 11 December 1785.
26 Lenoir Papers, Bibliothèque municipale d'Orléans, MS 1421–3, 1423, mélanges, 39.

and therefore a party in the parlement, but also he was in particular closely allied with d'Amécourt, who had hoped to succeed d'Ormesson as contrôleur and now desired to supplant Calonne.[27] Calonne had promised to recommend that d'Amécourt be made a conseiller d'état,[28] but this was not enough to satisfy him. The ministerial aspirations of parlementaires added another variation to inter-ministerial rivalries.

Calonne's loan was finally registered only 'at the king's express command' – the formula employed for a lit de justice which would not have encouraged subscribers. Moreover the parlement placed its objections in an arrêté at the end of the final form of the edict, a proceeding which was also, as Calonne observed, 'calculated to discredit the loan'.[29] As a result, Calonne never raised another loan: writing to the king in August 1786 he saw the origin of a National Bank in a loan to the state by the Caisse d'escompte:

It is a necessary resource to enable us to dispense with a new loan and supply the funds for the coming year.[30]

After the 1785 loan had been registered, Calonne sent the former contrôleur Bertin, himself the victim of parlementaire opposition, to quiz d'Amécourt. Bertin sent Calonne a résumé of this interview in the form of Calonne's accusations together with d'Amécourt's replies. These provide an insight into the discussions which generally took place between the ministers and the parti ministériel prior to the presentation of royal legislation. Calonne had had preliminary discussions with d'Amécourt in which it had been agreed that the loan should be registered 'after "representations", everything passing off amicably'. On 8 December there had followed, as was customary, a conférence in Miromesnil's apartments between the Keeper, Calonne (and probably Vergennes) for the government and d'Aligre, d'Amécourt, and the brothers Joly de Fleury, the parti ministériel, for the parlement.[31] At this meeting Calonne had defended his measures in a 'truly sparkling manner' but his very presence had excited some outspoken criticism. D'Amécourt had given Calonne to understand 'with a whisper and a wink' that this criticism would die down when the edict was discussed in the parlement's comités particuliers. Afterwards d'Amécourt asked Calonne for a copy of the memorandum he had read to the meeting and it was on d'Amécourt's subsequent use of this memorandum (which was read out in the chambre des enquêtes) that Calonne's criticism of d'Amécourt's conduct turned.

---

27 Prince de Talleyrand, *Mémoires*, ed. Duc de Broglie, 1891–2, 5 vols, I, 90–1; fonds Joly de Fleury, 607 fo. 95; A.N. K163 no. 8. 22.
28 Calonne Papers, P.R.O. P.C. 1/125.68.
29 ibid.
30 A.N. K677.104.
31 B.N. fonds Joly de Fleury, 607 fo. 76.

Calonne accused d'Amécourt of telling his colleagues that he had personally 'verified the falsity' of Calonne's accounting and of criticizing 'with studied *sarcasm* even the *various declarations in the preamble*', which gave a rosy picture of the future. Calonne's was a fair accusation: d'Amécourt had told Président Joly de Fleury that he was against registration.[32] D'Amécourt, however, was on firmer ground in refuting Calonne's last charge: 'registration with an arrêté tacked on which was calculated to discredit the loan': though the arrêté did indeed discredit the loan, it was the best d'Amécourt could do, 'given the disposition to ask the king to withdraw his edict and that an arrêté to this effect had obtained nineteen supporters etc.'.[33]

D'Amécourt's best, however, was not good enough for the king, nor indeed for Miromesnil, for whose benefit Calonne had asked Bertin to draft his report. Miromesnil confessed to the king that he distrusted d'Amécourt.[34] Vergennes and the Polignacs supported Calonne's demand for royal intervention to quash the offending arrêté. On the evening of 21 December, Bombelles records, the Polignac group was greatly agitated: the Duc de Polignac, 'pacing up and down', neglected his guests; 'the Duchesse only arrived when supper was served. M. de Vaudreuil collared her immediately; anger flashed from the eyes of this outspoken friend of the contrôleur-général'.[35] Louis needed little encouragement to chastise the parlement; it was said that when he was displeased with that body 'his whole physiognomy altered'. On 23 December, the king summoned the parlement to Versailles by lettre de cachet for what he termed in his diary an 'audience' rather than a 'lit de justice'. After chastising the parlementaires for publishing remontrances which were intended for his own, not public, consumption and for abusing his kindness to the point of 'criticizing his administration at all times and in all places', he told them, 'I am going to annul an arrêt which is as ill considered as it is disrespectful'. Then he took a piece of paper out of his pocket and gave it to Breteuil, whom the irony of the situation cannot have escaped, and told him to instruct the greffier-en-chef to record everything he had just said. To make sure Louis repeated: 'Is that quite clear? The arrêt must be printed as it now stands'. For the king, this was the central event of the 'audience', as his terse diary entry makes clear: '23 Decembre. Audience du parlement pour biffer ses registres'.

As the parlement was leaving, the king called back d'Aligre to tell him: 'I no longer want M. Dammécourt as the rapporteur of my affairs; you will give the keeper of the seals an alternative and he will report to me'. On 28 December Miromesnil told the king that 'the next day

32 ibid., fo. 111, cited in Stone, *Parlement of Paris*, 88.
33 Original italics; P.R.O. P.C. 1/125.68.
34 A.N. K163 no. 8. 7.
35 Marquis de Bombelles, *Journal*, ed. J. Grassion and F. Durif, Geneva, 1978–93, 3 vols, II, 96.

the premier président will give me a list of those gentlemen in the grande chambre whom he considers most suitable to carry out the duties of rapporteur of Your Majesty's business'. The king, however, did not find any of them suitable, or at least none of them was appointed. As d'Amécourt maliciously observes, 'we were a long time without a rapporteur de la cour. Finally the Abbé Tandeau was appointed'.[36] That evening the canopy of Calonne's bed collapsed on him, and he was buried beneath 'forty pounds weight' and unable to reach his bell. Rescued at last, he had himself bled twice, as a precaution or, according to Bombelles, as a publicity stunt. Wits made laborious puns on *ciel*, which is the French both for 'canopy' and for 'the Heavens'.[37]

Though this séance did not achieve the celebrity of the 'séance de flagellation', there was a realization among the participants that a critical situation had been reached. The procureur-général, Joly de Fleury, tried to effect a reconciliation but he found little appetite for one on the part of the parlement. D'Amécourt warned Miromesnil that there was talk of the parlement's formally protesting at the king's actions when it came to discuss them a week later, but Miromesnil replied that if that happened he would advise the king to summon 'the whole parlement' and once again 'score out with his own hand such a disrespectful arrêté'. However, Miromesnil at the same time confided to the king his growing sense of disquiet as his system for controlling the parlement began to show cracks:

I confess, Sire, that I am in a considerable state of anxiety, not out of fear of what will happen (because those who fear the parlements do not know or do not wish to know how little they are to be feared) but because I am pretty uncertain of the good faith of those with whom I have to deal.[38]

The situation further deteriorated the following March when the parlement denounced Calonne's re-coinage. This increase in the ratio paid by the Mint for gold and silver from 14.4 to 15.5 to 1 was necessary to prevent gold coins from being exported; the defective ratio had been primarily responsible for the crisis at the Caisse d'escompte in 1783. However, d'Amécourt and his allies presented the consequent reduction in size of the gold *louis* by one-sixteenth as a further chance for Calonne to line his own pockets. D'Amécourt was aided in this denunciation by the conseiller d'état, Foulon, who was Breteuil's alternative candidate to replace Calonne and who had his own following in the parlement. Foulon had previously had responsibility for the Mint and he simultaneously tried to detach Vergennes from Calonne by presenting him, as chef du conseil royal

36 This account is based on d'Amécourt's MSS *Journal* fo. 74 *et seq*; Miromesnil's letter is in A.N. K163 no. 8. 6.
37 Bombelles, *Journal*, II, 97.
38 Stone, *Parlement of Paris*, 89; A.N. K163 no. 8. 7, Miromesnil to the king, 4 January 1786.

des finances, with a memorandum critical of the re-coinage. The manoeuvre backfired, Vergennes backed Calonne, and Foulon was exiled.[39]

The action then moved to the dénouement of the Diamond Necklace Affair. Rohan, it will be remembered, had expressed a wish to be tried by the parlement and the king had now to decide whether to accede to his request. Miromesnil held that Rohan's office of grand almoner – it had been 'grand' only for two centuries! – did not automatically entitle him to trial by parlement since it was not a great office of state like that of the chancellor; he should be sent for trial to the châtelet 'si le roi ne lui donnait une attribution directe au parlement'.[40] On 25 August 1785 the king assembled a comité to decide the matter. Castries informs us that it included, apart from himself, the king, the queen, Vergennes, Breteuil, Miromesnil, 'etc.' [sic].[41] The queen had not attended ministerial comités before but on this one occasion she had extracted the king's promise that no minister should speak to him about the affair except in her presence. Vergennes and Castries argued that Rohan should be tried by the châtelet; the queen and Breteuil, with apparent magnanimity, said that his request for trial by parlement should be granted.

The magnanimity of Breteuil, in whose office the lettres patentes sending Rohan for trial in the parlement were drafted,[42] at first sight seems curious. However, he knew that he would have d'Amécourt, d'Aligre and the parti ministériel on his side. Unfortunately, this was not sufficient. Calonne and Vergennes lined up what d'Amécourt called 'the opposing camp', headed by Président Lamoignon, against them. It was the strength of this group, incidentally, which had enabled Lamoignon at the beginning of 1786 to advise Calonne that the Lemaître affair should be evoked to the parlement, where he would be 'absolute master of the case' and able to prevent damaging revelations about their authorship of anti-government pamphlets; whereas Miromesnil argued correctly that the matter concerned the state and should be subject to 'administrative law'.[43]

Vergennes's position in the Diamond Necklace Affair was coloured by obligations to the House of Rohan and he went to great lengths to secure the witnesses who could prove that the cardinal had been a dupe rather than an accomplice.[44] Calonne wanted to bring about Breteuil's fall, not only out of malice but also, as he told Lamoignon, because he wanted to move to the ministry of the maison du roi

39 D'Amécourt, MSS Journal, fo. 74.
40 Véri, MSS Journal, cahier 136.
41 Castries, Journal, Archives de la Marine, MS 182/7964 1–2, I, fo. 303.
42 Lenoir MS 1423, mélanges, 31–9.
43 J.M. Augeard, Mémoires secrètes, 1866, 141 ff.; A.N. K163 no. 8. 9 and 8; Miromesnil to the king, 15 and 17 January 1786.
44 Price, 'Vergennes and Breteuil', 311–36.

before the financial crisis which had always been expected in 1787 and which his personal difficulties with the parlement threatened to aggravate.[45] On this occasion therefore, Calonne was using the crown's patronage, which had enabled him to build up his faction in the parlement against the king. Moreover, not only was the king in effect subsidizing rival factions in the parlement, but also each, in the persons of d'Amécourt and Lamoignon, was headed by a ministerial aspirant.

When it became clear that Rohan was likely to be acquitted, members of the parti ministériel, who felt personal sympathy for the king and queen, strove at least to impose some lesser sentence on the cardinal for indiscreet conduct which would salvage the queen's honour and satisfy her vengeance. Apparently, the procureur-général, Joly de Fleury, concluded that Rohan should apologize before the court to the king and queen and resign his offices. D'Amécourt is said to have supported this line, but without success.[46] Instead, at the end of May 1786, Rohan secured a straight acquittal by twenty-six votes to twenty-three.

Calonne, however, had also miscalculated. Breteuil's ministerial career survived the affair: it was hard enough to dislodge a minister for the maison but one supported by the queen was virtually impregnable. Since Calonne could not now change ministries he would have to attempt to gain proper control of the parlement by breaking d'Aligre, who also had been weakened by the acquittal.

This forced Miromesnil, who had lain low during the trial, to act to save the parti ministériel he had nursed for twelve years. When Calonne chose this moment to resurrect d'Aligre's debts to the crown the premier président, dishonoured in the king's eyes and chronically ill, was inclined to throw in the towel.[47] Miromesnil prevented him and covered his tracks in a tortuous rather than balanced letter to the king, for the length of which he apologizes. In it Miromesnil admits the weakness of d'Aligre's excuse, that he had not realized that his debts to the crown had gone unpaid because of the death of two successive notaries in charge of his affairs. Nevertheless, Calonne was wrong in wanting to omit this justification from the arrêt du conseil annulling the contract. D'Aligre's opposition to Calonne was 'implacable', as he had demonstrated during the discussions on the loan of 1785 and the re-coinage:

M. le contrôleur-général is fully aware how disadvantageous it will be to have at the head of the parlement a leader always disposed to undermine his administration. He ardently desires that M. d'Aligre should go and I cannot blame him.

45 Augeard, *Mémoires secrètes*, 152.
46 Stone, *Parlement of Paris*, 74–5.
47 Auget de Montyon; *Particularités sur les ministres des finances les plus célèbres*, 1812, 260 n. a.

Nevertheless

It is not possible to force a premier président to retire; for that one would have to put him on trial. And whatever M. d'Aligre says about it I see clearly that at present he has no desire to hand in his resignation.[48]

The garde des sceaux was certainly in a position to create constitutional conventions but to say that a premier président could not be dismissed was a dangerous innovation. It was true that in practice the king did not have much control over the actual appointment of the premier président, since this was in effect determined by seniority: if Calonne had succeeded in breaking d'Aligre he would have been succeeded by Président d'Ormesson, not Calonne's ally Lamoignon. Nevertheless the premier président, unlike the présidents à mortier, held a revocable commission. To give him permanent tenure, like the chancellor, was for the crown to relinquish a vital measure of control over the parlement, for there was no procedure for exiling him and having another perform his functions. It is indeed amazing that Miromesnil could say, almost in the same breath, that d'Aligre was 'always disposed to undermine [Calonne's] administration' and yet that he could not be dismissed. What did Miromesnil expect Calonne to do? Probably exemplify the current maxim that it was ordinarily premier présidents who broke contrôleurs-généraux and not the other way round. It must have come as a genuine surprise to him when Calonne pulled the temple down about them both.

Calonne's failed attempt to discredit d'Aligre (he stayed on until 1788) completed the ruin of his credit with the parlement. His party had in any case been a transient configuration numbering clients of the Rohan (three judges) and 'antagonistes de la cour' (a further six) as well as those in his pocket.[49] They would not necessarily be available to support his financial operations. D'Aligre, who was angry at the way Calonne had dragged up his debts, even refused to speak about affairs with him without authorization from his colleagues.[50] According to Augeard the *parquet* and the *grand banc* (saving only Lamoignon and Brochet de Saron) went against him and only eight conseillers remained to him of the coalition that had saved Rohan.[51]

In December Miromesnil got wind of a manoeuvre by Breteuil and d'Amécourt to try and bring about Calonne's fall by having him denounced in the parlement for borrowing more money than was stipulated in the loan edicts (there had been a similar manoeuvre the previous January).[52] Calonne had left open the loans of Necker and Joly de Fleury as well as his own after they had been fully subscribed.

48 A.N. K163 no. 8. 14, letter of Saturday, 5 August.
49 Arneth and Flammermont, *Correspondance secrète*, II, 28–36.
50 Stone, *Parlement of Paris*, 89.
51 Augeard, *Mémoires*, 154.
52 A.N. K163 no. 8. 7, Miromesnil to the king.

Breteuil, who as minister for the maison had access to the records of the hôtel de ville which backed the rentes, was to supply d'Amécourt and his associates with the details. They hoped thereby to create a scandal and have the contracts for rentes in excess of the figure guaranteed by the parlement annulled; Calonne would be forced to resign and would be replaced with d'Amécourt. Nothing came of this, probably because Miromesnil advised the king to confront Breteuil over the matter. However, the climate was sufficiently soured for Miromesnil to advise the king that it was hopeless to attempt Calonne's plan of having the timbre and the lease of the crownlands registered in the parlement before the opening of the Notables.

This advice of Miromesnil's undermines the argument sometimes advanced that Calonne assembled the Notables because the parlement lacked the necessary prestige to endorse the measures – he assembled them because he could no longer get even conventional measures through the parlement – and weakens the general argument that the parlement came back in 1774 conscious of its weakness and that in 1787–8 it called for the Estates-General because it no longer had the capacity to withstand the demands of the royal despotism.[53] It may be objected that the troubles in the parlement stemmed from personal rivalries which the king for one, who was fully informed of them, should have put a stop to. Miromesnil may indeed have been right in saying that it was divisions within the ministry which undermined the king's authority in the parlement; in the case of Breteuil and Calonne, the difference was of politics not policy.

However, the implementation of the reform programme which the comité de gouvernement had been maturing since 1783 would inevitably have meant conflict between Calonne and Miromesnil himself over divisions which went beyond politics, touching as they did the organization of society and even the constitution, whether there was an attempt to implement them through the traditional structures or through the Notables. Miromesnil had after all undermined Turgot's less radical measures in the parlement. This struggle was too fundamental to be explained away in terms of Louis XVI's failure to hold a cabinet together. Miromesnil was reflecting parlementaire beliefs: no minister, not Miromesnil himself, could have got Calonne's whole programme through the parlement, given that the attempt to have even a part of it passed was abandoned. It was hoped that the Notables' endorsement would overcome parlementaire resistance.

Only a fundamental cleavage can explain why it was that the two constituent parts of the political system of the ancien régime – the absolute monarchy and the parlement – should have turned away from the system which gave them both their existence. Faced with the impasse of 1786 – a dilemma as stark as that which Echeverria has

---

53 This case is put most cogently by W. Doyle, 'The Parlements of France and the breakdown of the old regime, 1771–88', *French Historical Studies*, 1970 **VI**: 415–58.

Louis XV confronting in 1770 – Louis XVI ostensibly had two choices which lay within the framework of the ancien régime: instigate a coup such as Maupeou's or capitulate to the parlement. A coup was difficult because the parlement had not seriously violated the terms of the 1774 settlement; in particular it had not resorted to a judicial strike nor had it invoked the 'théorie des classes'. As Louis had lambasted the parlement on 23 December 1785, it was difficult to know what more he could do.

The alternative would have been to sacrifice Calonne and appoint d'Amécourt. This would have been akin to Louis XV's dismissal of Bertin and appointment of L'Averdy, a conseiller in the parlement, as contrôleur in 1763, after a period of parlementaire resistance. The humiliating tutelage to the parlement which followed and which was a formative influence on the young Louis XVI was not a precedent he would now have cared to follow. The imaginative escape from this dilemma which Calonne offered via the Notables, which would have put pressure on the parlement from a new angle, must have appealed to him.

In a sense, however, to bypass the parlements was more insulting to them than to mount a coup against them. As Castries noted on 28 December 1786, the day that the Notables were convoked: 'The parlement, anxious and discontented, says that the government wants to deprive it of its right of registration and that this step leads to the Estates-General'. Isolated voices among parlementaires, such as Malesherbes, had called for the Estates-General; at the time of the registration of Turgot's Six Edicts a few young conseillers had made a similar demand but to no avail. Président d'Ormesson 'did not disguise the fact that his motive [in opposing] was that it would lead to the destruction of the magistrature'.[54] As the last premier président of the parlement he was to see his prophecy fulfilled. Indeed, in the midst of their victory over Brienne and Lamoignon, they regretted the pledges which had been necessary to achieve it. Their insistence on the 'forms of 1614' for the forthcoming Estates-General was designed to sow dissension and paralyse their action. As Bombelles says of one of d'Aligre's speeches at this time: 'It shows the despair of the sovereign courts at having been taken at their word when they allowed themselves to be persuaded by a few hot-heads to call for the Estates-General'.[55] After Calonne had convoked the Notables, the calls of the 'hot-heads' had found a ready response. Not because the parlement was unable to resist royal demands in 1787–8 – they managed that very well – but out of pique that the king himself had experimented with a new polity. Only when it was too late did they stop to consider why he had done this and (reportedly) offer him

54 Véri, *Journal*, II, 8.
55 Bombelles, *Journal*, II, 257.

sufficient funds in April 1789 when they were no longer in a position to deliver them.

When the experiment with the Notables failed and also the subsequent coup which ex-Président Lamoignon mounted in May 1788, Louis not surprisingly decided that if he had to yield up his authority it was better to yield it to the nation than to the parlement. As he told the parlement in December 1788 when in extremis they tried to do a deal on a new constitution,

I have no reply to make to my parlement; it is with the assembled nation that I shall concert the measures appropriate to consolidate permanently public order and the prosperity of the state.[56]

56 A.N. XI B 8988.

CHAPTER TWELVE

The politicians and the public

Louis XV is supposed to have said, 'I appoint my ministers but the nation dismisses them'. Louis XVI, in his youthful political catechism, *Réflexions sur mes entretiens avec M. de La Vauguyon*, solemnly intoned, 'I must always consult public opinion; it is never wrong';[1] some five years later he put this resolution into practice by dismissing Maupeou and Terray against his better judgement. Public opinion had apparently arrived or, as contemporaries would have put it, had 'reached the very feet of the throne'. Warned about the consequences of restoring the parlement, Louis replied in November 1774: 'That may be true. It may be considered politically unwise, but it seems to me that this is the general will, and I wish to be loved'.[2]

Modern scholarship seems to confirm this view of the impact of public opinion on the closed world of royal government. Keith Baker considers that it was not just a force to be reckoned with, but one that the king found it convenient to recognize. Public opinion was a unified force which could be used to heal the wounds caused by the conflict between crown and parlement, 'it offered an abstract court of appeal to a monarchy anxious to put an end to several decades of political contestation'.[3] Thus also Malesherbes could depict the young king as 'a peacemaker in the temple of justice'.[4] There seems also to be agreement about *when* public opinion began to exert its role – from the mid-century. Mona Ozouf even suggests a precise date (1749), connecting the rise of opinion with literary events, especially the publication of Montesquieu's *De l'esprit des lois*.[5] (But may not the

1 J. Hardman, *Louis XVI*, New Haven, Conn., 1993, 35.
2 *Journal Historique*, 8 November 1774, VI, 301, cited in D. Echeverria, *The Maupeou Revolution*, Baton Rouge, La., 1985, 32.
3 K.M. Baker, 'Politics and public opinion', in J.R. Censer and J.D. Popkin (eds) *Press and Politics in Pre-Revolutionary France*, Berkeley, Calif., 1987, 264.
4 ibid., 226.
5 M. Ozouf, 'L'Opinion publique', in K.M. Baker (ed.) *The Political Culture of the Ancien Régime*, Chicago, 1987, 422.

creation of the vingtième, in peacetime, also in 1749 be a more likely cause?) All this, Baker argues, would have been unthinkable fifty years before. Under Louis XIV's absolutism, the king was the only public person, there was nothing public external to himself, least of all an opinion.[6]

Could this ever have been the case, bearing in mind that a book has been entirely devoted to *The Fabrication of Louis XIV*, or the 'selling' of an idealized version of the king?[7] If the king's was the only opinion, why bother mounting an elaborate propaganda machine? (Louis XV and his grandson, incidentally, were to have little interest in such exercises.) And if this had been the case, why did Louis XIV, in the nadir of the War of the Spanish Succession, appeal to his people by publishing the allies' terms for peace which included the demand that he use French troops to expel his own grandson from Spain? And if public opinion was not non-existent under Louis XIV, maybe it was not almighty under Louis XVI. For there lacked the precondition not only for its effective operation but also for its effective definition: representative institutions. It is necessary to discover not only how the influence of public opinion was exerted but also where it was located. Ozouf goes in search of it, in the company of police spies, to the public places and cafés. But this preoccupation with the *état des esprits* was an old one and pertains more to oppressive regimes than to more open ones. For our purposes, the best way to import some precision into a discussion of the role of public opinion is to examine some references to it by those themselves in governmental circles in an attempt to discover what they understood by it through the words they used to describe it.

When d'Ormesson lost office, his premier commis, Anson, consoled him with the thought that public opinion was on his side:

You have for you 'La Regina del mundo', opinion. It pleads loudly and clearly [for you] and in you it loses the best defender of its cause: all those who are submissive and attentive to its voice form the most majestic concert in favour of the man of virtue whom no one can reproach with the least inconsistency etc.[8]

However, if opinion really had been, as Anson suggests, 'the Queen of the World', why had it not saved his master? Indeed the number of occasions when public opinion brought down a minister is very small: the cases of Maupeou and Terray are the only unequivocal examples in our period and even with these the determinant pressure may well have been that of Maurepas who, however much he liked being applauded at the Opera, had been out of circulation since 1749

6 Baker, 'Politics and public opinion', 204.
7 P. Burke, *The Fabrication of Louis XIV*, New Haven, Conn., 1992; see also P.R. Campbell, 'Old regime politics', *Renaissance and Modern Studies*, 1989, XXXIII.
8 A.N. 144 A.P. 130 dossier 4. 1. 9, 12 November 1783.

(precisely the date selected for the rise of opinion) and thus had little acquaintance with it. Public opinion may have been responsible for the replacement of Brienne by Necker in 1788 though, as we have seen, Egret believed that Brienne fell because of a treasury crisis which Necker was appointed to resolve. Necker himself, however, gave as the reason for his refusal to serve under Brienne, 'I would be without strength and resources if I were to be associated with someone whose public reputation is unfortunately ruined and who nevertheless is believed to enjoy the greatest credit [at court]'.[9] (Note in passing Necker's use of 'nevertheless' to suggest that the king and queen are flouting public opinion.) These three, then, are the only examples of public opinion effecting ministerial changes, though they do occur at decisive turning-points in the reign.

To say, however, that public opinion rarely had the power to make or break ministers, is not to say that it did not influence them. Sartine fell in 1780 because of his quarrel with Necker over the naval estimates. Some months before that, however, Véri notes that

the public of Paris were blaming Sartine for this contretemps [a naval reverse] and speak only of driving him from office. I perceive, moreover, that M. de Maurepas himself is shaken by these popular murmurings [*bruits populaires*] and that if he had to hand a man recognized as capable of running the marine well, he would think only of providing M. de Sartine with an honourable retraite . . . this will be the fate of every minister whose department, *mis en activité*, does not meet with the success which the public desires.[10]

The ministers themselves were well aware that some ministries were judged by the public, others not, and this imposed a further hierarchy of desirability on the various departments. The service ministries were vulnerable when their departments were 'mis en activité', that is in time of war. The minister for the maison was not, however, according to his subordinate Lenoir, 'judged by general opinion'.[11] The foreign ministry, because of its esoteric nature, was in the same case: 'this veil [surrounding diplomacy] is only lifted by those who are in this career, restricted to a very small number of people and to men who are naturally discreet'.[12] (In this respect English foreign ministers were less fortunate: they tended not to survive successful wars whereas their French counterparts usually survived unsuccessful ones.) When, however, Vergennes attempted to step outside his sphere and to reach

9 A. d'Arneth and J. Flammermont (eds) *Correspondance secrète du Comte de Mercy-Argenteau avec l'Empereur Joseph II et le Prince de Kaunitz*, 1891, 2 vols, II, 203, Necker to Mercy, 21 August.
10 Abbé de Véri, *Journal 1774–80*, ed. J. de Witte, 1928–30, 2 vols, II, 30–4, 8 March 1780
11 Lenoir Papers, Bibliothèque municipale d'Orléans, MS 1421–3, 1423, résidus, 85.
12 Abbé de Véri, MSS *Journal*, Archives départementales de la Drôme, Valence, unclassified, cahier 118, November 1783: the time when Vergennes came nearest to disgrace.

for the ministériat, his pretensions 'did not cut ice, either with the public, or with his colleagues, or with the king'.[13]

One thing which should already be clear from these examples is that public opinion was not unitary. We have seen the 'public de Paris' whose 'bruits populaires' reached and shook Maurepas; the 'general opinion' which did not judge the maison; and an opinion against which the king and queen stood out in their defence of Brienne. Such diversity – and I shall give other examples – makes it difficult to accept Baker's view of public opinion as a unified point of reference. The reason for this diversity is not hard to find: English opinion was unified by its Parliament and the diffusion of its published debates. In France, however, the written political word came from such diverse sources as the publication of parlementaire remontrances, the preambles to royal edicts, the political press, mostly printed abroad but widely disseminated in France, and partisan pamphlets such as the two anti-Necker ones that Calonne clandestinely published in 1781.

To the end, Louis XVI persisted in regarding the publication of parlementaire remontrances not so much as a violation of the tenets of absolutism as a breach of faith. In the séance of 23 December 1785, Louis began by accusing the parlement of publicizing 'things which ought to remain in the secrecy of the intimate relations I permit it to have with me'.[14] Yet if the parlement sought publicity, so did the king who treated the preambles to his edicts as propaganda. A suggestion that Louis wrote them himself is mistaken,[15] but the ministers themselves often took personal charge of writing them. Thus the young d'Ormesson, supplying Turgot with a draft edict on a subvention territorial, assumed that the minister would want to write the preamble himself.[16] Pamphlets and the foreign press will be considered later but it should by now be clear that these various impulses would tend to create a variegated opinion.

Ministerial papers bring out not only this variety but also a confused reading of it by their authors. Thus in some notes on handling a public loan in January 1782, Vergennes considers 'the way of dealing with the people who will want to subscribe to the new loan and with the public'.[17] The rentiers, then, are not the same as the public; though in an age of loans rather than taxes, which by their nature need to be more popular than taxes, one might have imagined a practical equivalence. The following year, Joly de Fleury wrote to his brother,

---

13 ibid., cahier 123.
14 B.N. n.a.f. 22111, Lefebvre d'Amécourt, *Journal du règne de Louis XVI*, fo. 74.
15 This view has been propounded by G. and P. Girault de Coursac in *Louis XVI a la parole*, 1989, 10.
16 A.N. 144 A.P. 131 dossier 3. 2.
17 B.N. fonds Joly de Fleury, 1437 fo. 190, cited in M. Price, 'The Comte de Vergennes and the Baron de Breteuil: French politics and reform in the reign of Louis XVI', PhD thesis, Cambridge University, 1988, 159.

the procureur-général of the parlement, concerning his règlement setting up the comité des finances:

I know that the pretty ladies are protesting against my règlement but they can say and do what they like: the public opinion of Paris, of Versailles and of the provinces will oblige them to be silent. . . . it is only they [the ladies] who want to spend and . . . who find [the règlement] disagreeable.[18]

What, one might ask, did Joly mean by 'the public opinion . . . of Versailles'? The court? But this opinion is placed in antithesis to the 'pretty ladies', who must be taken to be the Polignac group whose pensions were threatened by the comité des finances. The population of the little town? It would seem a slight weight in the balance. The appointment of the Comte de Saint-Germain as war secretary was not, in Véri's view, 'welcome to the courtier soldiers, but very much so to the fighting soldiers and to the public of Paris and of the provinces'.[19] Again the contrast is between metropolitan and provincial opinion, which is at one among the general public, but divided among the specialists. Perhaps the most bizarre example of all comes from the pen of Bombelles. In April 1789, he claims that 'the *voix publique* designates the Baron de Breteuil' for the premiership.[20] Yet his appointment in July led directly to the storming of the Bastille!

Some references to the public (including perhaps Bombelles's) refer in fact only to our closed world. Thus one of Louis XVI's first acts was to write a letter to the first gentleman of his chamber suspending the strict application of the 1760 ruling on admittance to the honneurs de la cour but adding, 'I want you to spread it about among the public that only people of birth and recognized morality will be admitted – and not as young as heretofore'.[21] Obviously the 'public' here envisaged is very small indeed, since only a small proportion even of courtiers could aspire to the honneurs de la cour. Equally, the finer points of the working of government, our subject, were lost on the wider public, not because they were secret but because they were complicated. Thus Véri could say that 'in the ordinary language of the public', ministers were those who headed departments rather than the ministres who had the entrée to the conseil d'état;[22] in fact it was the general public which on this occasion was more aware of the reality of power. When Véri said that if Turgot moved from the marine to the contrôle 'it would be taking a drop in rank according to the common opinion', he means by this 'common opinion', the received opinion of initiates. Similarly when the king treated Ségur to silence

18 B.N. fonds Joly de Fleury, 2485 fo. 108, 13 March 1783.
19 Véri, *Journal*, I, 359.
20 Marquis de Bombelles, *Journal*, ed. J. Grassion and F. Durif, Geneva, 1978–93, 3 vols, II, 297.
21 A.N. C220, the king to the Duc d'Aumont, 9 July 1774, published in Courcelles, *Dictionnaire universelle de la noblesse de France*, 1820, 3 vols, I, Introduction.
22 Véri, *Journal*, II, 111.

after his appearance before the comité des finances, a treatment which, according to Véri, 'degraded [Ségur] before public opinion', again, only initiates learned of the minister's discomfiture.[23]

Despite the diversity of public opinions here displayed, most of the examples relate to an educated or at least a literate public; not to what we would call the general public or the 'people', which Necker characterized in his *Éloge de Colbert* of 1773 as 'toute sauvage'. In the reforms they presented to the Notables, however, Calonne and the king himself introduced this new element and with it perhaps a more menacing concept of the pressure it could exert. In November 1786 Calonne told the king that if there were clamours from the privileged orders,

their voice will be drowned by the *vox populi* which will necessarily prevail, especially since the establishment of . . . the provincial and district assemblies will give the government the help of that national interest which at present is null and which, well directed, can smooth all difficulties.[24]

Necker had intended his provincial administrations to deprive the parlements of the support of public opinion,[25] but Calonne goes further in both organization and intent: his assemblies were in three tiers going right down to the level of the parish; the introduction of the concept of a national interest set apart from sectional interests strikes a new note. The public opinion which hitherto had influenced government under the ancien régime had been precisely sectional interests, pressure groups, in short, Talleyrand's sociétés: 'France gave the impression of being composed of a certain number of sociétés with which the government had to reckon'.[26] Calonne repudiates this state of affairs, because his national interest gets its meaning only by being put in antithesis to sectional interests. His argument is related to Rousseau's distinction between 'public opinion' and the 'general will'. The 'national' interest is identified with that of the people. This is clear from Louis's attitude during the Notables. In Miromesnil's last audience, the king told him, 'that [the nobility and clergy] were opposing everything; that the people paid everything'; to which Miromesnil replied 'that he begged the king not to be prejudiced against any order or any corps'.[27]

The avertissement, which the avocat Gerbier drafted and the king touched up, was generally characterized as an 'appeal to the people'. In the Notables, Lafayette went so far as to say that 'even at Boston

23 Véri, MSS *Journal*, cahier 114; Baron de Besenval, *Mémoires*, ed. Berville and Barrière, 1821, 2 vols, II, 145.
24 A.N. K164.4, *Objections et réponses* . . .
25 Baker, 'Politics and public opinion', 238.
26 Prince de Talleyrand, *Mémoires*, ed. Duc de Broglie, 1891–2, 5 vols, I, 63.
27 Comte de Brienne and Loménie de Brienne, *Journal de l'Assemblée des Notables*, ed. P. Chevallier, 1960, 63.

this appeal would be considered seditious'.[28] Castries and Miromesnil thus characterized it to the king's face. Castries even talks to the king about 'the *seditious* distribution of [the avertissement] to all the *curés* of Paris and dissemination among the people', and adds, 'Would not Your Majesty be alarmed to see his subjects worked up against each other?'[29] Miromesnil, in his last letter to the king as a minister, warned him: 'I see that he [Calonne] is seeking to turn you against the bishops, against the nobles, against the magistrates, against your ministers. He is making a sort of appeal to the people which may have dangerous consequences.'[30] Thus Miromesnil presents the people in contrast to the entire political world, the establishment.

Calonne's attempt to direct public opinion was wholly unsuccessful, though he may have sown seeds which bore a doubtful crop in 1789. For an appeal to the people, the ironic salon tone of the avertissement was singularly inappropriate. Nor had Calonne's attempts to influence the financial markets through such hired pens as Mirabeau and Clavière proved more successful: both were essentially more concerned with their own interests, Clavière with his hopeless addiction to speculating (only Brissot's cronyism could have procured such a man the finance ministry in 1792) and Mirabeau with the chance of building a wider political career on the ruins of the ancien régime.[31] Calonne may have sensed the way Mirabeau's thoughts were moving: the first reference to an Assembly of Notables comes in a letter of 13 June from Mirabeau to Calonne;[32] immediately afterwards, Calonne got him out of the way by sending him for five months on an empty mission to Berlin which was tantamount to exile. Calonne's pamphlets were most successful when he found time to write his own, as in 1781. If he had lived, his 'worthy and much-lamented friend', Vergennes, could have taught him a thing or two about how to manipulate public opinion. He and Necker were the two greatest exponents of the art under Louis XVI. Ironically, although it was entirely characteristic of government during the reign, they used their skills to undermine each other – or at least Vergennes did.

Vergennes began by holding Necker in some awe as a miracle worker who could finance the war without recourse to new taxation: 'If he can finish the war without departing from that system,' he told Montmorin, 'he will be a very great man in his own domain'.[33] Only the condescending 'in his own domain' introduces a sneer. However, Necker's attack on Vergennes's personal friend Sartine showed clearly

28 ibid., 45.
29 My italics; Castries, *Journal*, Archives de la Marine, MS 182/7964 1–2, II, entry for 2 April.
30 A.N. K163 no. 8. 31.
31 On Clavière, see J. Bouchary, *Les Manieurs d'argent à Paris*, 1939–43, 3 vols, I, 11–111.
32 P.R.O. P.C. 1/125.48.
33 15 December 1779, cited in H. Doniol, *Histoire de la participation de la France à l'établissement des États-Unis d'Amérique*, 1886–, 5 vols, IV, 493.

that he intended going beyond his 'own domain', as, more directly, did his gauche attempt to put out feelers for peace with England.[34] When the king asked Vergennes to give him his written opinion of the *Compte rendu* and the desirability of 'entrusting the most sensitive position in the country [that of finance minister] to a foreigner, a republican and a Protestant',[35] Vergennes leapt at the opportunity. And in doing so, he introduces a new element into the discussion of public opinion, its subjectivity. He scoffs at 'M. Necker's version of public opinion', and this is a valid point. It was all very well for the king to say that he 'must always consult public opinion', but there needed to be a scientific way of locating the public's body and taking its temperature. In England, Parliament served this function and though this was a precedent that Vergennes abominated, it was better than allowing Necker to say he possessed a monopoly of interpreting public opinion. For Necker could be wrong in his reading of the public mood, for instance in 1788 when he failed to realize that the parlement had lost its following after its declaration on the organization of the forthcoming Estates-General.

In a classic passage, Vergennes criticizes Necker (and implicitly the king) in the following terms:

He finds this opinion in the spirit of innovation of the times, in the society of men of letters, of the Philosophes . . . or again in the plaudits given him by a section of the English Parliament . . .; finally in the ideas of reform and humanity which he himself propagates . . . Your Majesty has already made very considerable sacrifices to this spirit of innovation . . . which increases its demands and pretensions with every new favour.

Such, Sire, is the nature of the public opinion which M. Necker enlists, and which becomes his strength . . . since he has been deprived by the nature of his operations of the support of the true public opinion of this monarchy.
If 'the opinion of M. Necker' finally wins the day, if English and Genevan principles are introduced into our administration, Your Majesty can expect to see the portion of his subjects which now obeys in command and the portion which presently governs take its place.[36]

Vergennes concluded that Necker was undermining the traditional French monarchy and basing his conduct 'on the example of England, which publishes its accounts – an example for which Your Majesty's ancestors have shown such considerable and well-justified aversion'. In a sense he was right: the publication of the *Compte* was a natural consequence of the way Necker had changed the nature of public credit. His reliance on loans rather than taxes, and international loans rather than French ones, meant that people had to be persuaded not

---

34 R.D. Harris, *Necker: Reform Stateman of the Ancien Régime*, Berkeley, Calif., 1979, 208–17.
35 'Observations remises à Louis XVI et par ses ordres, le 3 Mai 1781', published by J.L. Soulavie, *Mémoires historiques et politiques du règne de Louis XVI*, 1801, 6 vols, IV, 149–59, 149.
36 ibid., 153.

coerced: as Necker himself observed, the mightiest prince on earth could not prevent international capital seeking the best return on its outlay.

In criticizing Necker's use of public opinion, Vergennes is not, as might an earlier absolutist, denying the existence or deploring the influence of public opinion as such. Rather he is distinguishing Necker's version of public opinion from what he calls, just as subjectively, 'the true opinion of France'. And he had always striven to make this 'true public opinion' not just known but prevalent. This he had sought to achieve through his own counter-manipulation of sections of the press.

In eighteenth-century France, the official purveyors of news were the *Gazette de France* and the *Journal politique*, under the aegis of the foreign secretary; the *Mercure de France*, under the minister for the maison;[37] and the *Journal de Paris*, under the keeper of the seals. So there was no one official line: news-dissemination was as fragmented as the ministry. The *Gazette*, however, was the most official of these organs. The American historian Jeremy Popkin examines in some detail what this publication was 'for', stressing its lack of narrative sense and its exclusive concentration on the king's meetings with members of his family and the various public corps. An English reader is more likely to appreciate that the *Gazette* was simply a court circular. Few ministers sought to import a political content into this publication, exceptions being Maupeou, who had the *Gazette* note the smooth installation of his new parlement, and Turgot, who used it to denounce what he deemed to be the conspirators behind the Guerre des farines.[38] Vergennes's correspondence with the king contains several references to inclusions for the *Gazette*, but there is no indication that either man sought a departure from its traditional role. Apart from the *Gazette*, readers had a choice between the partisan political pamphlets clandestinely printed in France and foreign political publications to whose import the authorities turned a blind eye.

The pamphlets were often written not by outsiders but by ministerial aspirants and indeed constituted part of the mechanism for entering the ministry. Notable pamphleteers included Calonne, who apart from the two he wrote against Necker, wrote or commissioned *Démocrite contre M. D'Ormesson*; Lamoignon, who wrote pamphlets against Miromesnil, when he was intriguing for his job in 1783–4; Sénac de Meilhan, intendant of Valenciennes, another contender for the finance ministry who wrote his *Liégoise* against Necker; Bourboulon, Artois's treasurer; and Augeard, farmer-general and the queen's secrétaire des commandements. Because governments were

---

37 R.M. Rampelberg, *Le Ministre de la maison du roi 1783–1788: Baron de Breteuil*, 1975, 184.
38 J.D. Popkin, 'The pre-revolutionary origins of popular journalism', in K.M. Baker (ed.) *The Political Culture of the Ancien Régime*, Chicago, 1987, 205–8.

not united it was possible to attack one member without inviting the wrath of the rest or creating embarrassment when the pamphleteer had achieved his purpose of entering government. Pamphlets tended to attack an already wounded prey – or one perceived to be – hence Bachaumont's observation that 'in France they were all too often the prelude to disgrace'.[39] The successful pamphleteer had to imitate the action of the vulture; this comes across strongly in Lenoir's account of a travail with the king:

The king summoned me and said in the presence of M. Amelot [secretary for the maison]: 'What do you think of these mischievous writings against the Keeper of the Seals that are doing the rounds: is the Chancellor de Maupeou responsible or the Président de Lamoignon?' I replied that I had no reason to suspect the Chancellor. The king replied, 'Whilst M. de Maurepas was alive, people did not defame the Keeper, *whom I greatly esteem*. I am aware that it is difficult for you to discover the authors of the ballads and pamphlets, since M. de Sartine couldn't during the exile of the parlements, but try to prevent these acts of malice one way or another'.
. . . I took the liberty of saying, 'Since Your Majesty permits me to put it about that you accord your estime to your Keeper, it will perhaps be a way to arrest the circulation of the libels against him which have failed to diminish Your Majesty's confidence in him'. And indeed, after I had put abroad what the king had said to me, the pamphlets against M. de Miromesnil came to an end.[40]

Writing anonymous pamphlets could be a rewarding but also a risky business, given the king's disapproval. Calonne and Lamoignon's determination to preserve the anonymity of their authorship of pamphlets against d'Ormesson and Miromesnil in 1783 explains the vicissitudes of the trial of Lemaitre, the greffier-en-chef of the conseil d'état, who had arranged for the clandestine publication of their productions. Lamoignon wanted his trial to take place in the parlement, where he would be 'absolute master' – and make sure Lemaitre did not blab.[41]

Control of foreign publications came within Vergennes's departmental brief of foreign secretary. The entry of political pornography, some of the grossest in the history of the genre, the *libelles*, he banned, and with some effect.[42] Foreign political periodicals such as the *Gazette de Leyde* and the *Courier de l'Europe*, he sought to influence or even censor.[43] The foreign publications had an anomalous position under the ancien régime. They were theoretically banned

---

39 Cited in Harris, *Necker*, 205.
40 My italics; R. Darnton, 'The memoirs of Lenoir', *English Historical Review* 85, 1970, 532–9, 542–3.
41 J.M. Augeard, *Mémoires secrètes*, ed. E. Bavoux, 1866, 141ff.
42 R. Darnton, *The Literary Underground of the Old Regime*, Cambridge, Mass., 1982, 196–200.
43 On these two periodicals see J.R. Censer and J.D. Popkin, 'The *Gazette de Leyde* under Louis XVI', in Censer and Popkin (eds) *Press and Politics*.

yet the Paris bookseller David had an official privilege for their distribution and the income from their delivery was a regular item in calculating the level of the 'ferme des postes'! And banned though they were, much of their information on France came from Vergennes. The bulk of the information on France used by the *Gazette de Leyde* came from a semi-official news bureau run by Pascal-Boyer under the personal direction of Vergennes. Another paradox: France's traditional policy of non-ideological alliances (under Louis XVI with American rebels and Dutch Patriots) meant that Vergennes's policies were in natural sympathy with those of the editor of the *Gazette de Leyde*, Luzac. They differed, however, on the merits of Necker; Vergennes did not see why the man who had become his ideological enemy should receive yet more publicity; rather he should be starved of what for him was oxygen. The *Gazette* was given no information on the events leading to Necker's fall. As regards the *Courier de L'Europe*, published in London, Vergennes went further, informing the editor of his wishes in an unattributable way by using the word '*on*' to refer to himself (Brissot, one of the correspondents, cracked the device). The editor was castigated for a laudatory article on Necker which was not repeated.

For three years after Necker's fall, Vergennes continued to starve the *Gazette de Leyde* of news relating to home affairs. This was the period of his ascendancy in home as well as foreign affairs, which revealed him in his true authoritarian colours. After his attempt at the ministériat failed, in the autumn of 1783, and he became just one of the comité de gouvernement, the supply of news resumed. The *Gazette de Leyde*'s issue of 21 September 1784 contained the first publication of a parle-mentaire remonstrance for many years. By the time of the Diamond Necklace Affair (1785–6), Vergennes was happy to see his valiant efforts to repatriate the witnesses who could prove Rohan's innocence presented in a favourable light. As in the American War, so in the Diamond Necklace Affair pragmatic motives (in the latter case his links with the House of Rohan) led to a conduct which made him seem a champion of liberty.

He died in 1787 and missed seeing the realization of the prophecies he had made to the king in 1781. Necker, however, the object of these criticisms, had ample leisure to reflect on the affections of the public, just as fickle as those of princes. When he resigned in 1790, Louis's sister Madame Elizabeth wrote:

Have you heard the great news that does not cause a stir in Paris? M. Necker is gone. He took such a fright at the threat of being hanged that he was unable to resist the tender solicitations of his virtuous wife to take the waters. The Assembly, on reading this phrase, laughed and passed to order of the day.[44]

44 Madame Elizabeth, *Correspondance*, ed. Feuillet de Conches, 1866, 145.

Conclusion

We have considered that the system of government under Louis XVI was worthy of examination in its own right, though we have cast the odd nervous glance over our shoulders towards the Revolution which brought it to an end. To some, our preoccupation with such matters as Breteuil's title of chef du conseil in July 1789 may seem as frivolous as his own strutting around organizing his secretariat in the hundred hours at his disposal before the fall of the Bastille. If the new power of the National Assembly could not comprehend Breteuil's title, why should we bother trying to make it comprehensible? Similarly, not everyone can rejoice with Laurent de Villedeuil on his reaching the safe haven of the maison du roi after traversing the choppy waters of the contrôle-générale, shortly before both ministries were to be transformed, though some may relish the frisson provided by the dramatic irony of the situation. In deference to such imagined objections, in this conclusion we shall adopt a more teleological standpoint and try to relate the political system in the last years of the ancien régime to its demise.

The system of government we have examined was for most of its span characterized by extreme informality, though the débâcle of the Assembly of Notables in 1787 led to a reaction, indeed an over-reaction, to this. At the heart of the informal system was the transference of the power of decision-making from the conseil d'état to ad-hoc comités. The use of the council became merely an occasional adjunct to the ministerial politics of Maurepas and Vergennes, a rubber-stamp or even a fiction. The basic unit of government was the travail royal; government became atomized. This was not apparent to the public, who were informed that measures were taken by the king 'on the advice of his council'. Did it matter? Fictions are not in themselves inimical to good government but this one meant that if a minister with an idea could persuade the king that it ought to be implemented (it was often easiest to closet the king during the autumn removals of the court to Fontainebleau as d'Ormesson did in 1783 and

Calonne in 1786) there was no preliminary, formal machinery for stopping him. The council was not consulted over rescinding the lease of the general farm in 1783 and was presented with a fait accompli over Calonne's measures. Thus proposals, which in a well-regulated system might never have got off the ground, travelled a long way and even became law or executive action. Then the ministers or interests which had been ignored asserted themselves and the measures were often defeated. Thus decisions which it has been supposed had the whole weight of government behind them and then were weakly withdrawn often represented merely the policy of one man. The volte-face or *reculade* is often a delayed reaction, though it was no less damaging to the regime for that. The one man was usually the contrôleur-général, partly because the stress occurred in the field of finance and partly because in the other ministries the dynamic traditions of the monarchy had faltered. But the contrôleur-général was seldom the most powerful minister. Seen in this light, the failure of reforms seems even more inevitable and the surprising thing is not that they failed but that a system existed which allowed them to appear above the surface.

The contrôleur-général, Calonne, at once the most creative and the most destructive force in politics, brought this system to an end in three respects. First, he put the need for ministerial unity at the centre of the political agenda. In 1786 he tried to remove his chief opponents in the parlement, the premier président and the rapporteur du roi (he failed to shift d'Aligre but made another attempt during the Assembly of Notables). The following year in the same spirit he tried to replace his opponents in the ministry with his own nominees. Although he was only partially successful, he did finally convince the king of the need for ministerial unity (the ministers of the 'king's party' had recognized it some time before) and thus ironically paved the way for the premiership of Brienne.

Second, by causing the Assembly of Notables to be convoked, he stepped outside the framework of the ancien régime, which resting on agreement, on fundamentals, between the king and the parlement, obviated the need for Assemblies of Notables or Estates-General.

Calonne's third contribution to a change of system was a negative one. The widespread if largely erroneous belief that the informal government of the period 1774–87 had enabled Calonne to consume vast amounts of money (the difference between Necker's *Compte* and his own) led to a stress on formal procedures. Not only was a committee of investigation into Calonne's management set up with d'Ormesson as its rapporteur, but also a revived if not rejuvenated conseil royal des finances now met regularly. An important benefit was the institution and publication of an annual budget which in itself did much to end the autonomy of the travail. But the dynamism and innovation of the earlier period were lost. Not only was there formality but a slavish revival of old forms: the conseil royal des finances, an official ministre principal, the cour plénière, the Estates-General. In a sense, the revival of the Assembly of Notables began this trend for Calonne, who would dearly like to have packed it, felt obliged to observe the same forms as when the body had last met in 1626. Malesherbes's suggestion that the provincial assemblies should nominate a National Assembly without distinction of order was rejected in favour of a slavish observance of the forms of the Estates-General. When Brienne had himself appointed ministre principal all he could think of was a mechanical codification of Maurepas's gossamer practices. Lamoignon had to remind the parlement of the antiquity of the cour plénière.

All this is of course purely a structural critique of the system; after all the regime was overthrown by a general insurrection. But the forces that were working in the country were working inside government too – in many ways began there – and it was precisely a general insurrection that the government had no intention of resisting: the Maréchal-Duc de Broglie, minister for war and generalissimo, told his field commander in the capital, 'if there is a general insurrection we cannot defend the whole of Paris'. This was a subjective appreciation: the latest historian of the royal army, S.F. Scott, considers that force could have been used with success.[1] Moreover, Broglie's attitude was a far cry from that prevailing in government circles at the beginning of the reign. Maurepas had considered that an increased readiness to use force was the necessary concomitant to the restoration of the parlement. This doctrine was tested during the Guerre des farines, which the king believed had been instigated by the parlement. After the bloody suppression of the Guerre des farines, Croÿ feared that the next step would be for the farmers-general to ask for troops to assist in the collection of taxes:[2] the 'military' collection of taxes was con-sidered to be the hallmark of a despotic regime such as that obtaining in Prussia or Russia.

Government thinking had changed radically by 1789. The regime was undermined not only by its mechanisms, such as whether decisions were taken by comités or councils, but also by the very spirit in which it was operated. Daniel Mornet in *Les Origines intellectuelles de la révolution française* said of the Abbé de Véri, our principal source and Maurepas's éminence grise, '[ses] jugements pourraient servir de conclusion à toutes les enquêtes de ce livre'.[3] He not only charts but also reflects the decline in respect for kingship and the king, whom he frequently calls disparagingly 'the young man'. He believed

1 S.F. Scott, *The Response of the Royal Army to the French Revolution . . . 1787–93*, Oxford, 1973, 59 and 80.
2 Duc de Croÿ, *Journal 1718–84*, ed. Grouchy and Cottin, 1906–7, 4 vols, III, 159.
3 D. Mornet, *Les Origines intellectuelles de la Révolution française*, 1933, 401–2.

that France would be a republic within fifty years and did not seem to mind. This in itself may not have mattered, but Turgot seriously proposed that he should be made the minister for the maison du roi. This lack of respect is also to be found in the diaries of Castries and d'Ormesson. Indeed few men in the ministerial milieu (the king, Maurepas, Vergennes and the odd contrôleur-général excepted) still believed in the administrative monarchy, and the number declined throughout the reign with the changing pattern of ministerial recruitment.

Some, like Miromesnil and Castries, inclined to a more aristocratic interpretation of the constitution. Others, like Turgot, Véri and Malesherbes, favoured a more democratic evolution. When Necker was introducing his provincial administrations, Turgot told Véri that he, Turgot, had not introduced them himself, because they would have diminished the king's authority:

As a citizen, I would have been delighted: but acting as a minister of the king, I made a scruple of abusing his confidence to diminish the extent of his authority. It is not that I did not plan to do it, but I wanted to wait until the king was older, experienced and mature enough to judge for himself rather than by another's lights.[4]

This conflict between duty as a minister of the crown and preference as a citizen, so strongly expressed in Castries's diary, was the thing that fatally undermined the regime's capacity to defend itself. To this lack of belief in itself the pre-Revolution introduced a new element: division between what would soon be called Left and Right. Paralysis was added to lack of self-belief.

4 Abbé de Véri, *Journal 1774–80*, ed. J. de Witte, 1928–30, 2 vols, II, 147.

Louis XVI's ministers, 1774–89

Date	Chef du conseil	Chancellor/ keeper of the seals	Foreign secretary	War secretary	Marine	Maison du roi	Finance minister
1774	–	Maupeou Miromesnil	d'Aigullon Vergennes	d'Aigullon du Muy	Boynes Turgot Sartine	La Vrillière	Terray Turgot
1775	–	Miromesnil	Vergennes	du Muy Saint-Germain	Sartine	La Vrillière Malesherbes	Terray Turgot
1776	Maurepas	Miromesnil	Vergennes	Saint-Germain	Sartine	Malesherbes Amelot	Turgot Clugny Necker/ Taboureau
1777	Maurepas	Miromesnil	Vergennes	Saint-Germain Montbarey	Sartine	Amelot	Necker/ Taboureau Necker
1778	Maurepas	Miromesnil	Vergennes	Montbarey	Sartine	Amelot	Necker
1779	Maurepas	Miromesnil	Vergennes	Montbarey	Sartine	Amelot	Necker
1780	Maurepas	Miromesnil	Vergennes	Montbarey Ségur	Sartine Castries	Amelot	Necker
1781	Maurepas	Miromesnil	Vergennes	Ségur	Castries	Amelot	Necker Joly de Fleury
1782	–	Miromesnil	Vergennes	Ségur	Castries	Amelot	Joly de Fleury
1783	Vergennes	Miromesnil	Vergennes	Ségur	Castries	Amelot Breteuil	Joly de Fleury d'Ormesson Calonne
1784	Vergennes	Miromesnil	Vergennes	Ségur	Castries	Breteuil	Calonne

Date	Chef du conseil	Chancellor/ keeper of the seals	Foreign secretary	War secretary	Marine	Maison du roi	Finance minister
1785	Vergennes	Miromesnil	Vergennes	Ségur	Castries	Breteuil	Calonne
1786	Vergennes	Miromesnil	Vergennes	Ségur	Castries	Breteuil	Calonne
1787	Vergennes Brienne (From August also ministre principal)	Miromesnil Lamoignon	Vergennes Montmorin	Ségur Comte de Brienne	Castries La Luzerne	Breteuil	Calonne Bouvard de Fourqueux Laurent de Villedeuil Lambert
1788	Brienne	Lamoignon Barentin	Montmorin	Comte de Brienne Puységur	La Luzerne	Breteuil Laurent de Villedeuil	Lambert Necker
1789 (until 16 July)	Breteuil	Barentin	Montmorin La Vauguyon	Puységur Broglie	La Luzerne La Porte	Laurent de Villedeuil	Necker

Map of the généralités of France

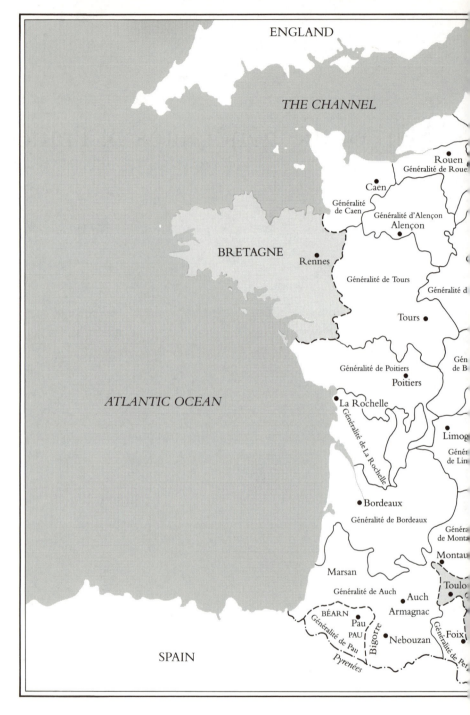

ENGLAND

THE CHANNEL

Rouen
Généralité de Roue

Caen

Généralité
de Caen

Généralité d'Alençon
Alençon

BRETAGNE

Rennes

Généralité de Tours

Généralité d

Généralité d

Tours

Gén
de B

ATLANTIC OCEAN

Généralité de Poitiers
Poitiers

La Rochelle

Généralité de La Rochelle

Limog

Généra
de Lin

Bordeaux

Généralité de Bordeaux

Généra
de Monta

Montau

Marsan

Toulo

Généralité de Auch
Auch

Armagnac

BÉARN

Généralité de Pau

Pau

PAU

Bigorre

Nebouzan

Généralité de Pe

Foix

Pyrénées

SPAIN

Note. The généralité was the administrative division ruled by an intendant.

The king's residences away from Versailles

In the summer and autumn the king spent considerable periods of time in his smaller palaces ringing Versailles, and it was in these that the most important decisions of the reign were taken: the decision to recall the parlements in 1774, to rescind the lease of the general farmers in 1783, to convoke the Notables in 1786 and to quash the proceedings of the National Assembly in 1789. Different protocol obtained in the smaller palaces: for instance at Versailles (and Marly) only the ambassadors of the Bourbon rulers (of Spain, Naples and Parma) were allowed to take up residence; elsewhere the representatives of all the powers could. Again, access to the king was more difficult even for the ministers away from Versailles but by the same token it was easier for favourite ministers to closet him in the smaller palaces. The king kept a record of the time he spent away from Versailles and the following abstract from it gives an extra dimension to the decision-making process.

1774: Choisy, 10 – 17 May; La Muette, 17 May – 16 June; Marly, 16 June – 1 August; Compiègne, 1 August – 1 September; Choisy, 5 – 10 October; Fontainebleau, 10 October – 10 November; La Muette, 11 – 12 November.

1775: Compiègne, 5 – 8 June; [Rheims, 9 – 16 June, for the Coronation]; Compiègne, 16 – 19 June; Choisy, 27 – 28 August and 5 – 9 October; Fontainebleau, 9 October – 16 November.

1776: Marly, 8 June – 11 July; Choisy, 17 – 21 August, 16 – 17 September, 4 – 9 October; Fontainebleau, 7 October – 16 November.

1777: Choisy, 15 May, 27 July – 3 August, 10 – 16 September, 24 – 25 September, 3 – 9 October; Fontainebleau, 9 October – 15 November.

1778: Marly, 17 May – 6 June; Choisy, 16 – 27 August, 20 – 27 September;

Fontainebleau, 5 – 6 October; Marly, 7 – 28 October; Fontainebleau, 28 – 29 October and 4 – 5 November.

1779: La Muette, 7 – 9 February; Marly, 25 April – 22 May; Choisy, 5 – 10 October; Marly, 13 – 31 October; Fontainebleau, 9 – 11 November.

1780: La Muette, 16 – 29 May; Choisy, 1 – 6 October; Compiègne, 8 – 11 October; Marly, 13 – 31 October; Fontainebleau, 7–9 November.

1781: Marly, 22 April – 20 May; La Muette, 5 – 16 September; Compiègne, 16 – 19 September; La Muette, 19 – 23 September; Fontainebleau, 5 – 7 November.

1782: La Muette, 20 – 23 January; Choisy, 8 – 19 June; Compiègne, 1 – 4 September; La Muette, 9 September – 30 October; Fontainebleau, 4 – 6 November.

1783: Compiègne, 31 August – 3 September; Choisy, 6 – 9 October; Fontainebleau, 9 October – 24 November.

1784: Compiègne, 29 August – 1 September; Fontainebleau, 11 – 13 October and 8 – 10 November.

1785: Rambouillet, 23 – 24 May; Saint-Cloud, 30 August – 4 September; Compiègne, 4 – 7 September; Saint-Cloud, 7 September – 7 October and 8 – 10 October; Fontainebleau, 10 October – 17 November.

1786: Rambouillet, 20 – 21 June; [visit to Normandy, 21 – 29 June]; Compiègne, 10 – 13 September; Choisy, 6 – 9 October; Fontainebleau, 9 October – 15 November.

1787: Fontainebleau, 5 – 9 November.

1788: Saint-Cloud, 19 May – 15 June (including five nights at Rambouillet).

1789: Marly, 14 – 21 June; Paris, 6 October – 31 December (Louis records his enforced residence in the capital as a 'voyage'!)

Note the extreme length of the king's absence from Versailles in 1774, when Maurepas worked on him to recall the parlement; the appearance of Rambouillet and Saint-Cloud (purchased in 1783 and 1784 respectively) from 1785; and the drastic curtailment of the 'voyages' during the crisis of 1787–9.

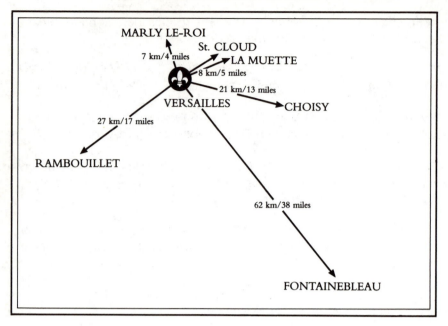

MARLY LE-ROI

St. CLOUD

7 km/4 miles

LA MUETTE

8 km/5 miles

21 km/13 miles

VERSAILLES

CHOISY

27 km/17 miles

RAMBOUILLET

62 km/38 miles

FONTAINEBLEAU

Glossary

The following short definitions are often necessarily approximations: words are best defined by their context.

acquits de comptant: exemption from audit by the **chambre des comptes**

adjoint: assistant

agiotage: speculation, especially on the **Bourse**

agrégation par fiefs: assimilation into the nobility by holding a noble fief

alluvions: land formed by river silt; claimed by the crown

almanach royal: official list of public functionaries

améliorations: economies

amovible: dismissable

ancien régime: literally 'former regime', that obtaining in France before the Revolution

anticipations: advances against future tax revenues

appanage: quasi-autonomous estates granted to **enfants de France**

arrêt: ruling, decree; an arrêt de conseil had legislative effect without registration by a **sovereign court**. An arrêt always stated that the measure had been adopted 'by the king in his council', although this was often a fiction

Assemblies of Notables: ad hoc bodies nominated by the king and representing the elite groups in society to give support for major measures

assignats: paper money issued during the Revolution with the confiscated churchlands as collateral

avertissement: 'warning' or 'preface', here the detachable preface to the publication of Calonne's 1787 measures

avocat: practicing lawyer with a degree in civil or canon law

avocat-général: assistant to the **procureur-général**

bail salzard: contract for the **General-Farm** 1780–6

bénéfices: remuneration

Bourse: Parisian stock-exchange

brevet d'appointement: royal instrument of appointment

brevet général (de la **taille**): the sum fixed for the taille for the coming year

cabinet: king's private room, c.p. English 'closet'; always a room, never 'the government'

cabinet noir: secret bureau instituted by Louis XV to open private correspondence

cadastre: register of land and its average yield

cahiers des doléances: list of grievances drawn up by representatives of the three orders for the Estates-General with a view to being embodied in royal legislation. The ensuing general legislation was often embodied in an **ordonnance**

caisse d'amortissement: sinking-fund instituted in 1784 in the hope of paying off the royal debt

caisse d'escompte: discount bank set up by Turgot in 1776 to foster commerce by lending at 4 per cent through a convertible paper currency

capitation: graduated universal poll-tax instituted in 1695

cautionnements: surety-bonds

chambellan: chamberlain

chambre des comptes: body charged with maintaining the royal domain and auditing the accounts of all royal agents handling royal funds

châtelet: the law court for the town of Paris

chef du conseil royal des finances: largely honorific post akin to the English first lord of the treasury

chevaleresque: nobility dating from before 1400

chevalier de Saint-Louis: knight of the military order founded by Louis XIV in 1693

choiseuliste: follower of the Duc de Choiseul, dismissed in 1770, died in 1786

cinquantième: innovative tax of one fiftieth payable by all in kind, instituted in 1725 and abandoned in 1727

comité: small group of ministers meeting in the presence of the king

commandant (-en-chef): adjoint of a provincial governor who performed all but his ceremonial functions

commissaire: official with a revocable commission from the king, c.f. **officier**

compagnie des Indes: pale imitation of the English 'East India Company', re-founded by Calonne in 1785

Compte rendu au Roi: statement of royal revenues and expenditures published by Necker in 1781

conférence: small group of ministers meeting in the king's absence

confiance (du roi): the king's personal regard

connétable: the supreme head of the army in the king's absence; suppressed by Richelieu in 1627

THE COUNCIL:

    conseil d'en haut: the council meeting to discuss foreign policy; generally called the conseil d'état under Louis XVI

    conseil d'état: either the conseil d'en haut or king's council generally

    conseil des dépêches: the council meeting to discuss home affairs

    conseil privé: the regular administrative and judicial body delivering the 'private' justice of the king as opposed to his public justice as given by the parlements

    conseil supérieur: tribunals set up by Maupeou to break up the large jurisdictions of the parlements, particularly that of Paris

    conseiller: judge

    conseiller d'ambassade: assistant to an ambassador

    conseiller d'état: judge in the **conseil privé**

    conseiller d'état d'épée: a **conseiller d'état** taken from the military nobility

contrôle-générale: the contrôleur-général's headquarters at Versailles

cordon bleu: the blue ribbon or sash worn by members of the military order of the **Saint-Esprit**

corps: a group of people with a collective personality; it is often said that the ancien regime consisted of corps rather than individuals

corvée (royale): the obligation of peasants to work so many days a year on the royal roads

cours des aides: sovereign courts judging matters relating to certain taxes, notably aides and the **taille**

cour des ministres: the front quadrangle of Versailles where the ministers had their bureaux

cour des pairs: the peers sitting in the parlement to judge one of their number (such as d'Aiguillon in the 1760s)

cour plénière: court established by Lamoignon in 1788 to register royal legislation for the whole of France; body envisaged in 1774 to pronounce forfeiture against the parlement

dame d'atours: 'lady-in-waiting' ranking below a **dame d'honneur** in the household of a royal lady

dame d'honneur: lady ranking immediately below the **surintendante de la maison de la Reine**

dauphin: heir to the throne

décision précise: the king's rejection of a candidate as a result of a fundamental objection

déficit: deficit, an import from England: adverse gap between revenue and expenditure

département des impositions: the bureau, under an **intendant des finances**, in charge of direct taxation: **taille**, **capitation** and **vingtièmes**

dérogeance: loss of nobility through engaging in demeaning acts or activities, such as retail trade; rarely, almost never applied

dette arrièrée: the unfunded 'war debt', e.g. unredeemed **lettres de change**

dévôt, parti dévôt: the ultra religious party headed by Louis XV's children

directeur des bâtiments du roi: junior minister (under Louis XVI, d'Angiviller) with responsibility not just for royal building but for the applied arts

disette de numéraire: shortage of coins, especially gold ones

domaine de la Couronne: what was owned by the king in his public capacity, theoretically inalieanable

domaine d'occident: excise duties on produce from the French West Indies

don gratuit: 'free gift' by the church to the crown in lieu of taxation

doublement: double representation sought and obtained by the third estate for the Estates-General of 1789

duché-héréditaire: hereditary dukedom

duché-pairie: dukedom with rights of peerage

échange: sale of lands or rights to the crown, usually at inflated price

échevin: 'alderman'

école militaire: military academy founded in 1751 for the sons of the nobility

économistes: alternative name for the **Physiocrats**

écuyer: esquire

édit: most solemn royal legislative act, formed by the registration of royal **lettres patentes** in the parlements

élection (pays d'): those areas of France where direct taxation was collected by the royal official known as the élu as c.f. the **pays d'états**, where the local estates raised the money themselves

encyclopédiste: supporter of the principles enunciated in the Encyclopédie edited by Diderot, often used pejoratively

enfants de France: children or grandchildren of the king

engregistrement: the process whereby a parlement converted royal **lettres patentes** into edicts

enquêtes (chambres d'): junior chamber in the parlements; in criminal cases they only dealt with offences punishable by fines

entrées de Paris: tax paid on goods entering Paris

entrées familières: *see* **grandes entrées**

Estates-General: assembly of the three orders of the kingdom: clergy, nobility and third estate

estime (du roi): the king's formal regard for an official

état civil: registers of birth, marriage and death. Since they were kept by the Catholic clergy, Protestants were technically bastards and unable to inherit until the edict of November 1787

état des esprits: the public mood as gauged by the police

état nominatif: list of pensions published by order of the National Assembly in 1789–90

exigible (dette): unfunded (debt)

FARMING (TAX)

    farmers général/fermiers-généraux: a syndicate who bought the right to the indirect taxes in return for a fixed advance to the crown. Contracts usually ran for six years

    ferme des postes: farm of the postal services

fonds d'avance: money put up by farmers to obtain a contract

franc: post-Revolutionary name for **livre**

frondeur: noble opponent of the crown, after the rebellion known as the Fronde (1648–52)

gabelle: salt tax

gaspillages: pecculation

généralité: administrative unit ruled by an intendant; there were 33 généralités in 1789

gens de robe: people who wore the lawyer's gown or robe

gens titrés: dukes

gent robine: colloquial reference to the **noblesse de robe**

gloire: concept developed particularly by Corneille of one's duty to oneself in one's appointed station in life

gouverneur/gouvernante des enfants de France: governor of the children or grandchildren of the king

gouverneur (de province): the king's representative in a province, by the eighteenth century largely a ceremonial post

grace d'éclat: a signal mark of royal confidence

grand aumonier: grand almoner, the head of the clerical establishment in the maison du roi

grand banc: the bench in the grand' chambre of the parlement, the **présidents à mortier**

grand conseil: rival jurisdiction to the parlement established in 1497 to judge those cases where the latter was expected to display bias. It replaced the parlement in 1771

grand maître des eaux et forêts: in 1789 24 of these enforced obedience to the laws governing the maintenance of the forest belonging to the royal domain

grand prévôt: officer responsible for maintaining order in the vicinity of the king's residence

grand seigneur: member of the court nobility

grand trésorier des ordres du roi: treasurer of the orders of chivalry

grand' chambre: the senior chamber in the parlements

grandes entrées: these conferred the right to sit in the king's cabinet rather than having to stand in the ante-chamber

grandes remontrances: attack on the administration of royal finances drafted by Malesherbes as **premier président** of the **cour des aides** in 1775

grands baillages: here, 47 tribunals set up by Lamoignon on 8 May 1788 to reduce the jurisdiction of the parlements

greffier: archivist of a court of law

guerre des farines: the 'flour war' of 1775 in response to Turgot's freeing of the grain trade

haute robe: senior members of the **noblesse de robe**

hobereau: poor country gentleman

homme de robe: member of the **noblesse de robe**

honneurs de la cour: the right to ride in the king's carriages and participate in the hunt, restricted to those whose nobility pre-dated 1400 or to ministers and their descendants

hôtel de la contrôle-générale: the contrôleur-général's Paris headquarters

impôt territorial: land tax based on a **cadastre**

inféodation des domaines: leasing out the royal domain, a device whereby Calonne sought in 1787 to get round the legal inalienability of the domain

intendant (de province): or **commissaire départi du conseil**, the ruler of a **généralité**

intendant des armées: an intendant attached to an army

intendant des finances: six (generally) powerful venal office holders heading the bureaux of the **contrôle-générale**; suppressed by Necker in 1777

intendants du commerce: as above, but dealing with commerce

lèse nation: crime instituted during the Revolution as a substitute for lèse majesté

lettre de cachet: order sealed under the king's signet ring (petit cachet), counter-signed by a secretary of state, to an individual or group; often implying constraint. These letters were folded and could not be read without breaking the seal

lettre de change: used to purchase supplies overseas during a war; capital and accrued interest were discharged together after the conclusion of peace

lettre ordre: unsealed letter of constraint from the king directly or from the minister for the **maison du roi**; under Louis XVI the usual instrument for exiling an ex-minister

lettres patentes: unfolded letters under the great seal; they only took legislative effect as an edict when registered by a sovereign court

lieutenant-criminel: the senior officer dealing with criminal matters in the **châtelet**

lieutenant-général de police: junior minister (created by edict in 1667) responsible for the police of Paris; the surbordinate of the minister for the **maison du roi**, but often having his own **travail** with the king

lit de justice: royal session in a sovereign court for the forcible registration of legislation. To distance themselves from the measure, parlements recorded that the registration had been performed 'at the express command of the king'. The theory behind the lit de justice was that the parlements were only exercising delegated authority and that 'in the presence of the delegator [that is the king] the powers of the delegate cease'. Extremist parlementaires denied the legality of the lit de justice

livre: unit of account worth 20 sous, later replaced by the **franc**; there were 24 livres to the pound sterling

livre tournois: the livre current in the Tourraine; it became the most widely used in France

louis: gold coin worth twenty livres

maison du roi: the king's household, the court

maître des requêtes: originally these attended the king to deal with suitors. In our period they were **rapporteurs** in the **conseil d'état**. Sometimes called 'primary matter' because of their protean quality: the classical recruiting ground of the intendants and hence (until the 1780s) the ministers

maréchal de camp: rank above colonel, lowest of the general officers

marine: the navy; the minister for the marine was also minister for the colonies

menin: official companion of the **dauphin** (generally about eight years his senior). Ex-menins were often made ministers (e.g. du Muy and Montmorin)

Mesdames Tantes: Louis XVI's maiden aunts, Adélaïde and Victoire; not forgetting Madame Sophie, the abbess, who kept on appartments at Versailles

minister for Paris: colloquial name for the minister for the **maison du roi**

ministre: minister with right to sit in the **conseil d'en haut**

ministre-ordonnateur: minister with independent control of funds

ministre principal: variant title for a premier ministre, held by Brienne 1787–8

National Assembly: successor name for the **Estates-General** (from June 1789)

noblesse d'épée: military nobility; in distinction to **noblesse de robe**

noblesse d'état: historians' term for ministers and high functionaries; generally lawyers

noblesse d'extraction: nobility dating back before royal ennoblements, that is before 1400

noblesse de race: similar to above

noblesse de robe: the legal nobility

notaire: lawyer's clerk

officier: one who has bought his office and whose remuneration (gages) is merely the interest on his advance: working for nothing and owning his job, he tended to be venal (in the modern sense), lazy and independent. For key positions, the king preferred to use **commissaires**

orders/estates: French society was legally divided into orders based on function and rank, thus clergy (the 'first' order), nobility (the 'second order') and the third estate

orders of chivalry: these were military (e.g. Saint-Louis and Saint-Esprit) or religious (e.g. the Knights of Saint-John)

ordonnance: ordonnances tended to cover a wide range of subjects (*see* **cahiers des doléances**), edicts only one; they were not used in our period: the so-called 'Ségur ordonnance' of 1781 restricting commissioned entry to the army to those with four generations of nobility was really only a règlement

ordonnateur: a functionary with spending powers dependent only on the king's signature; this meant he often had his own **travail** with the king

pair de France: (effectively) non-lawyers with the right to sit in the parlement and be tried by that body so constituted; kings discouraged the exercise of the former right

parlement: court of appeal also with administrative and political functions, particularly the right of registering royal edicts

parlementaires: members of the parlements

parquet/'gens du roi': the **procureur-général** and his twelve deputies plus the two or three **avocats-généraux.** The king's orders for the parlements were addressed through this channel and they pleaded his interests/the public interest. The parquet was literally the place in the parlement where the gens du roi stood

parti choiseul: *see* **choiseulistes**

parti ministériel: the government's party in the parlement

pays d'états: provinces which had retained their local estates, such as Brittany and Burgundy; they tended to pay less taxation as a result

philosophes: writers who popularized and sought to apply to society the teachings of Newton and Locke; often anti-clerical

pouvoirs intermédiaires: bodies mediating between the crown and the people, especially as defined by Montesquieu in **De l'esprit des lois**

Physiocrats: sect of economists founded by Quesnay and the Marquis de Mirabeau who believed that land was the basis of all wealth; advocated a single, universal tax based on a **cadastre**

piastres: Spanish gold coins; imported into France in times of **disette de numéraire**

place: office

premier commis: permanent head of a government department

premier consul: provençal mayor; Provence was the Roman *provincia*

premier écuyer: high officer in the maison du roi, at the head of the grande écurie (stables)

premier médecin: king's chief doctor; Louis XIII's did well (and were ennobled) because he was a hypocondriac

premier président: head of a court of justice

président à mortier: a president in the grand' chambre of the parlement, who was entitled to wear a mortar (a cross between a mortar-board and a top hat)

préventions (du roi): lightly-held prejudices

prévôt des marchands: mayor of Paris

procès-verbal: minutes

procureur-général: attorney-general, head of the **parquet**

produit net: clear profit after deduction of costs; term much used by the **Physiocrats**

provincial assembly: form of non-political devolution advocated by royal reformers and introduced by Brienne in 1787

rapporteur: official presenting the preliminary work (rapport) on a case or administrative/political matter

rapporteur du roi: king's political agent in the parlement

receveur des tailles: collector of the taille, one per **élection**

receveur-général: the head of (direct) tax-collection in a **généralité**; men of substance, they were 'faiseurs de services', that is they advanced money to the crown against future receipts

réformations: recoinages, generally a euphemism for a devaluation

régie: collection of taxes by salaried officials (régisseurs) rather than by a farm. Régies des aides, postes, poudres: collection of the duty on alcoholic drink, the post-office and the fabrication and sale of gun-powder (a state monopoly) by this method

régie intéressée: a hybrid between a farm and a régie: the régisseurs keep everything collected above an agreed figure

remontrances: criticisms of proposed royal legislation presented to the king

règlement: (internal) ruling

rentes: bonds, fixed interest securities, bought and sold like modern 'gilts' and Treasury bonds

rentes perpetuelles: undated bonds

rentes viagères: life-annuities

rentiers: holders of rentes

représentations: form of protest less severe than remontrances; Miromesnil envisaged that the **Assembly of Notables** might make représentations

Requête au roi: Calonne's defence of his ministerial conduct, published in London in 1788

résultat du conseil: archaism meaning minutes of a council meeting. These were no longer taken but its use in December 1788 to grant the third estate **doublement** captures something of the original flavour, consisting as it does of Necker's entire rapport as well as the decision. Does not, as often suggested, connote anonymity, rather the reverse

retraite: a retiring minister's financial settlement

révolte nobiliaire: resistance by nobility (and clergy) to royal attempts to tax them and remodel the parlements, 1787–8

robe, robin: the lawyer's gown and one who wore it

roi-fainéant: literally 'do-nothing king', originally applied to the later Merovingian kings

roturiers: non-nobles; usually used pejoratively

saint-esprit: the most prestigious of the orders of chivalry, founded by Henri III in 1578

séance de flagellation: Louis XV's lashing of the parlement (with his tongue) in 1766

séance royale: hybrid between a **lit de justice** in a parlement and free registration: also the royal session in the **Estates-General** on 23 June 1789

secret du roi: Louis XV's unofficial diplomacy

secrétaire du roi: holder of a sinecure whose purchase conferred transmissible nobility

seigneur/seigneurie: lord/lordship of a manor

société intime: here, Marie-Antoinette's social circle, the Polignac group

sol (pl. sous): twentieth of a **livre**

sols pour livre: 'shillings in the pound', supplementary taxation

sovereign court: one whose judgements were not subject to appeal, such as a parlement or **cour des aides**

subvention territorial: percentage land tax with no exemptions, especially that presented to the **Assembly of Notables**

supplément d'instruction: Calonne's attempt to narrow the basis of the Notables' discussion of his **subvention territorial**

sur-achat: 'cut' on bullion coined by the Mint

surintendant: prestigious title which enabled its occupant inter alia to 'signer en commandement', that is give executive authority to the king's wishes in the field concerned:

surintendant des finances: finance minister replaced by a contrôleur-général by Louis XIV. The surintendant could spend and authorize payment without the king's signature

surintendant de la maison de la reine: head of the queen's household; revived in favour of the Princesse de Lamballe in 1775

survivance/survivancier: the legal right to succeed an office-holder

tabac: tobacco duty

taille: effectively, poll tax paid by the peasants

terre d'exil: estate to which a minister was exiled

third estate/tiers état: legal and functional category to which all those who were not clergy or nobles belonged

timbre: stamp duty

traitement: payment

traites: customs duties (external and internal)

transfuge: one who has moved from a parlementaire career to one in the royal administration

travail/travail royal: a minister's (usually weekly) tête-à-tête working-session with the king; also the material he brought along to this meeting

trésor royal: the treasury

trésorier de la marine: treasurer to the navy

valet de chambre: 4 premier valets and 32 valets were the intimate as opposed to the ceremonial servants of the king. They were important in regulating access to the king

veniat: literally come! here used for the enforced attendance of a provincial parlement on the king; a reverse form of exile

vérification (parlementaire): the process which preceded registration of royal legislation; the crown saw it merely as a necessary formality, the parlement as a check on the measure's legality and utility

vérification (taxation): updating of the rolls recording liability to the **vingtième**

vérification des pouvoirs: 'checking credentials', here of the deputies to the **Estates-General**

vingtième: tax of one twentieth imposed by Machault in 1749; there could be one, two or (1783–6) three in place at any one time

Principal sources cited

For all French works cited, the place of publication is Paris unless otherwise stated. For all English works cited, the place of publication is London unless otherwise stated.

MANUSCRIPT SOURCES

The king

Archives Nationales (A.N.) K161, K163 and K164, 'cartons des rois'; communications to vastly outnumber those from the king; of special interest are K163 no. 8, a series of thirty-three letters from Miromesnil to the king, and K164 no. 3, correspondence with Vergennes.

A.N. AEI–4, the king's diary, a microfilm copy of the original in the Musée des Archives.

Archives de Vergennes (the Tugny Vergennes Family Archives), *Lettres de Louis XVI* (the complement to K164 no. 3).

Papers of ministers and those in the ministerial milieu

D'Amécourt, Lefebvre, rapporteur du roi in the parlement, Bibliothèque Nationale (B.N.) nouvelles acquisitions françaises (nouv. ac. fr.) 22103–12 (of special interest in his *Journal du règne de Louis XVI*, 22111, and the section Ministres de Louis XVI, starting at folio 1).

Bertin, B.N. nouv. ac. fr. 6498.

Brienne, A.N. 4 Archives privées (A.P.) 188.

Calonne, A.N. 297 A.P. (especially 297 A.P. 3 fos 1–137 relating to the 1787 Assembly of Notables); Public Record Office (P.R.O.) P.C. 1/125.

Castries, Archives de la Marine, *Journal de Castries*, MS 182/7964 1–2; A.N. A.P. 306, the Castries Papers, especially 306 18–24; B.N. nouv. ac. fr. 9509–10.

Joly de Fleury, B.N. fonds Joly de Fleury, especially 1432–44.

Lenoir, Bibliothèque municipale d'Orléans, MSS 1421–3 (fragmentary memoirs left by the lieutenant-général de police).

Malesherbes, A.N. 154 A.P. 11. 147.

Miromesnil, A.N. 158 A.P. 3 dossier 16, seventeen letters from Miromesnil to the parlementaire Duval d'Éprémesnil; B.N. nouv. ac. fr. 20073.

Montbarey, B.N. nouv. ac fr. 22901.

Montmorin, B.N. nouv. ac. fr. 14129 (correspondence with the ambassador to England, La Luzerne).

D'Ormesson, A.N. 144 A.P. 130–3; the minister's *Journal* is in 130 and the minutes of the comité des finances are in 131 dossier 5.

Véri, Abbé de, MSS *Journal*, Archives départementales de la Drôme, Valence, unclassified; the archives also contain de Witte's copy of this diary, of which cahiers 100–2 are missing in the original.

Vergennes, Archives des Affaires Étrangères (A.A.E.), Mémoires et Documents (M.D.) (France) 1375–1400.

The Assembly of Notables of 1787

Bibliothèque de l'Arsenal MS 3975–6; the minutes of the second bureau of the Assembly, presided over by the Comte d'Artois.

MS 3978; a fuller version of the preceding containing not only the formal opinions of the members but also the debates for the first two 'divisions'.

MS 4546; a diary of the bureau kept by the Duc de Montmorency-Laval, one of its members.

PRINTED PRIMARY SOURCES

Adhémar, Comtesse d', *Souvenirs sur Marie-Antoinette* . . ., 1836, 4 vols.

Allonville, Comte d', *Mémoires secrètes*, 1838–41, 10 vols.

D'Angiviller, *Mémoires*, Copenhagen, 1933.

Archives parlementaires; the official record of parliamentary proceeding begins with the Assembly of Notables.

D'Argenson, *Mémoires*, ed. M.E.J.B. Rathery, 1859.

D'Arneth, A. *Marie-Antoinette, Joseph II und Leopold II*, 2nd edn, Vienna, 1866.

D'Arneth, A. and Flammermont, J. (eds) *Correspondance secrète du Comte de Mercy-Argenteau avec l'Empereur Joseph II et le Prince de Kaunitz*, 1891, 2 vols.

D'Arneth, A. and Geffroy, M.A. (eds) *Marie-Antoinette: Correspondance secrète entre Marie-Thérèse et le Comte de Mercy-Argenteau*, 2nd edn, 1875, 3 vols.

Assemblée des Notables de 1787, *Procès-verbal*, 1788.

Assemblée des Notables, *Collection des mémoires présentées . . . par M. de Calonne . . ., précédée d'un avertissement*, Versailles, 1787.

Assemblée des Notables, *La Conférence du 2 mars 1787*, ed. P. Renouvin, 1920.

Augeard, J.M. *Mémoires secrètes*, ed. E. Bavoux, 1866.

Bachaumont, *Mémoires secrètes pour servir à l'histoire de la république des lettres*, London, 1777–89.

Barentin, *Lettres et bulletins à Louis XVI*, ed. A. Aulard, 1915.

Barentin, *Mémoire autographe sur les derniers conseils du Roi Louis XVI*, ed. M. Champion, 1844.

Barentin, *Mémoire pour M. de Barentin, ancien garde des sceaux . . . sur la dénonciation dans laquelle il est nommé et qui a donné lieu sur la plainte pour M. le procureur-général du roi au châtelet*, 1790.

Barnave, *Introduction à la Révolution française*, ed. G. Rudé, 1960.

Beauveau, *Mémoires du maréchal de Beauveau*, ed. Mme Standish, 1872.

Bernis, *Mémoires et lettres de François-Joachim de Pierre, Cardinal de Bernis*, ed. F. Masson, 1878, 2 vols.

Bertrand de Molleville, A.F., *Mémoires secrètes pour servir à l'histoire de la dernière année du règne de Louis XVI, Roi de France*, London, 1797, 3 vols.

Besenval, Baron de, *Mémoires*, ed. Berville and Barrière, 1821, 2 vols.

Boisgelin, *Lettres de Mgr de Boisgelin, Archevêque d'Aix à Mme de Gramont*, ed. A. Cans, 1902, *Revue Historique* **79**: 316–23; **80**: 65–77 and 301–17.

Bombelles, Marquis de, *Journal*, ed. J. Grassion and F. Durif, Geneva, 1978–93, 3 vols.

Bouillé, Marquis de, *Mémoires*, ed. Berville and Barrière, 1821.

Brienne, Comte de, and Loménie de Brienne, *Journal de l'Assemblées des Notables de 1787*, ed P. Chevalier, 1960.

Calonne, C.A. de (attrib.) *Les Comments*, 1781.

Calonne, C.A. de, *Lettre au Roi*, London, 1789.

Calonne, C.A. de (attrib.) *Lettre du Marquis de Caraccioli à M. d'Alembert*, 1781.

Calonne, C.A. de, *Réponse de M. de Calonne à l'écrit de M. Necker, publiée en Avril 1787*, London, 1788 (the appendix contains a letter of August 1786 from Calonne to the king concerning the Notables).

Campan, Madame, *Mémoires sur la vie privée de Marie-Antoinette, reine de France et de Navarre*, 1849, 2 vols.

Croÿ, Duc de, *Journal, 1718–84*, ed. Grouchy and Cottin, 1906–7, 4 vols.

Elizabeth, Madame, *Correspondance de Madame Elizabeth*, ed. F. Feuillet de Conches, 1865.

États-Généraux, *Recueil des documents relatifs aux États-Généraux de 1789*, ed. G. Lefebvre, 1953–70, 4 vols.

Fersen, Comte de, *Journal*, published by Klinckowström in *Le Comte de Fersen et la Cour de France*, 1878, 2 vols.

Flammermont, J. (ed.) *Rapport . . . sur les correspondances des agents diplomatiques étrangers en France avant la Révolution*, 1896.

Glagau, H., *Reformverstücke und Sturz des Absolutismus in Frankreich (1774–88)*, Munich, 1908 (an appendix contains letters between Calonne and the king on the subject of the Notables).

Lally-Tollendal, article on Necker, in M. Michaud, *Biographie universelle ancienne et moderne*, 1843–, 45 vols.

Lescure (ed.) *Correspondance secrète sur Louis XVI . . ., 1866, 2 vols.*

Lévis, Duc de, *Portraits et souvenirs*, 1813.

Louis XV, *Correspondance secrète inédite*, ed. M.E. Boutaric, 1866, 2 vols.

Louis XV, *Lettres à son petit-fils . . .*, ed. Amiguet, 1938.

Louis XVI, *Louis XVI a la parole*, ed. P. and P. Girault de Coursac, 1989.

Louis XVI, *Réflexions sur mes entretiens avec M. le Duc de La Vauguyon*, ed. E. Falloux, 1851.

Louis XVI, Marie-Antoinette et Mme Elizabeth, *Lettres et documents inédits*, ed. Feuillet de Conches, 1864–9, 6 vols.

Louis-Philippe, *Memoirs*, ed. and trans. J. Hardman, New York, 1977.

Luynes, *Mémoires du Duc de Luynes sur la cour de Louis XV, 1735–58*, ed. Dussieux and Soulié, 1860–5, 17 vols.

Malesherbes, *Nouveaux documents inédits*, ed. P. Grosclaude, 1964.

Mallet du Pan, *Mémoires et correspondances pour servir à l'histoire de la Révolution française*, ed. A. Sayous, 1851, 2 vols.

Malouet, *Mémoires*, 1874, 2 vols.

Marie-Antoinette, *Lettres*, ed. La Rocheterie and Beaucourt, 1895–6, 2 vols.

Marmontel, *Mémoires*, 1804, 4 vols in 2.

Miromesnil, *Correspondance politique*, ed. P. Le Verdier, 1899–, 4 vols.

Montbarey, *Mémoires du Prince de Montbarey*, 1826–7, 3 vols.

Montmorency-Luxembourg, Duc de, *Mémoires*, ed. P. Filleul, 1939.

Montyon, Auget de, *Particularités . . . sur les ministres des finances les plus célèbres*, 1812.

Moreau, J.N., *Mes souvenirs*, 1898–1901, 2 vols.

Morellet, Abbé de, *Lettres à Lord Shelburne depuis 1772 jusqu'à 1803*, ed. E. Fitzmaurice, 1898.

Necker, J., *Sur l'administration de M. Necker par lui-même*, 1791.

Necker, J., *De la Révolution française*, 1797.

Papon, Abbé, *Histoire du gouvernement français depuis l'Assemblée des Notables, tenue le 22 février 1787 jusqu'à la fin de décembre de la même année*, London, 1788.

Saint-Priest, Comte de, *Mémoires*, ed. Barante, 1929.

Sallier, G.M., *Annales françaises . . . 1774–89, 1813.*

Ségur, Comte de, *Mémoires ou souvenirs et anecdotes*, 1827, 3 vols.

Soulavie, J.L., *Mémoires historiques et politiques du règne de Louis XVI*, 1801, 6 vols.

Staël, Mme de, *Considérations sur . . . la Révolution française*, op. post., 1843.

Talleyrand, Prince de, *Mémoires*, ed. Duc de Broglie, 1891–2, 5 vols.

Vaudreuil, *Correspondance intime du Comte de Vaudreuil et du Comte d'Artois*, ed. L. Pinguad, 1889, 2 vols.

Véri, Abbé de, *Journal, 1774–80,* ed. J. de Witte, 1928–30, 2 vols.

Wéber, *Mémoires concernant Marie-Antoinette*, ed. Berville and Barrière, 1822, 2 vols.

SECONDARY WORKS

Antoine, M., *Le Conseil du Roi sous le règne de Louis XV*, 1970.

Antoine, M., 'Le Conseil des dépêches sous le règne de Louis XV', *Bibliothèque de l'École des Chartes* 1953, **8**: 158–298.

Antoine, M., 'Les Comités des ministres sous Louis XV', *Revue Historique de Droit français et étranger,* 1951.

Antoine, M., 'Les Conseils des finances sous le règne de Louis XV', *Revue d'Histoire Moderne et Contemporaine*, 1958, **5**: 161–200.

Antoine, M., *Louis XV*, 1989.

Ardaschef, P.M., *Les Intendants de province sous Louis XVI*, 1909.

Arnaud-Bouteloup, J., *Le Rôle politique de Marie-Antoinette*, 1924.

Baker, K.M., *Inventing the French Revolution*, Cambridge, 1990.

Baker, K.M., (ed.) *The French Revolution and the Creation of Modern Political Culture:* vol. I, *The Political Culture of the Ancien Régime*, Chicago, 1987; vol. II, *The Political Culture of the French Revolution*, ed. C. Lucas, Oxford, 1988.

Blanc, L., *Histoire de la Révolution française*, 1847–62, 12 vols.

Bluche, F., *Les Honneurs de la Cour*, 1957.

Bluche, F., *Les Magistrats du Parlement de Paris au XVIIIe siècle (1715–71)*, 1960.

Bluche, F., *Les Magistrats du Grand Conseil au XVIIIe siècle (1690–1791)*, 1966.

Bluche, F., *L'Origine des magistrats du Parlement de Paris (1715–71)*, 1956.

Bosher, J., *French Public Finances 1770–95*, Cambridge, 1970.

Bouchary, J., *Les Manieurs d'argent à la fin du XVIIIe siècle, 1939–43,* 3 vols.

Browne, R., 'The Diamond Necklace Affair revisited', *Renaissance and Modern Studies*, 1989, **XXXIII**, 21–5.

Burley, P., 'Louis XVI and a new monarchy', PhD thesis, London University, 1981.

Campbell, P.R., 'Louis XVI King of the French', in C. Lucas (ed.) *The Political Culture of the French Revolution*, 1988.

Campbell, P.R., 'Old regime politics', *Renaissance and Modern Studies*, 1989, **XXXIII**, 1–20.

Caron, P., 'La Tentative de contre-révolution de Juin–Juillet 1789', *Revue d'Histoire Moderne* 1906, **8**, 5–34, 649–78.

Castries, Duc de, *Le Maréchal de Castries*, 1956.

Censer, J.R. and Popkin, J.D. (eds) *Press and Politics in Pre-Revolutionary France*, Berkeley, Calif., 1987.

Chastellux, Marquis de, *Notes prises aux archives de l'état civil de Paris, brûlées le 24 mai 1871*, 1875.

Chérest, A., *La Chute de l'Ancien Régime, 1787–9*, 1884–6, 3 vols.

Cobban, A., *Ambassadors and Secret Agents: The Diplomacy of the First Earl of Malmsbury at the Hague*, 1954.

Courcelles, *Dictionnaire universelle de la noblesse de la France*, 1820, 3 vols.

Dakin, D., *Turgot and the Ancien Régime in France*, 1939.

Darnton, R., *The Literary Underground of the Old Regime*, Cambridge, Mass., 1982.

Dictionnaire de biographie Française (D.B.F.), ed. J. Balteau, A. Rastoul and M. Prévost, 1929–.

Doniol, H., *Histoire de la participation de la France à l'établissement des États-Unis d'Amérique*, 1886–, 5 vols.

Doyle, W., *The Parlement of Bordeaux and the End of the Old Regime, 1771–1790*, 1974.

Doyle, W., 'The Parlements of France and the breakdown of the old regime, 1771–88', *French Historical Studies*, 1970, **VI**, 415–58.

Doyle, W., 'The parlements', in K.M. Baker (ed.) *The Political Culture of the Ancien Régime*, Chicago, 1987.

Droz, J.F.X., *Histoire du règne de Louis XVI . . .*, Brussels, 1839.

Dull, J., *The French Navy and American Independence, 1774–1787*, Princeton, 1975.

Echeverria, D., *The Maupeou Revolution*, Baton Rouge, La., 1985.

Egret, J., *La Pré-Révolution française*, 1962.

Egret, J., *Louis XV et l'opposition parlementaire*, 1970.

Egret, J., *Necker*, 1975.

Fay, B., *Louis XVI ou la fin d'un monde*, 1955.

Félix, J., *Les Magistrats du Parlement de Paris, 1771–90*, 1990.

Fréville, H., *L'Intendance de Bretagne, 1689–1790*, Rennes, 1953, 3 vols.

Girault de Coursac, P., *L'Éducation d'un roi: Louis XVI*, 1972.

Gomel, H., *Les Causes financières de la Révolution française: les derniers contrôleurs – généraux*, 1893, 2 vols.

Granges de Surgères, Marquis de, *Histoire nobiliaire, 2,500 actes de l'état civil et notarial concernant les familles de l'ancienne France*, Nantes, 1895.

Granges de Surgères, Marquis de, *Répertoire historique et biographique de la 'Gazette de France'*, 1902–6, 4 vols.

Grosclaude, P., *Malesherbes*, 1961.

Gruder, V.R., *The Royal Provincial Intendants*, Ithaca, NY, 1968.

Hardman, J., 'Ministerial politics from the accession of Louis XVI to the Assembly of Notables, 1774–87', DPhil thesis, Oxford University, 1972.

Hardman, J., *The French Revolution . . . 1787–95*, 1981.

Hardman, J., *Louis XVI*, New Haven, Conn., 1993.

Harris, R.D., *Necker: Reform Statesman of the Ancien Régime*, Berkeley, Calif., 1979.

Harris, R.D., *Necker in the Revolution of 1789*, 1986.

Jougla de Morénas, *Grand Armorial de France*, 1934–52, 7 vols.

Labourdette, J.F., *Vergennes*, 1990.

La Chesnay des Bois, F.A. de, *Dictionnaire de la noblesse*, 3rd edn, 1863–76, 19 vols.

Laugier, L., *Un ministère réformateur sous Louis XV, Le Triumvirat*, 1975.

Laugier, L., *Turgot ou le mythe des réformes*, 1979.

Lever, E., *Louis XVI*, 1985.

Luçay, Comte de, *Les Secrétaires d'État en France depuis les origines jusqu'à 1774*, 1881.

Lüthy, H., *La Banque Protestante en France*, 1959–61, 2 vols.

Mandrou, R., *La France aux XVIIe et XVIIIe siècles*, 1974.

Mansell, P., *The Court of France, 1789–1830*, Cambridge, 1988.

Marion, M., *Le Garde des sceaux Lamoignon*, 1905.

Mathews, G.T., *The Royal General Farms*, New York, 1958.

Maupeou, J. de, *Le Chancelier Maupeou*, 1942.

Michaud, M., *Biographie universelle ancienne et moderne*, 1843–, 45 vols.

Mornet, D., *Les Origines intellectuelles de la Révolution française*, 1933.

Pimodan, Comte de, *Le Comte de Mercy-Argenteau*, 1911.

Price, M., 'The Comte de Vergennes and the Baron de Breteuil: French politics and reform in the reign of Louis XVI', PhD thesis, Cambridge University, 1988.

Price, M., 'The "Ministry of the Hundred Hours": a reappraisal', *French History*, 1990, **IV** (3): 317–39.

Ranum, O., *Richelieu and the Councillors of Louis XIII*, Oxford, 1963.

Renouvin, P., *Les Assemblées provinciales de 1787*, 1921.

Robinet, D., *Dictionnaire historique et biographique de la Révolution et de l'empire*, 1898, 2 vols.

Rogister, J.M.J., 'Conflict and harmony in eighteenth-century France: a reappraisal of the pattern of relations between Crown and Parlements under Louis XV', DPhil thesis, Oxford University, 1972.

Scott, S.F., *The Response of the Royal Army to the French Revolution . . . 1787–93*, Oxford, 1973.

Stone, B., *The Parlement of Paris, 1774–89*, North Carolina, 1981.

Stone, B., *The French Parlements and the Crisis of the Ancien Régime* North Carolina, 1986.

Tocqueville, A. de, *The Ancien Régime and the French Revolution*, ed. H. Brogan, 1966.

Van Kley, D.K., *The Jansenists and the Expulsion of the Jesuits from France, 1757–65*, New Haven, Conn., 1975.

Viollet, P., *Le Roi et ses ministres pendant les trois dernières siècles de la monarchie*, 1912.

Wick, D., 'The court nobility and the French Revolution: the example of the society of thirty', *Eighteenth Century Studies* 1980, **13**: 263–84.

Woëlmont de Brumagne, Baron de, *Notices généalogiques*, 1923–38, 9 vols.

Index

Significant entries are in bold.